MILLER'S

PRICE GUIDE

Affordable ANTIQUES

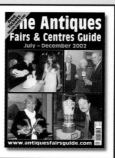

MILLER'S

PRICE GUIDE

Affordable ANTIQUES

MILLER'S AFFORDABLE ANTIQUES PRICE GUIDE

Created and designed by
Miller's Publications
The Cellars, High Street
Tenterden, Kent TN30 6BN
Telephone: 01580 766411
Fax: 01580 766100

Consultant Editor: Leslie Gillham
Project Co-ordinators: Caroline Bugeja, Léonie Sidgwick
Editorial Co-ordinator: Deborah Wanstall
Editorial Assistants: Joanna Hill, Maureen Horner
Designers: Philip Hannath, Kari Reeves
Advertisement Designer: Simon Cook
Jacket Design & Styling: Victoria Bevan
Advertising Executive: Jill Jackson
Advertising Co-ordinator & Administrator: Melinda Williams
Production Assistants: Gillian Charles, Helen Clarkson, Ethne Tragett
Production Controller: Angela Couchman
Additional Photography: Robin Saker
Indexer: Hilary Bird
US Advertising Representative: Katharine Buckley,
Buckley Pell Associates, 34 East 64th Street, New York, NY 10021
Tel: 212 223 4996 Fax: 212 223 4997 E-mail: buckley@moveworld.com

First published in Great Britain in 2003
by Miller's, a division of Mitchell Beazley,
imprints of Octopus Publishing Group Ltd

This edition published in 2004 by Bounty Books,
a division of Octopus Publishing Group Ltd
2–4 Heron Quays, London E14 4JP

A CIP catalogue record for this book is
available from the British Library

ISBN 0 7537 1083 8
ISBN13 9780753710838

Illustrations by CK Litho, Whitstable, Kent
Printed and bound by Toppan Printing Co (HK) Ltd, China

How to use this book

It is our aim to make this book easy to use. In order to find a particular item, consult the contents list on page 6 to find the main heading – for example, Silver & Plate. Having located your area of interest, you will find that sections have been sub-divided alphabetically. If you are looking for a particular factory, designer or craftsman, consult the index which starts on page 291.

BOWLS & DISHES • SILVER & PLATE 5

Miller's compares...

A. Silver sugar basket, embossed with foliate scrolls below a bail handle, on an oval foot, London 1806, 7in (18cm) wide, 10.25oz.
£250–320/$360–460 CGC

B. Silver sugar basket, with ribboned shield to either side, on a conforming foot, maker's mark of Alexander Gairdner, Edinburgh 1792, 5in (12.5cm) high, 8.5oz.
£400–480/$580–700 B(Ed)

The decoration on Item A appears to be a later addition to the piece and while Item B is smaller, the original simple decoration and the fluted shape make it more appealing to collectors. Item B also has a known maker's mark and is earlier in date adding to the price.

Soup ladles

Soup ladles were introduced around the 1740s, and earlier examples tend to follow the style of other tableware from the period. They were often sold in pairs.

Silver-gilt sugar bowl, by J. & J. Angell, embossed and chased with Oriental figures, scrolls and rocaille, London 1838, 4¼in (11cm) high, 13oz. The Angells frequently produced good embossed work of this kind.
£480–580/$700–850 S(O)

◄ **Silver sugar basket,** by William Edwards, with pendant grape cluster decoration, the body with pierced repoussé and etched bird design, blue glass liner, swing handle modelled as a vine, on a circular pierced foot, London 1856, 4in (10cm) high. A plainer example would be about £200–300/$300–450, but this is a particularly pretty item.
£480–580/$700–850 B&L

Further reading

Miller's Silver & Plate Buyer's Guide, Miller's Publications, 2001

Silver bowl, by Marshall & Sons, the body chased with flowers and leaves and engraved with initials, a family crest and motto, Edinburgh 1860–61, 6in (15cm) diam, 10.25oz.
£675–750/$975–1,100 NS

The look without the price

Charles Stuart Harris was one of the best of the Victorian silversmiths, and this example is almost as good as the real thing. An original in very good condition might fetch £10,000–15,000/$14,000–22,000.

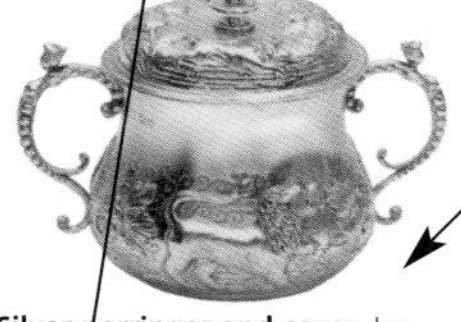

Silver porringer and cover, by Charles Stuart Harris, with 17thC-style decoration of lions and unicorns among foliage, with caryatid handles, the cover with turned finial, London 1901, 9in (23cm) wide, 26.75oz.
£300–350/$440–500 Bea(E)

Miller's compares
explains why two or three items which look similar have realized very different prices.

Information box
covers relevant collecting information on factories, makers, fakes and alterations, period styles and designers.

Price guide
these are based on actual prices realized shown in £sterling with a US$ conversion. Remember that Miller's is a price guide not a price list and prices are affected by many variables such as location, condition, desirability, whether it is a dealer or auction price (see the source code below) and so on. Don't forget that if you are selling it is quite likely you will be offered less than the price range. Price ranges for items sold at auction tend to include the buyer's premium and VAT if applicable.

The look without the price
highlights later items produced 'in the style of' earlier counterparts. It illustrates how you don't have to spend a fortune to have the original look.

Source code
refers to the Key to Illustrations on page 286 that lists the details of where the item was photographed. The auction icon indicates the item was sold at auction. The dealer icon indicates the item originated from a dealer.

Caption
provides a brief description of the item. It explains, where possible, why an item is valued at a particular price.

Further reading
directs the reader towards additional sources of information.

MILLER'S

Contents

Contributors

FURNITURE:
Leslie Gillham has worked for Gorringes, Bonhams and Phillips over the last 35 years. He now heads the Valuations Department of Gorringes, Sussex.

Lawrence Bright graduated from Southampton University with a degree in Fine Art Valuation and now works for Sotheby's Furniture Department. He has a particular interest in good English 18th-century furniture and also Arts & Crafts furniture.

CERAMICS:
John Sandon has been the International Director of Phillips' European, Pottery, Porcelain and Glass since 1988. Like his father, Henry Sandon, he lectures widely on antiques and has written books on porcelain and glass.

ASIAN CERAMICS:
Peter Wain is a leading specialist in Chinese and Japanese ceramics and works of art. He has written many books, broadcasts on television and given lectures all over the world on this subject.

SILVER & PLATE:
Hugh Gregory is a consultant valuer at Tennants Auctioneers and has worked since the mid-1970s as a freelance valuer. His interest in antiques began as a young child when at the age of 12 he joined the Antiquarian Horological Society. He has been a fellow of the Gemmological Association (FGA) since 1966.

GLASS:
Brian Watson has been dealing in antique glass since 1991. He attends the major fairs in London and his customers come from all over the world. Although his speciality is Georgian glass, over the last few years he has developed a particular interest in continental glass of the 18th century.

Elaine and Ian Bonnon have 20 years experience dealing in antique glass, specializing in 18th- and 19th-century pieces. They trade from their premises in Chandlers Ford, Hampshire.

PAPERWEIGHTS:
Anne Metcalfe deals solely in glass paperweights from Sweetbriar Gallery, Helsby, Cheshire. She wrote in 2000 *Miller's Paperweights of the 19th and 20th Centuries: A Collectors Guide*.

CLOCKS:
Sam Orr has a special interest in fine quality original English longcase and bracket clocks. He also stocks a good selection of French clocks, carriage clocks and chronometers in his premises in Hurstpierpoint, near Brighton, East Sussex.

Bob Schmitt began collecting clocks in 1969. In 1985 he and his wife moved to New Hampshire, USA, where they hold semi-annual clock and watch auctions.

WATCHES:
David Jackson is a watch and clock restorer, working in Kent. He specializes in older watches, French carriage clocks and English bracket clocks.

BAROMETERS:
Richard Twort discovered an interest in barometers and barographs when, as a school boy, he was put in charge of the school weather station. He is now a dealer in Somerset.

ANTIQUITIES:
Chris Belton has had a lifelong interest in history, archaeology and antiquities. After 25 years of dealing in antiquities from his shop, he now deals only by mail order from his business Ancient & Gothic.

ARCHITECTURAL:
Rupert van der Werff is head of the Garden Statuary and Architectural section of Sotheby's Sussex, Summers Place, Billingshurst, West Sussex.

ARMS & ARMOUR:
John Spooner's interest in antique arms and armour was initially fired by his great grandfather's shotgun dating to the mid-19th century. He started collecting over 40 years ago and turned his hobby into a business in 1980 but still regards it as a hobby. He lectures and has broadcast on the subject and appeared on British television in 'Going for a Song'.

BOXES:
Alan and Kathy Stacey are specialist dealers of the finest quality tea caddies and fine boxes. They have a world-renowned expertise particularly in the tortoiseshell and ivory field combined with 35 years experience in the antiques trade. They are members of both LAPADA and BAFRA.

DOLLS, TEDDY BEARS & TOYS:
Sheila and Marilynn Brass are North American Consultants for *Miller's Antiques Price Guides* and *Miller's Collectables Price Guides*. They have been licensed antique dealers for 26 years. Their collection of mechanical toys, doll's furniture and dollhouse miniatures is impressive and they frequently act as consultants to universities, publications, television stations and dealers. They also lecture on their extensive toy collection.

KITCHENWARE:
Janie Smithson married into a farming family and discovered an interest in country kitchenware. Along with her husband Skip, she has been dealing in antique kitchenware since 1988, and her particular enthusiasm is for early Victorian and dairy items. They show at the NEC, Alexandra Palace and the Battersea Decorative Fairs.

LIGHTING & TEXTILES:
Joanna Proops has been trading from her shop, Antique Textiles in Bath, in period textiles and lighting for the last 30 years. In 2002 she won the BACA Specialist Dealer award for costume and textiles.

METALWARE:
Mark Seabrook has been collecting antique metalware for 20 years. He deals through antique fairs such as the Chelsea Antiques Fair, NEC, West London and LAPADA. He also deals in oak and country furniture which complements the antique metalware perfectly.

RUGS & CARPETS:
Desmond North has been collecting and selling Oriental rugs for 30 years. He and his wife, Amanda, sell their rugs from home and hold sale exhibitions every May and October.

SCIENTIFIC INSTRUMENTS:
Charles Tomlinson has been a specialist dealer in antique scientific instruments for the last 30 years. He has a particular interest in antique slide rules and mechanical calculators.

SCULPTURE:
William Bevan bought his first Henry Moore sculpture in 1978 and from this grew his lifelong interest in sculpture. He started dealing in 1992 and has a particular affection for British and Italian sculpture, with a strong liking for Spanish and 20th-century Belgian work.

WOODEN ANTIQUES:
Daniel Bray MRCIS is a senior auctioneer at Bracketts, Tunbridge Wells. He has been an auctioneer for 6 years.

Dates	British Monarch	British Period	French Period	German Period	U.S. Period	Style	Woods
1558–1603	Elizabeth I	Elizabethan	Renaissance			Gothic	Oak Period (to c1670)
1603–1625	James I	Jacobean		Renaissance			
1625–1649	Charles I	Carolean	Louis XIII (1610–1643)		Early Colonial	Baroque (c1620–1700)	
1649–1660	Common-wealth	Cromwellian	Louis XIV (1643–1715)	Renaissance/ Baroque (c1650–1700)			Walnut period (c1670–1735)
1660–1685	Charles II	Restoration					
1685–1689	James II	Restoration			William & Mary		
1689–1694	William & Mary	William & Mary			Dutch Colonial	Rococo (c1695–1760)	
1694–1702	William III	William III		Baroque (c1700–1730)	Queen Anne		
1702–1714	Anne	Queen Anne					
1714–1727	George I	Early Georgian	Régence (1715–1723)	Rococo (c1730–1760)	Chippendale (from 1750)		
1727–1760	George II	Early Georgian	Louis XV (1723–1774)	Neo–classicism (c1760–1800)	Early Federal (1790–1810)	Neo–classical (c1755–1805)	Early mahogany period (c1735–1770)
1760–1811	George III	Late Georgian	Louis XVI (1774–1793) Directoire (1793–1799) Empire (1799–1815)	Empire (c1800–1815)	American Directoire (1798–1804) American Empire (1804–1815)	Empire (c1799–1815)	Late mahogany period (c1770–1810)
1812–1820	George III	Regency	Restauration Charles X (1815–1830)	Biedermeier (c1815–1848)	Late Federal (1810–1830)	Regency (c1812–1830)	
1820–1830	George IV	Regency					
1830–1837	William IV	William IV	Louis Philippe (1830–1848)	Revivale (c1830–1880)		Eclectic (c1830–1880)	
1837–1901	Victoria	Victorian	2nd Empire Napoleon III (1848–1870) 3rd Republic (1871–1940)	Jugendstil (c1880–1920)	Victorian	Arts & Crafts (c1880–1900)	
1901–1910	Edward VII	Edwardian			Art Nouveau (c1900–1920)	Art Nouveau (c1900–1920)	

Introduction

Among the seemingly overwhelming mass of information available to the antiques hunter today just two pieces of priceless guidance shine through like beacons, and they are – always buy what you like, and always buy the very best quality items you can afford. And that is where *Miller's Affordable Antiques Price Guide* comes in. It will demonstrate that buying quality and having a finite budget are not mutually exclusive conditions. In short it will illustrate that quality is often surprisingly inexpensive and that there are real bargains to be had out there if you just have the courage to ignore short term fashion fads.

In the field of furniture, Victorian pieces are better value than they have been for many years. Even some Georgian furniture is very affordable with pairs and single dining chairs and even bureaux being real snips. The latter frequently sell for half the figures they were making five years ago. If it is tables you are looking for, late 18th-century drop-leaf dining tables and pembroke tables of the same period are both currently selling for prices that are just too good to miss. Also remember that Victorian copies of the more expensive examples of Georgian furniture will give you the period look without the cavernously empty bank account that can accompany the purchase of the real thing.

If you are looking to build a collection of decorative ceramics, there is no shortage of items which come in well below the £1,000/$1,500 bench-mark, but if you are prepared to put up with a bit of damage then even more expensive pieces fall into range.

Silver and plate is no more exclusive than furniture and ceramics. A reluctance on the part of many young people with busy working lives to spend their valuable free time applying polish and elbow grease, and concern over security for such easily portable items means there are many bargains to be had. Particularly if you are prepared to accept good quality reproduction in lieu of the 18th- and 19th-century originals. A George III sugar basket (page 138) would fetch £400–500/$580–720 but settle for the George V copy illustrated and the price will be less than half that. Patch boxes, pill boxes, card cases, vinaigrettes and similar items of 'smallwork' can still be found in the £100–250/$145–350 price range.

If any area offers particularly good value it is probably that of antique glass. Some people are obviously put off by the thought of investing money in something that might be smashed to fragments at any moment. But this perfectly logical fear is an insufficient explanation since any good contemporary glass is also relatively expensive and yet it still finds its way onto the dining table and into the drinks cabinet. So why not start by checking out decanters which are both attractive and utilitarian. The George IV facet-cut pair (page 171) which will fetch £170–180/$250–260 stand as a good example of just how favourably prices compare with modern pieces. If you just want some nice practical and durable beer glasses with a bit of character you will do no better than good solid Victorian 'rummers' (page 175) which are still retailing at less than £50/$75. But if your tastes are more esoteric then remember you can buy any number of 18th-century English wine glasses for under £500/$720 a piece.

Miller's Affordable Antiques Price Guide is designed to provide the reader with not just a catalogue of prices but also practical tips on how to get the best out of today's market. After all, who knows when such favourable conditions will prevail again?

Leslie Gillham

Furniture

The publication of *Miller's Affordable Antiques Price Guide* has coincided with what is arguably the best opportunity to buy antique furniture in this price range for ten years. In fact, it is no exaggeration to say that certain lower-priced pieces are making little more than they were twenty years ago.

The cause of this market upheaval seems to be a major sea-change in the taste and, therefore, buying habits of younger homeowners with a trend towards more clean and uncluttered interiors, often with modern design predominating, but frequently incorporating a very good or unusual single antique item. This, along with the continued popularity of the country house look in certain areas of the property market, has helped to lead to a dramatic polarization of furniture prices with the finer pieces reaching formerly unimagined stratospheric price heights, while lesser items frequently pass seemingly unnoticed.

This new breed of buyer of antique furniture expects its purchases to be not only easy on the eye but also practical. Out of favour has gone the Georgian mahogany bureau because despite all its self-tidying usefulness (all you need to do is close the flap to complete your filing in one easy step) it will not comfortably support a computer, and in have come the Victorian library table and the pedestal desk for the precise reason that they will.

Delicate Victorian cabriole-legged chairs have fallen from fashion as a result of their tendency to break with repeated use. The trend is now for the far more robust late Georgian and early Victorian counterparts.

Out have gone Victorian nursing and prie-dieu chairs, and in have come big leather armchairs that will comfortably accommodate postprandial slumber.

Nor is the new order confined to the serried ranks of antique 'brown' furniture. It happily encompasses the sensuous lines and rich ornamentation of the type of 19th-century French confections that were once the stars of many an auction or fair stand. In particular, ebonized and boulle pieces which, not long ago, would have made £1,000–2,000/$1,500–3,000 at auction can now be found selling for markedly less, especially if their condition is not good. It is necessary to move into the realms of signed pieces or those with established exhibition track records before prices really perk up.

It would be easy to take a wholly negative view of current market trends but that would be very much a glass half-empty stance. Every uncertain market, whether in housing, stocks and shares, antiques or any other form of investment or commodity provides a great opportunity for the buyer brave enough to swim against the prevailing current. So it is that the present situation offers a wonderful opportunity to anybody looking to furnish a home today. For example, the chances are there to equip sitting rooms and dining rooms entirely in the late 19th-century taste for far less than it would have cost just a few years ago. If such slavish adherence to period authenticity holds no appeal then consider the possibility of achieving a particular look without paying the full price. For instance, a good set of Georgian dining chairs will cost a lot of money but a matched set – a collection of pairs or single chairs, all similar in appearance but originally from different sets – will do the job perfectly well for a fraction of the price of the real thing.

Leslie Gilham

Beds

Acquiring an antique brass and iron bedstead at an auction can be a hit-and-miss affair. There are several definite pitfalls to avoid. Firstly, check the structure. Does the bed come with its side runners and are they correct for the bed? Secondly, how much general damage is there? The charm of an antique bed is immense, but is it enough to overcome rust corrosion and dangerously sharp edges where the brass casing peels off?

Your bed can be renovated completely or repaired while keeping the look of its age by using the services of a specialist restorer. Bed bases and mattresses can be ordered to go with your bed, no matter what its size, length or shape, but these extra costs must be borne in mind from the outset.

Rocking cradle, with original paint, Continental, c1840, 46in (117cm) wide. This cradle would make an ideal log basket or an antique container for pot plants.
£280–320/$400–460 TPC ⊞

◀ **Cast-iron and brass bedstead,** finished in matt olive green, c1895, 42in (106.5cm) wide.
£450–500
$580–720 SeH ⊞

▶ **Cast-iron bedstead,** finished in black, c1875, 48in (122cm) wide. Although this is a simple bed it is made more desirable by the unusual flowerhead motif which is far more attractive than the normal straight vertical rails.
£520–575/$750–835 SeH ⊞

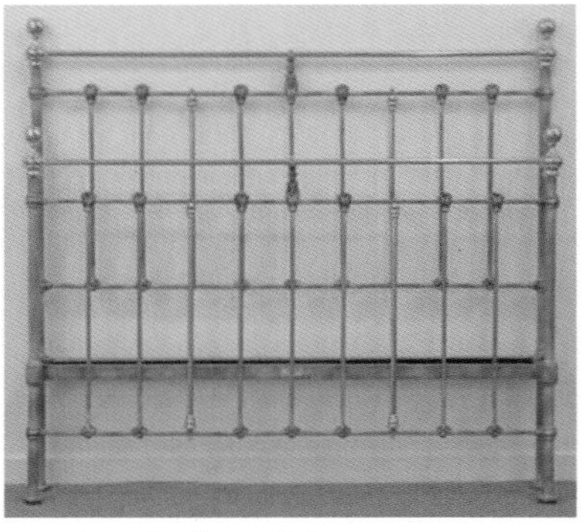

Cast-iron bedstead, finished in black, c1885, 60in (152.5cm) wide.
£700–800/$1,000–1,150 SeH ⊞

Bedsteads

These examples of antique bedsteads are cast-iron or cast-iron and brass, and generally the plainer the design the less they are worth. However, the retail cost of a genuine William IV mahogany four-poster bed would be at least £5,000/$7,500 while a later Victorian example with hand carving to the headboard and footboard would be around £3,000/$4,500.

Benches

Oak bench, 19thC, 101in (256.5cm) long.
£225–250/$320–360 WV

Oak settle, with a fielded four-panel back and loose cushion, seat boards later, 18thC, 72in (183cm) wide. This oak settle has seat boards of a later date and if completely original it could fetch in the region of £1,500/$2,000.
£650–750/$950–1,100 S(O)

Victorian ash hall bench, the arched panelled back with a central ebonized cartouche above a two-hinged seat and panelled front, on compressed bun feet and casters, 72in (183cm) wide. This is a very functional piece of furniture incorporating a seat and storage space for toys etc. If it had been made in oak rather than ash it would command a higher price.
£680–820/$700–1,175 CGC

Painted beech bench, with a rush seat, French, provincial, 1880, 51in (129.5cm) wide. This bench is a particularly good buy because the rush seating is already in good repair. Before buying pieces of rush or cane seating do ensure that it is in good order, or check the cost of repair with a professional restorer.
£800–900/$1,150–1,300 MLL

Oak settle, with linen-fold decoration, 20thC, 42in (106.5cm) wide. Linen-fold panelling is always popular and early examples are much prized, so a 17thC or 18thC piece of furniture of this type would be far more expensive than this 20thC reproduction.
£875–975/$1,300–1,400 PICA

Auction or dealer?

All the pictures in our price guides originate from auction houses and dealers. When buying at auction, prices can be lower than those of a dealer, but a buyer's premium and VAT will be added to the hammer price. Equally, when selling at auction, commission, tax and photography charges must be taken into account. Dealers will often restore pieces before putting them back on the market. Both dealers and auctioneers can provide professional advice, so it is worth researching both sources before buying or selling your antiques.

Bookcases

◀ **Mahogany stepped open bookcase,** with a later base, c1850, 30in (76cm) wide. Stepped bookcases, also sometimes known as waterfall bookcases, are perennially popular. A similar example dating from 30 to 40 years earlier might well cost £2,000–3,000/$2,900–4,350.
£320–380/$450–570 SWO

◀ **Satinwood bookcase,** with mahogany stringing and two astragal-glazed doors, 1875–1900, 50½in (128.5cm) wide. This seems a particularly good buy since satinwood is almost always a sign of a good quality piece.
£600–720
$870–1,000 B(Ba)

Edwardian mahogany dwarf open bookcase, the top with oval satinwood and harewood fan-shaped paterae and spandrels within wide satinwood beading, the stiles with conch shell inlay, 52¼in (133cm) wide.
£720–850/$1,000–1,230 Oli

Miller's compares...

A. Mahogany bookcase, the moulded and corbelled cornice above two astragal-glazed doors, c1780, 32½in (82.5cm) wide.
£260–300/$380–440 S(O)

B. Mahogany bookcase, the moulded cornice above two astragal-glazed doors, within glazed ends, c1780, 47¼in (120cm) wide.
£600–700/$870–1,000 S(O)

While each of these items began as the upper section of either a bureau bookcase or a secretaire bookcase, one is of markedly better quality than the other. Although Item B has a less complicated cornice which at first glance makes it appear less decorative, a closer look reveals that it is veneered whereas that on Item A is not. The use of veneers enabled the maker to gain the maximum effect from the distinctive grain and colour of the mahogany but it was also an additional expense. This attention to detail demonstrates the superiority of Item B over its counterpart.

Inlaid rosewood bookcase/ display cabinet, by James Shoolbred & Co, the drawer stamped 'Jas. Shoolbred & Co.', 1880–1905, 47¼in (120cm) wide. It is unusual for English makers and retailers to stamp their pieces. Usually, as in this case, it is an indication of quality which leads to a higher than average price for such a piece of furniture.
£720–850
$1,000–1,230 Bea(E)

◀ **George III mahogany bureau bookcase,** the upper section with plain pediments and dentil cornice, carved florets to the frieze, herring-bone crossbanding and astragal-glazed doors enclosing shelves, the bureau with fitted interior and fall-front above two short and three long drawers flanked by quarter turned reeded pilasters, on ogee bracket feet, 48in (122cm) wide. The proportions and differences in detail of this piece make it clear that it is a marriage – the bookcase top and bureau base originated from two separate items of furniture. This explains the modest price.
£750–900
$1,100–1,300
TRM

Mahogany two-stage bookcase, with moulded cornice, two brass-trimmed glazed doors enclosing shelves, protruding base with two walnut panelled cupboard doors, leaf-capped pilasters and beaded edging, on a plinth, 19thC, 50¾in (129cm) wide.
£800–1,000/$1,150–1,500 AH

Did you know?

All the major styles of bureau were also made in bureau bookcase form from c1690, in styles that matched other furniture of the period. They were invariably constructed in two pieces, the bookcase resting within the moulding on the bureau top (which is left unfinished), and held in place by screws.

◀ **George III mahogany bureau bookcase,** the dentil-moulded cornice above two astragal-glazed doors enclosing three shelves, the fall-front opening to reveal drawers and pigeonholes flanking a central cupboard and two book slides with four graduated drawers below, on shaped bracket feet, 37¾in (96m) wide. The price of this piece indicates a marriage. An original mahogany bureau bookcase would cost at least £1,500/$2,150. However, if you are satisfied with the marriage it is an opportunity to obtain a very pleasing piece of furniture for far less than the cost of a piece where both parts are original.
£850–1,000/$1,250–1,500 CGC

Chairs

Child's Victorian chair, with cane seat.
£20–25/$30–35 TAY

Beech and elm splat-back chair, c1890.
£70–80/$100–115 AL

► Sheraton-style mahogany elbow chair, with a rail back, downswept arms and stuff-over seat, on fluted front legs, repaired, c1800. Always keep an eye out for old repairs, especially to the legs, as this weakens the chair and can often make it unusable.
£90–100/$130–145 WW

Elm and beech chapel chair, c1890.
£55–60/$80–90 AL

Hall chairs

Hall chairs were made for large houses and were often carved impressively with the crests or coats-of-arms of the owners. The seats were often slightly dished so that the sitter did not slide off the highly polished surface, but they offered no comfort and were specifically intended for messengers or others waiting in their outdoor clothes.

Child's fruitwood chair, with rush seat, 1900.
£65–70/$95–100 MLL

Late Victorian walnut hall chair. This chair would originally have been one of a pair or a larger set. Its modest price is explained by its now being single.
£80–95/$115–140 TAY

Victorian walnut elbow chair, with inlaid banding, the domed back with a bobbin-rail open splat, with a rattan seat.
£90–100/$130–145 WW

◄ **Regency mahogany elbow chair,** the rope-twist and turned horizontal rail back with ebony stringing, with scrolling arms on front turned supports, the stuff-over seat on reeded sabre front legs with brass pads. This is a reasonable price for a period chair with two popular and stylish features – the rope-twist back and sabre legs.
£110–130
$160–190 WW

Victorian walnut lady's chair. This is an inexpensive chair as frames alone often sell for £120/$175. They are not always comfortable and, of course, the upholstery may not suit your existing colour scheme.
£150–180/$220–260 TAY

Set of four early Victorian mahogany side chairs, grained to simulate rosewood, with open buckle backs, on turned and carved front legs. The modest price indicates the current restricted demand for small sets of chairs. In this case good well-made, robust chairs are selling for £50/$72 a chair whereas a set of eight would command at least double that figure.
£170–200/$250–300 WW

Victorian chairs

Although chairs from the William IV and Victorian periods may lack the style and elegance of earlier chairs, they are often very well made. The best examples, with elegant French-style cabriole legs, are classics of English design.

Single chairs were essential in the drawing room for accommodating the wide skirts worn by ladies at that time, and consequently the seats were often slightly narrowed at the sides, with serpentine fronts. The French rococo style was popular for the boudoir and bedroom during the early Victorian period, often executed in walnut, gilded or painted soft woods, or papier mâché. Sheraton and Hepplewhite designs were reproduced from the 1870s onwards.

► **Child's folding wood steamer chair,** c1900.
£180–200
$260–300 ALA

◄ **Set of five late Victorian mahogany dining chairs,** with hoop backs and turned legs. This is a very good price for a practical set of chairs due to an unfashionable style and an odd number in the set.
£180–200
$260–300 B(W)

Set of six oak chairs, c1880.
£180–220/$260–320 AL

Child's high chair, with recaned seat, early 20thC. Caning was introduced to seat furniture shortly after 1660. It utilizes palms known as rattans which originate in the Malay peninsular. Rush seating which makes use of common rushes dates back to the medieval period.
£270–300/$400–440 DHA

Edwardian mahogany upholstered chair, on turned and fluted front legs, with buttoned scroll back and seat.
£180–220/$260–320 DA

◄ **Child's mahogany rocking chair,** the plain back with crest and loop handle, with shaped wing sides and commode seat, 19thC. This is quite a practical little chair with the former pot compartment providing storage space for toys etc. However, remember that little fingers can find their way under the rockers.
£200–220/$300–320 AH

► **Victorian oak hall chair,** the round back carved with three fish and on turned supports with lobed finials, the seat rail with turned pendant finials, one finial missing.
£240–260/$350–380 DN

Child's painted metal chair, decorated with tigers and trees, 1875–1900. This chair would sit just as happily in a modern interior as it would in a room of antiques.
£180–220/$260–320 MLu

The look without the price

Ash and elm high splat-back Windsor chair, Yorkshire 1840–90.
£270–300/$400–440 MIL

A similar chair of the same period but made of yew and elm instead of ash and elm would command a price of £600–800/$850–1,150 at auction and would retail well in excess of £1,000/$1,500.

George IV mahogany elbow chair, the back with a crest rail and back rail with a centred roundel, with tapering legs, some restoration.
£300–360/$440–520 DN

► **Oak swivel chair,** with leather seat, c1930.
£320–350
$450–500 COLL

Victorian walnut open armchair, requires reupholstering. This is a good example of the quality of the frame dictating the price regardless of the condition of the covering. But beware – quality traditional reupholstery can be an expensive business and cutting corners will be detrimental to the value of the item if you try to resell it.
£320–360
$450–520 SWO

***Faux* bamboo conservatory chair,** with embroidered cloth back and cane seat, French, 1900.
£300–350/$440–500 MLL

Walnut bergère, with scrolled and downswept reeded and fluted arms, upholstered, 19thC. As with many furniture terms, 'bergère' is used not altogether correctly. Often featured to describe a particular type of armchair and settee with caned sides and back, a bergère was originally any armchair with upholstered sides. This particular form of seating first appeared in France c1725 and gradually spread in popularity to other European countries displacing chairs with open arms. The name is now perhaps most frequently applied to a style of chair which was popular during the Regency period: often of square form but sometimes with a curved back and having caned sides, back and seat. Similar upholstered examples can be found but these usually date from a little later.
£300–360/$440–520 BR

The look without the price

Louis XVI-style oak armchair, the shaped floral-carved crest flanked by two finials over a lyre-carved and pierced splat, with serpentine arms and fluted uprights, rush seat, French, provincial, 1850–75.
£320–380/$450–570 NOA

Although described as Louis XVI-style, this chair is not a direct copy of an 18thC example. It merely incorporates elements of design of that period. The lyre back is the most distinctive feature although this also occurs in Sheraton and Regency English furniture. Altogether a bit of a mixture, but this offers a lot of style.

Dating chairs

Although there are few hard and fast rules when dating chairs there are certain pointers which can be looked for. One of these is to examine the way the seat frame is braced for strength. In the 18th century this was achieved by fitting and sticking a thin strut of wood across the front corners of the frame. In the 19th century this technique was quickly superseded by sticking and screwing a solid block into each corner. Although many 18th-century chairs have had their original struts replaced with the stronger and more durable blocks, the notches in the frame where the struts originally fitted should still be visible.

Pair of oak ladderback chairs, with rush seats, c1790–1810.
£325–360/$470–520 TRI ⊞

Set of six ash and elm wheelback chairs, 1900.
£330–365/$480–530 MLL ⊞

Walnut fauteuil, with a rush seat, French, 1870. French walnut furniture of this style and period is no longer as popular as it was. Also, always remember to check walnut furniture for woodworm as it is susceptible to attack. Be particularly careful that it has not been badly infested and then disguised with filler.
£330–365/$480–530 MLL ⊞

◄ **Pair of elm ladderback chairs,** with solid seats, 18thC.
£340–380/$480–550 TRI ⊞

► **Beech and elm slat-back armchair,** c1890.
£360–400/$520–580 AL ⊞

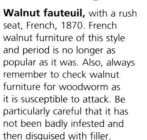

Set of four Victorian rosewood dining chairs, with carved back rails and turned legs. A set of eight chairs is the minimum desirable number – sets of less than eight are currently easy to buy.
£340–400/$480–580 TAY

Windsor chairs

Windsor chairs were unknown before the 1720s, and were originally found in Georgian taverns and coffee houses. The earliest examples have comb backs, plain turned splayed legs, and no stretchers. Cabriole legs suggest a date between 1740 and 1770. The hooped back was introduced c1740, and the wheel splat around 1790.

Gothic Windsors, recognized by the carving of their splats and their pointed arch backs, were made between 1760 and 1800. The most desirable wood is yew, followed by elm, but mahogany examples are always of good quality. Curved stretchers and carved and well-proportioned backs also add to the value. Some better quality Windsor chairs were stained black or japanned black or green and are more valuable in original condition – do not strip them.

Child's ash and elm Windsor armchair, c1830.
£350–400/$500–580 F&F

Walnut and upholstered low armchair, needlework fabric damaged, c1860. The cost of restoration of old needlework can be high so this must be taken into consideration when buying an item with damaged needlework upholstery.
£380–450/$550–650 S(O)

Yew, ash and elm Windsor chair, with a pierced splat, the elm seat on turned yew front legs and ash back legs, mid-19thC.
£380–420/$550–600 WW

Victorian walnut upholstered armchair, with padded button back and arms, on flower- and scroll-carved cabriole legs with brass casters.
£380–460/$550–670 DN

◄ **Victorian walnut and upholstered spoon-back easy armchair,** with button back and carved supports, on cabriole legs with casters. It is worth checking to make sure that walnut chairs of this period have not been attacked too seriously by the common furniture beetle (woodworm). This problem does not affect mahogany furniture.
£400–450/$580–650 WW

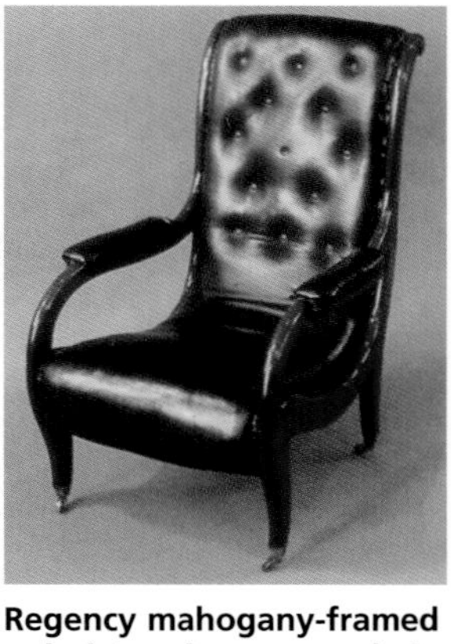

Regency mahogany-framed upholstered open armchair.
£400–450/$580–650 MAR

► **Victorian walnut reading chair,** with carved back pediment and fitted brass adjustable reading stand and candlestick.
£400–480/$580–700 TAY

Hepplewhite-style oak commode chair, c1800. Little is known of George Hepplewhite other than that he had a shop in Cripplegate, London. He died in 1786 and in 1788 his wife Alice published the *Cabinet Maker & Upholsterer's Guide* which was the standard guide to style for a wide range of simple domestic furniture.
£400–450/$580–650 MTay

Set of four rosewood-veneered buckle-back dining chairs, 19thC. The number of chairs in the set is more important than the wood used. Rosewood is more desirable in chairs of this type since it usually means the chairs are earlier than the mahogany examples.
£400–480/$580–700 TAY

► **Child's George III mahogany elbow chair,** the back with a pierced ribbon splat, with ribbon-carved scrolling arms and leather-covered drop-in seat.
£450–500/$650–720 WW

Mahogany carver dining chair, 1820. The term 'carver', used for an armchair in a set of dining chairs, evolved from the chair being used at the top of the table by the head of the house.
£450–550/$650–800 DY

The look without the price

George III-style mahogany wing chair, with acanthus-carved cabriole legs and scroll feet, c1900.
£430–500/$625–725 NOA

This chair has cabriole back legs, which is a sure sign of quality. A wing chair dating between 1760 and 1820 would cost between £1,000–1,500/$1,500–2,000 at auction with the upholstery not necessarily in perfect condition.

Set of four George IV mahogany dining chairs, one with arms, with ebony-strung crest rails, reeded backs, and drop-in seats. The more chairs there are in a set the higher the price per chair. A set of eight chairs like this, including an additional armchair, would command a price of £2,000–3,000/$3,000–4,400.
£450–550/$650–800 DN

Set of five ash spindle-back chairs, with rush seats, four with a shell-carved crest, one with later rockers, 19thC. The odd number of chairs in the set and the fact that the total is less than eight makes for a very affordable and useful set which can be fairly closely matched to additional chairs to build up a harlequin set.
£480–550/$700–800 DN

► **George III mahogany chair,** the shaped back with scroll-back top rail and solid shaped splat, the drop-in seat with shaped seat rail, on shell-carved cabriole legs with pad feet.
£500–600/$725–870 AH

Pair of walnut hall chairs, the backs pierced and carved with winged masks, griffons, putti and C-scrolls above seven barley-twist supports, the cane seats above pierced and carved frieze seat rails, on barley-twist legs and stretchers, late 19th–early 20thC. Carved oak chairs of the same period would be considerably cheaper while being similar in appearance. However, in this case, the use of the more expensive walnut and the finer than average carving has made for a superior pair of chairs.
£500–550/$720–800 RTo

Louis XVI-style fauteuil, 20thC. A genuine Louis XVI fauteuil – the French term for an armchair with open arms and upholstered elbow rests – would cost in the region of £1,500–2,000/$2,000–3,000.
£500–600
$720–870 S(O)

► **Pair of Regency mahogany side chairs,** with moulded curved top rails above horizontal foliate-carved splats.
£500–570/$720–825 B(Ed)

X-frame chair, with a cane seat, late 19thC.
£550–600/$800–870 GKe

Set of six George III mahogany chairs, with open bar backs and panelled top rails, stuff-over seats and ring-turned tapering front legs.
£560–640/$800–950 AH

◀ **Victorian mahogany open armchair,** the out-scrolled crest over a deep-buttoned back, with downswept scroll-end arms, on turned legs with casters.
£600–700/$870–1,000 NOA

▶ **Victorian mahogany library writing armchair,** with padded arms and back and sprung seat, on turned front legs with brass casters.
£600–700/$870–1,000 WW

The look without the price

Two genuine Louis XVI bergères – the French term for chairs with upholstered rather than open arms – would cost at least £2,000–3,000/ $2,900–4,400. If these chairs had been a pair it would have increased their value to £900–1,000/ $1,300–1,500, so they are an affordable way to furnish a stylish room. But beware of the cost of reupholstering them.

Two Louis XV-style giltwood bergères, the larger with a cartouche and a scroll-carved top rail above a padded back and side panels, with downswept arms and scroll terminals above a padded seat and carved apron on floral-carved cabriole legs, French, late 19thC, the other chair of similar form.
£600–700/$870–1,000 B

◄ **Walnut and leather desk chair,** c1870. The leather-covered back and arms makes for a more desirable chair than the usual all-wood type which would cost £200/$290 less.
£650–700/$950–1,000 GBr ⊞

► **Victorian walnut button-back open armchair,** the back carved with flowerheads and entwined ribbons, on moulded cabriole legs with casters.
£650–800
$950–1,150 Bea(E) ⚒

Set of six George IV beech dining chairs, formerly painted to simulate rosewood, with rosewood-veneered and brass marquetry crest rails, drop-in seats and sabre legs. While the practice of 'graining' beech to look like rosewood enabled the maker to produce an impressive set of chairs with less investment in the timber used, the results do not look cheap when done well. Such chairs can be very attractive and often restore well, so do not be tempted to strip them to their bare beech if they are a bit battered.
£680–800/$985–1,150 DN ⚒

Pair of late Victorian button-back chairs, the walnut frames with inlaid decoration. This type of chair has become unpopular in recent years and the fabric used to cover these particular examples would not have helped the selling price. However, they are strong and practical and at this price very inexpensive.
£700–800/$1,000–1,150 TAY ⚒

Scrambled sets

Because of their simple structure and design, a set of straight-legged chairs is easy to enlarge by 'scrambling'. This involves taking all the chairs apart, removing one or two members from each one, sufficient to make up a number of 'new' chairs, and by replacing these parts with new timber. The resulting set does not include a single totally new chair but a large number of repaired ones. To detect if a set has been scrambled, every member of each chair must be examined and compared with the rest of the set.

Harlequin set of eight George III mahogany dining chairs, with pierced vertical splats and drop-in seats. The term harlequin is used to denote that these chairs did not originate as a set but have been assembled as a group of near-matching items. The better the chairs match in a harlequin set the higher the price will be. In this case each chair has cost less than £100/$145.
£750–900/$1,100–1,300 CGC ⚒

◄ **Harlequin set of eight elm and fruitwood spindle-back chairs,** with shaped top rails and rush seats.
£780–850/$1,100–1,250 B(W)

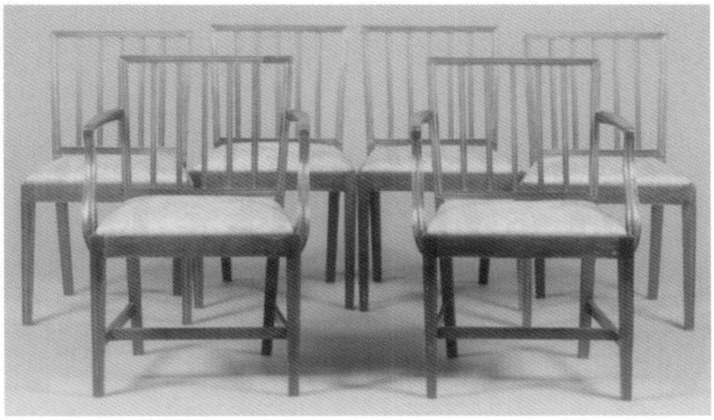

Set of six mahogany dining chairs, including a pair of armchairs, restored, c1800. This does not seem expensive which suggests considerable restoration. While cosmetic work is generally viewed as acceptable, obvious pinning and splicing of frames will devalue the items. Check for breakages where the arms are attached to the frames and splitting at the top of the front legs when chairs have drop-in seats such as these.
£780–850/$1,100–1,250 S(O)

Set of four carved oak and hide upholstered chairs, by Gillow, the lion mask and leaf-carved cresting with a hand-hold moulding to the reverse, the front legs with brass casters, stamped 'Gillow' and '8803', some seat rails with stencil '27891', c1894. This is not a popular style of dining chair and these four were probably part of a much larger set. However, the Gillow stamp ensures you are buying good quality furniture.
£800–950/$1,150–1,400 S(S)

X-frame beech chair, covered all over with moss-green velvet, with fringed trimmings, c1870.
£800–880
$1,150–1,275 RAN

Set of six cherrywood chairs, with rush seats, French, provincial, 1890.
£800–900
$1,150–1,300 MLL

◄ **William IV walnut upholstered salon chair,** with button back, the open padded arms on scroll- and flower-carved supports, with stuff-over seat, on turned tapering front legs with brass toes and casters.
£880–1,000
$1,300–1,500 AH

Chests & Coffers

Oak coffer, with carved decoration of oak and ivy leaves, 19thC, 39¾in (101cm) wide. This piece would have been a rather plain coffer if it were not for its Art and Crafts-style carving on the base. This enhances its rustic appeal and, for the private buyer who likes this type of look, it is good value. The top appears faded and dry and would benefit from a polish.
£160–190/$230–275 SWO

► **Elm blanket box,** 35in (89cm) wide. This price seems reasonable for this box. Elm has a lovely configuration to the grain which makes it more desirable than the more common pine examples. This piece also has a good colour.
£165–185
$240–270 MIL

George III oak mule chest, the top with a moulded edge, with six fielded-edge dummy drawers over three drawers, 52½in (133.5cm) wide. The price of this mule chest reflects the fact that it may have a later top. If the top had been original it would be worth between £800–1,200/$1,150–1,750. Originality is the by-word for collectors of oak furniture. The term 'mule chest' arises from the erroneous belief that this type of furniture was the hybrid product of a coffer and a chest of drawers. In fact, the mule chest originated in its own right during the late 16thC, although most examples date from the 17th and 18thC.
£300–350/$450–500 TRM

Beech wedding chest, Romanian, c1875, 45in (114.5cm) wide. This piece is primitive but unusual and charming. However, the price is more a reflection of its decorative rather than its overall market value. The date of 1875 would be far too late for serious collectors of country furniture, who prefer genuine pieces from before the early 18thC.
£200–240/$300–350 Byl

Chest or coffer?

The terms 'chest' and 'coffer' have become largely interchangeable although old wills and inventories suggest that small chests were often referred to as coffers. Another distinction was that coffers were made by specialist craftsmen, cofferers, while chests were originally made by carpenters and joiners.

◄ **Panelled oak coffer,** the plank lid with moulded edge and wire hinges, the front with an iron lock plate and clasp, with moulded stiles, on feet, late 17thC, 48in (122cm) wide. This piece would have fetched about £500–800/$720–1,150 if it had relief-carved detail on the front. Comparative coffers with carving usually start from £600–900/$870–1,300.
£300–360/$440–520 WW

George III oak and mahogany crossbanded mule chest, modelled as a dresser base, with canted corners, the hinged lid over five dummy drawer fronts and four real drawers, on ogee bracket feet, 64in (162.5cm) wide. This chest contains features that are typical of the period, ie crossbanded drawers, canted corners and ogee bracket feet. It is an extremely attractive piece of furniture at a very affordable price due to the impracticability of having to clear the top of items every time you want to use it.
£380–450/$570–650 BR

Oak coffer, dated 1640, carving later, 25in (63.5cm) high. This boarded chest is good value due to the carving being of a later date.
£445–495/$650–700 SEA

Oak mule chest, the interior with lidded compartment, the shaped fielded panel front above three drawers over a shaped apron, 18thC, 52¼in (132.5cm) wide. This is a good price for a mule chest, although the feet look partially damaged. In better condition it may have fetched £1,000/$1,500.
£720–850/$1,000–1,250 Oli

Oak six-plank coffer, the front carved with two bands of foliate scrolls, early 17thC, 37in (94cm) wide. This is a good price for this piece though that may be on account of its rather weak colour and the carving may be of a later date. If original, the value would be around £800–1,200/$1,150–1,750.
£420–500/$600–720 G(L)

Boarded chests

Early boarded chests are much sought-after in today's market. Their value greatly depends on a number of factors, such as originality, age, colour and rarity. For instance, some Tudor examples can make well above £5,000/$7,250, whereas good examples of 17th-century models start from around £1,000–1,500/$1,500–2,200. Please remember, however, that on many of them the carving is of a later, often Victorian, date. Original carving tends to be deeper and less stylized.

Oak and burr-elm chest, formerly with drawers, the top, panelled sides and two lower front panels of burr-elm, mid-18thC, 48in (122cm) wide. Any alteration to a piece of furniture, particularly a piece of oak furniture, is likely to devalue it since the purist dealers and collectors will no longer be interested in it. Such is the case with this piece. Although it is now lacking its drawers, the colour is good and if this piece were in original condition it could fetch in the region of £1,500/$2,200.
£850–1,000/$1,250–1,500 S(O)

Chests of Drawers

◄ **Edwardian mahogany Art Nouveau-style dressing chest,** with shaped mirror, the supports with stylized motifs, above two short drawers and one long drawer. This is a good example of how reasonable bedroom furniture of this period can be.
£220–260
$320–380 SWO

Mahogany and boxwood line-inlaid chest of drawers, with three short and three long graduated drawers, on bracket feet, c1800, 36in (91.5cm) wide.
£300–360/$440–520 HOK

Regency mahogany chest of drawers, the reeded rectangular top above two short and three long graduated drawers with a shaped apron below, on shaped bracket feet, 39½in (105.5cm) wide. A bowfronted chest of this period would command a price of £400–600/$580–870 at auction. This demonstrates what good value straight-fronted chests can be.
£300–360/$440–520 CGC

◄ **Walnut-veneered miniature Wellington chest,** with six drawers, on a plinth base, locking bar missing, 1860–70, 22in (56cm) high.
£400–480
$580–700 TF

Wellington chests

Wellington chests were first seen during the 1820s and are identified by their tall narrow shape, usually with seven drawers. Instead of each drawer having its own lock, they have a single locking mechanism in the form of a hinged flap on the right, which locks over the drawer fronts to stop them opening.

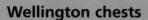

George III mahogany chest of drawers, the moulded top above two short and three long graduated drawers, on bracket feet, 40¼in (102.2cm) high.
£420–500/$600–720 CGC

Figured walnut miniature Wellington chest, with seven graduated drawers, the two locking bars with carved volutes, on a plinth base, mid-19thC, 21½in (54.5cm) high.
£420–500/$600–720 TF

Miniature furniture

There are differing theories regarding the origins of items of miniature furniture that are now so sought-after by collectors. Each explanation probably contains an element of the truth and, at least, they all help to add to the general charm and attraction of this specialist field.

The first hypothesis is that the pieces were produced by apprentices who were effectively being examined by their master prior to being recognized as craftsmen in their own right. This is an attractive and logical idea and would seem to be borne out by the high quality of much of the finished work. However, some examples are far less impressive than the best and would suggest either that the apprentice had yet to reach the required standard or that the furniture had been produced for another reason.

The second theory is that miniatures were produced as travelling salesmen's samples or as window dressing for the makers' shop premises. The latter is a particularly nice idea since it is argued that the use of small pieces of furniture for display complemented the small-paned 18th-century shop windows. Whatever its *raison d'être*, a good quality piece of miniature furniture is likely to be the subject of considerable competition in today's marketplace.

Late George III fruitwood and ebony-strung bowfronted chest of drawers, the cross-banded top above a slide and three long graduated drawers with brass handles, on bracket feet, 43in (109cm) wide. The use of fruitwood in chests of this type and period is most unusual since country makers (the main users of fruitwood) tended not to make bowfronted chests. The brushing slide over the drawers indicates a touch of quality so, overall, this price appears reasonable.
£480–580/$700–840 DN

Pine stippled chest of drawers, with two short drawers over three long drawers, 1880, 42in (106.5cm) wide. The tendency toward built-in bedroom furniture in the smaller home has resulted in a reduced demand for all but the very best quality large chests of the late 18th and 19thC. This can make for some real bargains if you shop around.
£450–500/$650–720 MLL

◀ **George III oak chest of drawers,** with two short and three long graduated cockbeaded drawers with brass swan-neck handles, on shaped bracket feet, 34½in (87.5cm) wide.
£500–600/$720–870 DA

George III mahogany chest of drawers, the top with moulded edge above two short and three long lockable drawers with brass swan-neck handles, on bracket feet, some moulding missing, 40½in (103cm) wide. This is a nice example of a good quality piece of late 18thC furniture which is both useful and good to look at without being too expensive.
£500–600/$720–870 PFK

Walnut dressing chest, the top with crossbanded border and moulded edge over two short and two long graduated drawers, each with feather-inlaid borders, early 19thC, 40in (101.5cm) wide. This is the lower section of a George II chest-on-chest with a later top set into the moulding which would have originally held the upper part in place. Its incomplete state accounts for the modest value.
£570–650/$825–950 AAR

◀ **Mahogany bowfronted chest of drawers,** with two short over two long drawers, 19thC, 35in (89cm) wide. This is another indication of the ready availability of early bowfronted chests in the £400–700/$580–1,000 price range.
£580–700/$840–1,000 B(W)

Chests of drawers

The majority of chests of drawers produced from the late 18th century onwards were practical pieces of bedroom or dressing room furniture. Sometimes of solid mahogany, but more often veneered on oak or pine, their quality can vary widely. The standard arrangement was either four long drawers of graduated depth or two short drawers with three graduated long drawers beneath. Some pieces were also fitted with what is usually referred to as a brushing slide.

By 1800 the straight-fronted chest had a popular alternative in the bowfronted variety, which continued in production throughout the 19th century.

George III oak chest of drawers, with two short over three long drawers with brass swan-neck handles, on ogee bracket feet. What appear to be original handles along with shapely ogee feet contributed to the higher than average price for this country-made piece.
£675–800/$975–1,150 HOLL

▶ **Mahogany-veneered chest of drawers,** with two short and four long drawers, on bracket feet, one foot replaced, probably Irish, early 19thC, 39½in (100.5cm) wide. Any mention of an Irish pedigree inflates the price range of a piece of furniture, in this case probably by about £200/$290.
£700–800
$1,000–1,150 WW

◄ **Mahogany chest of drawers,** the top with canted edge over a case fitted with three long graduated drawers, on bracket feet, 1850–75, 43½in (110.5cm) wide. This chest has probably been reduced in height by having the top drawer or drawers removed.
£700–800
$1,000–1,150 NOA

Transitional-style burr-walnut, mahogany and marquetry commode, the three drawers applied with gilt-metal mounts, the sides and back with chequer stringing, on cabriole legs, late 19thC, 35in (89cm) wide. The term 'Transitional' refers to the period when the main elements of Louis XV design began to be overtaken by the straighter less curvaceous lines of the Louis XVI era.
£700–850/$1,000–1,250 B

► **Mahogany and chequerbanded commode,** the top with canted angles, with four frieze drawers, on a plinth base on elongated bun feet, mid-19thC, 31½in (80cm) wide. The term 'commode' was first used to describe chests of drawers of the Louis XVI period. It was then adopted by the English to describe the French-influenced gracefully curved cupboards and chests produced in the mid-18thC.
£700–850/$1,000–1,200 B

◄ **Mahogany chest-on-chest,** on bracket feet, late 18thC, 44½in (113cm) wide. The faded colour makes this piece a real bargain since a richer hue would have resulted in paying at least £1,500/$2,175.
£850–1,000
$1,250–1,500
WW

Chests-on-chests

Chests-on-chests, or tallboys, were first made in the late 17th–early 18th century. They are sometimes prone to being married – made up from different pieces of furniture which may not even be of the same period. It is generally possible to tell when this is the case – for example, when a top looks too heavy for its base. The colour of the front of the two pieces should match, and the construction of the drawers in each piece should be the same.

Cupboards

Victorian mahogany pot cupboard, 31in (78.5cm) high. The price seems fair for this type of small cupboard. It would have increased if it had been one of a pair. Pairs of this type are more desirable because they are often bought as bedside cabinets. Look carefully at this type of furniture as these cupboards are sometimes made up from the pedestals of a contemporary sideboard. Check that the sides do not have signs of filled-in apertures where dowels would have been used to join the sideboard together.
£130–155/$190–225 TAY

Oak hanging corner cupboards, with dentil cornice, the fielded panel door enclosing shaped shelves, 19thC, 38in (96.5cm) high. A late 18thC corner cupboard would be more expensive. The split colour of the front may also attribute to it not making £500/$720.
£300–360/$440–520 WW

Pairs of bedside cupboards

Genuine old bedside cupboards and tables are sometimes 'paired' with later copies. When looking at what appears to be a pair both pieces should be inspected to ensure that the quality and figuring of the timber, construction and signs of age correspond. Signs of natural distressing should be comparable on both pieces, and any brass fittings, such as locks, hinges and handles, should match.

► **Walnut Queen Anne-style miniature cabinet,** c1930, 13in (33cm) high. The size of the piece indicates that it is perhaps an apprentice piece or made by the cabinet maker himself and taken around on his travels to potential customers. Miniature furniture is highly collectable and, if the piece had been Victorian, it would have been much more expensive. A good sign of quality is the amount of attention to detail. In this example, the cross-banded interior and handles are good indicators.
£200–240/$290–350 G(L)

The look without the price

The price for Arts and Crafts furniture greatly depends on who designed or made it. This piece represents the more commercial, mass-produced end of the market. At the other end of the spectrum, pieces by designers such as Ernest Gimson or Charles Annesley Voysey can make thousands of pounds, so if you like this style it is a very good price.

Arts and Crafts oak sideboard, with leaded glazed cupboard, the bowfronted base with two frieze drawers, over two panelled doors, 72in (183cm) wide.
£400–480/$580–700 AH

Pair of kingwood bedside tables, with three drawers, French, c1920, 15in (38cm) high. The price reflects the fact that these were made in the 1920s and not earlier. French Louis XV-style kingwood furniture was reproduced from the 1870s up to the 1930s. Earlier pieces tend to be better quality than those made in the 1920s, when cheaper versions were produced for the mass market.
£500–550/$720–800 MLL

► Oak food cupboard, with two panelled and spindle-filled cupboard doors enclosing a single shelf, adapted, early 19thC, 39½in (100.5cm) wide. It is possible that this item has been cut down from a larger piece with the lower cupboard section and two drawers having been removed, hence the price.
£500–600
$720–870 P(NW)

The look without the price

Painted pine standing corner cupboard, the moulded cornice with turned spheres above an astragal-glazed door and a panelled door, on a plinth base, 19thC, 84in (213.5cm) high.
£550–650/$800–950 DN

This piece is made from pine stained to look like oak or mahogany. Pine is a soft wood and does not lend itself to carving as well as other harder woods. If it had been made from mahogany the price would be nearer to £1,500–2,500/$2,150–3,600.

Edwardian satinwood cellaret, now converted to a magazine cabinet, painted with floral garlands and a vignette depicting a scene from classical mythology, with fitted interior, on square tapering legs and spade feet, 16¼in (41.5cm) wide. This piece is quite decorative despite its made-up appearance.
£550–650/$800–950 AH

Victorian mahogany sideboard, the mahogany-veneered back with applied scroll-carved centre shield and four pilasters, with an arch-panelled cupboard door to either side, both opening to reveal shelves, the left one with a cellaret drawer, 79in (200.5cm) wide. This price reflects the down-turn in the market value for Victorian pedestal sideboards which are currently out of fashion. Late 18thC examples are more desirable and have held their value to a greater extent.
£600–700/$870–1,000 Mit

◀ **Oak corner cupboard,** with mahogany crossbanding, c1825, 36in (91.5cm) wide.
£600–700/$870–1,000 NoC ⊞

George III oak dresser, with three frieze drawers over a central recess with ogee-panelled door, flanked on either side by two deep drawers, fluted corner quarter columns to the corners, on bracket feet. The price seems reasonable as it could be more in the region of £800–1,200/$1,150–1,750. The reason for the lower value could be its orange colour.
£600–720/$870–1,100 AH

Dressers

Dressers were first made in the 17th century and, despite the enthusiasm which prevailed from the 18th century onwards for mahogany sideboards, the oak dresser continued in use in dining rooms and kitchens through to the Edwardian era. After a decline in demand between the wars the dresser is once again one of the most sought-after pieces of furniture on the market.

The classic Welsh dresser base is fitted with cupboards with shallow drawers above them, while the same piece of furniture from southern England is more likely to have an open 'potboard' in place of cupboards.

George III oak dresser base, on stile feet, 59in (150cm) wide. The price seems a little low and this could be due to the colour.
£650–750/$950–1,100 CGC

The look without the price

This is a good example of early reproduction furniture and is based on late 17th-century models. If the piece had been original, the value would be between £2,000–4,000/$2,900–5,800, depending on colour and condition.

17thC-style oak low dresser, with moulded top above three geometrically moulded frieze drawers with turned split mouldings between, on turned baluster legs with bun feet, late 19th–early 20thC, 71¼in (81cm) wide.
£600–720/$870–1,100 CGC

Locate the source

The source of each illustration in Miller's can be found by checking the code letters below each caption with the Key to Illustrations, pages 286–290.

Mid-Victorian giltwood carved credenza, the serpentine Calcutta marble inset top within a leaf-carved border and frieze, above three arched glazed doors enclosing a velvet-lined interior and flanked by floral uprights and grotesque mask terms with a further bowed glazed arched door to either side, on a moulded plinth base, 84¾in (215.5cm) wide. The price seems good, probably because heavily-carved Victorian furniture is rather out of vogue. Examples of this type of credenza shape, but veneered in walnut with ormulu mounts, make around £2,000–3,000/$2,900–4,400.
£700–850/$1,000–1,250 B

George III oak dresser, on shaped bracket feet, 86½in (220cm) wide. This dresser is clearly a marriage, which brings the value down to its present level. If it had been completely original, the price would be £4,000–6,000/$5,800–8,700. It was probably bought for the base alone, since on its own that would have made the same price.
£950–1,100/$1,400–1,600 CGC

George III mahogany bowfronted linen press, with chequer- and line-inlaid decoration, the two panel doors over three long drawers, slides missing. The fact that this linen press is missing its original sliding trays is reflected in its relatively low value, although the lack of good colour may also be a contributory factor. Had both these factors been right, the price would have been around £1,500–2,000/$2,150–2,900. Nowadays the trays are sometimes taken out and the linen press used as a large television cabinet.
£900–1,000/$1,300–1,500 RTo

Linen presses

Linen, or clothes, presses were introduced c1750. Until 1780 many were made from mahogany, after which some were veneered in satinwood or walnut. Quality varies dramatically – some are highly sophisticated with fine carving or inlay, while others are simply constructed and unadorned.

The interiors of the upper part of most presses were originally fitted with sliding trays, many of which have now been replaced by hanging rails.

Desks & Writing Tables

◄ **Rosewood-veneered writing box,** with a fitted interior, c1860, 5in (12.5cm) wide. The price is fairly good probably because the interior is not complete, ie one of the inkwells is missing. If the piece had been in better condition it would have fetched £100–150/ $145–220. Even more desirable are those writing boxes made from coromandel wood. The interior fitments also vary in quality.
£50–60/$75–90 TAY

► **Oak table desk,** the slope opening to reveal a side compartment, 19thC, 20½in (52cm) wide.
£70–85/$100–125 WW

Edwardian lady's mahogany writing table, with inlaid decoration, the hinged lid opening to reveal a fitted interior with fold-out writing surface, stationery compartments and pen tray, top badly bowed. The price for this piece is reflected by the fact that it has a badly bowed top. If the condition had been better the value could have been £600–800/$870–1,150. Good quality Edwardian furniture, particularly Sheraton-style, is going through a renaissance in the present market. Writing furniture, such as Carlton House desks, are keenly sought-after. The elegant proportions and decorative inlays are well suited to modern tastes.
£250–300/$360–440 RTo

Miller's compares...

A. George III oak bureau, the fitted interior with drawers and pigeonholes, above four graduated drawers, on bracket feet, 43in (109cm) wide.
£480–550/$700–800 TAY

B. George III mahogany bureau, the fall-front enclosing a cupboard, pigeonholes and drawers, on bracket feet, probably Scottish, 40¼in (102cm) wide.
£800–950/$1,150–1,400
Bea(E)

Mahogany bureaux are much more expensive than oak. Item B appears to be partially missing its bracket feet which might account for its low value. With bracket feet it could fetch up to £1,500/$2,150, although the price of bureaux per se is very low at the moment due to the modern requirements of the computer, and even with bracket feet intact it is still possible to pick up bureaux like this for under £1,000/$1,500.

Late Victorian walnut-veneered davenport, decorated with boxwood floral marquetry panels, 21in (53.5cm) wide. The price here reflects the current market demise of davenports, particularly plain, later examples of which this is one. Earlier Victorian burr-walnut models with cabriole supports are more popular and can fetch £800–1,200/$1,150–1,750, although they have to be good quality and in good condition. Some Regency examples in rosewood are more desirable and can fetch up to £2,000/$2,900. A sign of quality is cedar-lined drawers.
£500–600/$720–870 TAY

Inlaid mahogany bureau, with satinwood banding and quadrant fan medallions, the shell-inlaid fall-front enclosing a cupboard, drawers and pigeonholes, above four graduated long drawers, on slender bracket feet, early 19thC, 37¾in (96cm) wide. This is a nice example although the inlaid motifs appear to be of a later date.
£900–1,000/$1,300–1,500 Bea(E)

Bureaux

The quality of the fitments and the amount of detail have a significant bearing on price. Some bureaux are fitted with a concealed well, which can be reached only from the inside by pushing back the covering slide to reveal a hollow section. In addition to a well, some have small pull-out 'secret' slides, disguised as pilasters, on either side of the central cupboard.

Fall-fronts are prone to splitting or cracking, especially in the hinge area. They are also liable to warp owing to the fact that they are made from one large piece of wood.

◄ **Edwardian mahogany secretaire cabinet,** the arched top above a chequer-strung fall enclosing a tooled green baize, pigeonholes and an arrangement of drawers with a pair of cupboard doors below, on splay legs with casters, 22in (56cm) wide. These do not sell well simply because they are not very functional. They have little storage space and the writing slope is far too high.
£550–650/$800–950 CGC

Victorian oak pedestal desk, with three frieze drawers and three drawers to each pedestal, on a plinth base with casters. This piece is the right value and quite a nice colour. Oak pedestal desks such as this are good buys compared with earlier William IV walnut counterparts, which can make £1,500–3,000/$2,200–4,400.
£900–1,000/$1,300–1,500 CGC

Prices

Desks and writing tables have steadily increased in price in recent years because a personal computer can be placed on them and still leave working space. For this reason the price of bureaux has remained static.

Mirrors & Frames

Mirrored wall sconce, 19thC, 10¼in (26cm) high.
£75–90/$110–130 SWO

Mahogany-framed swing toilet mirror, with later glass, on a stretchered frame with splay feet, 18thC, 14in (35.5cm) high. This is a very plain swing mirror.
£95–100/$140–145 WW

► **George IV mahogany table mirror,** on later bun feet, 19¾in (50cm) wide. This mirror is good value although it is a little plain in shape. Slightly earlier George III examples with serpentine outlines to the drawers and often with shield or oval backs are priced between £400–600/$580–870, though good examples can make over £1,000/$1,500. When buying a swing/toilet mirror there are often replaced elements, most commonly the feet, but sometimes the top and base are from different pieces.
£140–160/$200–230 DN

Miller's compares...

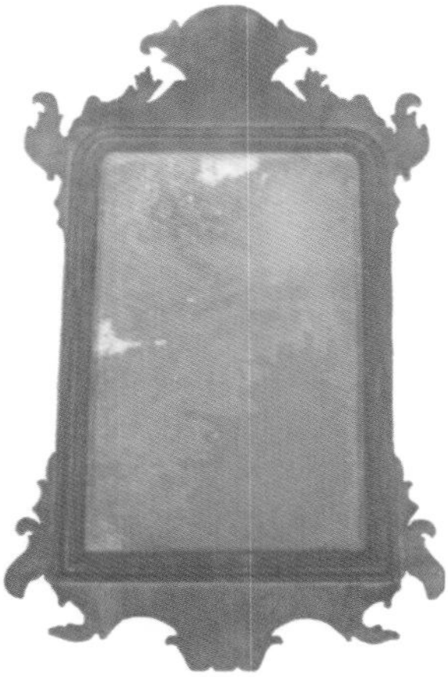

A. Mahogany-veneered fret frame mirror, late 18thC, 13in (33cm) high.
£95–110/$140–160 WW

B. Mahogany-veneered fret frame mirror, the glass with a gilt-leaf gesso edge to the moulded frame, late 18thC, 22½in (57cm) high.
£160–200/$230–290 WW

These types of small Georgian fret-carved mahogany mirrors range greatly in quality. Item A is rather plain and much smaller than Item B. Value increases with size, quality and decoration, as can be seen in Item B, which has parcel-gilt decoration. The fret-carved surrounds are often replaced. Look for any obvious differences in the grain and colour.

Mahogany-veneered fret frame mirror, with a later base, late 18thC, 35¼in (89.5cm) high. This is a nice mirror and has a good colour. It would have made more had the plate been original.
£150–180/$220–260 WW

Regency gilt pier mirror, the ball-decorated cornice above a frieze set with a lion's mask, with incised flashing and later painting, the bevelled rectangular glass with a reeded ebonized inner slip, with leaf-capped moulded pilasters, 28½in (72.5cm) high. There is some later painting and worn gilding on this item which may have some bearing on the low price. The cost of re-gilding is very expensive and can run into three-figure sums, so it may be better to buy a good quality example in the first place as it may prove to be cheaper in the long run.
£200–250/$290–350 WW

Mirrors

Mirrors or 'looking glasses' were being produced in Murano and silvered in Venice in the 16th century but were not made in England until a hundred years later. It was in Sir Robert Mansell's glass house in London in 1625 that they were first manufactured by the cylinder process (whereby cylinders of glass were blown, then slit open and laid flat), and then by the Duke of Buckingham at his famous glassworks at Vauxhall. The limitations of this production method meant that only small plates could be made so it was not unusual for several pieces of glass to be used to create a single mirror. By 1773, far larger and better quality plates were being produced at Ravenshead.

During the latter half of the 18th century and in the 19th century, framing styles changed dramatically from the airy full-blown carved giltwood confections of the Chippendale period to the heavier designs of the Regency and Victorian eras.

► **Mahogany dressing table mirror,** the moulded plate on leaf-carved cheval supports, over a box base with drawers, on rounded feet, 19thC.
£200–250
$290–350 HOK

Mahogany swing toilet mirror, with turned supports, the box base with three drawers, on turned feet, finials missing, early 19thC, 22in (56cm) high. This is a good example of its type. The feet appear original but may not be. Feet are the most commonly replaced elements to swing mirrors.
£200–250/$290–350 WW

◄ **Pierced, swept and gilded composition frame,** Continental, 19thC, 24¼in (61.5cm) high. Picture frames like this one are now frequently fitted with mirrored plates. This can prove very effective although the purist will always be happier with a genuine mirror.
£220–250
$350–380 Bon(C)

Mahogany travelling mirror, 19thC, 15½in (39.5cm) high.
£260–320/$330–460 SWO

Care of mirrors

If the silver backing of an antique mirror has badly deteriorated, repair should not be attempted as any restoration will always substantially devalue the piece.

There are three traditional methods used to clean the fronts of mirrors. The first is to wipe the glass with a lint-free cloth moistened with methylated spirits. The second is to wipe the glass with a lint-free cloth which has been wrung out in lukewarm water to which a few drops of ammonia have been added. The third is to lightly moisten a lint-free cloth with paraffin and wipe the glass. This last method works well but leaves a smell of paraffin in the air for some time. Whichever method is chosen, it is essential to avoid any moisture getting behind the glass, as this will cause further deterioration of the silvering.

Regency mahogany swing toilet mirror, the reeded frame supported by pilasters with urn finials, surmounted by a scrolling foliage crest surrounding Prince of Wales plumes, on acanthus-carved scrolling front legs, 30in (76cm) high. A good price for a well-carved Regency mirror.
£260–320/$380–460 WW

Gilt pier mirror, the cornice above a panel with a papier mâché scallop shell flanked by anthemia, the later bevelled plate with a reeded ebonized strip- and rope-twist pilasters, early 19thC, 46in (117cm) high. This is a good price for such a mirror.
£320–380/$460–575 WW

Pair of oval boudoir mirrors, with beaded gilt gesso frames, the wire plasterwork laurel borders with urn surmounts and ribbon-tied pendant bases, 19thC, 28in (71cm) high. The wire-framed gesso (plaster) decoration on mirrors of this type is easily damaged. On this occasion several pieces of ornamentation are missing and this is reflected in the price. The price of these were they undamaged would be £1,000–1,500/$1,500–2,150.
£500–550/$720–800 WW

► **Micro-mosiac easel mirror,** the frame decorated with panels of floral sprays and foliage on a powder blue and white ground, with spiral twist-glass borders and glass flowerheads, with bevelled glass, late 19thC.
£500–600/$720–870 Bea(E)

Convex mirror, the moulded ball-decorated frame with a gesso leaf border, with a reeded ebonized slip, 19thC, 21½in (55.5cm) wide.
£500–600/$720–870 WW

► **Late George III giltwood-framed overmantel mirror,** the ball-decorated cornice above a carved shell with acanthus leaves, flanked by figures in niches and stop-fluted Corinthian columns, side cornice moulding missing, later glass plate, 43in (109cm) high. This is a very good price for such a mirror. It could make in the region of £2,000–3,000/ $2,900–4,400. The balls are damaged which may have a bearing on the price. Also, the mirror plate looks new which will also effect the value.
£520–620/$750–900 Bea(E)

Mirrors & frames

A combination of a heavy tax on glass and the failure of English factories to produce large mirror plates tended to dictate the form and development of the mid-18th century mirror. To escape the duty and to avoid the costly import of large plates from France, two steps were taken. Old mirrors were recycled and sizeable mirrors were produced by contriving frames which, while they held multiple pieces of glass, gave the illusion of a single plate.

By the end of the 18th century the availability of large home-produced plates made it possible to create far bigger mirrors with much lighter frames. Perversely, the beginning of the 19th century saw the rise in popularity of a small example – the convex mirror. This was much favoured in the dining room since it enabled the butler to keep an eye on the progress of a meal without having to move about the room thereby distracting the diners.

Gilt gesso and carved wood-framed hall mirror, the arched scroll top centred by a basket of fruit, the sectional plates with applied open vine leaf and scroll-carved frame, restored, north Italian, 1800–50, 47¼in (120cm) high. This is a good price for a mirror such as this.
£580–680
$850–1,000 P(WM)

► **Etched Venetian glass wall mirror,** with a pierced scroll surmount, the bevelled plates within etched blue glass margins, Italian, c1910, 49in (124.5cm) high.
£820–900
$1,200–1,300 S(S)

Victorian overmantel mirror, the gilt gesso frame decorated in neo-classical revival style, the cornice with a flower frieze and oval paterae above the doric capital pilasters, 46½in (118cm) high. This is a good quality mirror.
£840–1,000/$1,220–1,500 WW

Screens

William IV rosewood pole screen, with woolwork shield-shaped crest, raised on a tapering lotus-carved support and concave platform base on compressed bun feet, 54¾in (139cm) high. This is a good pole screen at a low price. It should be £250–400/$360–580. Pole screens per se are not that sought after. They are bought for their decorative appeal and have little function.
£150–180/$220–260 CGC

Facts in brief

All fire screens were originally intended to protect those sitting around the hearth from the direct heat of the fire. Certain 18th-century examples were fitted with sliding panels so that the area of protection could be increased or diminished as the user required.

At some point, probably in the 19th century, cheval screens (the type comprising a panel supported on four outswept legs) started to serve the secondary purpose of standing in front of spent or unlit fires. This may have been to disguise the fact that the maid had not cleared away the ashes or simply to cover the grate during the summer months.

Pole screens were used specifically to protect the face and the cosmetic preparations used on the face from intense heat. This was not a requirement confined to the ladies since many gentlemen also made use of make-up, including the Prince Regent whose skin, as a result, was reported to have been waxen and almost copper-coloured by the time he was in his late forties.

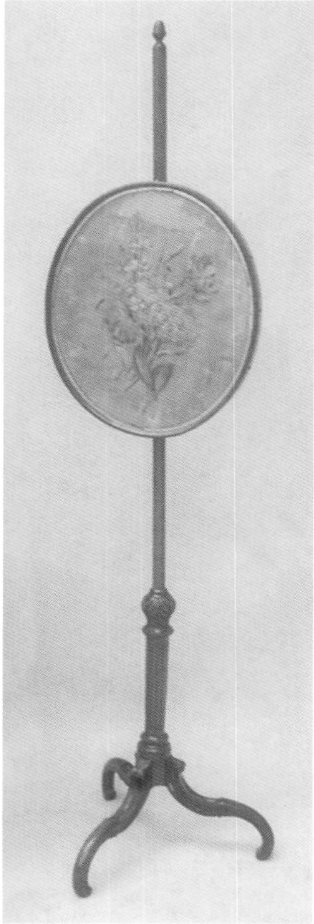

► **Walnut tripod pole screen,** the fluted column with acorn finial, on S-scrolled supports with acanthus-carved knees and scroll toes, 19thC, 56¼in (143cm) high. The price for this screen would have been higher if it were George III. Earlier George III examples in the Sheraton style made from satinwood are more desirable and fetch between £600–900/$870–1,300.
£280–350/$400–720 DD

Giltwood Louis XV-style threefold screen, the graduated panels with floral and foliate frames, containing shaped bevelled plates of glass above shaped fabric panels, each on scroll feet, 72in (183cm) high. This is a good quality screen.
£800–900/$1,150–1,300 B

Further reading

Miller's Late Georgian to Edwardian Furniture Buyer's Guide, Miller's Publications, 2003

Sofas

Beech-framed upholstered three-piece suite, with bobbin-turned stretchers, 1920s, sofa 52in (132cm) wide.
£250–300/$360–440 SWO

Settees & sofas

The word settee was used throughout the 18th century to describe any appropriate piece of seat furniture, whether it had a carved or upholstered back, while the term sofa came to be applied just to more heavily upholstered examples. Now the words are almost interchangeable.

Most settees of the 18th century, whether upholstered or carved, formed parts of suites and as such their designs matched those of the chairs in the suites. Also, since they were made to stand against walls, their backs were plain and unadorned.

The elegant French-influenced designs of the late 18th century gave way to the far heavier and extravagantly shaped pieces during the period of the Regency reigns of George IV and William IV. By 1860, the French taste had once again brought a lighter touch to the form of Victorian furniture, and the settee and the now popular chaise longue had taken on new curvaceous, organic lines. During the last quarter of the century the sumptuously upholstered and buttoned Chesterfield gained a level of popularity which it has never really relinquished.

Stained beech button-back sofa, c1860, 57in (145cm) wide. The price reflects the market for this type of Victorian sofa. It would have been more if it were made from mahogany and were less plain. The upholstery at the top is worn, which may have affected its price. In better condition this could make £900/$1,300.
£550–660/$800–960 S(O)

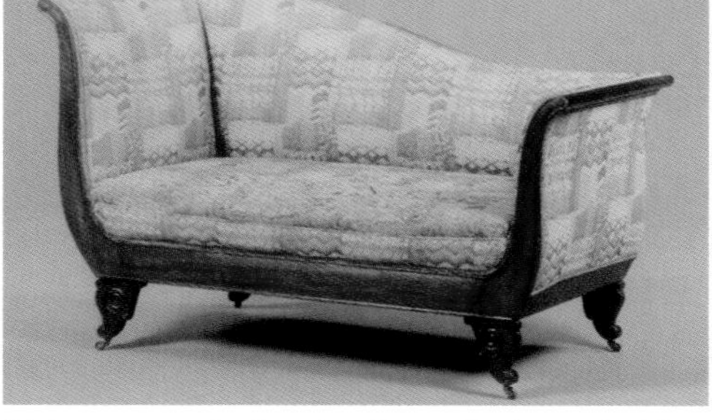

Mahogany sofa, French, c1830, 57in (145cm) wide.
£600–720/$870–1,050 S(O)

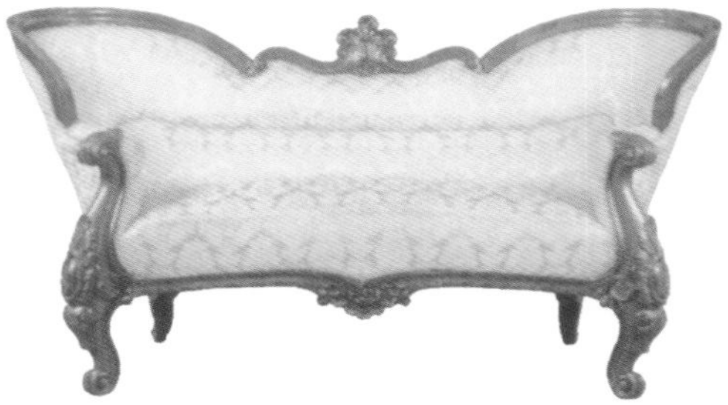

Louis XV-style mahogany twin-seater sofa, c1870, 77¼in (196cm) wide. This item is a very good buy as the upholstery appears to be immaculate.
£650–780/$950–1,130 S(O)

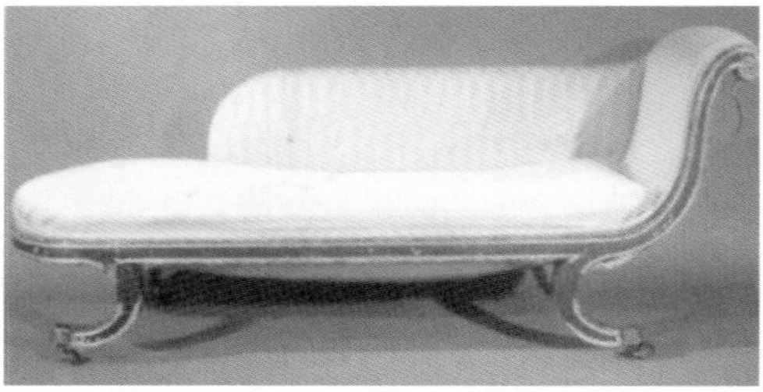

Regency chaise longue, the ebonized and gilt grooved frame on scroll legs with brass sabots, with a loose cover, 72in (183cm) wide. This is the sort of piece that interior decorators love, being simple but elegant. If it were in better condition it could make £800–1,200/$1,200–1,750.
£650–800/$950–1,150 WW

Chaises longues & daybeds

The Regency period saw the introduction of the chaise longue, a fully upholstered chair with an elongated seat and inclined back and arms. They were sometimes made in mirror image pairs, with headrests at opposite ends, but are now mostly found as single examples. The frames of Victorian chaises longues were often elaborately carved.

Mid-Victorian carved mahogany love seat, the tapering padded back with downswept carved arms on scroll supports, above a deep stuff-over seat on egg-and-dart carved bun front supports with brass cappings and casters. The price for this love seat is good, considering how unusual it is and that it does not need recovering. Love seat is a 20thC term to describe a small settee designed for two people. The first date back to the early 18thC. The French use the term *causeuse*.
£700–840/$1,000–1,220 B

Louis XVI-style four-piece giltwood and gesso salon suite, comprising a pair of fauteuils, a canapé and a side chair, French, c1900, canapé 46½in (118cm) wide. The price for this suite reflects the fact that it is incomplete, missing a side chair. The condition may also be poor. This type of Louis XVI revival salon suites were made in abundance in the last quarter of the 19thC and into the 20thC and they vary in quality. If this had been a whole set and in better condition it would have made £1,500–2,500/$2,200–3,600 at auction.
£850–1,000/£1,250–1,500 S(O)

George III-style mahogany and upholstered settee, restored, retipping, 19thC, 72¾in (185cm) wide. This is an elegant sofa, but the price reflects the fact that these types of sofa are not that desirable at the moment. The reason is that the seat tends to be too high and they are uncomfortable to sit on.
£900–1,000/$1,300–1,500 S(O)

Stands

Washstands

Washstands vary from simple tripod stands, sometimes wrongly known as wig stands, to small cabinets. They were made to hold a wash basin and a jug, and usually include a drawer for toiletries. Although they are no longer in demand for their original use, they are popular as decorative items for bedrooms or halls.

Victorian pine washstand, with all-over painted decoration and two frieze drawers, 48in (122cm) wide. This is an attractive piece and reflects the current taste for painted pine furniture. The two missing handles may have affected its value, but not by much as they are easily replaceable. The price for a good mahogany example from the same period would be from £300–500/$450–700.
£170–200/$250–290 SWO

◄ **Edwardian pine plant stand,** 26in (66cm) wide. If this stand had been made of mahogany rather than pine it would have made about £100/$145 more.
£85–95
$125–140 MIL

Mahogany whip and boot stand, with a brass handle, the domed top with pegs to a central tier with heel cups, with a base tray and plinth feet, early 19thC. This is a good buy. The fact that this has faded may have influenced the price.
£220–260/$320–380 WW

Sheraton period mahogany corner washstand, the later top with a single and two dummy drawers, the centre section with dummy drawers, on later socket feet, splash back removed, 23½in (59.5cm) wide. The missing splashback and later top account for the price. If everything were right it would make £300–500/$450–700.
£230–275/$330–400 WW

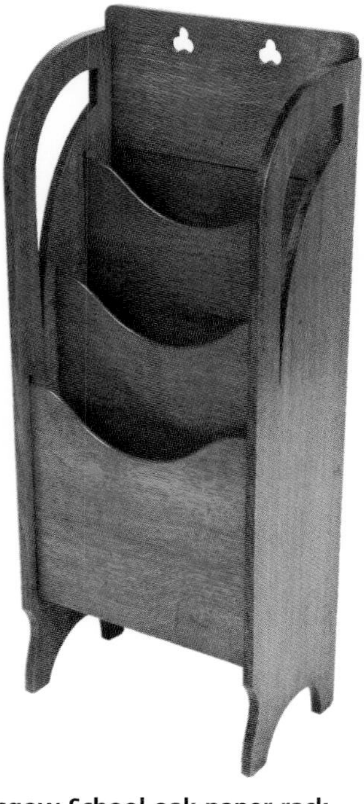

Glasgow School oak paper rack, Scottish, c1905, 15in (38cm) wide.
£350–385/$500–560 MTay

Victorian mahogany luggage stand, by James Shoolbred & Co, with a copper-banded edge, on turned tapering legs, 24¼in (61.5cm) wide.
£400–500/$580–720 Bon

Early Victorian mahogany luggage rack on stand, the slatted top on turned tapering legs and spool feet, 26¾in (68cm) wide.
£500–600/$720–870 B

Mahogany shaving stand, with mirror, c1890, 56in (142cm) high.
£550–600 $800–870 GBr

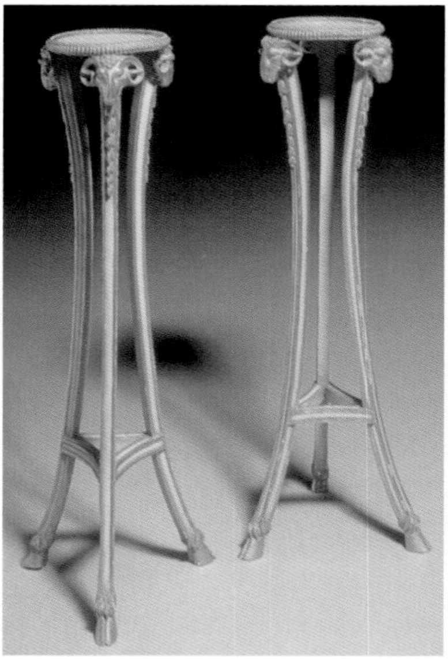

Pair of grey-painted and parcel gilt torchères, the dished tops with gadrooned borders on inswept supports headed by ram's head and husk decoration, on outswept legs and hairy hoof feet, 41in (104cm) high. These are a good buy. The gilding looks slightly worn, which may account for the price. They could easily make £1,000–1,200/$1,500–2,000.
£700–840/$1,000–1,220 B

Jardinières & stands

If the 19th century was the period of the jardinière, the last half of the 18th century was the zenith of the stand.

Stands were in abundance in well-appointed houses. There were stands for busts, candles, basins, Chinese jars, urns and even for tea kettles. They were fashioned out of delicately carved giltwood, wire and gesso, simulated bamboo, mahogany, satinwood and other fine woods.

These 18th-century styles were revived in the 1860s but by 1910 the Tottenham Court Road 'art furnishers and decorators', Norman & Stacey, were meeting a new public demand with carved hardwood examples imported from the Far East.

The relatively simple flower stand that is now recognized as a jardinière has evolved from a very complicated article. In the early 1800s, when the term was first used, ingenious designs abounded, so much so that George Smith's 1826 *Cabinet Makers' and Upholsterers' Guide* even contained a modest proposal for a combined jardinière and aviary.

Steps & Stools

Beech folding stool, c1920, 16in (40.5cm) high.
£30–35/$45–50 AL

Elm stool, c1890, 15in (38cm) high.
£35–40/$50–60 AL

Oak stool, c1920, 27in (68.5cm) high.
£50–55/$75–80 AL

Ash and elm country stool, c1835, 10in (25.5cm) high.
£60–70/$90–100 F&F

Ash and beech stool, c1830, 9in (23cm) high.
£50–60/$75–90 F&F

Mahogany stool, with drop-in seat, on tapering legs, partly restored, early 19thC, 21in (53.5cm) high. The price of this piece is low because it has been restored, which may mean that one of the legs has been spliced and re-attached.
£60–70/$90–100 WW

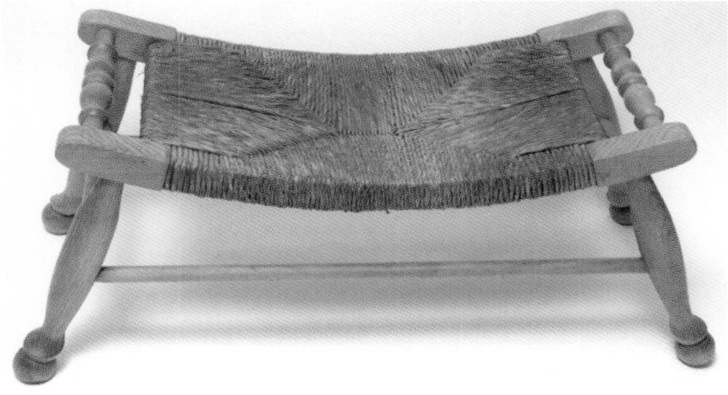

Oak stool, with a rush seat, 1900, 12in (30.5cm) high.
£70–80/$100–115 MLL

► **Victorian walnut piano stool,** with upholstered adjustable top, foliate-carved baluster column and three similarly carved downswept legs on scroll feet, c1860, 14¼in (36cm) diam. This is a good price. If it were in better condition it would make £200–300/$300–450.
£95–115/$140–165 WilP

Oak metamorphic library steps, c1890, 27in (68.5cm) high. These steps are a good price, particularly when a reproduction would cost more. The history of metamorphic library chairs/steps dates back to the 18thC but examples from this period are extremely rare. In the Regency period the firm of Morgan & Saunders patented a design for a mahogany armchair with scrolled arm rests, which has since become the most recognized model ever. In today's market, a Morgan & Saunders period example can make up to £10,000/$14,500. In the late Victorian era simpler types were made. This is a provincially made piece. Some examples dating from the same period, made from walnut with tiled backs, make between £300–500/$450–700.
£110–120/$160–175 AL

Mahogany piano stool, the revolving padded seat with central screw adjustment, on turned tapering legs, 19thC, 5in (38cm) diam. The fact that this stool is rather plain reflects its low price.
£120–140/$175–200 WW

Sycamore and ash milking stool, Welsh, 19thC, 11in (28cm) high.
£120–145/$175–210 CoA

Carved oak jointed stool, with later Victorian top, 17thC, 20in (51cm) high. The very good price reflects the fact that it has a later Victorian top. Joint stools are highly sought-after. They were first produced in the middle of the 16thC, and for the next hundred years became the standard seat furniture. They were originally made in sets but due to time and damage (many have severe woodworm), these are now very rare, and most stools that appear on the market are single, which makes them collectable items in their own right. Condition, colour and rarity are a key factor to understanding value. If the top of this stool had been original it would have fetched between £700–900/$1,000–1,300, though rare examples can make up to £7,000/$10,000, particularly earlier Tudor pieces. Examples made from yew wood are also rare and command good prices.
£160–180/$230–260 SuA

Miller's compares...

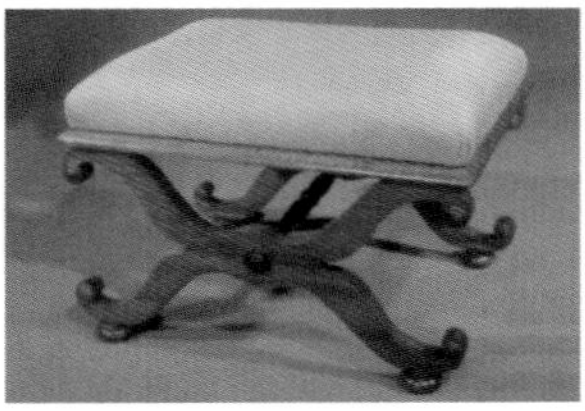

A. Early Victorian faded rosewood X-frame stool, with a detachable padded seat, with a turned stretcher and bun feet, 21½in (54.5cm) wide.
£165–185/$240–270 PICA

B. Victorian mahogany X-frame stool, the seat upholstered in silk and wool needlework, the base with a double baluster stretcher.
£650–780/$950–1,130 B&L

Item B, with its double baluster stretcher, is a more attractive design than Item A. Although the rosewood in Item A is a particularly popular wood, it is faded, and the padded seat compares less favourably with the silk and wool needlework of Item B.

Oak stool, c1890, 14in (35.5cm) high.
£165–185/$240–270 PICA

Revolving piano stool, c1880, 19in (48.5cm) high. This piano stool is probably walnut. Earlier George IV models with reeded turned legs and splayed feet (in the Gillow style) in mahogany can make £400–600/$580–870 or more.
£250–280/$360–410 RPh

Miller's compares...

A. Mahogany stool, with drop-in upholstered seat, shaped frieze, cabriole legs and pad feet, early 18thC, 15in (38cm) wide.
£400–480/$480–700 AH

B. Walnut stool, with drop-in seat, on cabriole legs with pad feet, mid-18thC, 20in (51cm) high.
£840–1,000
$1,175–1,500 WW

The price of Item B is greater than Item A because it is in better condition, made from walnut and, although slightly later in date, it is generally better quality, particularly the legs, where the carving is crisper. Item A is rather plain, the top is not shaped and the legs are fairly crude when compared to good examples, which can have carved knees, cabriole legs and well-carved claw-and-ball feet.

◄ **Edwardian mahogany and satinwood-banded dressing stool,** with trade label for Edwards & Roberts, 26in (66cm) wide. This piece is high quality and good value. A pair could fetch £1,500–2,500/ $2,200–3,600.
£450–550
$650–800 P(S)

► **Oak joined stool,** the top with channel-moulded edge and frieze, on turned legs, late 17thC, 22in (56cm) high. This stool is a good price and could have fetched between £800–1,200/ $1,200–1,750 if in better condition.
£580–650
$840–950 Bea(E)

Tables

Victorian mahogany occasional table, with inlaid satinwood stringing, on square tapering legs, the X-stretcher inlaid with a sunflower, 20in (51cm) wide. This is a good example of a late Victorian octagonal-top table, of which there are many. Usually in plain mahogany and selling for under £1,000/$1,500, this example benefits from the extra detail of the satinwood stringing and the central flower-head motif to the stretcher.
£150–180/$220–260 WW

Victorian walnut occasional centre table, the quatreform undertier on square tapering legs with carved chrysanthemums, 33in (84cm) wide. This is a typical late Victorian octagonal-top centre table of good design. The carved flowerheads on the legs are motifs used on Aesthetic furniture of the 1870s, so it could loosely be described as Aesthetic style. Tables such as this are fairly common and are often ebonized, and in those examples the flowerheads are often gilded. A nice feature is the fact that the undertier is higher up than on the more standard models which use the undertier as a stretcher.
£200–240/$290–350 WW

Centre tables

The term centre table is now widely used for almost any table designed to stand freely in the centre of a room and which is therefore of symmetrical form. Unlike pieces made for positioning against walls which have one side plain and undecorated, a centre table will look the same from all sides right down to having either two sets of opposing frieze drawers, or one real set and a dummy set. The most elaborate centre tables were intended for use in large halls.

Miller's compares...

A. Victorian mahogany centre table, on four square section supports with scrolled bases, 36¼in (92cm) wide.
£200–250/$290–350 WiLP

B. Rosewood centre table, on pierced trestle supports, with scrolled feet and casters, 19thC, 41¾in (106cm) wide.
£440–520/$640–755 AH

Item B is a similar style centre table to Item A, though it fetched more at auction. This is because it is made from rosewood, which is more desirable on this sort of furniture. It also has nicer detail in the unusual carved capitals of the trestle ends. The trestle ends of Item B are of nicely turned baluster form, whereas those of Item A are just square sections. The feet are also well-carved, terminating in gentle scrolls, compared with the plain turned feet of Item A.

George II oak tripod table, with a circular top and baluster stem, 27½in (70cm) diam. This highly practical period table is great value when compared with its mahogany counterpart which would command a price of £600–800/$875–1,150. The shape, lines and proportions being exactly the same as the more expensive variety.
£250–300/$360–440 S(O)

Victorian black lacquer and papier mâché snap-top chess table, the stem and base gilded with vine leaves and flowers. This would have been more expensive if it had carried the label for the firm Jennens & Bettridge, who were the most notable producers of papier mâché furniture in the 19thC. Papier mâché furniture is not always to everyone's taste but is popular with interior decorators as it is pretty and decorative. The market tends to fluctuate, although at the present time it is picking up again. This piece is functional as well as decorative, however, there is nowhere to store the chess pieces, unlike the typical Victorian wooden tables that have swivel tops which reveal a compartment for storage.
£280–320/$410–450 RTo

The look without the price

Many oak gateleg tables of this period have been altered or extensively repaired. The most common fault is that tops have been replaced either substantially or completely. In this example the missing drawer and other repairs will have led to a discounted price. An example in original condition could well fetch £2,000–3,000/ $2,900–4,350.

Oak gateleg dining table, on bobbin-turned legs, drawer missing, top probably a replacement, probably 18thC, 48in (122cm) wide.
£260–310
$380–640 G(L)

Types of tables

Perhaps no single item of furniture reflects better the explosion of affluence that took place during the 18th and 19th centuries than the table. Just two hundred years earlier, at the end of the 16th century, the dominant piece of furniture in this category was still the long oak dining table directly descended from the monastic refectory table, but by 1800, popular pattern books were bulging with a multitude of different varieties and designs, some practical and neat, others downright fanciful.

Life was certainly reflected in the art of the table. The card table was an essential item for any civilized drawing room since a mania for cards and gambling had swept the kingdom during the early part of the 18th century. So much so that the Countess of Hartford lamented in 1741 that it was a 'mortifying sight, that play should become the business of the nation from the age of 15 to fourscore'.

More intellectual activities also prevailed, however, and the library was an important statement of self-improvement and learning. Fine rooms demanded fine furniture, and the major makers and designers of the age, including Thomas Chippendale, Ince & Mayhew and Thomas Sheraton, responded with notable and original pieces.

The other great room in any house was the dining room but, curiously, no designs for dining tables are included in the pattern books of the period, although there are many different types and styles available, from the intimate gateleg to the opulent four-pillar table.

In common with other areas of furniture, the descriptions given to some tables have varied over the years so that the names by which they are currently known may not really reflect their original use.

Miller's compares...

A. Oak drop-leaf table, repair to top, mid-18thC, 39¾in (101cm) wide.
£300–360/$440–520 S(O)

B. Mahogany drop-leaf table, with pad feet, c1740, 46½in (118cm) wide.
£820–980/$1,180–1,425 S(O)

Item B made more money than Item A because it is a much better colour. The top of Item A has a repair and it is warped. Item B is in good condition and has a scalloped carved apron, whereas Item A is plain. The legs of Item B are well-shaped and nicely turned. All these factors reflect the differences in price.

► **Side table,** the banded top, frame and legs veneered in acacia, the frieze drawer veneered in mahogany, with oval embossed brass plate swing handles, Scottish, early 19thC, 36in (91.5cm) wide. The condition of the top of this table is poor and faded, the colour of the drawer does not match and could be later. A piece in good condition can make £700–1,000/$1,000–1,500.
£300–360/$440–520 WW

George III mahogany Pembroke table, with ebony stringing, reeded-edge top, frieze drawers with turned brass handles and square tapering legs with brass toes and casters, 39in (99cm) wide. Pembroke tables are a particularly good buy at the moment as their popularity is currently at rock bottom. However, it is hard to believe that prices will remain so depressed.
£320–380/$460–570 AH

Late Georgian mahogany tripod table, satinwood crossbanded and chequer strung, on a turned column with splayed legs, 29¼in (74.5cm) wide. This piece appears to be a very good buy. The shell inlay to the centre could possibly be an Edwardian addition.
£350–420/$500–600 DN

George III elm tripod table, with octagonal drop-leaf top, on a turned column and outswept legs, late 18thC, 21¼in (54cm) wide. This table would have made double the price if it had been in better condition. It is a good buy, and restoration would make this a good piece.
£350–420/$500–600 Bon

Gilt console table, with plaster and gesso decoration and marble top, the frieze on baluster knopped and reeded legs, with shaped undertier, marble cracked, 19thC, 65½in (166.5cm) wide. This piece is in very poor condition. The marble top is cracked and the gesso appears to be badly damaged. It is also plaster and not giltwood, which diminishes its value. In better condition it would fetch £800–1,200/$1,200–1,750.
£400–480/$580–700 WW

Tripod tables

The tripod table was introduced in England during the 1730s and was particularly popular in the Chippendale period. Most were of solid wood, although some later examples were veneered. Tops are usually round and were made so that they can tilt to a vertical position, allowing the table to be stored in a corner of the room when not in use. The top was fixed by means of two bearers and held in place with a brass catch. Some have a Birdcage support, where the whole mechanism fits onto the top of the pedestal. A peg through the stem allows the top to rotate, tilt, or be fixed in place.

The look without the price

This good quality copy of a George II low-boy represents excellent value since a genuine example could well make at least £1,000–1,500/ $1,500–2,200.

George II-style mahogany side table, with three drawers with brass handles, on turned tapering legs and pad feet, 34¼in (87cm) wide.
£400–480/$580–700 DN

► **George III snap-top tripod table,** the top with birdcage support, the centre turned column on downswept legs and pad feet, 30in (76cm) wide. This is a good price. Birdcage supports are more desirable than plain-stemmed. It could fetch £700–900/ $1,000–1,300.
£400–500/$580–720 Mit

Edwardian satinwood dressing table, the two hinged flaps enclosing lidded compartments, with a deep frieze drawer and four dummy drawers, on tapering legs with brass caps and casters, 35¾in (91cm) wide.
£480–570/$700–825 CGC

Arts and Crafts light oak dressing table, designed and patented by H. Lebus, the mirror above a fall-front recess with copper strap hinges, above one long drawer, c1901, 42in (106.5cm) wide.
£480–575/$695–835 G(L)

◄ **George III mahogany two-tier dumb waiter,** 31in (78.5cm) high. This piece has been cut down. Originally there would have been a third upper tier – although they do come with two tiers as well – in this case the upper tier is also a replacement. This is reflected in the price and had it not been altered it would have cost £1,200–1,800/ $1,750–2,600.
£480–580/$700–840 BR

Edwardian mahogany envelope card table, decorated with satinwood banding and boxwood string inlays, 30in (76cm) wide. This is a good price, the reason being that it is less sophisticated than other examples. Card tables in the Sheraton revival-style, usually in rosewood and often inlaid with urns and swags, are the best sellers and can sometimes fetch between £1,500–2,000/$2,200–3,000.
£500–600/$720–870 TAY

► **Mahogany work table,** with a single drawer, on turned legs, c1840, 28in (71cm) wide.
£500–550
$720–800 NAW

The look without the price

This is a classic example of a good-quality affordable 100-year old antique at a fraction of the cost of its original. Its design is based on a 1770 piece which would cost over £5,000/$7,250, depending on quality. When buying a demi-lune console or serving table, be careful because some of them have been cleverly adapted from the D-shaped ends of dining tables. Look at the underside to check whether there are signs where the bearers would have gone. Check the edge of the semi-circular top on dining tables as there is usually an overhang. The back of the top on a console/serving table should also jut out. This is because it goes against the wall, preventing the back legs from knocking into the skirting board.

Georgian-style mahogany demi-lune serving table, the top with foliate-carved edge, the frieze with an anthemion cartouche and paterae, on tapering square legs with spade feet, 54in (137cm) wide.
£500–600/$720–870 Bea(E) ⚒

Silvered carved side table/stand, the foliate and pierced carved frieze with a central drawer, on cabriole legs and ball-and-claw feet, 20thC, with elements of earlier carving in the frieze. This may have been the stand for a lacquered cabinet. Its modest price is explained by the fact that it will need to have a marble top cut for it if it is now to be used as a table.
£500–600/$720–870 B ⚒

Auction or dealer?

All the pictures in our price guides originate from auction houses ⚒ and dealers ⊞. When buying at auction, prices can be lower than those of a dealer, but a buyer's premium and VAT will be added to the hammer price. Equally, when selling at auction, commission, tax and photography charges must be taken into account. Dealers will often restore pieces before putting them back on the market. Both dealers and auctioneers can provide professional advice, so it is worth researching both sources before buying or selling your antiques.

► **Victorian mahogany drop-leaf table,** the rectangular top with two drop leaves, on bulbous reeded legs, the turned *toupie* feet on casters, 1850–75, 50in (127cm) extended. This is a fair price for the table. The legs are more attractive than on most Victorian drop-leaf tables which tend to be more plainly turned. The top is a little faded and needs a good polish.
£500–600/$720–870 NOA ⚒

The look without the price

17thC-style oak refectory table, c1920, 101½in (258cm) wide.
£500–600/$720–870 S(O)

This is a very good quality early 20thC copy of a 17thC-style refectory table. An original would cost at least £3,000–5,000/ $4,500–7,250. This piece is a very good buy and should have cost between £800–1,000/ $1,200–1,500.

► **George III mahogany Pembroke table,** with rounded oblong top, the shaped frieze with a single drawer with brass drop handles, on moulded chamfered legs, 36in (91.5cm) wide. This is a good Pembroke table with a figure on the mahogany top. The price reflects the general down-turn in popularity and, hence, the value of these tables.
£520–580/$750–850 AH

George III mahogany side table, the rectangular top with solid gallery above a single cockbeaded frieze drawer, on square tapering legs, 19¾in (50cm) wide. This piece sold for a very good price. It could have made £1,000–1,500/$1,500–2,200.
£520–580/$750–850 B(Ed)

Pembroke tables

Although the first Pembroke tables were used in England in the 1760s, Chippendale referred to them simply as breakfast tables. It was not until later in the century that Thomas Sheraton made them popular, claiming they were named after Lady Pembroke who first ordered one.

Early examples tended to have rectangular flaps but by 1800 the oval shape created by rounded flaps was the height of fashion. As the 19th century progressed, there was a return to a heavier form with D-shaped flaps and with some tables being supported on a central pedestal rather than legs.

Sheraton mahogany Pembroke table, the oval drop-leaf top above a flat end frieze drawer and dummy drawer with brass Dutch drop handles, the square tapering legs with ebony collars, 28¼in (72cm) wide. The low price of this piece may be accounted for by the fact that the top is damaged and the general lack of condition and quality.
£540–640/$800–950 WW

William IV rosewood work box, the hinged cover enclosing a later lift-out tray, on a knopped baluster stem and quatreform base, with flattened bun feet and brass casters, formerly fitted as a teapoy, cover cracked, 8½in (21.5cm) wide.
£550–660/$800–965 WW

Miller's compares...

A. Early Victorian mahogany work table, the twin-flap top with two frieze drawers and two dummy drawers each end, one formerly with divisions, with wood knob handles, on an open hoop stand with carving, the quatreform base on bun feet with casters, 22½in (57cm) wide.
£520–620/$750–900 WW

B. William IV mahogany-veneered work table, the twin-flap top banded in rosewood, the frieze with two drawers and two dummy drawers, on a shaped stem with gadroon moulding, the quatreform base on turned feet with brass casters, 18in (45.5cm) wide.
£660–800/$965–1,150 WW

The higher price of Item B is due to the better quality timber, the grain having a nice figure and the richer colour, in comparison to Item A.

► **Mahogany and rosewood crossbanded breakfast table,** early 19thC, 39in (99cm) wide. A possible explanation for the low price of this piece is that the top and base are a marriage. If not, it could easily make £1,200–1,800/ $1,750– 2,600.
£560–620/$815–900 NAW

George III oak side table, the moulded rounded rectangular top above a long drawer and two short drawers retaining the original engraved brass handles, on square chamfered legs, 28in (71cm) wide. This piece has poor colour and the condition is worn, which is reflected in its price.
£560–650/$815–950 CGC

Mahogany occasional table, the rectangular tilt-top crossbanded and inlaid with stringing, on a ring-and-vase turned stem with four reeded hipped splay legs and ball feet, 28in (71cm) wide.
£580–700
$850–1,000 WW

Tilt-top tables

The fashion for round tables which could be used for dining, playing games or simply as occasional tables increased during the beginning of the 19th century.

Some table tops can be tilted so that the table can be placed against a wall when not in use in order to take up less space. The top of the table rests on a block which is supported by a pedestal. If the top has always rested on the block there will be signs of this, often quite subtle, on the underside in between the bearers. The pedestal is usually tenoned onto the block for maximum strength. Owing to the inevitable shrinkage of the block, these tenons often stand slightly proud of the block and this will cause corresponding marks on the underside of the top.

To establish whether the top has always been associated with its bearers, examine the underside carefully for marks of other bearers or plugged holes which would indicate that the top has been on another table and has perhaps been cut down. Next, examine the base to see whether it belongs with the block. There should be no suspicious signs underneath the block indicating that an alteration may have taken place – for example, where the top may have been cut down from a larger table to fit the base.

William IV rosewood-veneered centre table, the rectangular top above a drawer and frieze drawers with brass knob handles, the tapering pillar on a quatreform base, on ebonized bun feet with casters, 42¼in (107.5cm) wide. This is a very good buy at this level, and could have made at least £800/$1,200. The difference between this and one that costs £3,000–4,000/$4,500–5,800 is down to quality of the timber and its relative simplicity compared to more sophisticated models, which have more carving to the base and feet. Faded colour will also affect price.
£580–700
$850–1,000 WW

Georgian-style mahogany three-tier buffet, with blind fret-carved back and two frieze drawers, on cluster column supports and cabriole legs with claw-and-ball feet, early 20thC, 50in (127cm) wide. This is very good quality. The blind fret-carved gallery back and frieze are in the Chinese Chippendale style of the 1750s and 1760s, but the buffet is a later Victorian form. It could have made £800–1,200/$1,200–1,750.
£600–700/$870–1,000 Bea(E)

Victorian rosewood and marquetry envelope card table, with a frieze drawer, on turned supports linked by a plateau, 22in (56cm) square. This example appears to be faded and the legs are probably later additions; it should have square tapered legs, which probably accounts for the low price.
£640–770
$920–1,100 G(B)

Card tables

The tops of some card tables have projecting dished corners to hold candlesticks. Alternatively, some have pull-out slides fitted into splayed corners. Cloth-lined receptables were also provided for gaming counters.

The look without the price

Edwardian mahogany Pembroke table, with satinwood banding and stringing, the moulded-edged oval top above a frieze drawer with turned brass handles, on square tapering legs with brass toes and casters, with shaped cross stretchers and a small undershelf, 33in (34cm) wide extended.
£660–800/$965–1,150 AH

This Pembroke table is based on a late 18thC Hepplewhite design and it is nice quality, that is, the timber is good and it is well made. Smaller Pembroke tables tend to be more sought after than the larger examples. A related late 18thC example would cost between £1,200–1,800/$1,750–2,600.

Work tables

Special tables designed for silk and thread embroidery and needlework were introduced in the second half of the 18th century. They were usually compact, the interior fitted with compartments for reels, bobbins and so on, sometimes with a silk pouch or bag beneath. Original bags are rarely found today, but replacements, often in pleated silk, are generally acceptable. Later Victorian examples often had solid wood pull-out bags, sometimes conical, on a carved tripod support. Papier mâché and walnut, inlaid with mother-of-pearl and gilt embellishments, became fashionable at this time.

► **Victorian walnut work table,** the top with marquetry inlay, the tapering lidded box top with corner brackets, enclosing a fitted interior, the turned stem on four cabriole legs, with petal-carved feet on brass casters, 20in (51cm) wide.
£680–820
$1,000–1,180
WW

Mahogany D-end dining table, with one drop leaf, on square tapering legs with brass terminals and casters, early 19thC, 63½in (161.5cm) wide. The price of this table seems quite reasonable considering that it requires restoration. This type of table, with numerous legs, is simply not as popular as the pedestal variety due to the leg restriction common to this style.
£700–840/$1,000–1,235 DN

Oak gateleg table, with two frieze drawers, early 18thC, 51in (129.5cm) wide. Many oak gateleg tables of this period have been altered or extensively repaired. The most common fault is that tops have been replaced either substantially or completely. In this example the missing drawer and other repairs will have led to a discounted price. An example in original condition could well fetch £2,000–3,000/$3,000–4,500.
£700–840/$1,000–1,235 WW

Regency painted and gilded console table, with later green marble top, gadrooned rim and moulded frieze, on square section supports headed by lion masks, with applied florettes and lion's paw feet, on a moulded plinth, 16¾in (42.5cm) wide. This table is very good quality. The price would have been much higher if it had been a pair, possibly £1,500–2,000/$2,200–3,000.
£720–860
$1,000–1,270 AH

► **Regency rosewood card table,** with baize-lined D-shaped fold-over top, on a turned simulated rosewood column with four downswept legs, 35in (89cm) wide. This may be a marriage, which would account for the low price, but it is a nice example.
£750–900
$1,100–1,300
DMC

Pair of mahogany side tables, each with a D-shaped top over a banded and centrally carved frieze, one with a concealed drawer, on tapering square legs, 1775–1800, 48in (122cm) wide. These tables are a very good buy. Although plain, they still could make double the price.
£800–950/$1,150–1,380 NOA

Regency mahogany pedestal table, the tilt-top inlaid with ebonized lines and ebony dots, the ring-turned stem with four similarly inlaid splayed legs and ball feet, one leg damaged, 19¾in (50cm) diam. This has a nice warm colour and is a good size table – a very good buy.
£800–950
$1,150–1,380 Bea(E)

Side tables

Side tables, sometimes used as serving tables, became fashionable from c1730 and remained popular until the Regency period. Early examples often had marble tops and were heavily carved. Chippendale developed a lighter style, and the emphasis during the late 18th century was on restrained elegance. A grander style returned during the Regency period, exemplified by the designs of Thomas Hope and George Smith.

George III mahogany tripod table, the tilt-top on a turned vase-shaped stem, with down-swept legs and ball feet, 20in (51cm) wide. Although the top is warped, which means it is probably original, this may account for the lower price.
£800–950
$1,150–1,380 AH

Rococo-style carved wood ebonized console, with a white marble top, above a pierced frieze and inscrolled legs, Isherwoods trade label, 19thC, 55¼in (140.5cm) wide. This piece has good quality carving. The fact that it carries the paper label of the firm who made it also adds to its value. If it had been gilded it may have made more.
£850–1,000/$1,250–1,500 HOK

Victorian games and work table, veneered in burr-walnut, the swivel fold-over flap-top with restored inlay, and a chequer and backgammon board, with a fitted frieze drawer and a work box, with twin turned supports and stretchered and carved splay legs, 27in (68.5cm) wide.
£900–1,000/$1,300–1,500 WW

► **Late George III mahogany and satinwood crossbanded fold-over tea table,** the frieze drawer with later painted husk swags, on tapering legs with spade feet, 37in (94cm) wide. This is a very good price for a fine card table. It could easily fetch between £1,500–2,500/$2,300–3,600. The value of card tables has remained static for some time and they can be bought fairly cheaply at the moment, particularly Regency or later models. Pairs are less common, hence they are keenly sought after. If this had been a pair, it would fetch £5,000–8,000/$7,250–11,500
£900–1,000/$1,300–1,500 B(O)

The look without the price

The price reflects the fact that this table has a later base, which originally would have been marble, and would cost £1,500–2,500/$2,200–3,600. This is a particularly good buy when you consider that specimen marble tops, usually larger than this, sell as single items for as much as £6,000/$8,500. Be careful, though, because there are a number of fakes on the market, which are described as being late 19th–early 20th century, but are modern.

Specimen-marble table top, the square white marble panel inset with a radiating segmented panel of various marbles and semi-precious stones, on a later gilt-metal base, some chips, Italian, 19thC, 16¼in (41.5cm) wide.
£850–1,000
$1,250–1,500 Bon

Games tables

Card tables are occasionally described as games tables. Chess and draughts were popular during the 18th and 19th centuries, although backgammon and *tric-trac*, a French variant of backgammon, also featured.

Most Victorian games tables are veneered in rosewood or walnut and stand on pedestal bases which are often elaborately carved.

Towel Rails

Beech towel rail, c1920, 30in (76cm) high.
£35–40/$50–60 AL

Beech towel rail, c1890, 34in (86.5cm) high.
£60–75/$90–110 AL

Hardwood towel rail, c1920, 35½in (90cm) high.
£55–60/$80–90 AL

Miller's compares...

A. Stained beech towel rail, c1880, 31in (78.5cm) high.
£90–100/$130–145 AL

B. Mahogany towel rail, c1840, 24in (61cm) wide.
£300–335/$440–480 RPh

The fact that Item B is more expensive than Item A is due to it being made of mahogany.

Whatnots & Butler's Trays

Early Victorian whatnot, veneered in burr-satin walnut, the galleried top above a central tier and a base drawer, turned supports and legs, on brass casters, 17in (43cm) wide.
£480–580/$700–850 WW

Whatnots

Whatnots were first seen in the late 18th century, mostly made from mahogany. They usually have three, four or five tiers, sometimes with a drawer at the bottom.

Mahogany whatnot, with three rectangular tiers, slender turned supports with spiral ball finials, small drawer below with conforming knob handles, on brass casters, lower tier division missing, probably Regency, 18¼in (46.5cm) wide.
£700–800
$1,000–1,150 Bea(E)

► **Mahogany butler's tray,** on a later stand, 37in (94cm) wide.
£800–950
$1,150–1,380 S(O)

Regency mahogany butler's tray, the hinged shaped gallery pierced for carrying, on a turned X-shaped stand, 27¼in (69cm) wide. Be careful when looking at these kind of items as the stands are often a marriage.
£750–900/$1,100–1,300 CGC

Miscellaneous

Set of George III mahogany hanging shelves,
27in (68.5cm) wide.
£385–425/$570–620 F&F

Early Victorian carved oak dumb waiter, the lobed dished revolving tray with a moulded edge and anthemion decoration, above a carved pierced frieze of acorns and oak leaves, on short moulded legs and paw feet, 23¾in (60.5cm) diam. This piece is nicely carved and is a good buy.
£550–650/$800–950 B

Mid-Victorian walnut canterbury, 19¾in (50cm) wide. This is an unusual shape with a good colour and in good condition. It could have made £1,000/$1,450.
£600–720/$870–1,000 B

Ceramics

The plethora of antiques programmes on television these days show that Antiques appeal to very different markets. The BBC *Antiques Roadshow* concentrates on the more expensive end of the market, showing valuable discoveries worth thousands of pounds, with very few pieces priced below £1,000/$1,500. At the other extreme, programmes such as more 'popular' daytime shows feature antiques and collectables at the lower end of the price league. Pottery and china accounts for a surprising proportion of the discoveries made at boot or garage sales. Viewers at home share the enthusiasm shown by the TV contestants and many people bring along their boot sale purchases to show me at the *Antiques Roadshow*.

These various television shows and the widespread availability of Miller's Guides are inspiring a new generation of ceramic collector. The academic knowledge needed to distinguish between different 18th-century china factories is rare these days, whereas the world of 'collectables' is a much easier substitute. Collecting sets of modern productions is simple, and increasingly popular. While I understand the appeal of modern collectables, antique pottery and porcelain seems to me to be surprisingly reasonably priced by comparison. There is a certain joy in owning something centuries old, and as this section shows, early ceramics don't have to be expensive.

Miller's Affordable Antiques Price Guide is intended to be just that, a guide to collecting inexpensive antiques, and not a guide to 'cheap' antiques. In compiling the captions for the ceramics section, I have attempted to explain why each object is good value and therefore worth collecting. Some porcelain that is high quality is under-rated. Of course, plenty of other pieces are inexpensive for the simple reason that they are less appealing. It is a question of finding the right balance.

The main reasons pieces are under-valued are because they are out of fashion, by minor makers or are damaged in some way. Victorian and 20th-century ceramics have increased in popularity at the expense of Georgian and Regency porcelain. Consequently some 18th-century porcelain fetches far less than it deserves. Collectors seek top makers like Derby, Meissen or Worcester, but plenty of less well-known names in Staffordshire or Dresden supplied the same marketplace with designs that were only marginally inferior. The price difference between top and lesser-known makers can be extreme.

Reviewing the present market in pottery and porcelain, I am aware of changing attitudes to damage. Serious collectors are digging deeper into their pockets to buy pieces in original condition. The price difference between perfect and damaged porcelain is growing wider, while even in the pottery field damage makes much more difference than it used to. I can understand this, for there is a special pleasure in owning antique porcelain in mint condition. I always advocate buying perfect specimens if you can afford them, but an interesting, damaged example should never be dismissed. Defective pieces that are rare or very decorative, are well worth buying as long as the price correctly reflects the damage. Relatively common porcelain, on the other hand, that can easily be found in perfect condition, should be avoided if there is even the slightest hint of damage. **John Sandon**

Baskets & Boxes

◄ **Porcelain casket,** by Bodley & Co, with turquoise floral decoration, c1878, 9in (23cm) wide. Bodley is a little-known maker and therefore good value. This is a useful object for a modern home.
£50–60/$75–90 G(L)

Pottery money box, with a mottled brown glaze, Scottish, c1880, 3½in (9cm) high. This money box would appeal to collectors of regional pottery. It is a typical Scottish shape and glaze, and a good introduction to Scottish pottery at this price.
£70–80/$100–115 SAAC

The look without the price

Far removed from Meissen quality, this box is still pretty. The poor condition of the mounts lets it down, but they could be regilded. An 18thC Meissen original would fetch £4,000+/$5,800+.

Samson porcelain box and cover, painted with figures and flower sprays, cross mark, early 20thC, 3¼in (8.5cm) wide.
£65–80/$95–115 WW

Derby porcelain chestnut basket and cover, decorated in blue and white with moulded flowers and leaves on a basket-work ground, the interior painted with a pagoda landscape, damaged, stand missing, c1760, 7½in (19cm) diam. This piece can be displayed without showing the damage. In perfect condition it would fetch up to £1,000/$1,500, even without its stand.
£140–170/$200–250 WW

► **Royal Worcester porcelain basket and cover,** cream-glazed with pierced decoration, standing on three paw feet, c1903, 8in (20.5cm) diam. Undecorated white porcelain can look unfinished and is rarely expensive, but this is still a superb Gothic design.
£90–100
$130–145 G(L)

◄ **Delft-style pottery oval box,** decorated in blue and white, the hinged lid with lovers beneath a tree, the sides with flowers and foliage, marked 'HL.S', probably French, 19thC, 3¾in (9.5cm) wide. Crudely-painted porcelain boxes are disappointing, but in delft-style this cheaper painting has charm.
£140–170/$200–250 WW

Pottery money box, modelled as a house, decorated in blue, yellow, black, red, green and brown, slightly damaged, c1830, 4in (10cm) high. Charming money boxes can often be inexpensive.
£145–160/$210–230 NAW

Porcelain snuff box, modelled as a stag's head, naturalistically coloured, with a hinged silver-coloured metal lid, 19thC, 2½in (6.5cm) high. Novelty boxes make lovely collections, but watch out for reproductions. This is a rather crude example, hence the low price.
£170–200/$250–290 WW

Clarice Cliff pottery beehive honey pot, decorated with pastel Autumn pattern, 4in (10cm) high. The lid on this pot is not the original one, which significantly reduces the price. Finding an original lid would be very hard. The correct lid would have decoration that reflects the colours and pattern on the base.
£180–220/$260–320 G(L)

Clarice Cliff pottery beehive honey pot, decorated with Crocus pattern, slight rubbing, 3¾in (9.5cm) high. Collectors sometimes only collect honey pots, and this is the instantly recognizable Crocus pattern, making it a desirable piece.
£190–230/$275–330 G(L)

Staffordshire blue and white pearlware dessert basket, with pierced sides, decorated with Willow pattern, c1810, 11½in (29cm) wide. Pearlware baskets in other patterns can be expensive, but the Willow pattern is common and less desirable. It would have been more costly with the original stand which is missing.
£220–270/$320–390 G(L)

► **Meissen porcelain snuff box,** gilt interior, missing mounts and cover, restored, regilt interior, 1750–60, 3in (7.5cm) wide. A complete snuff box would be very expensive at £5,000/$7,250. This is an excellent way to acquire a finely painted box, but restoration that hides the detailed painting should be avoided.
£240–280/$350–410 S(O)

Wemyss pottery honeycomb dish and lid, decorated with a beehive and bees, c1920, 7in (18cm) wide. It is nice to find a honey box complete with its stand. This is a charming object that would suit a modern home.
£550–600/$800–870 RdeR

Victorian Sunderland lustre pottery two-handled box and cover, transfer-decorated with a naval scene, inscribed 'The flag that's braved a thousand years, the battle and the breeze', 1850–60, 5in (12.5cm) high. Naval ceramics are popular with collectors and this is an unusual shape. It would have been more expensive if it commemorated an actual battle.
£380–460/$565–670 G(B)

► **Strasbourg faïence pottery basket,** French, c1760, 7in (18cm) wide. 18thC French Faïence offers excellent value for money. Plates and dishes are common, but delicate baskets are hard to find.
£700–800
$1,000–1,150 US

Miller's compares...

A. Wemyss earthenware pig, decorated in green with shamrock leaves, one leg restored, 6in (15cm) wide.
£380–460/$570–670 G(L)

B. Wemyss earthenware pig, painted with pink roses, impressed mark and ochre script mark, one ear and a foot restored, 6in (15cm) wide.
£780–950/$1,150–1,400 DN

Item A is decorated with the popular but simple shamrock design, while Item B is particularly well-painted with an elaborate and complicated rose design. Both have slight repairs, but as these pigs chip so easily, repair to a foot or an ear does not make a great deal of difference to the price.

Candlesticks

Derby porcelain candlestick group, with Cupid kneeling before flowering bocage raised on a high scroll base, candle-holder missing, minor chips, c1770, 7½in (19cm) high. The absence of the nozzle is a serious defect, but otherwise this is in surprisingly good condition. It shows how inexpensive Derby figures can be. It would otherwise cost £300–400/$450–580 complete.
£170–200/$250–290 WW

Bow porcelain candlestick, on a high rococo base, sconce missing, trumpet damaged, minor damage, c1770, 9¾in (25cm) high. The damage to the flowers and trumpet is to be expected, but the absence of the nozzle is much more significant. Bow figures of this period are generally out of favour. If complete, it would cost £600–800/$870–1,150.
£320–380/$460–560 Bea(E)

Derby porcelain candlestick, modelled with a shepherdess standing before flowering bocage with a lamb at her feet, on a scrolling base, restored, c1770, 10¾in (27.5cm) high. Some restoration is usual on Derby figures. Heavily restored figures should be avoided. A good single figure would be £500/$720, a pair £1,200/$1,750.
£200–240/$290–350 WW

Wedgwood pottery candlestick, decorated in blue and white with a floral pattern, c1840, 8½in (21.5cm) high. Undamaged examples such as this are rarely seen.
£500–550/$720–800 GN

Staffordshire porcelain miniature taperstick, decorated with a leaf design and loop handle, c1835, 4in (10cm) diam. This is a popular field for collecting, but the lack of an identifiable maker's name keeps the price down.
£240–265/$350–385 WWW

Porcelain chamberstick, by H. & R. Daniel, the dark green ground with gilded detail, c1840, 1¾in (4.5cm) high. This is dearer than many single-colour and gold tapersticks; evidence of Daniel as the maker would account for this.
£425–475/$620–690 DIA

Derby (c1748–present)

- Founded before 1750, probably by Andrew Planché.
- Planché was bought out by John Heath and William Duesbury in 1756.
- In 1770 they bought the Chelsea factory, and the period until 1784 is known as Chelsea-Derby.
- Robert Bloor bought the company in 1811. Due to Bloor's illness it was managed by James Thomason until 1848.
- Different factories were established in the 19th century. The present factory is known as Royal Crown Derby.

Cups, Mugs & Tea Bowls

◄ **Gaudy Welsh porcellaneous cup and saucer,** decorated with Tulips pattern in cobalt blue and burnt orange, 1840–90, saucer 5½in (14cm) diam. Made cheaply in Staffordshire, it was very popular in South Wales, hence the name. It is very decorative and generally inexpensive.
£40–50/$60–75 CoHA

Gaudy Welsh porcellaneous miniature mug, decorated with Grape pattern No. 1104, 1840–90, 2in (5cm) high. The miniature size is popular with collectors and early examples are worth seeking. This one is crudely painted.
£45–55/$65–80 CoHA

Gaudy Welsh

Pottery and porcelain known as Gaudy Welsh was produced as an inexpensive form of tableware for the working classes during the 19th century by factories in north east England, the Midlands and south west England, but only to a minor extent in Wales. It was therefore never intended to be classed together under one generic term. However, it became popular, particularly in the United States, where it became known as Gaudy Welsh and the name has become common internationally, although in the past it has also been called Cottage Swansea and Cottage Lustre.

There are over 200 shapes and patterns of this distinctive ware, many of which are based on the early Imari ceramics, and the colours are predominantly burnt orange, cobalt blue and shades of green.

Gaudy Welsh porcellaneous cup and saucer, decorated with Grape pattern No. 1104, 1840–60, saucer 5¾in (14.5cm) diam.
£45–55/$65–80 CoHA

Pair of Gaudy Welsh porcellaneous mugs, decorated with a chinoiserie design, 1830–45, 2½in (6.5cm) high. Chinese panels on Gaudy Welsh do not generally add to the value but they can be very charming. Avoid pieces where the lustre is worn.
£50–60/$75–90 CoHA

Porcelain cup and saucer, with Sèvres mark, French, Paris or Limoges, c1860, saucer 4½in (11.5cm) diam. Thin and delicate with rich colouring. Inexpensive as not by a known maker, but the quality is very high.
£50–60/$75–90 JOA ⊞

Porcelain moustache cup, decorated in colours with an aerial view of the Newcastle Exhibition, 3½in (9cm) high. This is an interesting historical piece. The exhibition view would date this to a time when gentlemen had large moustaches.
£70–85/$100–125 SAS ⚒

Moustache cups

Moustache cups were fitted with a shaped china trough across the drinking side of the rim to keep the gentlemans' moustache from reaching the liquid. Varied collections of moustache cups can be formed; most were cheaply made in Germany but examples by major factories are expensive.

Gaudy Welsh porcellaneous cup and saucer, attributed to Hilditch, decorated with Hexagon pattern, 1825–35, saucer 5½in (14cm) diam. An effective, bold pattern. Attributing makers is very difficult with Gaudy Welsh.
£50–60/$75–90 CoHA ⊞

Gaudy Welsh porcellaneous cup and saucer, decorated with Pinwheel pattern No. 612, 1840–60, saucer 6in (15cm) diam. A nice fancy pattern with an interesting handle shape.
£55–70/$80–100 CoHA ⊞

Gaudy Welsh porcellaneous cup and saucer, decorated with Tricorn/Powis pattern, cup cracked, 1835–50, saucer 5½in (14cm) diam. In any collecting field, some patterns are less frequently found, others are more decorative. A specialist dealer will usually charge more for better examples with interesting patterns than a general trader so it is worth looking around. This cup and saucer is cracked and this would greatly affect the price.
£80–90/£115–130 CoHA ⊞

Miller's compares...

A. Meissen porcelain tea bowl, painted in puce with flower sprays, brown line rim, crossed swords mark and impressed mark '66', rim chips, c1750, 3½in (8.5cm) diam.
£75–90/$110–130 WW

B. Meissen porcelain tea bowl, one side painted with lovers in a garden, the other with a reclining figure playing a pipe, within gilded borders, crossed swords mark, impressed marks and gilt marks, c1740, 3in (7.5cm) diam.
£500–600/$720–870 WW

The rim chips on Item A have not affected the price greatly. Odd cups are keenly collected in English porcelain, but odd Continental cups represent excellent value. Item B, with a Watteau figure in Italian comedy style, represents Meissen at its best with top quality painting. Item A, which was produced ten years later, is from an ordinary Meissen tea service, and although not particularly exciting it is still good value.

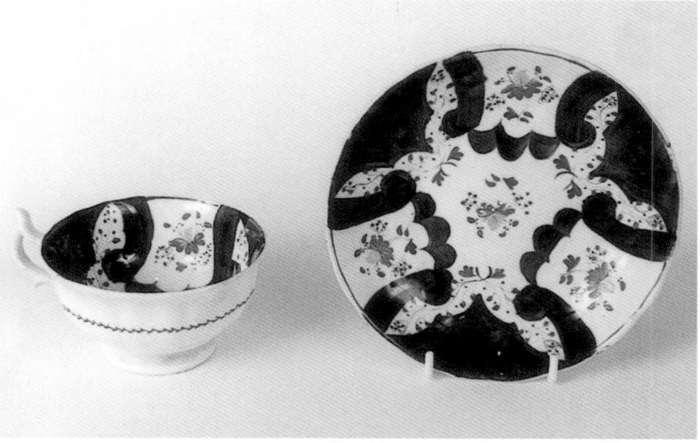

A Gaudy Welsh porcellaneous cup and saucer, decorated with Marigold pattern, 1830–50, saucer 5in (12.5cm) diam.
£80–90/$115–130 CoHA

Factory X, Y & Z

When the collector David Holgate researched the New Hall factory, he identified three contemporary factories whose names were not known. They were designated Factory X, Factory Y and Factory Z, but positive identification is still lacking.

Further reading

Miller's Antiques Price Guide,
Miller's Publications

Factory Z porcelain coffee can, decorated with a band of scrolling foliage in gold, 1805–10, 2½in (6.5cm) high. Single coffee cans represent a very popular collecting field. Any straight-sided can will always cost more than an odd tea cup. Prices vary greatly between dealers.
£80–100/$125–145 MER

Porcelain *famille rose* cup and cover, decorated with cornucopia and flower sprays, damaged, Chinese, 18thC, 5½in (14cm) high. This is a good quality piece and in perfect condition would be worth £600/$870.
£85–100/$125–145 SWO

► **Porcelain mug,** decorated in colours with flowers, inscribed in gold 'When this you see remember me, And bear me in your mind, Let all the world say what they will, Speak of me as you find', c1850, 3¼in (8.5cm) high. Lack of firm attribution keeps the price of such mugs affordable. If dated it would be worth a little more.
£110–120/$160–750 WW

Doccia porcelain coffee cup, c1770, 2¼in (5.5cm) high. 18thC odd cups from Continental factories are cheap compared to English cups and it can be useful to learn about the maker. This is a typical Doccia design and represents excellent value.
£85–100/$125–145 WW

Pottery spongeware mug, decorated with birds, cracked, Irish, 19thC, 3¾in (9.5cm) high. A basic, crude mug, the value of which lies in its local attribution.
£100–110/$145–160 Byl

Locate the source

The source of each illustration in Miller's can be found by checking the code letters below each caption with the Key to Illustrations, pages 286–290.

Miller's compares...

A. Bow porcelain coffee cup, white-glazed, moulded with prunus sprays, with an ear-shaped handle, small rim chip, c1760, 2½in (6.5cm) high.
£100–120/$145–175 WW

B. Bow coffee can, painted with Cross-legged Chinaman pattern, with a figure in a sampan on the reverse, 1747–52, 3in (7.5cm) high.
£950–1,000/$1,400–1,500 G(L)

Single coffee cups such as Item A are a great way to collect and learn about a factory. Bow is famous for its white porcelain copies of Chinese Fujian *blanc-de-chine* and they are not particularly rare. The early blue and white of Item B appeals to many collectors and this can is a good early Bow example. A can is always much more expensive than a cup.

Worcester porcelain saucer, with a blue-scale ground, decorated with gilt scroll reserves of flowers, underglaze blue fretted square mark, minor wear, small nick to footrim, c1770, 5in (12.5cm) diam. Odd coffee cups are expensive compared to odd saucers, as there are very few saucer collectors. This is an excellent example from Worcester's golden age.
£110–130/$160–190 S(O)

Rockingham porcelain tea cup and saucer, pattern No. 561, decorated in orange, blue, green, iron-red and gold with flowers, leaves and grapes, red printed mark to saucer, c1830, saucer 4in (10cm) diam. Japanese or Imari patterns on English Regency and later porcelain offer an excellent opportunity to form a worthwhile collection. If you compare this quality with Gaudy Welsh of similar date – this is a bargain in view of the workmanship.
£130–150/$190–220 WW

Worcester

Founded in 1751 by Dr Wall, William Davis and others, the factory continues at Worcester to the present day. Early Worcester porcelain was the most successful in England and consisted mainly of tea and coffee services and dinner ware. Transfer-printing was introduced by the mid-1750s, at first in black, and in blue and white by c1757.

In 1783, the factory was bought by Thomas Flight for his sons, who were joined in 1792 by Martin Barr trading as Flight & Barr. Owing to changes in partnership, the company became Barr, Flight & Barr (1804–13) and Flight, Barr & Barr (1813–40). There were also several other factories in Worcester at that time.

► **Derby porcelain mug,** with a brown line rim, with a grooved loop handle, some restoration, 1760–70, 5½in (14cm) high. The cheap price reflects the damage and restoration. If restored without excessive spraying, it is a great example from which to learn. If heavily over-painted it is not so desirable.
£130–160/$200–230 WW

Set of three Royal Crown Derby porcelain cups and saucers, decorated in the Imari palette with Japan pattern, date cipher for 1889, saucer 4in (10cm) diam. These are an 1880s copy of an 1820s design. When designs are copied later they can often fall outside the interest of collectors which is reflected in the price.
£130–160/$190–230 WW

◄ **Minton porcelain cup and saucer,** decorated in blue and gold, 1885–90, saucer 6in (15cm) diam. This pattern reflects the Aesthetic Movement and, as a piece of Victorian design, costs more than other blue and gold cups and saucers.
£120–130/$175–190 JOA

Miller's compares...

A. Worcester porcelain tea bowl and saucer, printed with Fence pattern, 1775–80, bowl 3in (7.5cm) diam.
£130–150/$190–220 G(L)

B. A Worcester saucer, painted in underglaze blue with Cormorant pattern, workmen's mark, 1754–56.
£720–850/$1,000–1,250 LFA

The Fence pattern on Item A is now mass-produced and printed in great quantities. It is technically fine, but the life has gone out of it. Item B, however, of twenty years earlier, reflects the beauty of English blue and white – a painted pattern, light and of superb design unspoilt by a border.

Worcester porcelain reeded tea bowl and saucer, painted in blue and gold with flowers and foliage, 1785–90, saucer 4in (10cm) diam. Worcester gilding in the 1780s is high quality but prices are never very high making it a good buy. Always avoid rubbed pieces.
£140–160/$200–230 S(O)

Porcelain teabowl and saucer, Dutch-decorated, Chinese, Qianlong period, 1736–95, saucer 4in (10cm) diam. Chinese porcelain painted in Holland is interesting historically, but messy, and its appeal is limited to academic collectors.
£140–180/$200–260 GLD

Worcester porcelain coffee cup, decorated in blue with Canonball pattern, crescent mark, c1765, 2¼in (5.5cm) high. Single coffee cups are increasingly expensive. This one is cheaper because it is a common pattern.
£150–180/$220–260 WW

► **Worcester porcelain fluted trio,** with scalloped rims, decorated with *guilloche* bands on pale blue borders, c1770, saucer 4in (10cm) diam. The border pattern is smart, but without a painted centre the piece is less desirable. Most Worcester collectors are interested in earlier pieces, but when this was made it was the height of fashion.
£150–180/$220–260 WW

Nanking **cargo porcelain tea bowl and saucer,** decorated with Chrysanthemum Rock pattern, c1750, bowl 3½in (9cm) diam.
£160–180/$230–260 RBA

Factory Z porcelain trio, printed in grey with baskets of fruit in gilt-edged panels, early 19thC, saucer 4in (10cm) diam. This is among the highest quality and most elegant of early Staffordshire porcelain teawares and costs more as a result (see Factory Z information box page 71).
£160–190/$230–275 WW

◄ **Meissen porcelain tea cup and saucer,** white-glazed, moulded with prunus sprays, blue crossed swords mark, mid-18thC, saucer 4in (10cm) diam. Meissen white porcelain of 1720–40 is expensive, but from 1750 the interest is in colourful wares. White porcelain of this period is excellent value.
£170–200/$250–290 WW

◄ **Worcester porcelain coffee cup,** painted in polychrome enamels with three Chinese figures in a garden, with a grooved loop handle, c1765, 2½in (6.5cm) high. Worcester coloured coffee cups are readily available and can form varied collections. They tend to be expensive compared to Continental or Chinese cups, but more fun.
£190–230/$275–330 WW

Meissen porcelain *hausmalerei* saucer, painted in underglaze blue with a bird in flight among flowering shrubs, painted in overglaze enamels in shades of iron-red, green and ochre with flowerheads, a woman, a cockerel and a village, rim chip, blue crossed swords mark, impressed number 36, c1750, 5in (12.5cm) diam. A single chipped saucer is the only way to collect desirable *hausmalerei* decorations at a modest price. As such it is a good learning piece painted by F. J. Ferner.
£170–200/$250–290 DN

► **Meissen porcelain cup and saucer,** the cup decorated in pink with a gilt interior, the saucer decorated in green, crossed swords mark, German, 19thC, saucer 4in (10cm) diam. The low price of this item suggest that there may have been some restoration. In perfect condition expect to pay £700+/$1,000+.
£200–240 $290–350 WW

Victorian pottery loving cup, decorated with Crimean War battle scenes, 7in (18cm) high. Dating from the time of the Crimean War, it shows the brutality of the battles. A poignant piece of history at a bargain price.
£200–250/$290–360 G(L)

Pair of Worcester Flight & Barr porcelain coffee cans, decorated with gilt scrollwork and foliage on an orange ground, incised 'B' marks, c1800, 2¾in (7cm) high. Flight & Barr gilding is of good quality and value.
£230–280/$330–410 WW

Worcester *trembleuse* cup and saucer, with fluted decoration within a flower and lambrequin border, rim chip to cup, 1758–60, cup 3in (7.5cm) high. This is an uncommon shape and very elegant. If it had been in perfect condition it would be worth £500–700/$720–1,000.
£250–300/$360–440 G(L)

Porcelain blue and white tea bowl and saucer, Chinese, Kangxi period, 1662–1722, saucer 4½in (11.5cm) diam. These busy patterns are not as desirable as the more plain and artistic ones.
£225–250/$325–360 GLD

Worcester porcelain fluted coffee cup and saucer, painted with flower sprays within gilt and turquoise borders, 1775–78, saucer 4in (10cm) diam. The later Worcester coloured wares from the 1775 period used to be very costly 25 years or more ago. Fashions have changed and pretty examples such as this are undervalued now.
£230–280/$330–410 WW

► **Salt-glazed earthenware mug,** with a white metal mount and brown-glazed upper half, moulded in relief with hunting scenes and a 'Punch Party' plaque, base with glued repair, handle with riveted repair, late 18thC, 8¼in (21cm) high. A fine example of 18thC stoneware, the price reflecting significant damage. Limited variety of designs and shapes means that brown stoneware is generally expensive.
£240–280
$350–410 DN

Wedgwood pottery mug, transfer-printed in blue with Water Lily pattern, star crack, impressed mark, 1811–20, 5in (12.5cm) high. This is an uncommon shape and a very popular pattern. The price reflects a crack at the base. Damage makes a big different to Wedgwood values.
£250–300/$360–440 DN

Porcelain custard cup and cover, painted in blue, Chinese export, c1775, 3in (7.5cm) high. Custard cups are highly collectable because of the vast variety available and their ease of display. However, they must have their lids to be of full value.
£250–300/$360–440 US

Pottery blue and white loving cup, attributed to Bathwell & Goodfellow, hair crack, rim chip, 1818–23, 6½in (16.5cm) high. Mugs, jugs and loving cups are less expensive in the blue-printed pottery compared to plates and platters.
£300–360/$440–520 DN

Did you know?

- One of Wedgwood's earliest lines was cream-coloured earthenware, printed or painted, known as Queensware due to Wedgwood achieving the Royal patronage of Queen Charlotte in 1765.
- Wedgwood's factory was named 'Etruria' as the first productions copied Etruscan pottery from the Greek colonies of Southern Italy.
- Excavations at Pompeii and Herculaneum inspired Wedgwood to develop jasper ware with classical subjects modelled in relief.
- Collectors seek interesting colours in Wedgwood stoneware, such as 'Cane ware', 'Drab ware' and 'Rosso Antico' (a rich red pottery).

► **Bristol porcelain coffee cup and saucer,** unmarked, c1770, saucer 4in (10cm) diam. A classic example of shape and decoration associated with this English hard paste factory. Prices of items from these rarer factories are likely to rise.
£260–300
$380–440 WW

Liverpool porcelain saucer, probably by Richard Chaffers, painted in blue with a formal pattern of peony plants and bamboo leaves between diaper and whorl borders, a flowerhead in the centre, chipped, c1760, 4¾in (12cm) diam. Liverpool coffee cups are expensive but saucers have far fewer collectors. The chip keeps the price down.
£280–320/$400–450 P

◄ **Vienna-style porcelain cup and cover,** painted with a panel of the Rape of the Sabine Women on a ground of blue, brown and pink panels decorated with raised gold, blue shield mark and titled, knop reglued, 19thC, 3½in (9cm) high. Finely painted, but the saucer is missing and cups of this quality without saucers are not generally expensive and form lovely collections.
£300–360/$440–520 WW

John and Jane Pennington porcelain breakfast/broth cup, painted in blue with sprigs, the inside rim with a formal border, 1785–90, 4½in (11.5cm) diam. A very rare object from a small Liverpool factory, but the shape is unattractive. An academic piece for a specialist collector.
£320–380/$460–575 P

Pottery creamware coffee cup and saucer, polychrome-painted, the cup with Neptune, the saucer with Diana, in a pink-ground panel surrounded by terms, urns of flowers and leaves, reglued rim chip to saucer, impressed 'W' marks, late 18thC, saucer 4in (10cm) diam. Continental creamware does not have many collectors and as a result this unidentified cup and saucer is very affordable, despite being a high quality and elegant piece.
£350–420/$500–600 S(O)

► **Creamware pottery mug,** inscribed 'William Hall' within a flower garland, haircrack and rim chip, late 18thC, 4½in (11.5cm) high. Inscribed names are interesting, but without a date and only limited floral painting it is not decorative enough to be expensive.
£350–420
$500–600 S(O)

Vienna porcelain coffee can and saucer, the can painted with a panel entitled 'le temps fait passer l'amour', rim chip to saucer, minor wear, shield marks in underglaze blue, impressed mark, Austrian, c1804, saucer 4in (10cm) diam. Cabinet cups and saucers from leading Continental factories are always expensive, although Vienna is more reasonably priced than others. The saucer is worn and this affects the value.
£420–480/$600–700 S(O)

Longton Hall porcelain saucer, painted in blue with a formal Chinese riverscape, restored chip to rim, painted mark, 1755–60, 4½in (11.5cm) diam. A single chipped saucer is the only way to buy an example of rare Longton Hall blue and white at this price.
£440–520/$650–750 P

◄ **Sèvres porcelain custard cup and cover,** French, c1770, 3in (7.5cm) high. This is an attractive object and an appealing example of the Sèvres soft paste porcelain, in a very typical style. When undamaged a pretty shape like this is good value.
£450–500
$650–720 US ⊞

Sèvres porcelain cup and saucer, painted by Mme Maqueret with a colourful frieze of scrolling leaves and flowers reserved with three roundels, each containing a blue monochrome landscape, within gilt rims, rim chips to cup, saucer probably married, crossed LS marks, painter's mark, dated 1789, saucer 6¾in (17cm) diam. This is an exciting decoration from Sèvres. It is cheap because the cup and saucer do not match, it is chipped, and from the late 1780s.
£480–580/$700–850 B

► **Wemyss pottery mug,** painted with cherries, with a red border, c1890, 6in (15cm) high. Wemyss is typically expensive, and cherries cost more than some of the other patterns.
£550–600
$800–870 RdeR ⊞

Pair of du Paquier porcelain tall cups, c1740, 3in (7.5cm) high, and a du Paquier Imari-style fluted tea bowl. This is made by a rare Vienna factory with charming decoration. These were a very good buy for exciting pieces. Odd cups in early Continental porcelain can be incredible value.
£650–800/$950–1,150 S(NY)

Worcester porcelain tea cup and saucer, painted in coloured enamels in the London studio of James Giles with sprays of European flowers and leaves, within a gilt dentil rim, painted with crossed swords and numeral 9 marks in underglaze blue, with entwined handle, 1768–70, cup 2½in (6.5cm) high. An uncommon example from the Giles workshop, but the pattern is a little sparse so the price is modest.
£700–850/$1,000–1,250 LFA

◄ **Vienna-style porcelain cup and saucer,** Austrian, late 19thC, saucer 4½in (11.5cm) diam. Not from the main Vienna factory, but a richly-decorated example showing good workmanship.
£750–850/$1,100–1,250 MAA ⊞

Dishes & Bowls

Late Victorian porcelain sweetmeat dish, 4½in (11.5cm) wide. This box is missing its cover which completes the grapes form, hence the very low price.
£5–10/$10–15 OD

Pair of Copeland earthenware oval dishes, with shaped gilded rims, printed and enamelled with holly and berries, small chips, impressed mark and date code for 1888. Seasonal decoration for Christmas was a Copeland speciality. Because they seem inappropriate for the rest of the year they rarely fetch much money.
£40–50/$60–75 G(L)

◀ ***Famille rose* bowl,** the interior decorated with a central floral design, Chinese, c1860, 8in (20.5cm) diam.
£45–50
$65–75 FRY

Clarice Cliff bowl, decorated with Passion Fruit pattern, with matching cup, saucer and plate, c1936, 8in (20.5cm) diam. These two 1930s shapes and patterns on mushroom grounds have yet to take off with collectors, hence the low value.
£95–115/$140–165 G(L)

Cauldon blue and white dish, printed with a chariot in a classical landscape, c1900, 10in (25.5cm) diam. This is an 1830s design which was later reissued, but decorative nonetheless.
£80–100/$115–145 DHA

► **Cauldon blue and white spittoon,** the rim with a border of roses in panels, the sides decorated with three romantic-style Continental scenes, printed mark, 1905–20, 7¾in (19.5cm) diam. An unusual and surprisingly decorative shape, as long as you do not think about the original contents! A reissue of a much earlier pattern keeps the price down.
£100–120/$145–175 DN

Bow leaf-shaped pickle dish, painted in underglaze blue with a bunch of grapes within foliage, c1760, 4in (10cm) wide. While it is nice to collect porcelain pickle leaves in fine condition, chips to the rim are usual and do not detract from the decoration, but they do keep the price down.
£100–120/$145–175 G(L)

Arts and Crafts bowl, No. 301, decorated with tulips on a Wedgwood blank, TG monogram, dated October 1930, 10½in (26.5cm) diam. Because this Wedgwood bowl was painted by a relatively unknown amateur painter, it does not appeal much to collectors. However, it is very decorative.
£100–120/$145–175 G(L)

***Famille rose* Compagnie des Indes spoon tray,** decorated with flowers, Chinese, 18thC, 4½in (11.5cm) wide.
£100–120/$145–175 WW

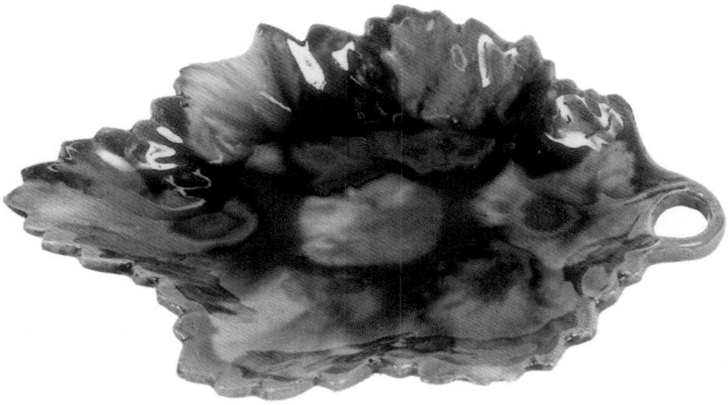

Dunmore leaf-shaped dish, decorated in green, brown and black, 1870–1900, 10in (25.5cm) wide. This is coarse and crude, but of interest because it is from a Scottish pottery. The glazes are particularly rich.
£110–120/$160–175 SQA

Compagnie des Indes

A generic term for Chinese export porcelain made specifically to European order and design. The name was used after the late 17th century when other East India Companies (other than the Dutch) began taking a large share of its china trade. Now an old-fashioned term, it is rarely used.

► **Blue and white printed pottery meat dish,** decorated with Pagoda pattern, c1800, 21in (53.5cm) wide. Willow-type Chinese patterns cost less than rustic European scenes, country houses or Indian palaces.
£110–130/$160–190 MCC

Wedgwood blue and white meat platter, printed with flowers and fruit around a geometric paterae, impressed mark, short hair crack, 19thC, 20in (51cm) wide. Gothic designs are unusual in pottery and this is very impressive. It is by a good maker but the crack brings the value down.
£120–150/$175–225 WW

Clarice Cliff Fantasque bowl, decorated with Melon pattern, 1930–31, 6in (15cm) diam. The Melon pattern shows Clarice Cliff's awareness of contemporary art, and in particular, the Cubists. This pattern, which perfectly suits the bowl shape, is a mid price Art Deco range, popular both in the 1930s and now.
£120–150/$175–225 G(L)

Potted meat dish, Little Nell & Grandfather, by Ridgway, from Humphrey's Clock series, 1830, 4in (10cm) diam. Small shapes for pâté, hors d'oeuvres and pickles are well worth collecting in blue-painted earthenware. Avoid stained and discoloured examples.
£125–140/$180–200 GN

Victorian Wedgwood blue majolica-type fruit bowl, with moulded fruit decoration and silver-plated mount, 10in (25.5cm) wide. An interesting Victorian design by a good maker. The dull colour of the plain glaze means that it is not very expensive.
£130–155/$200–225 G(L)

Chinese Export shell-shaped pickle dish, decorated in underglaze blue with a peony within a scrolling border, a cell border to the handle, minor chips, 18thC, 5¼in (13.5cm) wide. Chinese Export pickle dishes are far cheaper than English pickle shells and represent incredibly good value.
£145–160/$210–230 DN

Delft blue and white bowl, painted with boats, pagodas, rocks and a date palm, hairline crack and chips to foot, mid-18thC, 9in (23cm) diam. Small chips and fine glaze cracks have little effect on delft. This is English delft and many plates, and bowls especially, are good value.
£150–180/$220–260 WW

Swansea Pottery pearlware titled sauce tureen stand, painted by Thomas Pardoe, with an Upright Trillium, impressed mark, repair to one end, 1802–09, 9in (23cm) wide. This is an odd stand from a tureen and has been damaged and repaired. This is an inexpensive way to buy an interesting piece of Welsh pottery by a major artist.
£150–180/$220–260 S(O)

Blue and white meat platter, entitled 'Vintage', transfer-printed with floral cartouches and a landscape, with a shaped border, 1840s, 18½in (47cm) wide. This is an impressive size and a fantastic piece of crowded Victorian design that looks wonderful hanging on a kitchen wall.
£170–200/$250–300 SWO

◄ **Set of three blue and white miniature pottery tureens,** decorated with Kite-Flying pattern, repair to one foot, c1830, largest 4¼in (11cm) wide. Miniature pieces of blue and white have obvious appeal and considering their rarity are reasonably priced.
£170–200/$250–300 WW

Miller's compares...

A. Wemyss fern pot, painted with Strawberries pattern, c1900, 5in (12.5cm) wide.
£180–200/$250–300 RdeR

B. Wemyss dog bowl, 'Qui Aime Jean Aime Son Chien', c1920, 6¾in (17cm) diam.
£550–600/$800–870 RdeR

Values of Wemyss are all down to rarity. Item A is a decorative pattern that looks very modern. Strawberries are uncommon, so even this small bowl is expensive. Item B is decorated with sweet peas which are even rarer. A dog bowl is extremely uncommon which makes this the more valuable item.

Worcester blue and white junket dish, with shaped rim, moulded with scallop shells and scrolls, painted with flowers and leaves, rim chips and hairline crack, open crescent mark, 1760–70, 9½in (24cm) wide. Big pieces of blue and white Worcester can be remarkable value. The damage on this piece brings the value down. If it had been in perfect condition one would expect to pay £600–800/$870–1,150.
£170–200/$250–300 WW

Moulded cabbage leaf dish, by Samson, Paris, painted with flowers in gilt reserves on a blue scale ground, 1880–1900, 7½in (19cm) wide. This is a very convincing copy of Worcester, but in hard paste porcelain.
£180–200/$250–300 RAV

► **Meissen dessert dish,** decorated with Onion pattern in blue with stylized flower, c1890, 12in (30.5cm) diam. This pattern survives in large numbers and is rarely expensive as a result. When the Meissen crossed swords mark appears in the design this is a good sign.
£200–220/$300–320 MAA

◄ **Sèvres-style dish,** the central gilt monogram supported by cupids over a musical trophy within a burnished gilt frame on a turquoise ground, Chateau des Tuileries and 1844 printed marks, with cancelled S.74 in green, date code for 1874, 13½in (34.5cm) diam. This is a late copy in Sèvres style with added decoration of putti and coloured ground. The 'LP' cypher was original on a white and gold service, the rest of the decoration was added later.
£250–300/$360–440 CGC

Insurance values

Always insure your valuable antiques for the cost of replacing them with similar items, regardless of the original price paid. Both dealers and auctioneers can provide a valuation service for a fee.

Copeland & Garrett pottery pot pourri bowl with reversible pierced cover, from the Botanical Series, printed in blue with a flower spray within floral borders, moulded loop handles, printed circular mark around 'late Spode' 1833–47, 7¼in (18.5cm) diam. This is an uncommon shape and is very good for display.
£250–300/$360–440 DN

Pair of Vienna salts, with flower design and gilding, c1792, 3½in (9cm) diam. Salts are rare in porcelain. Vienna is generally inexpensive and these are good value considering their rarity and charm.
£300–350/$440–500 US

Bow chamfered rectangular dish, painted with peony, rockwork and a willow tree, the border with panels of flowers, small chips. c1760, 9½in (24cm) wide. This is an early and uncommon piece of Bow. The flatware is thickly potted and suprisingly cheap.
£320–380/$465–565 WW

Pair of salt-glazed stoneware moulded dishes, with scalloped rims and pierced trelliswork borders, decorated with diaper designs and scrolls, one dish cracked, mid-18thC, 12¼in (31cm) diam. White saltglaze from Staffordshire is crisply moulded but dull in colour. Hard and durable, many survive and can be surprisingly cheap. They are worth collecting for the quality of the moulding.
£350–420/$500–615 WW

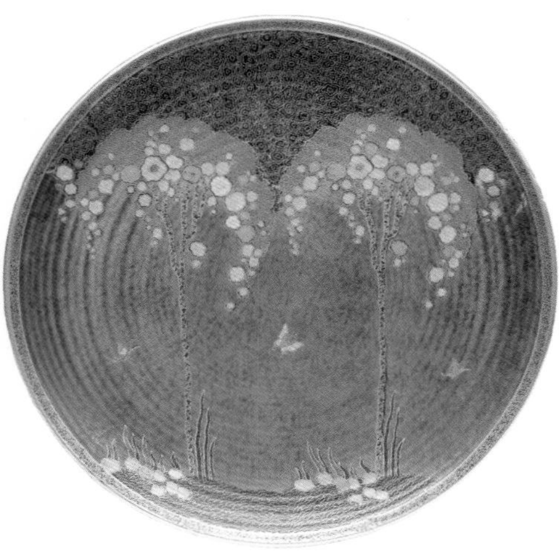

Crown Devon fantasy landscape charger, with flowering trees against a blue ground, 15¼in (38.5cm) diam. Although Crown Devon lustreware is collectable, the pottery does not command the heady heights of the similar Wedgwood lustre designed by Daisy Makeig-Jones. While not as fine as Wedgwood quality, it is still well made, and perhaps this makes Crown Devon under-valued by collectors.
£300–350/$440–500 G(L)

Moorcroft bowl, decorated with anemones on a dark blue ground, 20thC, 9½in (24cm) diam.
£320–400/$460–580 G(L)

Minton & Boyle three-part vegetable tureen, decorated with Tonquin pattern, c1830, 13in (33cm) wide. It is unusual to find all three parts of a vegetable tureen together. This is not an expensive pattern, but an elaborate shape by a good maker.
£350–400/$500–580 GN

Jacob Marsh blue printed pottery fruit bowl, with moulded decoration and rural scenery, 1804–18, 10in (25.5cm) diam. A lavish shape like this is great for display and makes a refreshing change from dinner service shapes.
£350–400/$500–580 GN

Pair of Royal Worcester square dishes, the centres painted with fruit, the borders with panels of flowers on a yellow and gilt ground, puce marks, c1908, 9in (23cm) square. The quality of the central fruit paintings suggest they are by a senior artist and had they been signed, they would have cost twice as much.
£360–430/$550–625 WW

Malachite comport, by F. & R. Pratt, entitled 'Hop Queen', c1855, 10½in (26.5cm) diam. Pot lids and other Pratt colour printed wares were expensive in the 1970s and have risen little since. Most are now seriously undervalued.
£400–450/$580–650 DHA

Blue printed pottery soup tureen and cover, from the Pineapple Border Series, each side depicting a view entitled 'Slingsby Castle, Yorkshire', the interior depicting Dalberton Tower, Wales, the cover with a ruined abbey, with a border of flowers and scrolls inside the rim and around the pedestal foot, blue scroll-mounted handles, damaged and repaired, printed title mark, 1820–30, 13½in (34.5cm) wide. This is a magnificent piece of blue-painted earthenware with a popular scenic view decoration. Because of the damage the price is modest but it still displays very well.
£400–500/$580–720 DN

◄ **Semi-china pearlware meat dish,** with canted sides,from the English Scenery Series, printed with boats in full sail in a river landscape, within a flower and C-scroll border, printed title mark in blue, c1825, 18½in (47cm) wide. Extensive English views with frames of fancy borders take up a lot of room, but if you have the space to display a collection, this is a marvellous object.
£400–500/$580–720 LFA

Bow meat plate, with chamfered sides, painted in the Kakiemon style with Quail pattern, c1758–60, 12½in (32cm) wide. Collectors of English porcelain, Bow especially, like smaller pieces. This dish is large and therefore not as popular, so consequently you get a lot for your money.
£400–480/$580–700 WW

Delft dish, probably Bristol, painted in green, blue and iron red with stylized leaves and flowers, blue line rim, 18thC, 13¾in (35cm) diam. A splendid dish from the first half of the 18thC, in remarkable condition. Within this price range it is possible to buy some superb dishes.
£400–500/$580–720 WW

Soft paste porcelain Chelsea-style two-handled tureen and cover, the ciselé gilt sides and cover with vignettes of birds within gilt frames, rubbing to gilding, gilt anchor mark, French, 1850–1900, 8¼in (21cm) wide. Technically a fake of Chelsea, but the gilding is superb and it deserves recognition in its own right.
£400–500/$580–720 S(O)

Worcester shell-shaped pickle dish, with stylized shell moulding under the rim and a curled handle to one side, printed with Marrow pattern, depicting a marrow growing in a garden surrounded by mushrooms, walnuts, peas and small berries, the shell rim edged in dark blue, minor firing crack to handle, crescent mark, 1770–75, 5¼in (13.5cm) wide. If this dish did not have any cracks it would cost £650/$1,000.
£480–570/$700–850 P

► **Stevenson blue printed pottery meat dish,** with Springer Spaniel pattern, depicting a spaniel flushing a gamebird from cover, within a floral border, impressed maker's surname, 1820–30, 14¼in (36cm) wide. This printed pattern has obvious appeal and even a small platter is expensive. Values of blue and white depend on rarity and the decorative nature of the pattern.
£500–600/$720–870 DN

Adams soup tureen and cover, decorated with Lions pattern, with scroll-mounted handles and knop, printed in blue with an animal scene and floral border, damage to cover, base cracked, 1820–30, 12½in (32cm) wide. Even damaged and lacking a stand this is a sought-after piece because of the popularity of the pattern. Printed designs with prominent animals tend to be expensive.
£500–600/$720–870 DN

Philip Christian leaf-shaped pickle dish, applied with a thin looped stalk, the sharply-serrated rim heightened with tiny blue arrows, painted in dark blue with three separate floral sprigs, the underside moulded with veins, small chip on the tip of the leaf, 1765–70, 4¼in (11cm) wide. This rare pickle leaf is in very good condition. To a specialist collector of pickle dishes, nice examples by the lesser makers are very desirable. The price reflects this.
£550–650/$800–950 P

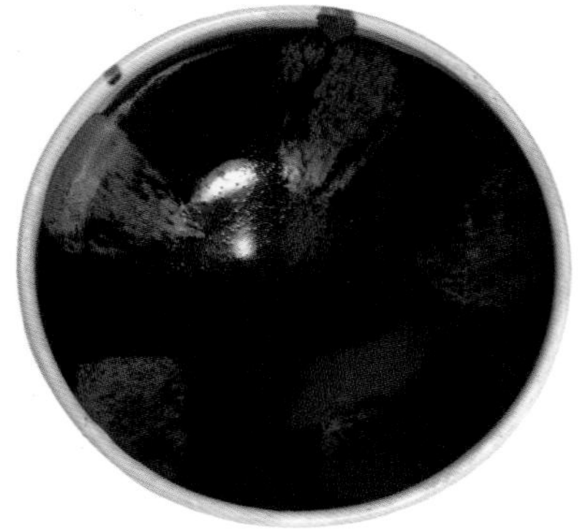

◄ **Tea bowl,** Chinese, Song Dynasty, 12thC, 7in (18cm) diam. Many Song Dynasty stonewares are now being copied. It is advisable to buy from a reputable dealer.
£610–680
$875–975 GLD

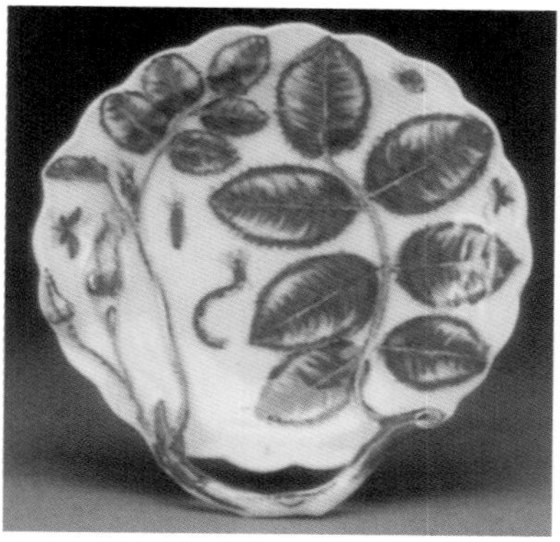

Worcester blue and white sweetmeat dish, decorated with Blind Earl pattern, moulded with a rose spray, crescent mark in underglaze blue, glaze starcrack to base, c1765, 6¼in (16cm) diam. This is a very attractive design, and without the crack would be worth £2,200–2,500/$3,200–3,500.
£650–750/$950–1,100 S(O)

Victorian Ironstone octagonal footbath, with serpent handles, and a matching water jug, both damaged, footbath 19in (48.5cm) wide. These are impressive items, despite the limited colouring. The damage makes them cheaper.
£650–800/$950–1,150 G(L)

Locate the source

The source of each illustration in Miller's can be found by checking the code letters below each caption with the Key to Illustrations, pages 286–290.

Minton majolica game pie tureen and cover, the cover moulded with naturalistic dead game on a bed of leaves, cracked and chipped, impressed marks, 13½in (34.5cm) wide. Majolica game tureens can sell for thousands, but this is the most common model, with unpopular dead game on top. Few people appreciate that you can buy good Minton majolica for under £1,000/$1,500.
£750–850/$1,100–1,250 S(O)

Blue and white bowl, Chinese, Ming Dynasty, Wanli period, 1573–1619, 9in (23cm) diam. Emperor Wanli was the last of the great Ming Emperors. This is an excellent opportunity to purchase a good piece of Ming porcelain for less than £1,000/$1,500.
£750–850/$1,100–1,250 GLD

Spode pottery soup tureen and cover, from Indian Sporting series, the body printed with The Hog at Bay, the cover with Hunting Buffalo within a border of animals, with moulded loop handles, body glued, cover cracked, printed and impressed upper-case marks, 1815–25, 15in (38cm) wide. The severe damage is reflected in the price of what would have been a very costly tureen at £4,000–5,000/ $5,750–7,250. An extensive restoration would make this more presentable.
£750–900/$1,100–1,300 DN

► **Porcelain tureen, cover and stand,** French, c1800, 12in (30.5cm) wide. This is a good size and a very impressive shape, although by a minor maker. Without the name of Sèvres or similarly famous maker, the value is modest.
£800–900
$1,150–1,300 US

Pair of Meissen cylindrical ice pails, painted with fruit sprays within puce scale borders, gilded details, crossed swords and star mark, German, c1780, 9¾in (25cm) wide. These have been heavily restored, which is reflected in the low price. However, because they are so splendid, it would be worth considering proper modern restoration which would make them look wonderful once again.
£800–950/$1,150–1,380 WW

◄ **Worcester pickle shell,** painted in blue with Two Peony Rock Bird pattern, with and leaf motifs repeated around the rim, workman's mark, 5in (12.5cm) wide. What makes this example an exception is the excellent condition. There is not a chip or a blemish. It is more expensive than many pickle dishes, but the quality of the piece stands out.
£850–950/$1,250–1,380 P

Figures

◀ **Porcelain centrepiece,** the floral-encrusted bowl supported by three maidens playing lyres, German, early 20thC, 8in (20.5cm) high. This piece is mixed-up rococo revival style. Not much quality, but as a decorative piece it has certain appeal.
£45–55 $65–80 G(L)

Two Staffordshire figures of Lord Byron and the Maid of Athens, c1860, 7in (18cm) high. Not particularly sought-after models, but very well coloured. The price is low for a pair as these are quite damaged.
£50–55/$75–80 DAN

Smoking monkey match striker, late 19thC, 3in (7.5cm) high. Such examples are well worth collecting today if they are of good quality.
£50–55/$75–80 JOA

Biscuit porcelain centrepiece stem, modelled as The Three Graces, c1850, 11½in (29cm) high. White biscuit figures are rarely expensive.
£60–70/$90–100 G(L)

Pair of Victorian Staffordshire pottery horses, from a shipwreck, 4in (10cm) high. Some white Staffordshire figures have recently come from a shipwreck which is interesting if the date of the wreck is known.
£85–95/$125–140 SER

Further reading

Miller's Ceramics Buyer's Guide, Miller's Publications, 2000

◀ **Minton parian group,** 'Naomi and her Daughters in Law', damaged, incised numerals '183', year cipher for 1876, 10½in (26.5cm) wide. A very popular model full of Victorian sentiment. Quite common and consequently affordable today.
£100–120/$145–175 F&C

Staffordshire condiment, in the form of a portly gentleman, c1870, 6in (15cm) high. This pepper pot is of particularly good quality.
£100–120/$145–175 DHA

Figure of Mercury and Cupid, painted in coloured enamels with gilt detailing, possibly Meissen, Mercury missing both arms from the elbows, Cupid missing his left leg, other chips, crossed swords mark painted to the back of the base, mid-18thC, 8¾in (22cm) high. The damage is so extensive that restoration is not economical.
£110–130/$160–190 WW

Staffordshire porcelain pastille burner, decorated with applied polychrome flowers, damaged, 1855–60, 7in (18cm) high. There has been little price movement for many years, so Staffordshire cottages are now excellent value.
£100–120/$145–175 NAW

► **Minton-style porcelain flatback model of Don Quixote,** riding a horse, on an oblong base inscribed 'Don Quichotte', sword hilt and left arm restored, c1830, 6in (15cm) high. This is a very thin profile figure and in spite of the severe restoration is good value.
£130–160/$190–230 WW

Pair of Victorian Staffordshire figures of a fisherman and his wife, c1880, 13in (33cm) high. These are likely to be Scottish, and while rather crude, they have lots of naive charm.
£130–160/$190–230 G(L)

Victorian Staffordshire portrait spill vase group of Robin Hood and Little John, on a titled oval base, c1860, 15in (38cm) high. The unpopular white colouring of this piece keeps the price low.
£110–130/$160–190 G(L)

Model of a cupid hiding under a shoe, c1880, 6in (15cm) high. An affordable Continental porcelain ornament with little surface detail, but plenty of charm.
£135–160/$195–230 JOA

Staffordshire figures

Victorian Staffordshire figures were intended to be viewed on a mantlepiece from the front only, and consequently the backs were neither modelled nor painted; hence the name 'flatbacks' for such pieces. Many figures were simple, but highly decorative, images of children or lovers.

From the 1840s there was a demand for portraits of famous people, whose features were copied from journals or the covers of popular printed music. In an age when the public rarely knew what famous people truly looked like, potters sometimes reused discontinued moulds to represent more topical individuals. Some figures were even wrongly named, such as a portrait of Benjamin Franklin labelled as George Washington.

Some popular figures were produced for many years and often require a close examination to determine whether they are earlier or later examples; this can greatly affect the value. As there are many fake Staffordshire figures on the market it is important to learn the correct 'feel' of genuine pieces, and it is advisable to buy only from reputable dealers and auctioneers.

Porcelain Sitzendorf-style figural centrepiece, the pierced basket supported by a shepherdess and lamb on a rose-mounted base, c1890, 19in (48.5cm) high. A decorative rococo-style Dresden centrepiece. Not a great work of art, but impressive and good value at this price.
£140–160/$200–230 BR

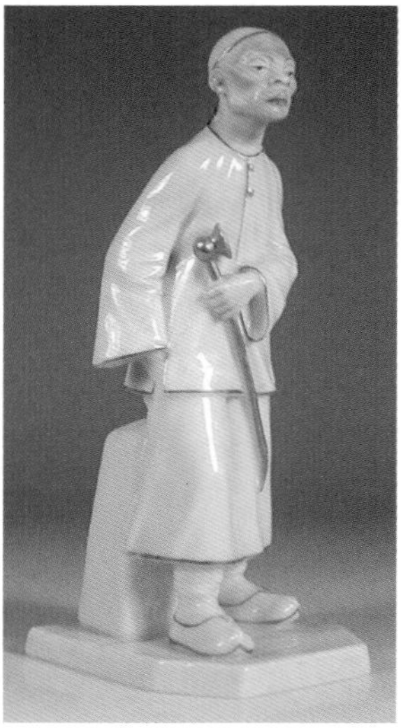

Royal Worcester figure of a Chinaman holding a pipe, decorated with gilt and enamel details, some restoration, impressed and printed marks, c1882, 6¾in (17cm) high. James Hadley's Countries of the World series is relatively inexpensive these days, each figure costing £200–300/$300–450 in good condition, and as affordable as this one when repaired.
£140–170/$200–250 WW

Miller's compares...

A. Staffordshire bust of Voltaire, on a restored socle, 19thC, 6in (15cm) high.
£150–180/$220–260 G(L)

B. Staffordshire bust of Homer, on a simulated marble socle, early 19thC, 5¼in (13.5cm) high.
£250–300/$350–440 G(L)

Classical figures are unpopular at the moment, and as a literary subject Item A would be expected to make more than Item B.

Staffordshire group of two figures and a deer, c1860, 7in (18cm) high. This model has plenty of detail and original colouring.
£145–160/$210–230 DAN ⊞

Pair of Victorian copper lustre Staffordshire chimney dogs, 1870–80, 10in (25.5cm) high. The separate front legs are a good sign on this nice matching pair with popular decoration.
£150–180/$220–260 G(L) ⚒

Pottery toy, press-moulded as a cockerel, minor frit to coxcomb, c1780, 4in (10cm) high. A very crude piece, but with a nice glaze and charming naïve appearance.
£190–220/$275–320 Bea(E) ⚒

Porcelain model of a poodle, with a bird in its mouth, 1830–40, 2½in (6.5cm) high. This would have originally been one of a pair, and a single dog can be bought for a lower price.
£145–160/$210–230 SER ⊞

Porcelain figure of a cherub, walking on spring flowers, decorated in polychrome pastels, probably French, 1880–90, 14in (35.5cm) high. A sentimental Victorian subject and a good size, hence the price. Rather kitsch, but with obvious appeal.
£150–180/$220–260 G(L) ⚒

◄ **Staffordshire figure of a gentleman sportsman,** standing beside a gun dog on a mound base, early 19thC, 7in (18cm) high. Figures of this type vary greatly in detail and modelling. This is an average example and, if genuine, a good buy at this price.
£180–215/$260–310 G(L) ⚒

The look without the price

Pair of Staffordshire collie dogs, c1890, 11in (28cm) wide.
£170–200
$250–300 AH ⚒

Staffordshire collie dogs dating from around 1860 are more valuable than the later ones, and would cost in the region of about £1,000+/$1,500+.

Staffordshire model of a deer, with bocage, on a mound base, c1815–20, 5¾in (14.5cm) high. This was originally one of a pair with a stag. The bocage is in reasonable condition and therefore this piece is good value for a single model.
£190–230/$275–330 G(L)

The look without the price

Parian porcelain figure of Rebecca at the Well, standing by a spring with an urn, wearing loose robes, on a rockwork base, firing crack and slight damage, c1860, 21¾in (55.5cm) high.
£220–260/$320–380 Bea(E)

Parian is mostly dominated by Minton and Copeland and unmarked examples by minor makers are rarely expensive. This one is large in size and the minor damage is not really a factor. A Minton piece of superior quality would be worth £1,000+/$1,500+.

Pair of Staffordshire flatback models of goats, above sleeping figures of a boy and girl, painted with coloured enamels, minor damage, mid-19thC, 11in (28cm) high. Unusual animal groups are popular with Staffordshire collectors and these are extremely good value for a matching pair.
£200–240/$300–350 WW

Two similar models of cats, by William Kent, some enamel flakes, chips to ears, early 20thC, 7¼in (18.5cm) high. These are 100-year-old reproductions of Staffordshire cats from the 1850s which are now hard to find, therefore, William Kent copies are increasing in value. Take care to avoid modern fakes.
£220–260/$320–380 DN

Pearlware model of a recumbent ewe, the base painted in shades of ochre, green and brown, restored, c1790. A fine early model which would cost £1,000/$1,500 if perfect. This one is badly damaged and requires costly restoration to hide the unsightly breaks.
£220–260/$320–380 DN

► **Pair of Samson porcelain Mansion House dwarfs,** 19thC, 7in (18cm) high. Samson made very good reproductions of early porcelain figures and although these examples are hard paste they fool many novice collectors. Samson is surprisingly good quality and many inferior fakes are wrongly attributed to him.
£220–260/$320–380 G(L)

Royal Copenhagen figural group of Hans and Trine, by Christian Thomsen, with a treetrunk behind, on a shaped circular base with gilt rim, impressed 'CmTn' to rear, green printed marks, blue wavy lines, inscribed '1783', 1925–30, 9in (23cm) high. Royal Copenhagen figures have not built up a significant secondary market yet and there are bargains to be found. This example is the work of a senior modeller and is well-coloured.
£250–280/$360–410 B

Walton group of a sheep and lamb, the waisted base with raised ribbon and 'Walton' on the reverse, bocage restored, 1820–30, 6¾in (17cm) high. A Walton mark is a bonus and adds to the interest of this piece, as does the lamb. Perfect examples are hard to find and sell at a premium, most have some damage as in this case.
£260–300/$380–440 Bea(E)

Staffordshire pottery clock group, c1860, 12in (30.5cm) high. This piece is of interest because of the unusually complicated clock with birds on top, adding to the value.
£260–280/$380–410 DAN

A biscuit porcelain figure of Nelson, wearing full naval uniform, standing before a pedestal draped with a cloak, c1830, 12¾in (32.5cm) high. White biscuit figures are not widely popular and can be inexpensive. This example is very rare and might fetch a much higher price. A specialist Nelson collector would be prepared to pay more.
£260–300/$380–440 S(O)

Derby model of a cow, before a flowering tree, on a pad base, one horn restored, c1770, 3½in (9cm) high. The flowers on this piece are not particularly detailed and the cow also lacks detail. However, the condition is sound, and for a popular Derby animal this is good value.
£260–300/$380–440 WW

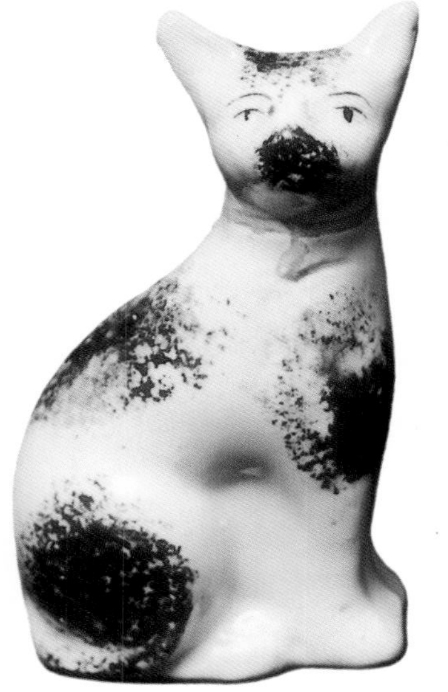

Staffordshire seated cat, 1845, 3½in (9cm) high. Cats are very collectable and early Staffordshire cats are hard to find. This lacks detail, keeping the price down, but it has charm.
£270–300/$400–450 WWW

Further reading

Miller's Staffordshire Figures of the 19th & 20th Centuries: A Collector's Guide,
Miller's Publications, 2000

Majolica model of a cockerel, standing before leaves and flowers forming a vase, some damage, incised marks, Continental, early 20thC, 13in (33cm) high. This is a crude Continental copy, but reasonable value when compared with the very high price of Minton majolica.
£280–320/$400–450 WW

Victorian Staffordshire clockface group, modelled as a royal coat-of-arms, painted in naturalistic colours, on an oval base, 9½in (24cm) high. An inexpensive piece because of the lack of detail. It should have gilding and a clock face. Royal arms models are very desirable.
£300–350/$440–500 G(L)

Derby figure of Milton, wearing a puce-lined robe, his left elbow resting on three large books and a scroll all on a pillar, on a scrolling base, painted with pale-coloured enamels and gilt, minor damage, c1765, 11¼in (28.5cm) high. An early piece with only minor damage, so it is excellent value.
£280–340/$400–500 WW

Parian ware group from Shakespeare's King John, entitled 'Prince Arthur and Hubert', after Beattie, modelled as a kneeling Prince embracing a seated Hubert, raised on a stepped oval base, 19thC, 17in (43cm) high. This is a large, finely-modelled parian group, but inexpensive because it is not by a major maker and is an unpopular historical subject.
£300–375/$440–570 AH

Pair of Royal Worcester shot enamel figures of a French fisherboy and fishergirl, c1890, 8in (20.5cm) high. This pair illustrates how inexpensive Victorian Royal Worcester figures have become. Ten years ago these might have made £500–600/$720–870. It is vital to buy figures in perfect condition.
£300–350/$440–500 G(L)

Pair of Pratt ware figures representing Spring and Autumn, from the Four Seasons Series, modelled as classical maidens, Autumn holding a sheaf of corn and a sickle, Spring holding a cornucopia of flowers, Spring restored to base, 1810–20, 8¾in (22cm) high. The titles on the base do not match. A fully matching set of four will always sell at a considerable premium. This price also reflects the fact that they have been restored.
£325–375/$470–570 DN

The look without the price

Pratt ware polychrome-decorated figure of an actor, leaning against a tree stump, hat and one hand restored, early 19thC, 9½in (24cm) high.
£325–350
$470–500 S(O)

This is a rare and very charming model. The price was kept down by the restoration, as a replacement hand is hard to restore. If it was in perfect condition it could fetch £1,000/$1,500.

Staffordshire porcellaneous model of a hound, with black patches and spots, chained to a green rockwork base, enamels re-touched, mid-19thC, 4¾in (12cm) high. This is a powerful model, but the repainting has affected the price, otherwise it could sell for about £450/$650.
£350–400/$500–580 WW

Staffordshire figure of a man, wearing a black hat and jacket, red waistcoat and yellow breeches, with one basket containing a rabbit, the other tipped and spilling broken eggs, c1810, 5½in (14cm) high. Although broken eggs was a popular allegory, the price of this piece is kept down by the sombre colouring, plain base and the fact that the figure is looking down.
£350–400/$500–580 JHo

Cross Reference
See Sculpture (page 270)

Pair of Royal Worcester porcelain figures of a young boy and girl, wearing Regency-style costume, each carrying a basket, standing against a tree trunk, with hand-painted faces and gilt decoration, on a naturalistic base, printed pink mark, impressed No. 88023, gilt monogram BT, date letter T for 1882, 9¾in (25cm) high. The gilt letters BT would be the mark of the gilder Henry Bright. Expect to pay £550–600/$800–870 for a perfect pair.
£375–450/$560–650 BLH

Pottery hen tureen and cover, modelled as a chicken sitting on eggs, the lower section ozier-moulded, fully coloured, some small chips, c1900, 8¾in (22cm) wide. Staffordshire hen tureens, while not exactly uncommon, are always sought after. Value depends on age and colour.
£400–475/$580–700 DN

Insurance values

Always insure your valuable antiques for the cost of replacing them with similar items, regardless of the original price paid. Both dealers and auctioneers can provide a valuation service for a fee.

Derby group of Jason and Medea at the alter of Diana, the goddess on a tall plinth with the two mortals at her feet, painted with coloured enamels with gilt details, some repairs, incised mark 'N31', 1770–80, 11¾in (30cm) high. It is inevitable that a complex group such as this will have some repair and, at this price it may be extensive. Even so, it is a large classical group from Derby and is very good value.
£400–480/$580–700 WW

Derby model of Asia, from the Four Quarters of the Globe Series, modelled as a young girl standing before a recumbant camel, c1770, 7in (18cm) high. This is an attractive subject, but is one of a set of four. It is not modelled to scale particularly well and is therefore unpopular, however, unrestored examples are worth seeking.
£400–480/$580–700 WW

► **Pearlware figure of the goddess Flora,** wearing classical robes, a lamb and a hound at her feet, on a square plinth base inscribed 'Floro', the frieze moulded in relief with an acanthus leaf band, some chips and losses, c1800, 13in (33cm) high. Well modelled with unusual colouring, and in good condition. Classical figures are not as popular as English subjects, so this large example is good value for money.
£480–550/$700–800 DN

◄ **Bow figure of a young woman,** holding a birdcage, decorated in coloured enamels, some restoration, c1765, 8¼in (21cm) high. Bow figures on later scroll bases (1765–70) are generally undervalued, but this is also less expensive because of extensive restoration.
£480–550/$700–800 LFA

Parian seated figure of Hamlet, plume and scabbard restored, c1860, 15in (38cm) high. This is a large figure with theatrical interest, but by an unknown maker. It is also an unpopular historical subject which is reflected in the price.
£450–550/$620–720 JAK

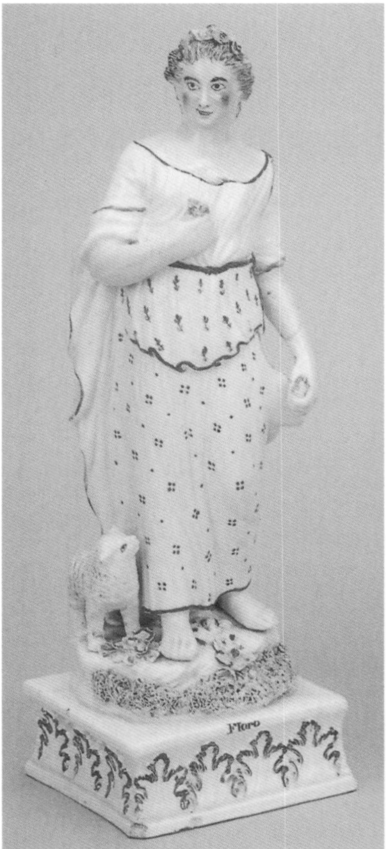

Minton parian figure of Clorinda, by John Bell, from Tasso's *Gerusalemme Liberata*, c1850, 14in (35.5cm) high. Clorinda was a pagan warrior who was mortally wounded by her lover, a Christian nobleman, who failed to recognize her in her armour. This is a quality piece by a good maker and a famous modeller. Clorinda was very popular in Victorian times and sold in great numbers. The fact that she looks down puts off many buyers today.
£500–550/$720–800 JAK ⊞

Pair of Derby porcelain figures of a youth and a maiden, playing musical instruments and wearing floral dress, among bocage, on a scroll-moulded base, with gilt embellishment, late 18thC, 8¼in (21cm) high. A good size pair in nice condition, later than some Derby figures but a good match and highly decorative. They appear undervalued, like most Derby figures.
£550–700/$800–1,000 AH ⚒

Staffordshire pottery group of a courting couple, before a blossoming tree, on a rockwork base, c1820, 8in (20.5cm) high. The figures appear stiff and there are some losses to the bocage making this good value.
£500–550/$720–800 JHo ⊞

Pair of Royal Worcester figures representing 'Joy' and 'Sorrow', by James Hadley, each depicting a classical maiden with a bird, chip to base edge of Sorrow, wear to gilding, puce printed marks and shape Nos. 2/57, c1919, 9½in (24cm) high. Figures weeping and struck with grief are never popular. Joy and Sorrow were made in many versions and in several sizes. This pair are well coloured and in good condition and fetched a good price as a result.
£600–725
$870–1,000 S(O) ⚒

Royal Dux figure of a water carrier, c1900, 24in (61cm) high. Single Royal Dux figures are far less popular than pairs, and the subject is not as appealing as a nubile female. Other subjects will command higher prices.
£500–550/$720–800 JOA ⊞

Derby figure of Neptune, sitting on a green dolphin, c1775, 9½in (24cm) high. Figures that were popular in their day are common now. This figure turns up regularly for sale.
£750–900
$1,100–1,300 DMa ⊞

Flatware

Nursery plate, with puce decoration, c1830, 3½in (9cm) diam. Miniature plates are easy to collect and do not take up much room. This has a particularly pleasant image.
£35–40/$50–60 IW

► **Earthenware wall plate,** enamelled and gilded with flowers on a cream ground, French, late 19thC, 15in (38cm) diam. This is very decorative, but would be worth more if it had a maker's name.
£50–60
$75–90 G(L)

◄ **Porcelain saucer from the *Tek Sing* cargo,** the centre decorated with an aster, c1820, 4½in (11.5cm) diam.
£50–60
$75–90 RBA

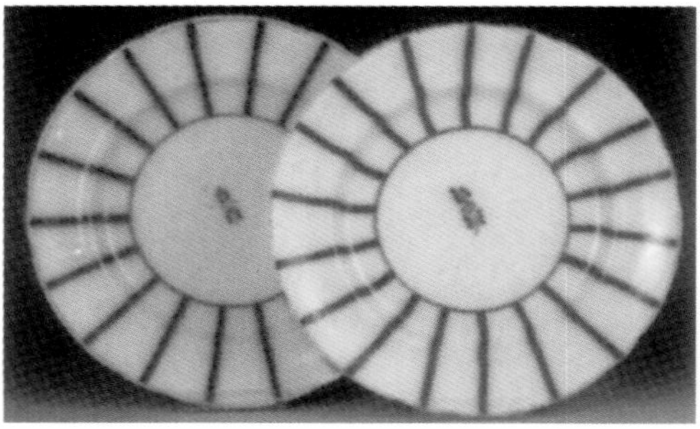

Davenport pottery part service, comprising eight plates, an oval bowl and three dishes, decorated with blue radiating stripes, impressed marks, 19thC. If you are creating a collection, it is often better to have one good piece rather than several mediocre items.
£50–60/$75–90 WW

Imari plate, depicting two figures beneath a tree, Japanese, c1920–30, 10in (25.5cm) diam. This plate has a decorative value only.
£60–65/$90–95 FRY

Coalport plate, painted with a central rose and panels of flowers on a gilt-decorated pink ground, c1840, 9½in (24cm) diam. Single plates from good quality Victorian dessert sets can be excellent value. This one has raised gold decoration which is always a good sign.
£70–85/$110–125 WW

◀ **Derby plate,** with brightly-coloured floral decoration and gilding, c1888, 8in (20.5cm) diam. A bold pattern, but it is only a coloured-in print, not hand-painted. Derby Crown Porcelain Co is a good maker.
£75–85
$110–125 JOA

Saucer from the *Tek Sing* cargo, decorated with peony and magnolia, c1820, 4½in (11.5cm) diam. This is an attractive pattern.
£80–90/$115–130 RBA

Blue and white plate, decorated with a village scene, early 19thC, 9½in (24cm) diam. This rural scene pattern was made by many makers and is not a rare subject. Single blue-printed plates are well worth collecting.
£80–90/$115–130 DHA

Hichozan plate, Japanese, Meiji marks and of the period, 1868–1911, 9in (23cm) diam. This is a good opportunity to buy a colourful and decorative antique porcelain plate for less than £100/$145.
£80–90/$115–130 FRY

◀ **Meissen dessert plate,** decorated with onion pattern, with gold trim, c1890, 8½in (21.5cm) diam. The pierced rim and gold trim makes this a de luxe version of an Onion pattern plate. It has the crossed swords mark on the front which is a good sign.
£90–100
$130–145 MAA

Pair of creamware plates, probably Liverpool, printed in black with a three-masted galleon, with pheasants on the rims, one rim chipped, c1785, 9½in (24cm) diam. These are lovely plates with a popular shipping subject. They are rubbed which keeps the value down.
£100–120/$145–175 G(L)

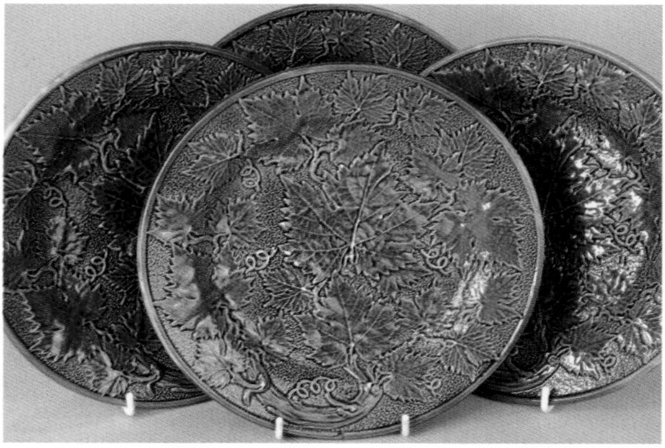

Four pottery leaf-moulded plates, green glazed, with ribbed backs, 19thC, 8¼in (21cm) diam. These are a good colour and popular with collectors. Marked examples would be a better buy.
£110–130/$160–190 SWO

Dish from the *Tek Sing* cargo, with spiral lotus pattern, c1820, 6in (15cm) diam. Shipwreck cargo is often of historical interest rather than merit.
£120–130/$175–190 RBA

Nine matching Victorian leaf-moulded plates, green glazed, 9in (23cm) diam. Green-glazed dessert plates were very popular in the 1840s–50s and remained in use until the 20thC. It is important to look at the quality of the moulding. Marked examples are more desirable.
£120–140/$175–200 DA

► **Monogrammed plate,** enamelled with the initials JEP, late 18thC, 9½in (24cm) diam. This is an opportunity to buy a good piece of Chinese Armorial porcelain for less than £150/$215.
£140–170
$200–250 WW

Staffordshire blue and white plate, from the Shipping series, printed with a sailing ship in a square panel on a ground of fruiting branches and shells, c1820, 10in (25.5cm) diam. A very good pattern and hard to find in good condition. This is excellent value.
£150–180/$220–260 WW

Clarice Cliff side plate, decorated with Honolulu pattern, 1933–35, 7in (18cm) diam. This is one of Clarice Cliff's most exotic and collectable patterns. Although this example has significant wear, buying slightly damaged or worn items of Clarice Ciff is an affordable way to own rare patterns. This particular plate, if it were perfect, would fetch £500–800/ $725–1,150.
£150–180/$220–260 G(L)

SAMSUNG
12:45
Mon, 7 Jan
ChatON
Camera
Samsung Apps
SONY
10:35
WALKMAN
Album
Movies
Playstation
NOKIA
Nokia MixRadio
4oD

HUAWEI
09:59

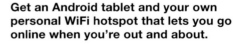

Wemyss plate, with a brown-painted cockerel, c1900, 5in (12.5cm) diam. A small but bold and very distinctive Wemyss painting of popular appeal and also for the specialist market.
£150–200/$220–290 RdeR

Clarice Cliff cup and saucer, decorated with Solomon's Seal pattern, with solid triangular handle, and a Crocus pattern salt, 1935–40, 10in (25.5cm) diam. This is the type of mixed lot that you may find at an auction. The cup and saucer are decorated in a part lithograph and part hand-painted design on Clarice Cliff's classic conical shape. However, the Crocus mustard pot is an entirely hand-painted design and if it had its original cover it would possibly be worth more than the cup and saucer due to the freehand design.
£160–190/$230–275 G(L)

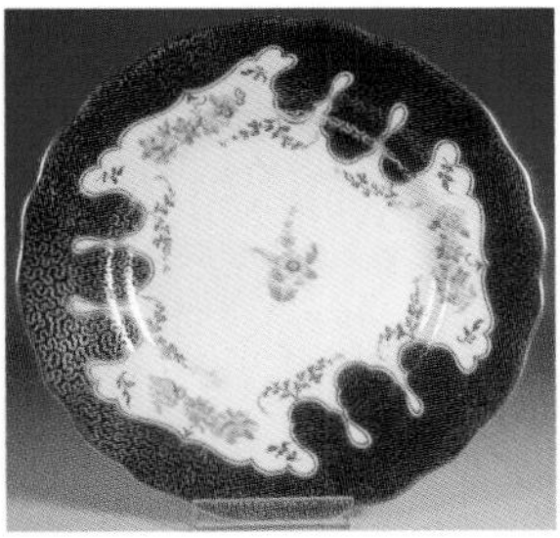

Set of ten bone china dinner plates, 19thC, 9¼in (23.5cm) diam. These plates are by a minor maker and would be best used rather than displayed as the quality is basic.
£160–190/$230–275 WW

Set of four Royal Crown Derby bone china dinner plates, painted with flower sprays by C. Gresley, date coded 1937, 10in (25.5cm) diam. The central painting is by a top artist, Cuthbert Gresley, but the borders are rather dull. It is difficult to obtain signed plates, so these would be good value at this price. Richly decorated border plates by Gresley would be very costly.
£160–190/$230–275 G(L)

Miller's compares...

A. Blue and white plate, decorated with Stevenson Castles pattern, c1820, 9in (23cm) diam. This is an unrecorded series.
£180–200/$260–290 SCO

B. Blue and white plate, from the Riley Hunting series, c1820, 10in (25.5cm) diam.
£270–300/$400–440 SCO

This is a vast field and new patterns are being written up all the time. The value of single plates depends on rarity and a rare pattern will always make more. Item B has an interesting scenic view and achieved a higher price. Certain well-known named patterns fetch much more than others. Prominent figures and animals are usually costly. If a plate is £200/$290 or more, the market should be well researched and understood by the purchaser.

Set of twelve Nymphenburg porcelain dessert plates, each painted in magenta with a bouquet of flowers, within a Greek key and moulded border, 19thC, 8¼in (21cm) diam. In the 19th/20th centuries Nymphenburg was one of many small German china factories. There is limited collectors' following, but the quality is good and they are good pieces for use.
£190–230/$275–330 SWO

Pair of *famille rose* plates, painted with floral sprigs, Chinese, Qianlong period, 1736–95, 9½in (24cm) diam. Condition is very important for these plates. Check carefully that there are no hair cracks or chips to the rim. If perfect, they are good value at £100/$145 each.
£190–230/$275–330 G(L)

◄ **Sunderland teapot stand,** decorated with a ship and inscription, 'Thou God Seest Me' to the reverse, c1840, 7½in (19cm) diam. A distinctive Victorian object and in good condition.
£200–225
$290–325 NAW

Vienna plate, painted with a spray of fruit and flowers and scattered blooms and butterflies, the gilt-edged rim with a gilt scrollwork border alternately terminating with a leaf and a bunch of grapes, border to edge of well slightly worn, shield mark in underglaze blue, impressed date code 805 and 85, painter's numeral 87 in puce for Franz Solnek, 1805, 9½in (24cm) diam. A good plate dateable to 1805, from an important collection, yet Vienna is not fashionable and the price is modest. Old Vienna porcelain is undervalued.
£200–240/$300–350 S(O)

◄ **Wedgwood creamware plate,** of royal shape, printed in black with a riverside scene, 1785–90, 10in (25.5cm) diam. This item has Liverpool printing on a Wedgwood plate. Rim chips or rubbing make a big difference to the value.
£220–245/$320–350 DHA

Royal Worcester bone china plate, painted with a still life study of fruit, signed 'H. Ayrton', within a tooled gilt rim, printed black factory mark to base, minor wear, c1954, 10¾in (27.5cm) diam. The price of this plate is low because of minor wear, but also because the factory mark is in black, indicating a post-war production. Fruit plates from the 1920s or 1930s, marked in puce or purple, sell for twice as much.
£220–260/$320–380 RTo

Worcester hexagonal teapot stand, with rich Kakiemon-style decoration on a blue-scale ground, with fluted sides, chip to rim exterior, minor surface scratches, open blue crescent mark, c1785, 6in (15cm) diam. This dates from the William Davis or Flight period (after the Dr Wall or First Period) and the price reflects this. A small chip also makes a difference to the price. However, teapot stands are popular with collectors.
£235–290/$340–425 S(O)

Further reading

Miller's Ceramics Buyer's Guide, Miller's Publications, 2000

The look without the price

A good quality 18th-century *famille rose* piece of large size. This would achieve £800/$1,150 if perfect, but a damaged piece can still be excellent decorative value.

***Famille rose* circular dish,** the centre painted with a flowering peony, large chip, enamel flaking, Chinese, Qianlong period, 1736–95, 15½in (39.5cm) diam.
£235–280/$340–410 S(O)

► **Worcester blue and white saucer,** painted with a fisherman and buildings beneath trees, workman's mark, 1755–60, 4¾in (12cm) diam. A very nice odd saucer and fantastic value as there are not many saucer collectors. The moulding on this one is excellent.
£240–280
$350–400 WW

Pair of Meissen ornithological soup plates, from the Marcolini period, painted with exotic birds within a foliate swag border and shaped gilt dentil rim, one rim chipped, blue crossed swords and star marks, c1800, 8¾in (22cm) diam. Sets of Meissen from the late 18thC are more plentiful than might be imagined. Soup plates are always cheaper than flat plates as they are harder to display. These are great value.
£240–280/$350–400 DN

Sunderland teapot stand, by Dixon & Co, Garrison Pottery, c1840, 7½in (19cm) diam. A good, busy pattern. Shipping subjects are popular in Sunderland pottery.
£250–275/$360–400 NAW

***Famille rose* plate,** decorated in bright enamels with peonies, insects and sprigs, Chinese, Qianlong period, c1760, 7in (18cm) diam.
£250–275/$360–400 NAW

◄ **Nantgarw 'chocolate edge' dessert plate,** painted by Thomas Pardoe, minor haircrack to rim, impressed 'Nantgarw C.W.', 1821–23, 8½in (21.5cm) diam. A crack in Welsh porcelain, however tiny, makes a huge difference to the value.
£250–280
$360–400 S(O)

Stubbs blue printed pottery plate, decorated with fruit and flowers, 10in (25.5cm) diam. Busy, all-over patterns of flowers and fruit are surprisingly expensive in blue-printed pottery.
£270–300/$390–440 SCO

Locate the source

The source of each illustration in Miller's can be found by checking the code letters below each caption with the Key to Illustrations, pages 286–290.

◄ **Wemyss Gordon plate,** painted with roses, c1890, 8in (20.5cm) diam. Roses are common on Wemyss, although a plate like this is unusual.
£270–300/$400–440 RdeR

Blue and white plate, Chinese, Kangxi period, 1662–1722, 8in (20.5cm) diam. This is a good quality piece of late 17thC Chinese blue-and-white, showing the dragon rising from the sea, but it must be in perfect condition to maintain the price level.
£270–300/$400–440 GLD

Spode hot water plate, from the Indian Sporting Series, with two spouts and loop handles, one spout with feather-moulded integral cover, printed in blue with 'Death of the Bear' within a border of animals repeated around the exterior, crack to rim, printed title mark and printed and impressed upper-case maker's name, 1815–25, 9¾in (25cm) diam. 'Death of the Bear' is a popular print on plates, but is much rarer on a hot water plate, doubling the price.
£280–320/$400–460 DN

► **Pair of Coalport plates,** the centres brightly-painted with birds, the blue borders decorated with scrollwork, slight wear, 1810–15, 8¾in (22cm) diam. These two plates are from a dessert service and are reasonably priced, although the slight rubbing to the gold does make quite a difference to the price. 'Stacking wear' on a decorative plate always reduces the value.
£280–350/$400–500 WW

Miller's compares...

A. Shaped Meissen plate, painted with a butterfly on a flowering branch, the border with flower sprigs, rim chip, crossed swords mark and impressed '16', mid-18thC, 9¼in (23.5cm) diam.
£270–320/$400–460 WW

B. Meissen plate, painted with the *Schmetterlingsdekor*, a butterfly on a flowering branch, brown-edged rim, crossed swords in underglaze blue, impressed '61', c1740, 10in (25.5cm) diam.
£410–450/$600–650 S(O)

Meissen collectors prefer small shapes rather than plates but these have a distinctive pattern. Item B is slightly earlier than Item A and is in perfect condition, whereas Item A has a rim chip.

► **Royal Worcester cabinet plate,** with central riverscape panel and royal blue and pink border, signed 'H. Davis', c1912, 8¾in (22cm) diam. Raised gold in the border is a sign of quality and the centre is painted by a top artist. However, the low price reflects some damage.
£280–350/$400–500 G(L)

Pair of blue and white circular dishes, Chinese, 1875–1925, 13¼in (33.5cm) diam. An excellent opportunity to purchase a highly decorative pair of large Chinese blue and white dishes for less than £300/$440.
£280–350/$400–500 SWO

The look without the price

This rare Chinese *famille verte* dish is of the highest quality and if perfect would be worth up to £3,000/ $4,400. An excellent opportunity to acquire a damaged example at 10 per cent of the optimum value of a perfect example.

Famille verte **circular dish,** the central panel decorated with geisha and deer pulling a cart, restored, Chinese, Kangxi period, 1662–1722, 18thC, 15¼in (38.5cm) diam.
£280–350/$400–500 SWO

Bow plate, with colourful flower sprays and sprigs and a brown line rim, 1755–60, 8in (20.5cm) diam. This example is quite uncommon, but sparsely decorated and fire-speckled, and is excellent value at such a modest price.
£280–350/$400–500 WW

◄ **Herculaneum plate,** from the India Series, c1820, 10in (25.5cm) diam. Indian views are among the most interesting subjects on blue-printed plates, especially when the source of the print can be traced. Much depends on the individual rarity.
£290–325
$425–470 GN

Bristol plate, decorated in colours with a bowl of fruit, 1760, 9in (23cm) diam. What may seem a dull pattern is actually rare, which is why this English delft plate is so costly.
£300–335/$440–500 JHo

► **Charlotte Rhead tube-lined charger,** with a colourful floral decoration, 1930s, 16½in (42cm) diam.
£300–400
$440–580 G(L)

***Famille rose* plate,** decorated with a dog and a buffalo, the rim with a gilt and iron-red scroll, rim chips, Chinese export, Qianlong period, 1736–95, 9in (23cm) diam. A good example of Chinese famille rose with European taste. The rim chips have had a major effect on the price. If perfect, this would achieve £800–1,000/$1,150–1,500.
£300–360/$440–500 DN

The look without the price

The Three Friends of Winter are bamboo, pine and prunus blossom. This 17th-century plate has a spurious Ming mark. However, this does not have an effect on the price as the design is contemporary with the date of manufacture. An unusual piece, very much in the Chinese taste. A good buy at £350/$500, even with the crack. If perfect it would be £800/$1,150.

Octagonal plate, with rounded canted corners, reserved in white with The Three Friends on a powder-blue ground, crack, Chenghua mark, late Ming dynasty, 17thC, 8in (20.5cm) diam.
£320–370/$450–550 DN

◄ **Spode blue and white plate,** from the Indian Sporting Series, decorated with 'Death of The Bear', impressed mark, c1810, 10in (25.5cm) diam.
£340–380
$500–550 NAW

Pair of blue and white plates, from the Shipping Series, each printed with a sailing ship in a square panel, on a ground of fruiting branches and shells, 1820–30, 9in (23cm) diam. There is no advantage in a pair of plates with identical patterns. Most collectors want only one. Some central shipping prints are rarer than others.
£350–420/$500–615 WW

Sèvres-style plate, the centre decorated with a portrait of a lady, signed 'Brun', French, late 19thC, 10in (25.5cm) diam. Richly decorated with lavish raised gold, this is a good decorative plate.
£400–450/$580–650 MAA

Prices

The price ranges quoted in this book reflect the average price a purchaser might expect to pay for a similar item. The price will vary according to the condition, rarity, size, popularity, provenance, colour and restoration of the item, and this must be taken into account when assessing values. Don't forget that if you are selling it is quite likely that you will be offered less than the price range.

Chelsea plate, from the Duke of Cambridge service, brightly-painted with fruit, leaves and insects, some damage, red anchor mark, c1755, 9¼in (23.5cm) diam. An exciting Chelsea plate with Royal connections, although this was not a single service. This item is badly cracked and worn. In such condition this should have been an inexpensive plate, but the provenance of the service makes a big difference.
£400–500/$600–720 WW

► **Pair of Chamberlain's Worcester dinner plates,** with central armorial within a blue and gilt border, 19thC, 9½in (24cm) diam.
£440–520/$650–750 G(L)

Five Victorian majolica shell-shaped plates, and a comport, on dolphin feet, 9in (23cm) wide. These copies of Wedgwood, by a smaller English maker, are costly because of the strength of the majolica market. The shapes appeal to decorators.
£440–520/$650–750 SWO

Cantagalli pottery wall charger, decorated with Persian pattern, 19thC, 15¾in (40cm) diam. Cantagalli, an Italian maker of fakes and reproductions has enjoyed a renewed interest recently with a London exhibition. This copy of Isnik is set to rise further.
£440–540/$650–800 SWO

Set of four Spode soup plates, printed in blue with Chase after a Wolf pattern, impressed and printed marks, c1820, 9¾in (25cm) diam. These reflect the correct auction estimate for Spode Indian Sporting pattern plates and are good value. Collectors like single plates and sets are not worth any more.
£450–500/$650–720 S(O)

◄ **Pair of Imari plates,** decorated with vases of flowers within a border of cranes, chrysanthemum and peony issuing from rockwork, one cracked, Japanese, 18thC, 8½in (21.5cm) diam. These are the very best quality Imari. If both plates were perfect the price would be £800/$1,150.
£450–550/$650–800 DN

◄ **Vienna-style plate,** probably Bohemian, c1890, 9½in (24cm) diam. This plate was decorated in either Dresden or Vienna with a spurious Vienna mark. The quality of the raised gold is exquisite and the workmanship of detail deserves to be appreciated in its own right.
£500–550
$720–800 DcA

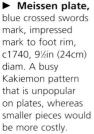

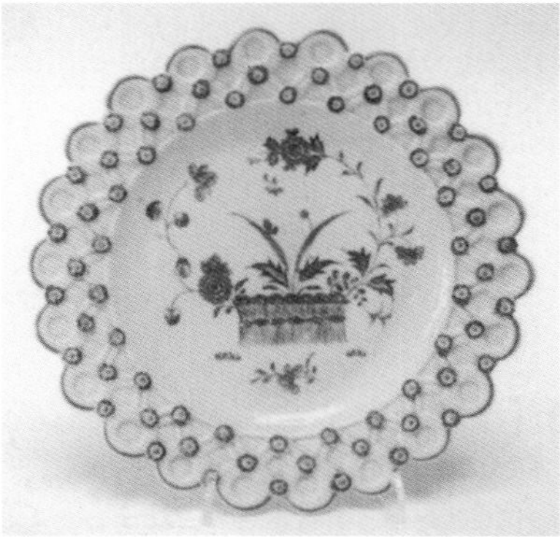

Derby plate, painted in puce monochrome with flowering branches and a banded hedge in Kakiemon-style, picked out in gold, the basket-moulded lobed border applied with puce and gilt flowerheads, c1760, 7¼in (18.5cm) diam. This is a rare and exciting plate, however, puce monochrome painting is unpopular, and therefore relatively inexpensive. The shape is typical of the period.
£500–550/$720–800 LFA

► **Meissen plate,** blue crossed swords mark, impressed mark to foot rim, c1740, 9½in (24cm) diam. A busy Kakiemon pattern that is unpopular on plates, whereas smaller pieces would be more costly.
£500–600
$720–870 WW

Insurance values

Always insure your valuable antiques for the cost of replacing them with similar items, regardless of the original price paid. Both dealers and auctioneers can provide a valuation service for a fee.

Pair of Worcester blue scale plates, painted with summer flowers within vase and mirror-form cartouches, gilt borders and rims, minor wear to gilding and enamels, blue square marks, c1770, 7¾in (19.5cm) diam. Not uncommon, but undervalued, these plates were worth more 30 to 40 years ago but have been out of fashion since. There has been an increase again in the past few years, but perfect examples deserve to increase further.
£550–600/$800–870 Bon(C)

◄ **Hot water plate,** decorated with Winemakers pattern, c1820, 10in (25.5cm) diam. A hot water plate in one of the most sought-after and expensive patterns in blue-printed pottery. It is a very special collectors' piece.
£720–800/$1,000–1,150 GN

Jars & Canisters

Two lobed jars, decorated in underglaze blue with scrolling lotus, south east Asian, 15thC, 3¼in (8cm) high. This is a good opportunity to purchase genuine Ming ceramics for £50/$75 each. These charming small storage jars are not the best quality, as they were mass-produced for sale throughout the Far East, but their free and quick painting style gives them a charm of their own.
£90–100/$130–145 DN

Creamware tea canister, 1765–75, lid missing, 4¾in (12cm) high. This example is a nice shape with English painting and it typically lacks a lid.
£240–270/$350–390 IW

◄ **Oil jar,** bottom missing, French, regional, 18thC, 25in (63.5cm) high. These coarse and heavily-weathered garden jars appeal to decorators.
£250–360/$360–520 CF

► **Slip-glazed pot,** Mataban, Burmese, 16th–17thC, 12in (30.5cm) diam. Burmese ceramics are not as collectable as Chinese ceramics but have a charm of their own. They can often be found in the Far East for very affordable prices.
£350–400/$500–580 GRG

◄ **Green-glazed tea canister,** Chinese, mid-19thC, 6in (16cm) high.
£380–460
$565–665 G(L)

► **Blue and white spice jar and lid,** Chinese, Kangxi period, 1662–1722, 3½in (9cm) high. Small lidded jars of this period are much sought-after by collectors. They must have the original lid and be perfect – without the lid they are worth half the amount.
£600–680
$880–1,000 GLD

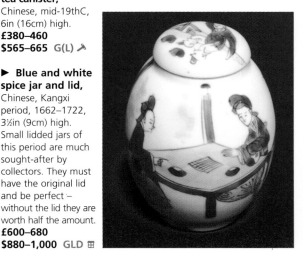

Jugs & Ewers

Lustreware commemorative jug, relief-moulded with General Hill and Lord Wellington between flags, both with an impressed title, chipped and cracked, early 19thC, 5in (13cm) high. These military hero jugs were so popular that they are now very common. Therefore, for a piece of collectable history they are very inexpensive.
£70–85/$100–125 WW

Alcock relief-moulded bone china milk jug, modelled with a gypsy encampment in a wood fanning a cauldron, the reverse with figures in a tent beneath trees, handle cracked, moulded mark, mid-19thC, 5½in (14cm) high. The crack makes a huge difference to the price. It is, however, a splendid and rare jug.
£80–100/$115–145 WW

► **Satyr jug,** spout restored, c1835, 4½in (11.5cm) high. Satyr- or Bacchus-head jugs were very popular from the 1770s onwards. These curious novelties tend to be undervalued.
£100–110/$145–160 DHA

► **Savoie pottery jug with lid,** French, 1900, 10in (25.5cm) high. This is a crude but fun piece of ceramic.
£80–90
$115–130 MLL

Meissen jug, decorated with Onion pattern, c1870, 2½in (6.5cm) high. A pretty shape in this popular pattern. This is not a rare object but charming all the same.
£85–95/$125–140 MAA

► **Milk jug,** painted with pink roses on a blue and gilt ground, 19thC, 6¼in (16cm) wide. This is not attributable to a maker, but is very well decorated giving it charm and richness.
£120–150
$175–220 WW

Victorian Staffordshire water jug, in the form of a begging black and white spaniel, 10½in (26.5cm) high. The enamel on this jug is flaking which reduces its value. It would be worth having it repainted.
£120–145/$175–210 G(L)

◄ **Copeland Spode water jug,** decorated in Hawkweed pattern with printed and hand-coloured floral decoration, c1890–1900, 11in (28cm) high. Water jugs on their own are much more affordable than if they were part of a washset.
£130–160
$190–230 G(L)

► **Victorian Meigh & Sons blue, white and grey water jug,** transfer-printed with a view from the Northern Scenery Series, cracked, 8in (20.5cm) high. A grey print is never popular and together with a crack makes this item quite inexpensive.
£140–170/$200–250 G(L)

Clarice Cliff cream jug, in Gayday pattern, with matching cup and saucer, early 1930s, 4in (10cm) high. Gayday is one of the most common Clarice Cliff patterns. The traditional shape and common pattern makes this an affordable starting point for a Clarice Cliff collection.
£140–170/$200–250 G(L)

Insurance values

Always insure your valuable antiques for the cost of replacing them with similar items, regardless of the original price paid. Both dealers and auctioneers can provide a valuation service for a fee.

◄ **Set of three Grainger Worcester earthenware jugs,** transfer-printed with Willow pattern in blue with gilt decoration, 1866, largest jug 8in (20.5cm) high. Although manufactured in Worcester, these jugs are basic and functional and not the best quality, hence the lower price.
£160–190/$230–275 G(L)

◄ **Pottery jug,** printed in black with a view of the Crystal Palace, commemorating the Great Exhibition, c1851, 9½in (24cm) high. This basic piece of pottery commemorates such an important event, which makes it an interesting Victorian collectable in itself.
£200–240
$290–350 SAS

Royal Worcester cream jug, by John Stinton, painted with Highland cattle, 1900–10, 3¼in (8.5cm) high. This jug was painted by a top artist. If the same painting appeared on a vase it would be worth much more as teawares do not command the same prices.
£180–220/$260–320 G(L)

Miller's compares...

A. Lowestoft sauce boat, decorated with foliage in underglaze blue within leaf-moulded reserves, c1770, 6¾in (17cm) wide.
£200–230/$275–330 G(L)

B. Worcester sauce boat, decorated with two panels of men in boats against a moulded ground, c1760, 5½in (14cm) wide.
£300–350/$440–500 G(L)

Lowestoft porcelain was produced from the latter part of the 18thC and had no formal trademark, with many items being unmarked. While most Lowestoft is costly, sauce boats are the exception, which accounts for the lower price of Item A. Worcester is an important factory and was noted for outstanding painted decoration although Item B is not a good example. Worcester sauce boats are remarkably plentiful and great value too but as Item B is 10 years earlier than Item A, this has also reflected in the price.

The look without the price

Majolica pewter-mounted milk jug, cracked, 19thC, 7in (18cm) high.
£200–240/$290–350 G(L)

If this milk jug had been Minton it would have been much better quality and at least three times the price.

Victorian Mason's Ironstone Imari water jug, cracked, 13in (33cm) high. This is a large piece of Mason's Ironstone and a splendid shape. Unfortunately, the crack is rather unsightly. It can, however, be restored but the repair cost must be considered. A perfect example could fetch in the region of £700–800/$1,000–1,150.
£200–240/$290–350 G(L)

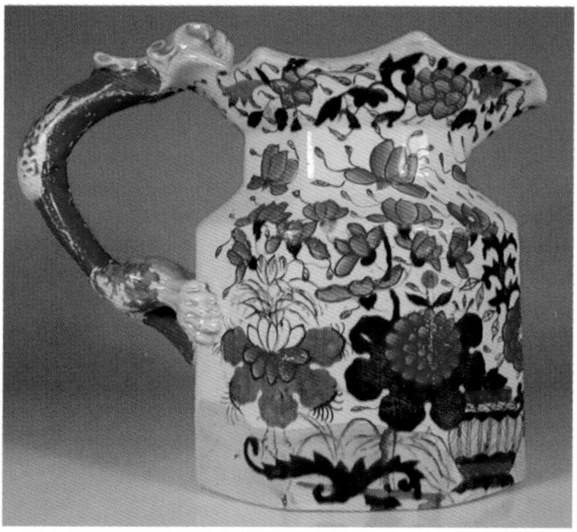

◄ **Mason's Ironstone Imari jug,** with a dragon handle, decorated with vases of flowers and leaves, blue-printed mark, c1830, 8in (20cm) high. This is a classic Mason's Ironstone pattern and a fair size. Some rubbing has kept the price down.
£220–270
$320–390 WW

The look without the price

Cantagalli majolica ewer, painted in polychrome with five warriors to one side and a castle to the reverse, painted cockerel mark, 1850–1900, 11¼in (28.5cm) high.
£260–300
$380–440 WW

This is a convincing copy of a 16thC Urbino painting, although the shape is a giveaway. The real thing would cost in the region of £10,000/$14,500, so this Victorian copy is a very good buy.

Royal Worcester ewer, with floral decoration on a cream ground, with a dragon handle, date code for 1884, 6in (15.5cm) high. This is a small ewer in blush ivory with a decorative handle. Prices are currently static so now is the time to buy if they appeal to you.
£250–300/$360–440 MAR

Bow fluted sauce boat, with angular scroll handle, painted in underglaze blue with buildings in a Chinese river landscape, the interior with an emblem, within a flower panelled diaper band, tiny rim cracks, c1758, 7¼in (18.5cm) long. Sauce boats are plentiful and currently undervalued regardless of the factory. This item is a lively shape and particularly well painted and is not expensive.
£320–390/$470–550 LFA

► **Pair of Caughley sauce boats,** the blue-printed sides with chinoiserie river scenes, c1785, 8½in (21.5cm) wide. Pairs of sauce boats are not so easy to find but these heavy printed patterns are unpopular. This price reflects damage as one handle is cracked.
£350–420
$500–600 AH

Worcester milk jug, painted with Mandarin figures, c1770, 4in (10cm) high. This rare shape would have made a higher price if in better condition, but the rubbing has had a big effect on the value.
£350–420/$500–600 G(L)

Minton Florentine miniature ewer and bowl, c1825, bowl 4¼in (11cm) diam. Miniature tablewares in blue and white are not all that expensive, but miniature jugs and bowls are sought after. This example is by a good maker and in good condition.
£425–475/$620–690 GN

Pearlware cow creamer and cover, painted with black and iron-red trefoil patches, tail restored, c1825, 6¼in (16cm) wide. This is a Welsh example, well coloured with great spirit. Repair to a tail is not that serious.
£550–650/$800–950 DN

Creamware cow creamer with milkmaid, sponge-decorated in ochre, blue and black, on a moulded base, early 19thC, 6½in (16.5cm) wide. Cow creamers have increased in price recently and deservedly so. This one has lovely character, with a milkmaid on the base, which adds to the interest. Minor damage is usual. Watch out for reproductions.
£580–700/$900–1,000 AH

Services

A Staffordshire 36-piece tea service, pattern No. 213, decorated in gold and blue, 19thC. A service such as this represents good value, although it requires a lot of storage space.
£100–120/$145–175 SWO

A Minton 33-piece earthenware part dinner service, including soup tureen, printed with Eagle Japan pattern in blue, 1879. This is good value if you intend to use it, but with large sets like this the plates are often chipped and worn. Tureens are sometimes sold on their own.
£160–190/$230–275 G(L)

A Grainger's Worcester 20-piece dessert service, painted with forget-me-nots, damaged, c1830. This is an excellent price, providing that the damage is not too severe.
£160–200/$230–300 WW

A Berlin 35-piece part service, with moulded and reticulated borders decorated in cerise and gilt, minor damage, factory marks, late 19thC. The plain centres on this service and the fact that red borders do not fit into most household colour schemes accounts for the lower price.
£170–200/$250–300 WW

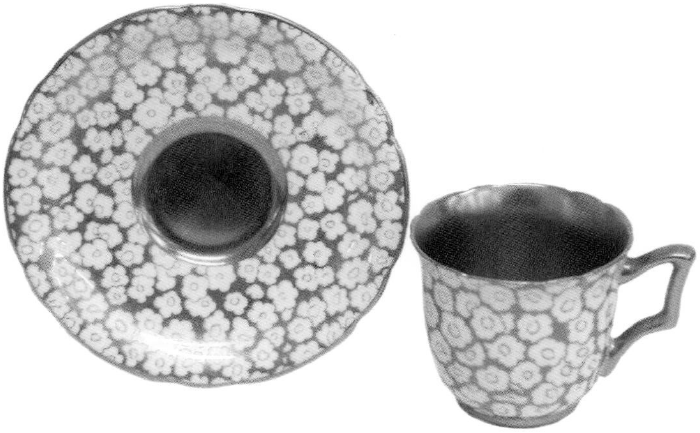

◄ **A Royal Worcester 12-piece coffee service,** with gilt floral decoration, retailed by Aspreys, early 20thC, cased. The six cups and saucers have never been removed from their box. This pattern is unusual but the white and gold decoration is not very popular, keeping the price low.
£180–220/$260–320 G(L)

An Art Deco Paragon part tea service, painted with a floral decoration, two cups cracked, 1930s. Although not as collectable as Clarice Cliff or Susie Cooper, Paragon china does command high prices due to the quality of Art Deco design and production.
£180–220/$260–320 G(L)

A 22-piece dessert service, each printed and painted with bunches of flowers within gilt cerise borders, possibly Ridgway, c1845. There are a number of possible reasons for the low price of this service. Red borders are not popular, the central sprays are rather small, it is likely to be damaged, and few homes have room to store a full dessert service.
£220–260/$320–380 CGC

A 24-piece dessert service, with gilded pink rose borders, c1830. The low price of this service reflects the extensive damage, particularly to the dish and plate.
£250–300/$350–450 G(L)

A Dresden 35-piece part tea and coffee service, painted with flower sprays within gilt scroll edges, early 20thC. Although not by a major maker, this service is thin and delicate with pretty painted flowers.
£350–420/$500–600 BR

A George Jones part dessert service, comprising two tall and two short comports and 12 plates, printed with roses, ribbons and swags within a raised gilt border, pattern No. 21140, crescent marks, c1890. George Jones is a Staffordshire firm and this service is delicate porcelain with an elegant pattern.
£400–480/$580–700 Bea(E)

Locate the source

The source of each illustration in Miller's can be found by checking the code letters below each caption with the Key to Illustrations, pages 286–290.

► **A 17-piece porcelain part tea service,** painted with garden flowers in reserves on a cobalt blue ground with trellis gilding, c1825. The price reflects the fact that this service is not by a known maker.
£400–500/$580–720 SHSY

A Barr, Flight & Barr 22-piece part tea and coffee service, each decorated with a band of blue flowerheads and leaves within gilt dentilled rims, teapot knop missing, some damage, impressed crown over initials marks, c1810. Sold as a set, this service is less attractive, and there is some damage, but if it was split it would undoubtedly command a considerable profit. In 1810 this was considered a very modern design.
£420–500/$600–720 S(O)

A Royal Crown Derby 25-piece tea service, decorated in Imari style with King's pattern, with stylized Oriental flowers, three cups cracked, printed marks, c1910. If in good condition, Royal Crown Derby from this period is good value.
£470–520/$700–750 S(O)

A Royal Worcester 17-piece bone china part dessert service, printed and painted with views within gilded claret borders, named verso and signed 'C. Creese' and 'I. Hendry', date code for 1933. The scenes are coloured-in prints and the ground colour is rather unpopular, but the plates would sell individually for at least £100/$150 each.
£500–600/$720–870 G(L)

A Copeland & Garrett 30-piece dessert service, decorated in green and gold, c1840. The strength of the green colouing and the fact that the centres are unpainted might not be to everyone's liking, and may account for its low price.
£700–800/$1,000–1,150 WW

A porcelain part dinner service, comprising 60 pieces, the centres printed and painted with a peony and other flowers within a decorative border, some damage, c1840. Most dinner sets in this style are pottery. This porcelain copy of Mason's is not easy to identify but this is good value for a set of this size.
£780–950
$1,150–1,400 Bea(E)

A Staffordshire dessert service, comprising two square serving dishes and six plates, with painted centres and gold-decorated pale green border, pattern No. 318, c1835. Although there are only eight pieces in this service it is an attractive pattern and the full centres make this a good set to display.
£800–950/$1,150–1,380 Bea(E)

Stands

Derby inkwell, early 19thC, 5in (12.5cm) diam. This example in Imari style is missing the centre and the top of the handle is rubbed.
£160–180/$230–260 JOA

► **Staffordshire pottery watch stand,** c1850, 12in (30.5cm) high. If the figures on this watch stand had been portraits then the value of this piece would increase.
£265–300
$385–440 DAN

Derby porcelain inkstand, with three urn-shaped pots and looped handles, painted with vignettes depicting landscapes on a gilded deep blue ground, on lion's paw feet, early 19thC, 11¾in (30cm) wide. There is some rubbing to the gold, but it is unusual that all the lids have survived. Derby inkstands are usually in poor condition and sell cheaply as a result. However, this was a good find.
£280–325/$410–470 AH

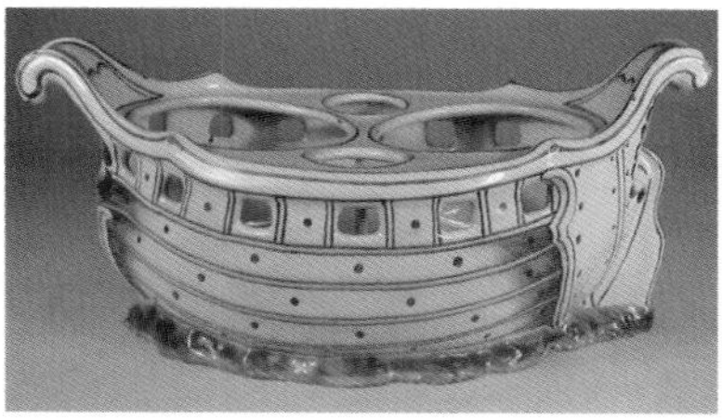

Strasbourg faïence cruet stand, modelled as a galleon, painted in puce and brown, on a sea base, 18thC, 10½in (26.5cm) wide. French faïence is generally undervalued and this is a rare piece of 18thC pottery. It lacks its bottles but it still commanded a good price.
£350–400/$500–580 WW

◄ **Bretby jardinière and stand,** in yellow, green and pink, marked, c1897, 33½in (85cm) high. Bretby is an acquired taste, but does have a limited following. Large majolica jardinières and stands only sell well if they are by popular makers.
£550–600/$800–1,000 HUN

► **Majolica triangular stick stand,** relief-moulded with leaves and fruit against a dark blue ground, 1880–90, 22in (56cm) high. Probably by a small British or American maker, this has good colouring and a dramatic shape which makes up for the lack of quality.
£800–950
$1,150–1,300 G(L)

Tea & Chocolate Pots

Worcester teapot, the bulbous, fluted body with an associated lid, handle restored, 18thC, 5¼in (13.5cm) high. This item is inexpensive because the Lowestoft lid does not match the teapot, there is damage to the handle and cover and there are unsightly firing defects all over. At this price it is a good buy for a new collector.
£85–100/$125–145 SWO

Majolica pineapple-moulded teapot and cover, decorated with a green and honey-coloured glaze, some damage, late 19thC, 8¾in (22cm) high. When this was made it was copying the collectable Whieldon ware of the 18thC. Now it is Majolica that is collectable. The fact that it was made by a minor maker and has slight damage keeps the price down.
£160–200/$230–290 WW

► **Belleek teapot and cover,** in Grass pattern, First Period, 1863–90, 4in (10cm) high. Teapot collectors like Belleek because the Irish potters came up with more exciting designs. The colouring works well here. However, Belleek needs to be perfect in order to command high prices.
£280–350/$400–500 SWO

A pair of Beswick pottery character teapots, from the David Copperfield series, entitled 'Pegotty and Dolly Varden', 20thC, 6in (15cm) high. Doulton is the big name in character jugs and wares, but there is growing interest in other makers. Beswick items are also worth looking at.
£100–120/$145–175 G(L)

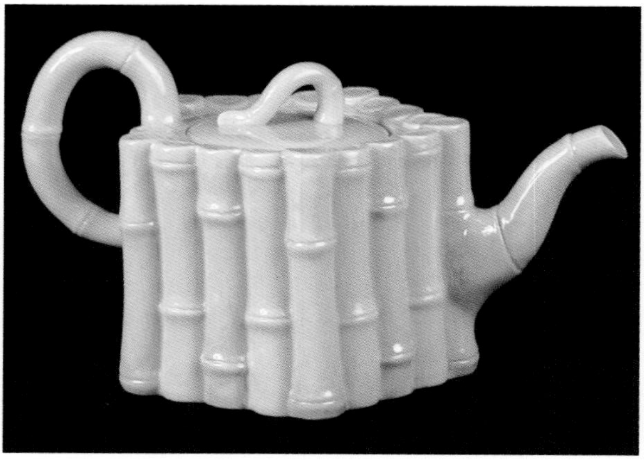

Belleek bamboo teapot and cover, First Period, 1863–91, 5in (12.5cm) high. This is an unusual shape and an interesting design. It also dates from the desirable First Period. Assuming it was perfect, this is a very good buy at this price.
£170–200/$250–300 SWO

Miller's compares...

A. Worcester Flight, Barr & Barr teapot, cover and stand, decorated with scattered pink roses and floral sprigs, some wear to gilding, impressed mark, c1815, 7in (18cm) high.
£300–350/$440–500 S(O)

B. Barr, Flight & Barr teapot, cover and stand, decorated with canted square reserves painted with flowers against a maroon ground, knop glued with minor nicks, small chip to spout, impressed and puce printed marks to stand, 1804–13, 7in (18cm) high.
£700–800/$1,000–1,150 S(O)

The difference in price between Item A and Item B is not due to the different names, as production did not alter with the name change. Item A is cheaper because the decoration is sparse, whereas Item B is much more decorative with better flower painting. The wear to the gilding on Item A is just as devaluing as the minor damage and restuck knop to Item B, but Item B is still the more popular of the two.

◄ **Wemyss bullet teapot,** painted with cockerels and inscribed 'Bon Jour', c1920, 4in (10cm) high. Wemyss teapots are uncommon and hard to find without cracks and staining.
£350–400
$500–580 RdeR

The look without the price

This is an exact copy of a Minton Majolica Japanese actor teapot. The Minton example is worth £2,500/$3,600, so this unknown maker provides a great look without the price.

Majolica teapot and cover, modelled as a sitting Oriental, holding a *Noh* mask which forms the spout, some repair to cover, 19thC, 8¼in (21cm) high.
£400–475/$580–700 WW

Meissen porcelain chocolate pot and cover, with flower knop and scroll-moulded spout and handle, painted with decorated yellow rococo panels, fruit and sprigs of flowers, crossed swords mark, late 18thC, 6in (15cm) high. This is probably c1770. Always check that the lid is a correct match. If in good condition, this is a good buy. Meissen wares of the late 18thC are not expensive.
£550–650
$800–950 Bea(E)

Toby Jugs

Staffordshire pottery Toby jug, wearing a blue coat, yellow waistcoat, pale brown breeches, grey stockings and a black hat and shoes, chipped, c1850, 9in (23cm) high. Mid-19thC Toby jugs can be undervalued and the quality of some pieces can be disappointing. The enamels on this example have deteriorated.
£100–120/$145–175 F&F ⊞

Toby jug, modelled as Wellington, with treacle glaze, c1860, 7in (18cm) high. Brown-glazed Toby jugs are generally inexpensive. This one is a rare commemorative and consequently is good value at this price.
£115–130/$165–190 DHA ⊞

Further reading

Miller's Antiques Price Guide, Miller's Publications

◄ **Prattware Toby jug,** wearing a dark ochre coat, spotted waistcoat, yellow breeches, ochre-striped stockings, light brown hat and shoes, the face with brown details and warts, hat restored, small chip to base, hairline cracks to underside, 1800–10, 9¾in (25cm) high. The extent of damage and restoration reduces the value of Toby jugs. This Prattware jug would be £600–900/$870–1,300 if not repaired, however, the colouring is nice and bright.
£250–300/$350–450 P(Ba) ⚒

Toby jug 'Hearty Good Fellow', holding a foaming jug with blue borders in his right hand, and raising a goblet in his left, wearing an underglaze blue coat, blue spotted cravat, blue-striped stockings and buckles picked out in yellow-brown, hat and goblet replaced, some crazing, c1820, 10½in (26.5cm) high. The 'Hearty Good Fellow' is a popular model and this is an early example. It is inexpensive because the hat and glass are completely replaced. In good condition this item could achieve £650–900/$950–1,300.
£250–275/$360–560 P(Ba) ⚒

► **Staffordshire Toby jug,** c1860, 8½in (21.5cm) high. The cross-legged Toby jug is quite a common model.
£325–365/$470–530 RAN ⊞

Ashtead Potters Johnnie Walker Toby jug, by Percy Metcalfe, in bright enamel colours, wearing a red frock coat and grey top hat, base inscribed 'Johnnie Walker Born 1820 Kilmarnock still going strong', small chips to enamels, painted marks and edition No. 444, 1926–36, 15in (38cm) high. This item is of interest because the maker, Ashtead, and the modeller, Percy Metcalfe, are well-known and it is of interest to collectors of advertising.
£400–450/$600–650 P(Ba)

Pearlware Toby jug, wearing a highly-glazed blue coat, holding a jug with a blue design, c1800, 10in (25.5cm) high. The limited colouring of this jug helps keep the price down. If found, early jugs in unrestored condition are very good value.
£400–500/$580–720 JBL

► **Prattware Toby jug,** decorated in browns and ochres, holding a small jug, c1800, 10in (25.5cm) high. This is a Prattware example, and the jug it holds is unusual. The value of these jugs is currently low so it is well worth buying one like this, if in perfect condition.
£550–650/$800–950 JBL

◄ **Prattware Toby jug,** modelled as a sailor, seated on a chair above a chest of dollars, with an anchor resting between his feet, c1800, 11¾in (29.5cm) high. This wonderful early sailor jug is extensively damaged, otherwise it would be £1,500–1,700/$2,150–2,450. Modern restoration would be expensive, but could make this into an excellent display piece.
£475–575/$700–850 P(Ba)

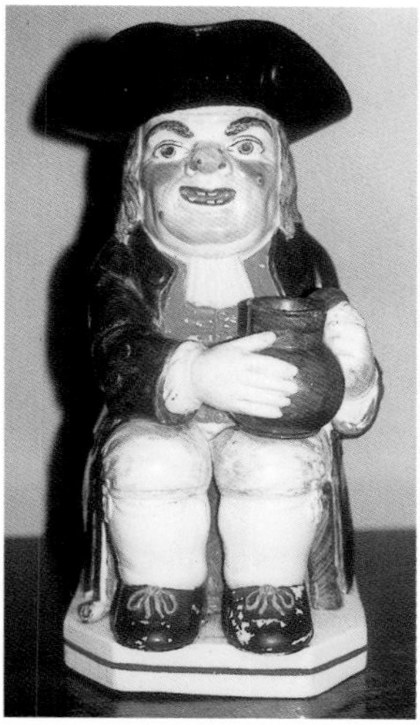

Toby jug, possibly by Neale & Co, wearing a blue waistcoat and a brown coat, c1810, 10in (25.5cm) high. This make of Toby jug always has finger nails and enamel colouring where the jug is fired and glazed. It is then painted and fired again which makes it prone to flaking. The hats are often repainted. This is a particularly good quality early Staffordshire creamware Toby jug. If this is unrestored, it is good value.
£450–550/$650–800 JBL

Vases

Watcombe pottery vase, c1920, 5¾in (14.5cm) high. Devon pottery is a growing market and this is an interesting shape. Avoid examples where the glaze has flaked off.
£60–70/$90–100 DSG

Celadon vase, Chinese, 19thC, 7in (18cm) high. This is a very late copy of a much earlier piece from c12thC.
£65–75/$95–110 FRY

Satsuma vase, painted with birds on blossom-laden boughs, gilt-enriched, on a shaded orange ground with a brocade border to the neck, impressed mark 'Taizan' and six-character mark 'Great Japan', early 20thC, 9½in (24cm) high. This has good 20thC Art Deco colouring for this price.
£100–120/$150–175 PFK

◄ Delft ribbed baluster vase and cover, decorated with panels of figures and birds between green borders, monogrammed 'PK', 20thC, 13¼in (33.5cm) high. This item is a reproduction but is very decorative for the price.
£100–120/$145–175 WW

Doulton Lambeth onion-shaped vase, marked X3258 to base and printed mark, probably 1885–90, 8in (20.5cm) high. This vase has unusual colouring but it is not an expensive piece as Doulton made a lot of vases.
£100–120/$145–175 SWO

Doulton Lambeth

Influenced by John Sparkes, head of the Lambeth School of Art, Henry Doulton set up an art pottery studio in the late 1860s to develop a new range of art stonewares. By the 1880s the company was employing more than 200 staff, with designers such as Hannah Barlow and George Tinworth producing highly individual work.

In 1877, Henry took over a Burslem manufacturer of domestic earthenwares which, under his leadership, established a reputation for high-quality tableware and ornaments.

Pair of Satsuma vases, decorated with figures in landscapes beneath Mount Fuji, damage to one rim, gilt marks, Meiji, Japanese, 1868–1911, 6¼in (16cm) high. These vases are quite affordable as there are many examples in existence.
£100–120/$145–175 WW

► **Porcelain vase,** with moulded dragon handles, painted with figural scenes on a gilded turquoise ground, Japanese, early 20thC, 2¼in (5.5cm) high. This is great workmanship for the money. Japanese porcelain vases are not expensive.
£100–120
$145–175 AH

Pair of Satsuma vases, decorated with figures in landscapes beneath Mount Fuji, damage to one rim, gilt marks, Meiji, Japanese, 1868–1911, 6¼in (16cm) high. These vases are quite affordable as there are many examples in existence.
£100–120/$145–175 WW

Royal Worcester vase, puce mark, c1895, 3½in (7.5cm) high. This is an interesting shape and reasonably priced with only minor wear. These items would be more popular if the colouring was stronger.
£110–130/$160–190 WW

◄ **Pair of Derby Crown Porcelain Co pear-shaped vases,** the bodies decorated in raised gold and brown enamel with flowering leafy branches, painted factory marks, date codes for 1887, 6¼in (16cm) high. The raised goldwork on these vases is of good quality and they are by a top maker. However, the ground colour is unpopular, but at this price they are of excellent value.
£120–150/$175–220 WW

◄ **Pair of polychrome hexagonal baluster vases,** decorated with orange prunus, Japanese, 19thC, 9in (23cm) high. These have excellent decorative value, although are not important collectors' pieces.
£140–170
$200–250 WW

Bottle-shaped vase, with later enamel decoration, Chinese, 19thC, 11½in (29cm) high. This piece is over-decorated to the point where the fine original decoration is almost obliterated, hence the lower price.
£150–180/$220–260 G(L)

Miller's compares...

A. Derby frill vase, with a reticulated shoulder, applied with twin mask heads, flowers and foliage, damaged, c1765, 8in (20.5cm) high.
£150–180/$220–260 WW

Frill vases are unpopular and inexpensive at the moment. Item A, although it is painted with attractive insects, lacks a lid and is damaged therefore reducing the value. Item B is complete, in good condition and is also quite a rare piece of 18thC English rococo porcelain, all of which contributes to it achieving a higher price.

B. Derby pot pourri vase and cover, one side painted with two birds, the other with butterflies, fruit and foliage, all applied with flowers, leaves and scrolls, minor damage, c1760, 11½in (29cm) high.
£700–850
$1,000–1,250 WW

Porcelain spiral-moulded vase, with a flared neck, one side painted with a house beside a river, the other with a rich flower spray on a gilt-decorated cerise ground, c1830, 8in (20.5cm) high. This is an interesting shape with good, bright gilding but because the maker cannot be identified the price is reduced.
£150–180/$220–260 WW

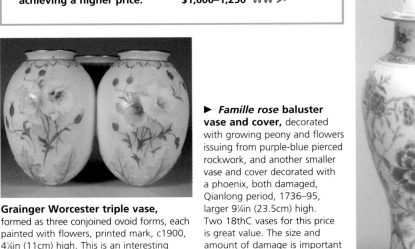

Grainger Worcester triple vase, formed as three conjoined ovoid forms, each painted with flowers, printed mark, c1900, 4¼in (11cm) high. This is an interesting shape and has very delicate painting with a hint of Art Nouveau style. Grainger tends to be cheaper than Royal Worcester but, in many cases, is just as good.
£160–190/$230–275 WW

► ***Famille rose*** **baluster vase and cover,** decorated with growing peony and flowers issuing from purple-blue pierced rockwork, and another smaller vase and cover decorated with a phoenix, both damaged, Qianlong period, 1736–95, larger 9¼in (23.5cm) high. Two 18thC vases for this price is great value. The size and amount of damage is important when assessing their value. The larger vase, if perfect, could make £300/$440, the smaller vase £200/$290 at auction.
£150–220/$220–320 DN

Porcelain ovoid vase, painted with a large vase of flowers with a gilt-edged panel on a blue ground, 19thC, 8¼in (21cm) high. This is not by an identified name like Royal Worcester or Minton and this keeps the price down. For a big, hand-painted Victorian vase this is good value.
£190–230/$275–330 WW

The look without the price

These two vases are late 19th–early 20thC copies of Dutch Delft. If you wanted to buy genuine 18thC originals you could end up paying in the region of £500–700/$720–1,000.

Pair of blue and white vases, c1900, 8¾in (22cm) high.
£200–220/$290–320 WW

Ironstone water/slop pail, with floral decoration on a green ground, missing cover, c1850, 12in (30.5cm) high. This is from a washstand set by a lesser known maker. The size makes it a good decoration piece for a modern bathroom or bedroom.
£220–270/$320–390 G(L)

Blue and white ovoid vase, decorated with figures in a landscape, Chinese, 19thC, 11½in (29cm) high. This is a well painted 19thC copy of Kangxi.
£220–270/$320–390 WW

Royal Worcester pot pourri vase and cover, date code for 1888, 8in (20.5cm) high.
£240–300
$350–440 MAR

► **Minton oval vase and cover,** with gilt handles and a tall stem, decorated with a *pâte-sur-pâte* panel of Cupid and Venus, gilded details, one handle repaired, gilt mark, c1900, 8½in (21.5cm) wide. This shows the importance of perfect condition on later English porcelain. This *pâte-sur-pâte* vase by A. Birks would be £1,300–1,500/$1,900–2,200 if the handle had not been repaired.
£240–300/$350–440 WW

Della Robbia vase and cover, decorated by Harry Pearce with geometric leaf designs, chips to cover, factory marks, c1900, 8in (20.5cm) high. This rare Art Pottery is keenly collected but this example is relatively inexpensive because the design is somewhat clumsy and the glaze poorly controlled. Better pieces of Della Robbia are more expensive.
£260–325/$380–470 WW

Moore Bros porcelain centrepiece, modelled as a leaf bowl encrusted with brown and gilt acorns and oak leaves, supported by three cherubs on a triform base, the gilt base with black Greek key design border, impressed and printed factory marks, late 19thC, 8in (20.5cm) high. Moore Bros porcelain is very prone to cracking and discolouration. If this was perfect it would be a good buy. Because so much is defective, the price of Moore Bros has fallen over the years and good, perfect pieces are worth buying. The low price here is due to some damage.
£325–380/$470–570 RTo

Bristol pearlware pottery vase, c1830, 7in (18cm) high. This is an interesting shape. The painting is very crude but this does not matter if it can be attributed to a provincial maker such as Bristol or Swansea. Local collectors are always keen to acquire these pieces.
£290–325/$425–470 DAN

Meissen pot pourri vase and cover, the basket-moulded body painted with flowers, raised on a flower and leaf-strewn base with a hound stalking two partridge, some damage, German, 18thC, 8¼in (21cm) high. The price reflects severe damage and various parts missing, possibly a figure of a huntsman and the knop to the cover. A perfect example vase would be worth £1,000–2,000/ $1,500–2,900.
£350–425/$500–620 WW

► **Staffordshire pottery spill vase,** c1815, 8½in (21.5cm) high. This is a rare model. It is inexpensive because the animals are dead game, which is never a good selling point.
£360–400/$520–580 DAN

Wemyss pottery vase, possibly by E. Sandland, painted with dragonflies among reeds, with blue-green base and rim, painted marks to base, 6¾in (17cm) high. This is an attractive Wemyss vase and very good value.
£325–380
$470–570 Bea(E)

Meissen two-handled vase, with waisted neck and domed and fluted gilt foot, painted with sprays of flowers within gilt borders, applied with two entwined serpent handles, fitted for electricity as a lamp, foot drilled, wear to gilding, some re-gilding, blue crossed swords mark, late 19thC, 23¼in (59cm) high. Large vases are usually made in sections and bolted together, so unless the neck is cut down – in this case it is not – the lamp fitting adds to the decorative use of this vase. It is inexpensive because it has snake handles and severe rubbing to the gilding. Meissen gold is impossible to restore convincingly.
£400–480/$580–695 DN

Pair of Royal Worcester two-handled vases, the turquoise ground painted with panels of orchids, one damaged, the other with heavy crazing, black printed marks, shape 1969, c1901, 11in (28cm) high. These are huge vases by a major artist, Frank Roberts. They show that damage greatly affects Royal Worcester, as these would be worth £5,000/$7,250 if in perfect condition. When turquoise enamel is crazed it becomes unstable and can flake off. Crazed turquoise grounds should be avoided.
£470–520/$680–740 S(O)

Pair of Derby vases, c1830, 6½in (16.5cm) high. Unfortunately, there is much flaking to the enamels, rubbing to the gold, and the left handle has been restored.
£575–650/$850–950 DeA ⊞

Hexagonal baluster vase, each panel decorated in underglaze blue with figures in a river landscape, neck missing, Chinese, Kangxi period, 1662–1722, 11¾in (30cm) high. This vase has been cut down from a larger one. The excellent painting and colour of this piece, if perfect, would give it a value of £2,000/$2,900.
£500–600/$720–870 DN

Wucai meiping, painted in red, green and underglaze blue with Chinese boys dancing among rocks on a terrace, while a lady looks on, Chinese, c1650, 7¼in (18.5cm) high. This vase is excellent value if in perfect condition. The value for such a vase should be £1,000/$1,500.
£600–700/$870–1,000 CGC

◀ **Belleek centrepiece,** trumpet-shaped with frilled pink rim, on a basket-effect base encrusted with flowers, black printed mark to the base, Second Period, 1891–1926, 12in (30.5cm) high. This item achieved a low price because it was Belleek Second Period, rather than First Period. It is also important to check the condition of the modelled flowers. A lot of chips make quite a difference to value.
£500–600/$720–870 DA

Miscellaneous

Ceramic feeding cup, with fleur-de-lys design above the spout, c1900, 2½in (6.5cm) high. Large numbers of feeding cups were made in coarse pottery, decorated only with the emblem of a medical institution. If you are collecting try to look for variety.
£10–12/$15–17 DHo ⊞

► **Stoneware flower pot,** by Hackwood, decorated in blue and white, 1815–20, 6in (15cm) diam. This pot is an interesting shape and good quality but by a minor maker and the stand is missing, hence the lower price.
£50–60
$75–90 OD ⊞

Porcelain egg cup, pattern No. 3119, c1840, 2¼in (5.5cm) high. Egg cup collectors like to seek porcelain examples from before 1860 so these can be expensive. However, this one is not by a major maker, hence the lower price.
£75–85/$110–125 AMH ⊞

Pair of Volkstadt easel mirrors, one damaged, late 19thC, 10in (25.5cm) high. These damaged mirrors look unsightly and are understandably inexpensive. However, it would be easy to replace the glass and that alone would make a big difference.
£120–150/$175–220 G(L) ⚒

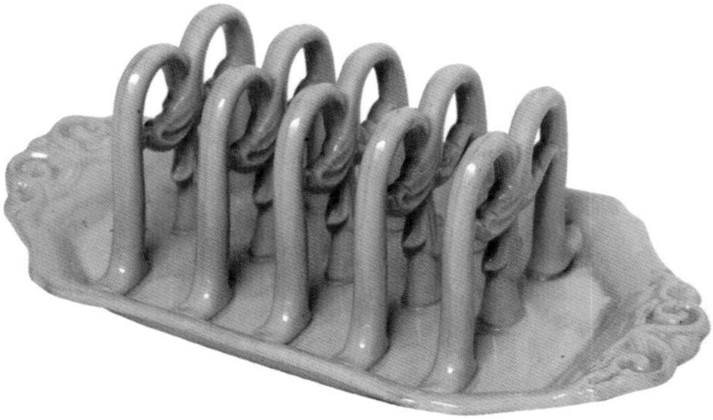

Copeland glazed blue pottery toast rack, c1870, 9in (23cm) wide. Most ceramic toast racks from the Continent are inexpensive. It is difficult to find marked English makers.
£140–160/$200–230 HUM ⊞

◄ **Pottery wall plate,** moulded with masks and fruiting foliage, stamped 'E. Bingham, Castle Hedingham', late 19th–early 20thC, 9in (23cm) diam. Castle Hedingham is an acquired taste. To the initiated this is collectable Art Pottery, but only worth buying if you like it.
£150–180/$220–260 SWO ⚒

◄ **Wall plaque,** inscribed 'Prepare to meet thy God', with olive border, impressed Wallace & Co, c1840, 6½in (16.5cm) diam. Only a true Newcastle or north east pottery collector would appreciate that this blue border is rarer than the black border.
£160–180
$230–260 IS

Minton majolica flower trough, impressed marks, date code for 1871, 10¾in (27.5cm) wide. This is an uncommon piece of Minton majolica, but a dull shape and colouring keeps the price down.
£160–200/$230–290 WW

Wedgwood Queensware *veilleuse* and fittings, painted in the Dutch style in shades of iron-red, blue and green with Oriental flowering shrubs, birds and insects, repaired, impressed marks, date code for 1884, 11in (28cm) high. This was a plain white Victorian Wedgwood *veilleuse* for medical use. The painting was added later. With repair it would purely be for a piece of decoration.
£160–200/$230–290 DN

◄ **Copeland parian wall bracket,** one leaf chipped, marked 'Ceramic and Crystal Palace Art Union Copyright Reserved Copeland', dated 1877, 8in (20.5cm) high. This is a significant piece of Victorian design, however, wall brackets are very hard to sell and are never expensive.
£180–220
$260–320 WW

► **Pair of Wedgwood blue jasper ware bulb pots,** some damage, missing one cover and central bulb holders, late 18thC, 6¼in (16cm) high. These bulb pots are still very good value.
£200–240
$290–350 DA

◄ **Wemyss pin tray,** painted with cockerels, c1900, 3½in (9cm) wide.
£225–250/$325–360 RdeR

Belleek oval tray, in Echinus pattern, chip to underside rim, Second Period 1891–1926, 15¾in (40cm) wide. A large piece of Belleek, but trays take up a lot of room and are therefore inexpensive. This item being from the Second Period keeps the price modest.
£280–320/$400–450 SWO

Staffordshire porcelain two-handled tray, with pierced and acanthus-moulded gilt handles enclosing a large enamelled floral spray, on a gilt-lined footrim, slight rubbing and wear, mid-19thC, 14¼in (36cm) wide. This is a good quality visiting card tray. Sometimes these have overhead handles which are prone to damage. If original and perfect this is good value.
£300–360/$440–520 WL

Miller's compares...

A. Delft blue and white flower brick, probably Liverpool, with one central hole and 18 smaller holes, painted with flowers, the sides painted with birds, some restoration, c1760, 5¼in (13.5cm) wide.
£375–425/$560–620 S(O)

B. Delft blue and white flower brick, the exterior painted with flowers within a fence, 18thC, 5¼in (13.5cm) wide.
£800–950/$1,150–1,300 G(B)

Item A has some restoration whereas Item B is perfect. This would account for the price difference. While chips make little difference to Delft, restoration should always be avoided if you can afford a perfect one.

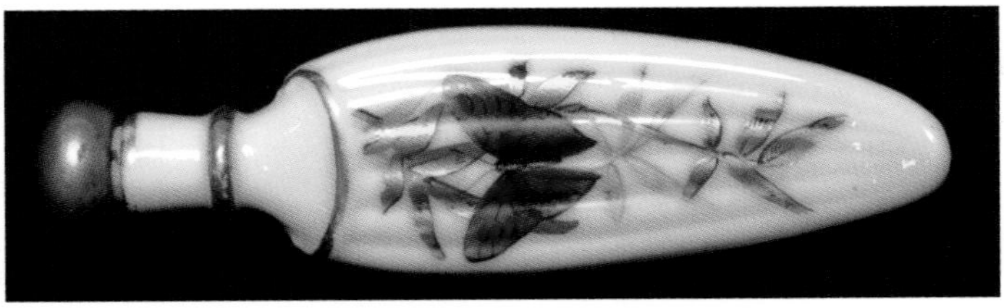

◄ **Worcester scent bottle,** c1880, 4in (10cm) high. Royal Worcester is a good maker and scent bottles are especially sought-after. This example has the correct stopper which is very important.
£350–400/$500–580 TH

Spode Carmanian series drainer, printed in blue with Citadel near Corinth pattern, with a simple band of stringing to the edge, stained, impressed lower-case mark, 1810–20, 8½in (21.5cm) wide. This is a very popular pattern and a sought-after shape. The big problem here is the staining. A buyer will take the gamble that chemical cleaning will remove the staining, but this needs to be done professionally.
£450–550/$650–800 DN

Pair of Sevrès-style porcelain plaques, painted with Watteauesque figures in landscapes within gilded and turquoise borders, one with incised marks, 1850–1900, 13¼in (33.5cm) high. This is a late 19thC copy of 18thC painting. They are not collectors items but they are very decorative to frame and hang on a wall.
£475–575/$700–850 WW

◄ **Imari *kendi*,** rim restored, some crazing, spout replaced, Japanese, late 17th/early 18thC, 8¼in (21cm) high. This is a rare piece of Japanese porcelain, but restoration makes a big difference to the value. If perfect, the price should be £1,200/$1,750.
£500–600
$720–870 S(Am)

Royal Worcester fern pot, by James Hadley, some wear to gilding, impressed and puce printed marks, impressed Y9, c1887, 6¾in (17cm) high. This is an uncommon shape and in good condition, although as it is one of a pair it looks incomplete without its partner.
£770–900/$1,100–1,300 S(O)

Pair of Coalport letter racks, the pink ground painted with titled views, 'Brock House, Salop', and 'Willey Park, Salop', red-painted titles, one with haircracks, printed Society of Arts mark, 6¾in (17cm) wide, c1820. These two local views will appeal to a specialist Coalport collector. Although pink is not a popular colour and there is some damage, letter racks are hard to find as matching pairs.
£825–1,000/$1,200–1,500 S(O)

Porcelain floral enamelled brush washer, Xuantong mark, 1909–11, 4in (10cm) square.
£850–1,000/$1,250–1,500 GLD

Silver & Plate

To any collector of silver and plate, or indeed anything however frivolous, the imposition of a price ceiling would appear to seriously curtail the choice of items available. As the following pages will show this is far from the case. There is a considerable selection of attractive articles available particularly between 1840–1940.

In the past it would seem that people were happy to accept copies of items made in previous times, a practice that today, is sadly unacceptable. For instance, the Edwardians were adept at interpreting, in their jolly way, architecture of the Queen Anne period.

The situation with silver and silver-plated items is similar. In the late 19th and early 20th centuries particularly charming pieces were often made by copying many earlier styles. The quality of these 'reproductions' is often superior to the originals, and if it were not for the date of the hallmark, they would receive far greater appreciation and value. It is worth looking out for such pieces, always bearing in mind quality and solidity. These pieces were made to be used!

An example is the existence of many christening mugs that were made during the early 20th century. They were usually handmade and of superb quality. An indication of this is that occasionally one sees pieces of this type hallmarked for the Britannia Standard (95.8%) compared with the usual Sterling Standard (92.5%). For instance, a George I half-pint mug would be worth four to six times its later counterpart only for the reason of its greater age. The later mugs often receive scant attention as they appear to be defaced by the engraving of the dedication to the original recipient. This should not be seen as a deterrent to buyers. Incidentally inscriptions of any age should never be erased as little benefit is gained.

Another good area in which to build a collection is that of condiments. Late Victorian copies of Georgian pierced and engraved mustard pots, for example, abound in the salerooms. A good mustard pot in the style of c1770, although made over a century later, can be obtained for about £150–250/$220–360; the original would be in the region of £500–600/ $720–870. The only difference between these two pots is that of the hallmark and perhaps the patina. Sugar baskets of a similar style and period make another comparison and show a similar price difference for the same reasons.

Larger pieces of silver, though of course of lesser appeal because of their greater bulk, can be good value. The humble three-piece tea set, that wedding present staple of years gone by, can be found in infinite variety. Often made in an earlier style and frequently of high quality they are still useful items, it is only today's pace of life that apparently prohibits time being given to the maintenance and use of such things. As they are sadly out of fashion at the moment a good set, probably of a Georgian or Regency style, can be bought at auction for about £10/$15 per ounce. For the average tea set this would be a price in the region of £400–700/$580–1,000. One would need plenty of space and enthusiasm to collect tea sets but all collectors should have at least one good example. A change in fashion could result in the best of these representing very good value.

There has been a recent revival in the popularity of *épergnes* of the Edwardian period. Once shunned, these elaborate pieces with an arrangement of vases often beautifully cast and pierced, are now back in fashion. Although these are generally not of an earlier style they indicate how prices can wax and wane with popularity. To reiterate my earlier comments 'Look at the piece before you look at the hallmark!' **Hugh Gregory**

Bowls & Dishes

George V silver sugar bowl, 6in (15cm) wide. This classic Art Deco shape is popular with many collectors.
£50–60/$75–90 G(L)

George V silver pedestal bonbon dish, with scroll handles, 9in (23cm) wide.
£95–115/$140–165 G(L)

◄ **Pierced silver bowl,** by William Comyns, with blue glass liner, London 1897, 4in (10cm) diam. Examine glass liners for chips and cracks as unusual shapes may be difficult to replace.
£110–135
$160–200 CoHA

The look without the price

17thC-style silver porringer and cover, by Nathan & Hayes, the body engraved with birds among vine branches, Chester 1906, 5in (12.5cm) high, 10.25oz.
£130–160/$200–230 L

This piece shows that a good reproduction can be as pleasing as the original, which would be worth £5,000–8,000/ $7,500–11,500.

Pair of embossed silver nut dishes, 1920, 3in (7.5cm) diam. As simpler decorations are currently more popular, ornate pieces can be an affordable alternative.
£140–160/$200–230 G(L)

◄ **Pair of boat-shaped silver bonbon dishes,** London 1894, 5½in (14cm) wide. If you are unsure whether an item is genuine, check the hallmark for further information, such as place and date of manufacture. International hallmarks denote varying standards of silver.
£150–180/$220–260 TMA

George V pierced silver sugar basket, with blue glass liner, 4½in (11.5cm) high. An early Georgian original dating from 1714–1811 would be worth £400–500/ $580–720.
£160–200/$230–300 G(L)

Edwardian silver pedestal sugar bowl, decorated with a shepherd and a woman picking fruit, Irish, 6in (15cm) wide. Good Edwardian copies are just as good quality as the 18th-century originals.
£180–220/$260–320 G(L)

◄ Silver rose bowl, by Horace Woodward & Co, with fluted moulded body and shaped reeded rim, London 1905, 7¾in (19.5cm) diam, 18oz. Although this is an attractive item, it is not particularly rare. An embossed rose bowl would be more valuable.
£220–260
$320–380 S(O)

Shaped and pierced silver fruit basket, with reel-cast rim and swing handle, Chester 1924, 10½in (26.5cm) diam.
£200–250/$300–360 TMA

◄ Edwardian silver-plated breakfast dish, with two liners, the fan-fluted revolving cover engraved with a monogram, ivory thumbpiece, 14in (35.5cm) wide. These are interesting items to collect, but rather bulky.
£230–280
$330–400 WW

Silver bowl, by R. & W. Sorley, on a circular foot, the rim and foot with a raised band of C-scrolls, London 1902, 7in (18cm) diam, 12.25oz.
£250–300/$360–440 PFK

Miller's compares...

A. Silver sugar basket, embossed with foliate scrolls below a bail handle, on an oval foot, London 1806, 7in (18cm) wide, 10.25oz.
£250–320/$360–460 CGC

B. Silver sugar basket, with ribboned shield to either side, on a conforming foot, maker's mark of Alexander Gairdner, Edinburgh 1792, 5in (12.5cm) high, 8.5oz.
£400–480/$580–700 B(Ed)

The decoration on Item A appears to be a later addition to the piece and while Item B is smaller, the original simple decoration and the fluted shape make it more appealing to collectors. Item B also has a known maker's mark and is earlier in date adding to the price.

Silver fruit bowl, by John Aldwinckle and Thomas Slater, embossed with masks, fruit, scalework and scrolling panels, on four scrolling foliate feet, London 1892, 18.25oz. In view of the partnership of good makers, the workmanship and the weight, this is an inexpensive piece.
£300–350/$440–500 Bea(E)

Silver-gilt sugar bowl, by J. & J. Angell, embossed and chased with Oriental figures, scrolls and rocaille, London 1838, 4¼in (11cm) high, 13oz. The Angells frequently produced good embossed work of this kind.
£480–580/$700–850 S(O)

◄ **Silver sugar basket,** by William Edwards, with pendant grape cluster decoration, the body with pierced repoussé and etched bird design, blue glass liner, swing handle modelled as a vine, on a circular pierced foot, London 1856, 4in (10cm) high. A plainer example would be about £200–300/$300–450, but this is a particularly pretty item.
£480–580/$700–850 B&L

Silver bowl, by Marshall & Sons, the body chased with flowers and leaves and engraved with initials, a family crest and motto, Edinburgh 1860–61, 6in (15cm) diam, 10.25oz.
£675–750/$975–1,100 NS

The look without the price

Charles Stuart Harris was one of the best of the Victorian silversmiths, and this example is almost as good as the real thing. An original in very good condition might fetch £10,000–15,000/ $14,000–22,000.

Silver porringer and cover, by Charles Stuart Harris, with 17thC-style decoration of lions and unicorns among foliage, with caryatid handles, the cover with turned finial, London 1901, 9in (23cm) wide, 26.75oz.
£300–350/$440–500 Bea(E)

Boxes

Silver *aide-mémoire*, the covers embossed with acanthus leaves, leather interior with ivory sheet, Birmingham 1896, 4in (10cm) high. These items are always relatively inexpensive.
£90–100/$130–145 BR

► **Silver box,** by George Gillet, embossed in the style of a Dutch tobacco box, London 1881, 6in (15cm) wide, 4oz.
£120–150
$175–225 S(O)

Miller's compares...

A. Silver note and card case, by Frederick Marston, engraved with initials and foliate borders, the blue silk-lined interior with ivory tablets for six days of the week, Birmingham 1865, 4in (10cm) long.
£120–160/$175–230 WW

B. Silver card case, by Frederick Marston, the cover depicting Westminster Abbey, the reverse with inscribed shield, Birmingham 1859, 4in (10cm) high, 2oz.
£750–900
$1,100–1,300 S(O)

Both these card cases are by Frederick Marston and while Item A also has a silk lining and writing tablets, it is the decoration on the outside that makes the difference in price. Cases decorated with well known places are desirable not only to card case collectors but also those interested in the location. While the engraved scrolls and foliage of the Item A are pretty, the view of Westminster Abbey makes Item B far more collectable and thus more valuable.

Silver patch box, by Samuel Pemberton, with vermicelli pricked cover, Birmingham 1810, 1in (2.5cm) diam.
£120–150/$175–225 S(O)

Silver pill box, by Walker & Hall, Birmingham 1911, 1¾in (4.5cm) diam.
£125–145/$180–200 BEX

► **Silver vinaigrette,** by Lawrence & Co, Birmingham 1833, 1¼in (3cm) wide. Vinaigrettes are significantly smaller than snuff boxes and should have a grille, either plain or elaborate, under the lid. Check that small pill/snuff boxes are not vinaigrettes missing their grille – even without a hinge there will be a thumb indentation under the lid.
£200–235/$300–340 CoHA

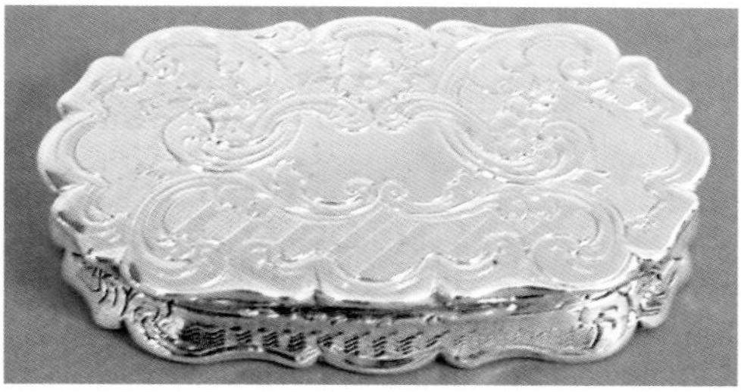

◄ **Silver vinaigrette,** engraved with scrolls and foliage, c1850, 1¾in (4.5cm) wide. It is wise to check the hinges for damage as repair can be costly.
£200–250
$300–360 G(L)

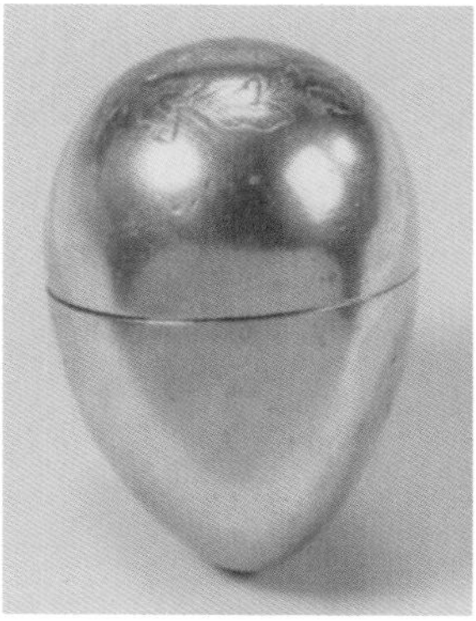

Silver vinaigrette, with initialled gilt pierced domed cover, maker's mark 'IL' on grille, c1800, 1¾in (4.5cm) wide, 1oz.
£250–300/$360–440 S(O)

Miller's compares...

A. Two silver vinaigrettes, by William Phillips and John Thorpe, upper initialled 'BJ', lower initialled 'MJ', with foliate-pierced grille, Birmingham 1814 and 1822, larger 1½in (4cm) wide.
£250–300/$350–450 S(O)

B. Two silver vinaigrettes, by Taylor & Perry and George Unite, lower formed as a book initialled 'EB', upper with foliate engraving and inscribed 'JH to JMC', Birmingham 1835 and 1853, larger 2in (5cm) wide, 1oz.
£400–480/$580–700 S(O)

The vinaigrettes in Item B are more valuable than the earlier one in Item A as the upper one is larger than most and the lower one is in the form of a book which is unusual and more sought-after. The two in Item A are of a common size and style although the engraving is pretty, which improves their desirability.

Silver combination patch, thimble, needle and bodkin case, c1800, 4in (10cm) long.
£300–350/$440–500 LBr

◄ **Walnut shell *necéssaire*,** with silver-capped ruby glass scent bottles and metal funnel, lid damaged, mid-19thC, 2in (5cm) long. Without the damage to the lid this unusual piece might be worth a further £100/$145.
£300–350/$440–500 S(O)

The look without the price

This is a copy of a late 18thC snuff box. The methods of manufacture are still very similar today, and the best way to tell the difference between an original and a copy is by looking at the hallmark. If this item had dated from 1790 it could be worth £500–600/$725–870.

Silver trinket box, by James Dixon & Sons, Sheffield 1920, 3½in (9cm) wide.
£300–325/$440–470 BEX

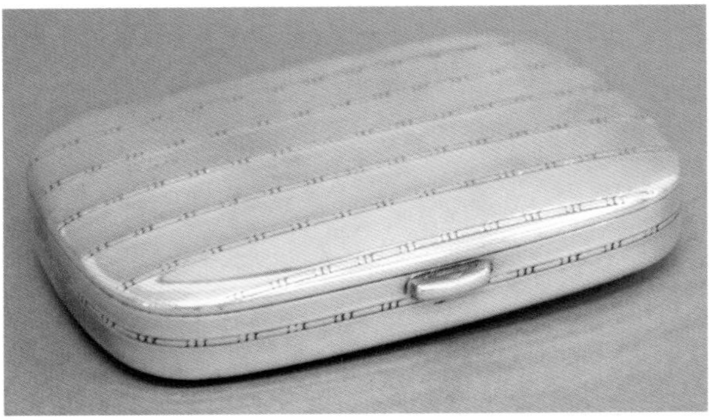

Engine-turned silver cigarette case, Continental, import mark for 1909, 3½in (9cm) wide. Continental items of this kind are not as desirable as British examples; hand-engraving is unlikely to increase the price significantly.
£350–400/$500–580 G(L)

Silver toothpick case, by Samuel Pemberton, with cut corners and bright-cut decoration, monogram, Birmingham 1790, 3¼in (8.5cm) wide, 1oz. Toothpick cases are not as valuable as as snuff boxes.
£380–450/$575–675 Bea(E)

Silver snuff box, by E. Edwards II, London 1846, 3in (7.5cm) wide. Plain boxes of this type and date are always good value because of their lack of decoration.
£400–450/$580–650 SHa

Further reading

Miller's Silver & Plate Buyer's Guide, Miller's Publications, 2001

◄ **Silver vinaigrette,** by Nathaniel Mills, depicting the Scott Memorial, Birmingham 1854, 2in (5cm) high. Nathaniel Mills, of Birmingham, is one of the most well-known specialist silversmiths, hence, boxes by him are popular with collectors.
£400–480/$580–700 G(L)

Silver and horn snuff mull, Scottish, c1910, 1¼in (3cm) diam. Snuff mulls are rarely marked and are interesting to collect in all their varieties.
£550–600/$800–870 BEX

Silver, silver-gilt and niello snuff box, by Louis Alexandre Bruneau, the cover depicting a hunting scene, the lip inscribed 'D Franchismme', French, c1820, 3½in (9cm) wide. Engraved hunting scenes on snuff boxes became very popular in Britain from the beginning of Queen Victoria's reign, although they appeared much earlier on Continental pieces.
£550–650/$800–950 S(O)

Dressing case set with silver fittings, by William Neal, the fitted interior containing ten bottles or boxes, London 1851, 11¾in (30cm) wide. Fittings have very often been removed, and this may be the case with this example.
£680–800/$1,000–1,150 S(O)

Silver-gilt snuff box, by Latty Brothers & Co, applied and engraved with flowerheads and scrolls, with presentation inscription '...to the Mess of the 2nd West York Yeomanry Cavalry...', Indian, Calcutta c1840, 4¾in (12cm) wide, 11.75oz. Snuff boxes were popular as gifts and, although inscriptions can devalue larger items such as sauce tureens, on the inside of snuff boxes they only affect the value if they have been added later.
£750–900/$1,100–1,300 TEN

Silver table cigar box, by J. Millward Banks, Birmingham 1893, 11½in (29cm) wide. Cigarette or cigar boxes tend to be much plainer than this, therefore, the decoration accounts for the higher price.
£720–850/$1,000–1,250 Bea(E)

Chased and engraved silver tobacco box, by Mark Edward Cornock, London 1707, 4in (10cm) diam. The design on this box was almost certainly added at a later date, which accounts for the low price.
£800–880/$1,150–1,275 LBr

Candlesticks

Set of four Sheffield-plated telescopic candlesticks, with foliate borders, c1815, 6½in (16.5cm) high. This type of candlestick is collectable when in good condition. If perfect and original these can make £500–700/$700–1,000.
£350–420/$500–600 S(O)

Pair of Georgian Sheffield-plated candlesticks, the single knop baluster columns on dished square bases with gadrooned rims, 9½in (24cm) high. Any wear will expose the underlying copper. A little wear on raised decorations can be attractive, but bear in mind it will only get worse and avoid items with large patches
£420–500/$600–720 TMA

► **Pair of Regency-style silver table candlesticks,** by J. K. & Co, with baluster stems and shaped circular bases repoussé decorated with shells, leaves and scrolls, loaded, bases worn, Sheffield 1826, 12in (30.5cm) high. These candlesticks are often worn on the high spots.
£600–700/$870–1,000 L

Pair of silver candlesticks, with spiral chased square sconces, baluster knop stems, on square gadrooned-edge bases, loaded, Sheffield 1896, 10¾in (27.5cm) high.
£580–700/$850–1,000 TRM

Pair of table candlesticks, with detachable nozzles, maker's mark worn, Birmingham 1932, 10¾in (27.5cm) high, 20oz. Check corners for damage on square bases as this will affect the price.
£360–400/$550–580 Bea(E)

Beware

The metal rod with which a loaded candlestick is weighted is often set in pitch or plaster of Paris. Sometimes this may begin to disintegrate, in which case it will rattle if gently shaken.

Pair of silver desk candlesticks, by John Carter, with column stems, on square bases later engraved with the Nelthorpe crest, London 1773, 6¼in (16cm) high. Smaller items such as these candlesticks often have crests rather than coats-of-arms. English crests may be accompanied by a motto below the crest; in Scottish examples it generally appears above.
£800–950
$1,150–1,400 S(O)

Condiments

Pair of George V silver salts, boat-shaped on rectangular bases, 3in (7.5cm) high. This style of salt boat is prone to splitting at the point where the foot joins the body – always check carefully for signs of damage and repair. Repairs with silver solder can be difficult to spot.
£100–120/$145–175 G(L)

Silver pepperette, engraved with the nelthorpe crest, on a spreading foot, London 1810, 3in (7.5cm) high, 1oz. While sets of pepperettes command a premium, single examples are not undesirable and are a more affordable option.
£100–120/$145–175 S(O)

Victorian silver-plated condiment set, by Elkington & Co, fitted with a set of six cut-glass condiments, 10in (25.5cm) wide.
£110–130/$160–200 G(L)

Pair of silver salts, by Urquhart & Hart, decorated with wriggle-work bands, London 1793–94, 3½in (9cm) wide. The hollow ball-and-claw supports make these examples less desirable.
£240–280/$350–400 S(O)

◄ **Silver-mounted cut-glass condiment bottle,** c1780, 5in (12.5cm) high. Bottles such as this usually form part of a cruet frame containing various bottles and casters for condiments. The frames were very often damaged by the weight of the bottles, and the handles turned into toasting forks. As a result, sets were often separated leaving individual items such as this.
£180–220/$250–320 G(L)

► **Silver pepperette,** by Wakelin & Taylor, the vase-shaped body engraved with the Sutton crest, with a pierced capstan cover, London 1785, 4in (10cm) high, 2oz. The cap and body are engraved with the same crest, suggesting that they are original.
£240–280/$350–400 S(O)

► **Silver-gilt enamel salt,** by Marius Hammer, with scalloped plique-à-jour rim and two dragon head handles, Norwegian, early 20thC, 2in (5cm) wide. The price of this item is a reflection of the good quality and unusual design.
£380–450/$575–650 S(O)

Pair of silver salt cellars, by Edward Wood, the undersides engraved with the Nelthorpe crest, London 1741, 3in (7.5cm) diam, 9oz. These cellars are good value – they are well marked and not too thin or worn.
£240–280/$350–410 S(O)

Set of four silver salts, by Emes & Barnard, crested above initial, the inverted rims with shell and acanthus edging, the lobed bowls on flaring, fluted polygonal bases, London 1833, 3¾in (9.5cm) diam, 17.5oz. This kind of salt needs a glass lining or gilded interior as salt is extremely corrosive. Always check for corrosion damage as it will affect the price.
£440–520/$650–750 Bea(E)

Collection of silver cruet wares, comprising a pair of ribbed and crested pedestal pepperettes by Thomas Daniel, London 1805, a pair of ovoid pepperettes, and a single square-section pepperette by Robert Hennell, London 1804, 3in (7.5cm) high, 10oz. Job lots bought at auctions can be a good opportunity to start a collection as they often contain a wide variety of interesting items.
£400–480/$580–700 S(O)

► **Silver salt,** by Liberty & Co, in the Japanese Aesthetic taste, modelled as a chrysanthemum, 1893, 4in (10cm) high. Pieces designed by particular companies have a strong body of collectors and will appeal to both silver enthusiasts and specialist collectors, consequently making them more expensive.
£450–550/$650–800 ALiN

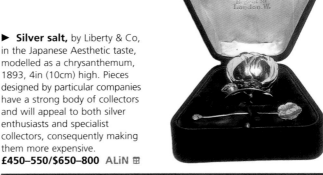

► **Pair of silver novelty pepperettes,** modelled as cockerels with detachable heads and hinged wings, German, c1900, 5in (12.5cm) high, 13oz. Novelty pepper pots can make an interesting collecting area. Pairs tend to be more valuable than individual ones, although single examples are still sought after.
£550–650/$800–950 S(O)

Cups, Mugs & Tankards

Silver-gilt replica of the Palm Leaf Cup, Sheffield 1907, 6in (15cm) wide. This is an Edwardian replica of an exhibit in the British Museum – the original is likely to be a one-off and priceless.
£100–120/$145–175 TMA

◄ **Sheffield-plated tanker,** by Tudor & Leader, c1760, 7½in (19cm) high. The copper colour on the handle and raised decoration shows that the plate has worn thin. This kind of damage will increase, so the tanker is probably best used only as a display item.
£175–200
$250–290 S(O)

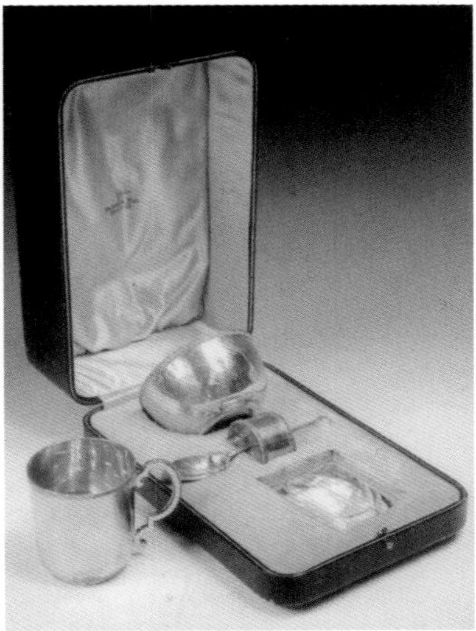

Silver four-piece christening set, by Walker & Hall, comprising a mug with chevron edge and moulded scroll handle, a matching porringer, rat-tail spoon and napkin ring, Sheffield 1915, mug 3in (7.5cm) high, 8oz, cased. Some christening mugs come with matching cutlery, the spoon often being badly worn. Mugs are very sturdy and tend to be in good condition. Bear in mind that although damage can detract from the price, silver sets are still popular christening gifts and minor damage may be acceptable.
£130–160/$200–230 CGC

Silver trompe l'oeil mug, by Viktor Sawinkow, Russian, Moscow 1869, 4½in (11.5cm) high. Trompe l'oeil work is unique to Russian silver. Prospective buyers should be aware of the great number of modern reproductions now available and are advised to seek expert advice before purchasing.
£250–280/$350–400 S(O)

The look without the price

Silver beaker, engraved with flowerheads, Russian, Moscow 1743, 4in (10cm) high, 2oz.
£250–320
$350–450 S(O)

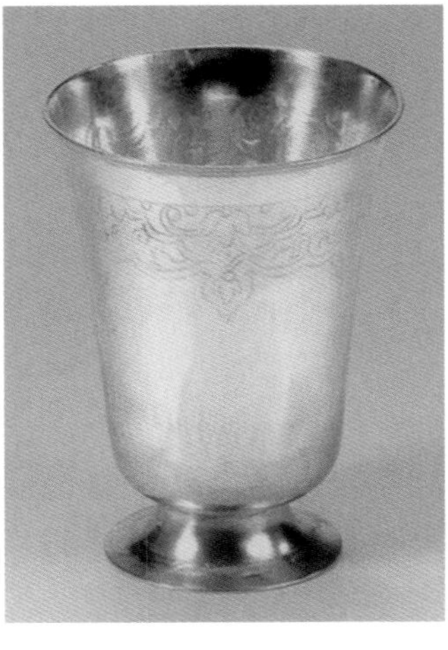

If this beaker had been more ornately decorated with a gilt interior and chased decoration, and by a named maker, it could have made £500/ $700. Russian silver was mainly produced in Moscow and St Petersburg, each city having several outstanding makers.

Miller's compares...

A. Silver mug, by Edward Farnell, later engraved with a crest and motto above initials 'FLD', London 1792, 4in (10cm) high, 9oz.
£330–360/$475–525 S(O)

Item B is the more valuable than item A for two reasons; firstly the weight of the mug is 5oz heavier than Item A, so contains more silver and is sturdier. Secondly, Item B has a better provenance with an identifiable crest and interesting history attached.

B. Silver mug, by Thomas Lambe, engraved with Pattinson armorial, London 1788, 4¾in (12cm) high, 14oz. The motto *Ne vile pretiosa* (Valuable things out of a base one) was adopted by Hugh Lee Pattinson of Alston, Cumberland (1796–1858) alluding to his discovery of a process for the separation of silver from lead in 1829 which he patented in 1833.
£550–650/$800–950 S(O)

Silver-mounted coconut cup and cover, 1875–1925, 6in (15cm) high. Coconuts used in these items would probably have been imported by sailors and then mounted in silver and sold in Britain.
£350–400/$500–580 G(L)

Silver cup, by John King, London 1772, 6¾in (17cm) high. These items are sadly no longer practical but are a good way to buy affordable silver, providing they are undamaged and the hallmarks have not been erased.
£650–750/$950–1,100 S(O)

Silver half-pint mug, the girdle applied and later initialled 'MH', with tapered cylindrical scroll handle, marks rubbed, Britannia period, c1715, 3½in (9cm) high, 6oz. Rubbed marks will limit the appreciation of a piece.
£350–400/$500–580 S(O)

Silver thimble toddy cup, by C. H. Cheshire, inscribed 'Just A Thimble Full' Birmingham 1891, 2in (5cm) high, 1oz. This inscription was very popular on Victorian toddy cups.
£350–420/$500–600 S(O)

► Pair of silver barrel beakers, by Peter and William Bateman, London 1806, 6in (15cm) high. In perfect condition these would make £1,000–1,800/$1,500–2,500.
£900–1,000
$1,300–1,500 S(O)

Cutlery & Serving Implements

◄ **Silver-plated bread fork,** with mother-of-pearl handle, c1910, 6in (15cm) long.
£18–20/$25–30 HO ⊞

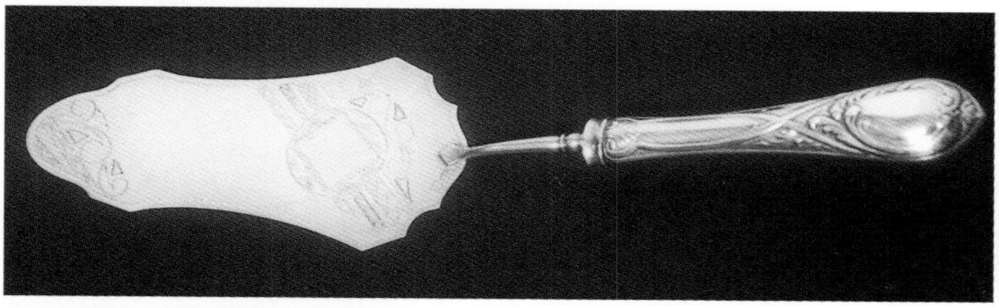

► **Cake slice,** with hand-engraved blade, Russian, c1860, 10in (25.5cm) long, 84 Zlotnik. *Zoloto* means 'gold' in Russian. The Russians have three silver standards: 84 (.875), 88 (916.6) and 91 (947.9).
£50–55/$75–80 Gla ⊞

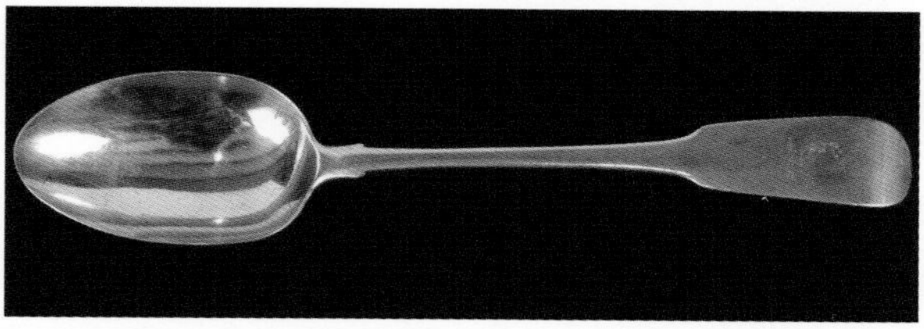

◄ **Silver spoon,** by Richard Garde, Irish, Dublin 1822, 9in (23cm) long. Irish silver is very collectable – mainly because there is little available. Generally it is estimated that the ratio of London to Dublin period silver is 150:1, hence as supply will not increase, Irish silver prices are likely to remain strong.
£70–90/$100–130 CoHA ⊞

Four silver Fiddle pattern forks, 1819, 9oz. The tines are rather worn and a set of six would be worth £150–170/ $220–250.
£80–100/$115–145 SWO ⚒

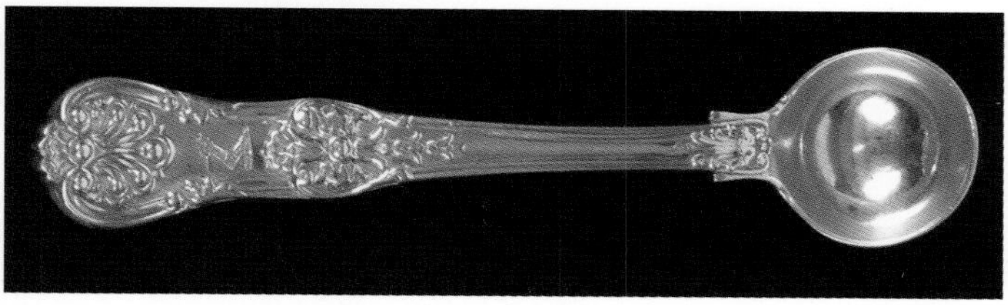

Pair of silver King's pattern salt spoons, by William Eaton, London 1843, 4½in (11.5cm) long. As with salt cellars, always check the condition of salt spoons as salt corrosion can seriously damage value.
£80–110/$115–160 CoHA ⊞

► **Victorian silver knife, fork and spoon christening set,** in a leather case, 6½in (16.5cm) long. These represent good value.
£100–120/$145–175 G(L) ⚒

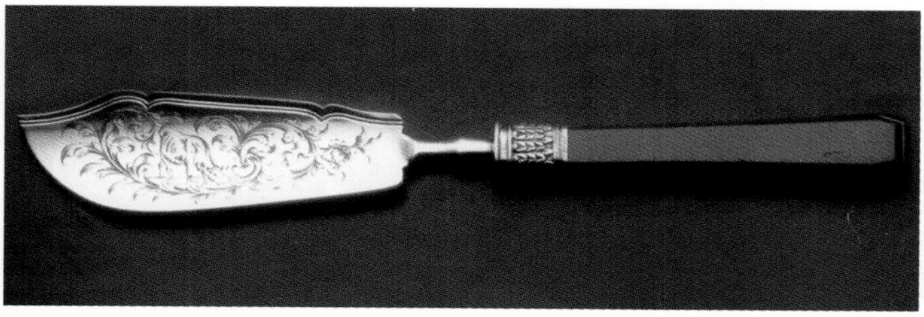

◄ **Silver butter knife,** by Elizabeth Eaton, engraved with a cow drinking in a river surrounded by engraved flowers and foliage, hardstone handle, London 1856, 8in (20.5cm) long. The pretty engraving and hardstone handle make this an attractive piece.
£100–120/$145–175 S ⚒

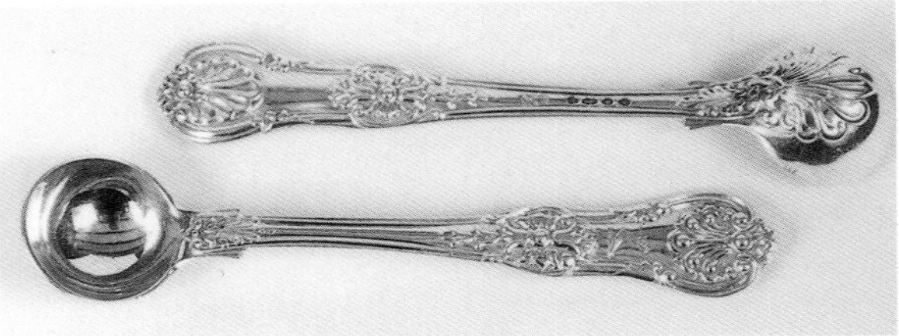

Two silver King's pattern salt spoons, by William Eaton II, London 1843, 5in (12.5cm) long. William Eaton II was a prolific maker and does not command the premium prices of slightly earlier makers such as Paul Storr.
£100–150/$145–225 CoHA

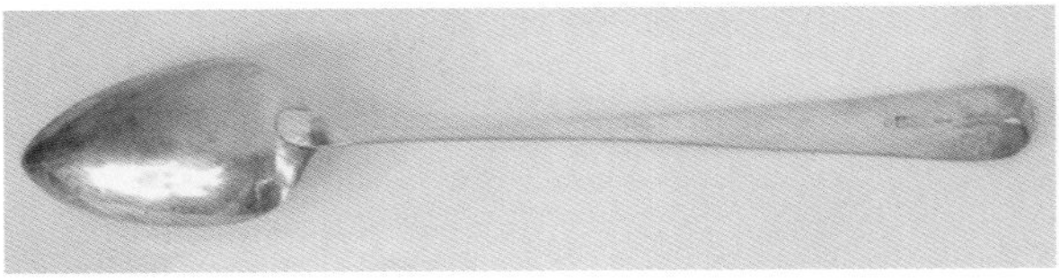

Silver Old English pattern gravy spoon, maker's mark N?, Edinburgh 1810, 12¼in (31cm) long, 2.75oz. Scottish silver is particularly collectable.
£120–150/$175–225 CGC

Set of 12 silver apostle spoons, with matching sugar tongs, Sheffield 1894, in original box. Early apostle spoons rarely survive in sets and are more often found individually. The Master (Christ) commands the highest price, but value depends on wear and there are a lot of fakes on the market. A Victorian reproduction makes an affordable alternative to the real thing.
£120–140/$175–200 BR

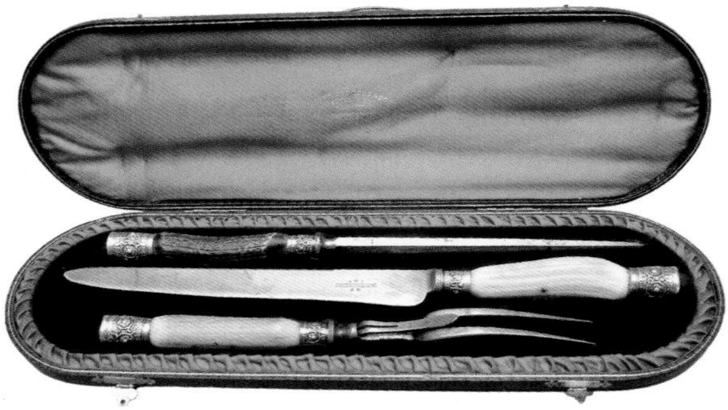

◄ **Victorian three-piece silver carving set,** with stag horn handles, in original box. A carving set by a named maker, such as Allen & Darwin, with a uniform horn colour and more elaborate silver decorations can be worth between £280–325/$410–470.
£130–155/$190–225 G(L)

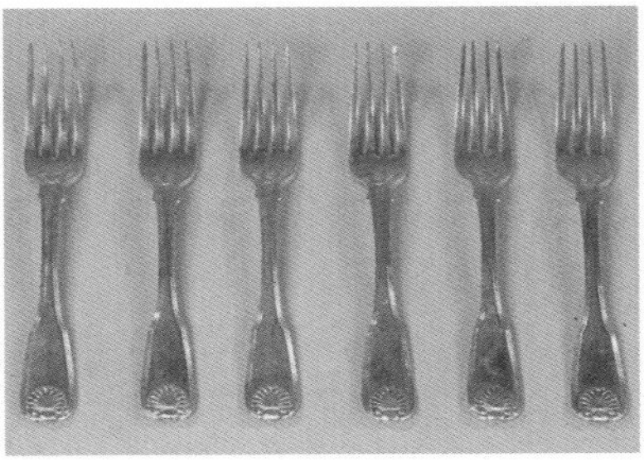

Set of six silver Fiddle, Thread and Shell pattern table forks, by William Eley and William Fearn, backs engraved to the back with a crest and motto, London 1804, 17.5oz.
£160–200/$230–300 PFK

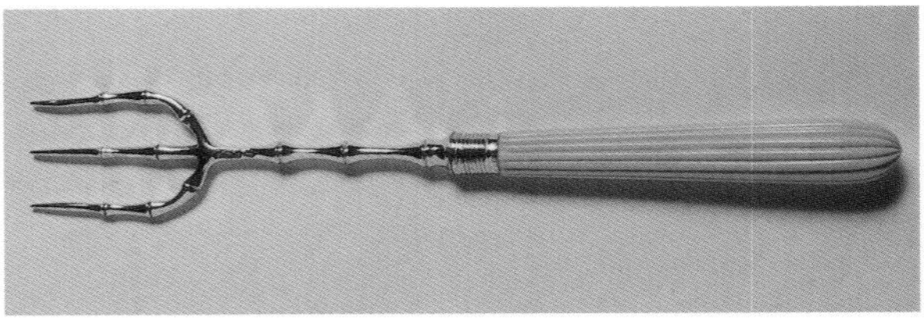

Silver bread fork, by James and William Deakin, with ivory handle, Sheffield 1895, 9in (23cm) long. This is a nice example of aesthetic style.
£200–220/$300–320 BEX

► **Silver basting spoon,** by Charles Hougham, London 1788, 12in (30.5cm) long.
£225–250/$325–360 CoHA

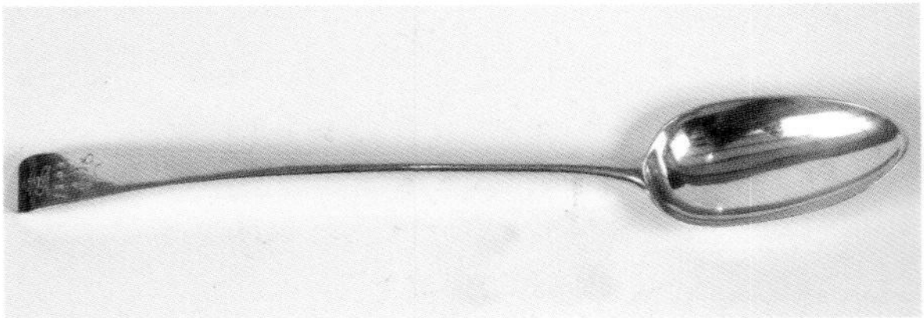

The look without the price

Set of nine silver table forks, by Georg Jensen, with stylized foliate stems, with seven matching dessert spoons and four matching cake forks, 1946.
£260–300/$380–440 G(L)

Complete cutlery sets often demand a premium. A 68-piece Georg Jensen set can make £4,000/$5,800, while smaller, incomplete sets can be an affordable way to buy examples of good quality silver by known makers. Also, part sets such as this can be usable in daily life as smaller numbers suit modern eating habits.

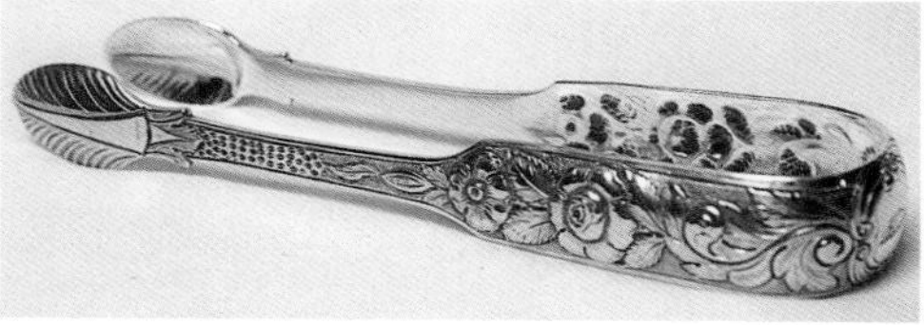

Pair of silver sugar tongs, by James Le Bas, Dublin 1835, 6in (15cm) long. Sugar tongs are an inexpensive way of starting a collection.
£250–280/$350–400 WELD

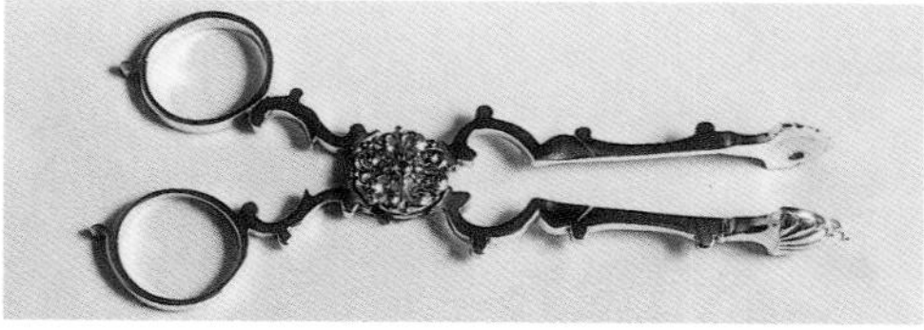

Pair of silver sugar nips, c1860, 5in (12.5cm) long. Hinged sugar nips preceded spring sugar tongs around 1790–1800.
£260–300/$380–440 BEX

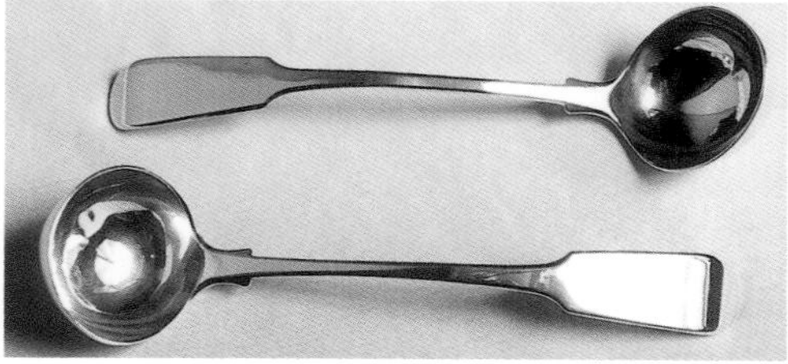

Pair of silver ladles, by Mitchell & Russell, Glasgow 1820, 6in (15cm) long. Ladles such as these can be used as sauce or toddy ladles.
£260–300/$380–440 BEX

Set of six silver table forks, by Peter Walker, 1870, 8in (20.5cm) long.
£260–300/$400–440 HCA

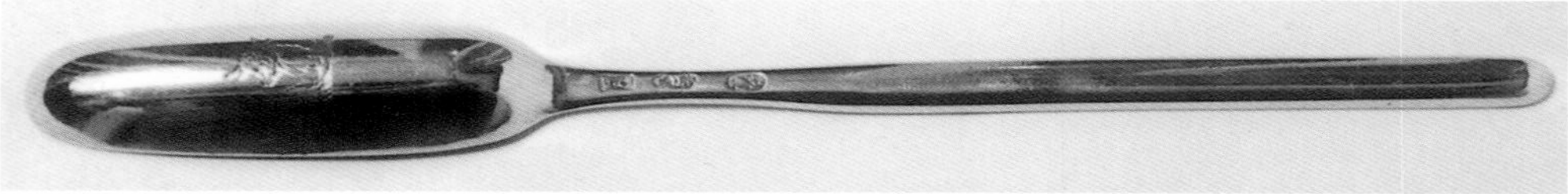

Silver marrow scoop, by J. Craig, Dublin c1765, 9in (23cm) long.
£260–300/$380–450 SIL

Marrow scoops

Marrow scoops were made in enormous quantities from the 17th century onwards. They were used to scoop out bone marrow, which was considered a great delicacy at the time.

Scoops are always the same size with a large and a small end to cater for different bones. They are plain in design but can have a crest on the wider end. Most scoops now available were made in the mid- to late 18th century and earlier examples are consequently more expensive.

Silver and ivory travelling apple corer, Birmingham 1857, 4½in (11.5cm) long. Apple corers are not all that common and are no longer practical, so are mostly collected for their novelty value.
£300–350/$450–500 CoHA

Silver bead Stilton cheese scoop, by George Adams, engraved with a crest and motto, London 1859, 3.5oz. These should be quite heavy to resist bending.
£300–350/$450–500 B(L)

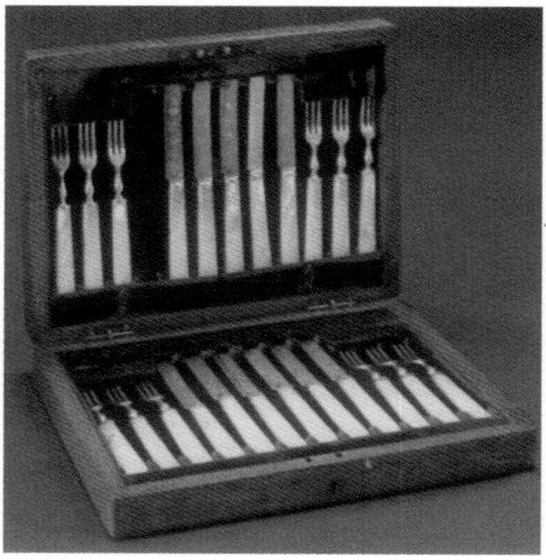

Set of silver fruit knives and forks, by Elkington & Co, with mother-of-pearl handles, Birmingham 1903, one knife missing, in an oak case. If complete, this set would have made £400–500/$580–720.
£260–320/$380–450 S(O)

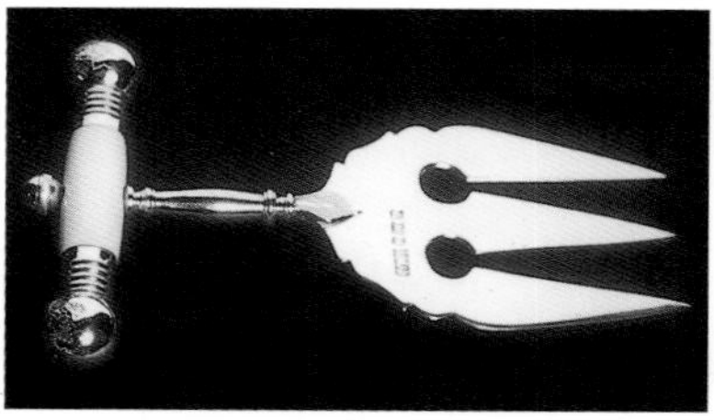

Silver bread fork, by Harry Wigfull, with ivory handle, Sheffield 1896, 5in (12.5cm) long.
£320–350/$460–500 BEX

Miller's compares...

A. Pair of silver sugar nips, by J. Rosenthal, London 1890, 5in (12.5cm) long.
£270–325/$400–470 BEX

B. Pair of silver sugar nips, c1730, 4½in (11.5cm) long.
£450–500/$650–720 BEX

Although Item A is much prettier than Item B, the latter is earlier in date and therefore warrants a higher value.

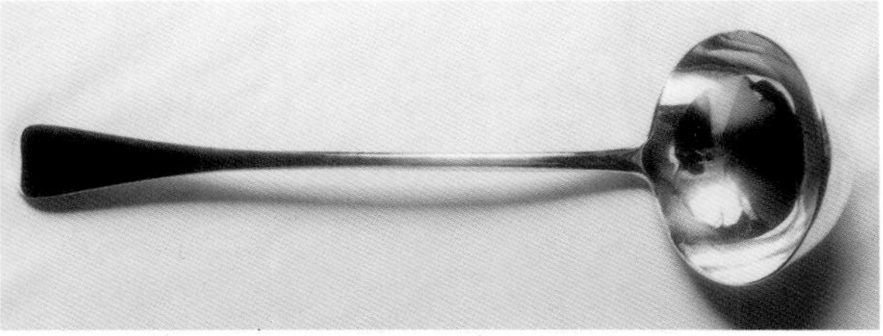

Silver soup ladle, by The Goldsmiths and Silversmiths Co, London 1901, 13in (33cm) long.
£320–360/$460–520 BEX

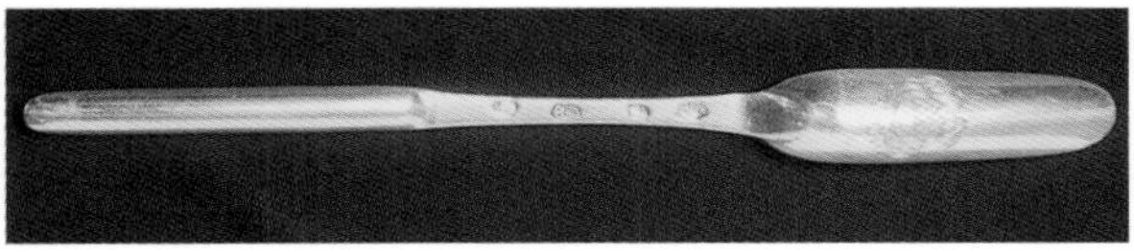

Silver marrow scoop, by C. Skinner, Dublin 1759, 9in (23cm) long. The Dublin hallmark makes this piece very desirable to collectors.
£350–400/$500–580 WELD

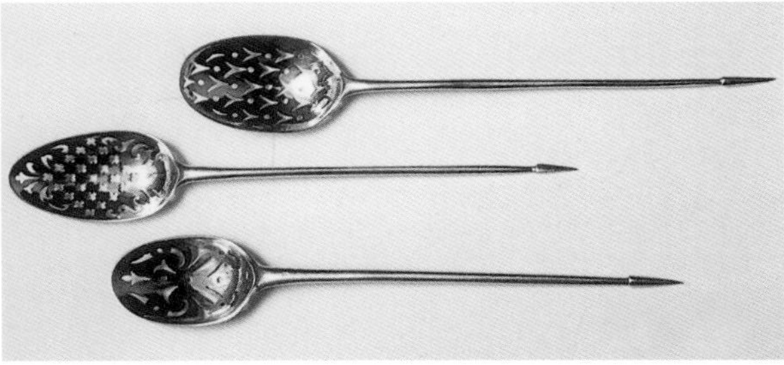

Three silver mote spoons, c1750, 5in (12.5cm) long. These would have been used for picking tea leaves or other residue from drinks, and the spike is for clearing the teapot spout.
£350–400/$500–580 HEB

► **Boxed set of silver teaspoons,** by D. Moulang, decorated with a harp design, Dublin 1895, 6in (15cm) long. Sets of tea and coffee spoons can be an interesting collecting area due to the variety of unusual designs.
£400–440/$580–650 SIL

Soup ladles

Soup ladles were introduced around the 1740s, and earlier examples tend to follow the style of other tableware from the period. They were often sold in pairs.

Set of silver fish servers, by S. Barraclough & Sons, with ivory handles, Sheffield 1910, in a fitted box 14in (35.5cm) long. Even the plainest examples such as this one are always saleable and collectable.
£350–400/$500–580 BEX

The look without the price

Quantity of King's pattern table silver, comprising four tablespoons, ten table forks, 12 dessert spoons, 13 teaspoons, four sauce ladles, two butter knives, a pair of sugar tongs, two salt spoons, a fiddle shell teaspoon and a quantity of silver-plated flatware, by various makers, single-struck, initialled 'J', Edinburgh 1838–60, 64oz.
£380–450/$575–650 S(O)

King's pattern became popular during the Regency period and is still made today. A full set is always worth more, and if these pieces were by one maker, such as George Adams, with one date they would fetch £600–900/$870–1,300.

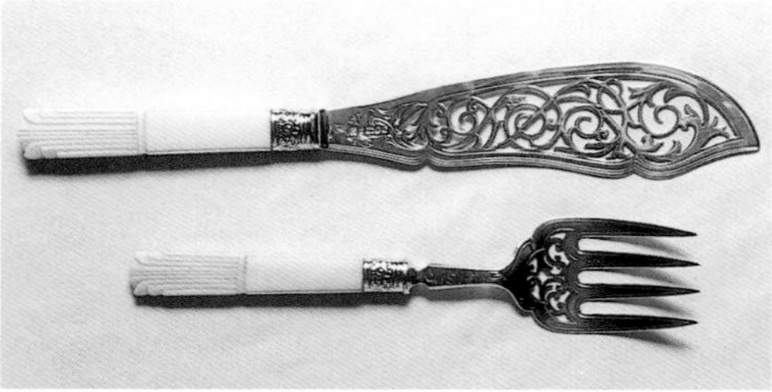

Set of silver fish servers, by R. Martin and E. Hall, with ivory handles, Sheffield 1865–66, knife 12in (30.5cm) long. From the mid-19thC, fish slices were made with a matching fork and called fish servers. Slices prior to the 19thC could have been made for either gateaux or fish and often had a turned wooden handle. Victorian items such as this can be particularly decorative thanks to the pierced decoration.
£400–450/$580–650 BEX ⊞

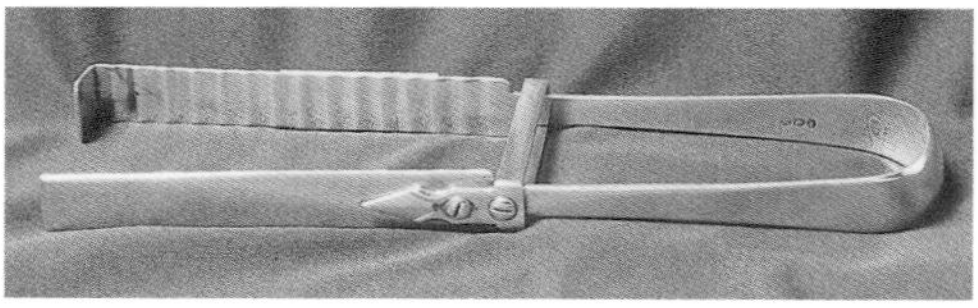

Pair of silver asparagus/chop tongs, by Eley & Fearn, London 1807, 9in (23cm) long. Asparagus tongs dating from the late 18thC tend to have bright-cut engraved decoration, while 19thC tongs such as these have a broader grip, and handles start being decorated to match services.
£450–500/$650–720 HEB ⊞

Silver soup ladle, by Thomas Chawner, London 1772, 13in (33cm) long. This item is more valuable than a plain ladle because of the shell bowl and bright-cut engraving on the handle which is sought-after by collectors.
£550–600/$800–870 BEX ⊞

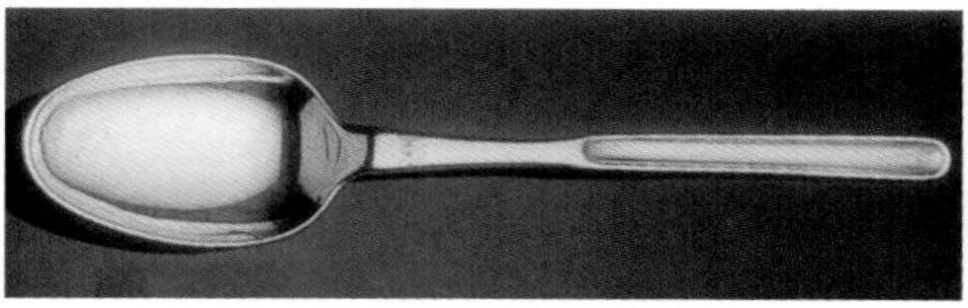

Silver marrow spoon, by James Ker, with faceted drop heel, engraved with a cypher of the Earls of Hopetoun, assay master Archibald Ure, Edinburgh 1734, 9in (23cm) long. The Edinburgh mark is not rare, but is desirable on an unusual piece such as this. If it had a Scottish provincial mark is could fetch between £1,000–1,500/$1,500–2,200.
£720–800/$1,000–1,150 B(Ed) ⚒

Set of silver fish servers, by George Adams, London 1864, 13in (33cm) long. George Adams was a plate worker who registered his mark in London in 1840. Plate was originally the term for domestic wares made of silver and gold. It is often confused with Sheffield plate, leading to the mistaken idea that early wrought plate was Sheffield plate, which was not the case.
£450–500/$650–720 BEX ⊞

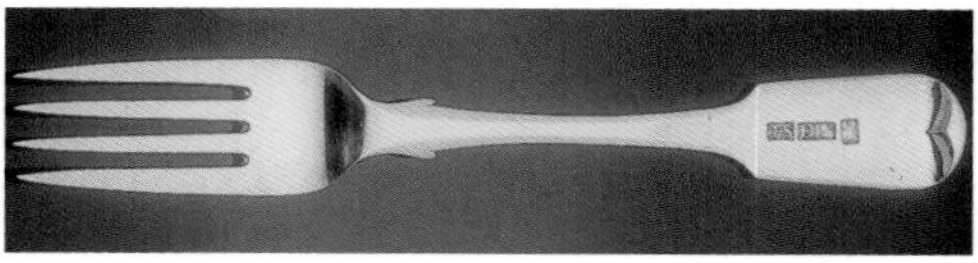

Silver Fiddle pattern table fork, by Thomas Stewart, three marks TS, ELN, St Giles, 1820–30, 8½in (21.5cm) long, 2oz. Scottish provincial silver is highly sought-after by private collectors, especially pieces such as this broad fork which probably originates from Elgin. Those from Forres, Tain and Ellon are especially rare, and if this were from Tain it might fetch £1,000/$1,500 or more.
£500–600/$720–870 B(Ed) ⚒

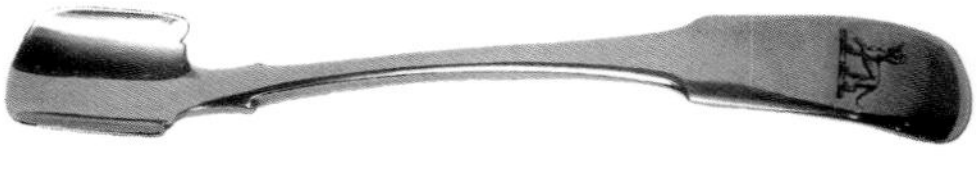

Silver Stilton cheese scoop, by West & Co, Dublin 1811, 7in (18cm) long. These types of spoons were often converted from tablespoons and basting spoons. This may be an example of such a spoon as it looks out of proportion.
£675–750/$975–1,100 WELD ⊞

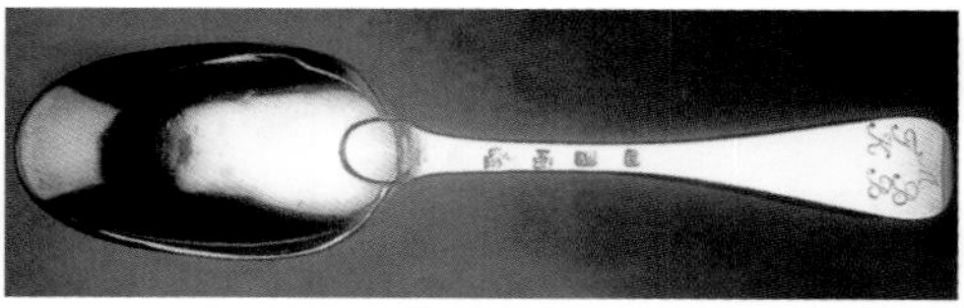

Set of five silver Hanoverian pattern tablespoons, by Edward Lothian, with faceted drop heel, engraved initials M/TB/KB, assay master Archibald Ure, Edinburgh 1737, 9oz. Nice marks on good Scottish spoons make them 30 to 50 per cent more valuable than, say, London examples. If there were six of these spoons, they would be worth £900–1,000/$1,300–1,500.
£800–950/$1,150–1,400 B(Ed) ⚒

Jugs & Sauce Boats

Silver cream jug, with gadrooned rim, 1812. These jugs are collectable if in good condition, as their variety is infinite.
£75–90/$110–130 G(L)

► **Silver milk jug,** the lobed compressed body engraved with the Sutton crest, marks rubbed, London c1815, 2¾in (7cm) high, 7oz.
£100–120
$145–175 S(O)

Silver cream jug, by Alexander Field, London 1807, 3in (7.5cm) high.
£240–275/$350–400 GLa

Silver cream jug, with wooden handle, raised on a lobed pedestal base, original gilding, Russian, Moscow 1842, 4½in (11.5cm) high. The interior gilding on this jug helps protect the inside from corrosion.
£280–320/$400–450 GLa

The look without the price

Victorian silver helmet-shaped cream jug, with George II-style design.
£130–150/$190–220 G(L)

An original George II cream jug could make £2,000–5,000/ $2,900–7,250, depending on date, maker, condition and decoration. This Victorian copy is an affordable alternative at £130–160/$190–220, while giving the impression of something more valuable.

Silver cream jug, by Nathaniel Appleton and Anne Smith, with pressed bead pattern to rim and scalloped pedestal foot, with acanthus scroll handle, London 1780, 3½in (9cm) high.
£320–370/$470–530 GLa

Silver cream boat, by S. Herbert & Co, with a flying scroll handle and crimped beaded rim, on three hoof feet, London 1768, 3in (7.5cm) high. This cream boat is a typical example from the mid-18thC. The bulbous form, flying scroll handle and waved edge decoration are all common features from this period.
£350–400/$500–580 GLa ⊞

Silver inverted pyriform cream jug, by John Pollock, with later chasing, London 1744, 3¾in (9.5cm) high. Later chasing makes this item worth £120–180/$175–260 less at auction.
£380–420/$550–600 GLa ⊞

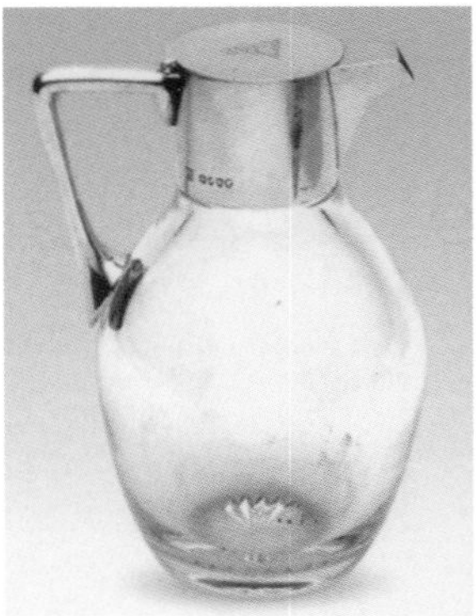

Silver-mounted baluster claret jug, by J. W. Hukin & J. T. Heath, crested, London 1885. Hukin & Heath produced a variety of tableware during this period, designed by such noted designers as Christopher Dresser. This jug is characteristic of the Modernist style produced at the time.
£400–480/$580–700 Bea(E)

◄ **Silver cow creamer,** in mid-18thC style, Dutch, c1890, 5in (12.5cm) long, 5oz. The price of cow creamers varies according to the size, weight of silver and finish of the decoration. This example is a simplistic representation typical of the 18thC taste. Had it been a more realistic finish it could be worth over £1,000/$1,500.
£400–480/$580–700 S(O)

Silver wine jug, by Bernard Muller, in the form of a Bacchus mask with embossed fruiting vine, simulated branch handle, Continental, Import mark for Chester 1901. Bacchus, the Roman god of wine, is often used as decoration on wine antiques.
£500–600/$720–870 RBB

The look without the price

Sheffield-plated sauce boat, with flying scroll handle and engraved initials to base, c1790, 9in (23cm) wide.
£375–425
$560–620 S(O)

A silver sauce boat of this period would be £500–800/$720–1,150. However, much depends on the weight and shape.

The look without the price

While made by the same company, this is not actually a matching pair of sauce boats. Had they been matching they could be worth an additional £300/ $440. Single sauce boats from this period can be bought for £100–150/ $145–220, proving that a pair is worth more than double the price of a single sauce boat.

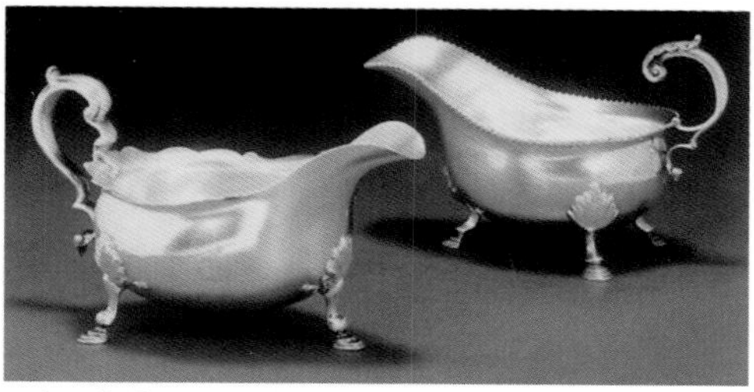

Pair of silver sauce boats, by The Goldsmiths & Silversmiths Co, on pad supports, London 1913, 7½in (19cm) wide, 20oz.
£450–550/$650–800 S(O)

◄ **Edwardian hobnail-cut glass claret jug,** with silver mounts. Always check that the stopper fits properly and that it appears original. Also, glass handles on claret jugs are often cracked or chipped, therefore the condition of the glass should always be checked.
£500–600/$720–870 G(L)

Pair of silver sauce boats, by William Comyns & Sons, with collet supports and gadroon borders, London 1901, 7in (18cm) wide, 21oz. Sauce boats are usually made in pairs and single ones are less desirable, hence together these are worth more than if they were sold singly.
£500–600/$720–870 S(O)

Facet-cut glass claret jug, by William Gibson and John Langman, with silver cover and scroll handle, Birmingham 1885, 10½in (26.5cm) high.
£600–700/$870–1,000 S(O)

Silver ewer, with putto finial, with mask-capped scroll handle, on a circular foot, pseudo Nurnberg marks, importer's mark of Edwin Thompson Bryant, import mark for London 1896, probably German, 12¾in (32.5cm) high, 28oz.
£850–1,000
$1,250–1,500 Bon

► **Silver water jug,** by Tiffany & Co, with embossed decoration, the scroll handle engraved with shell decoration, monogram, maker's mark, American, late 19thC, 7in (18cm) high, 25oz. If this jug were by a different maker it may be worth around half as much, but it would not be of the same standard of workmanship.
£950–1,000/$1,400–1,500 Bon

Salvers & Trays

Arts and Crafts-style silver-on-copper tazza, by Elkington & Co, embossed and chased with swans in a classical setting, with bluebirds, doves, parrots and insects within flowering sprays, late 19thC, 8½in (21.5cm) diam. When looking at electroplated items, check that the borders are in good condition. Electroplated examples are less easily damaged than Sheffield Plate as the borders and feet are not filled with lead. However, if there is damage, it is rarely worth repairing.
£35–42/$50–60 TMA

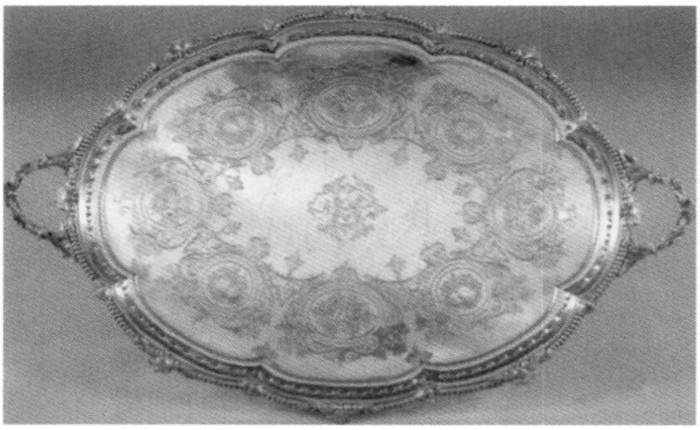

Silver-plated Welbeck plate and serving tray, by the Alex Clark Manufacturing Co, with beaded and leaf-scrolled edge, the centre engraved with a monogram within a border of floral cartouches, c1900, 30in (76cm) wide. These items can fetch as much as £250–350/$360–500, depending on decoration and quality.
£170–200/$250–300 PFK

Pair of silver dishes, by Elkington & Co, Birmingham 1890, 14½in (37cm) diam, 34oz. These decorative items are a typical example of the Victorian taste for embellishment. They are not to all tastes, but they are a good buy.
£650–750/$950–1,100 S(O)

Miller's compares...

A. Silver salver, by Richard Rugg, with a shell and scroll border, London 1762, 7in (18cm) diam.
£300–350
$450–500 S(O)

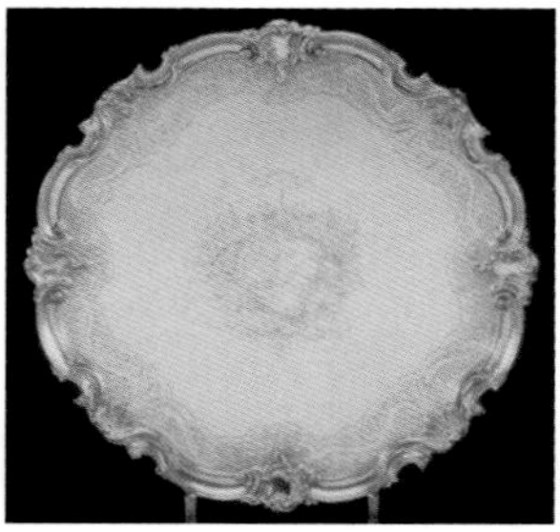

B. Silver salver, by William Eley, the centre engraved with an armorial, London 1833, 11¼in (28.5cm) diam, 26oz.
£880–1,000
$1,275–1,500 S(O)

Item B is more valuable because it is larger, more stylish and has elaborate decoration, while there are many similar examples like Item A on the market today.

Silver serving dish, by Paul Storr, engraved with an armorial, London 1799, 12½in (32cm) long, 23oz. The quality of these pieces is excellent and will last for many centuries, due to the thickness of the silver used. Paul Storr's work is not only collectable, but still very practical for everyday use.
£740–880
$1,100–1,275 S(O)

Tea & Coffee Pots

► **Silver biggin,** with a cane handle, 1893, 14oz. Biggins are not very sought-after, hence the low price.
£140–170/$200–250 G(L)

◄ **Silver hot water jug,** by Charles Stuart Harris, with wooden handle and knop, maker's mark worn, London 1882, 7½in (19cm) high, 9.5oz. The pattern on this hot water jug and many other Victorian beverage sets can be referred to as fluting as well as reeding.
£80–95/$115–140 Bea(E)

Silver demi-fluted compressed teapot, 1838, 17oz. These often suffer from excessive wear or damage.
£150–180/$220–260 G(L)

Silver miniature teapot, with floral finial, relief-decorated with chinoiserie, with reeded scroll handle and foliate-capped spout with tapering stopper, on four bracket feet, maker's mark of Joseph Willmore, Birmingham 1840, 1½in (4cm) high. This chinoiserie design is often seen on silverware of the period and reflects the growing interest in Far Eastern design at that time.
£200–250/$300–350 Bon

Miller's compares...

A. Bachelor's silver demi-fluted teapot, with sugar bowl and milk jug, late 19thC, 12.5oz.
£120–140/$175–200 G(L)

B. Bachelor's silver three-piece compressed tea service, by W. and J. Barnard, with semi-reeded lower body and gadroon and foliate rims, London 1892, 21oz.
£250–300/$350–450 Bea

The quality and weight of Item B is greater, and it is a more attractive style, reminiscent of c1820. Item A is commonly seen in sale rooms which makes it more affordable and easier to start a collection.

Silver three-piece tea service, with lobed lower section, the milk jug and sugar bowl with reeded handles, maker's mark 'E.H.', London 1882, 16.5oz. Be aware that cleaning silver using harsh modern chemicals or extreme buffing will, in time, wear down delicate decoration and engraving. If in doubt as to how to care for an item it is best to seek specialist advice.
£200–250/$300–360 DD

Silver three-piece tea service, by J. Gloster, part faceted, the teapot with wooden handle and button, Birmingham 1926, 18oz, cased. Wooden handles on tea and coffee pots from this period can suffer damage at the join from heat and over use. Be aware that chemical silver cleaners may strip the patina of these handles.
£250–300/$350–450 S(O)

Silver miniature tea service, comprising teapot, hot water jug, sugar basin, milk jug and two-handled tray, c1912, in original box 7in (18cm) wide. Tea trays are generally found with later tea services.
£300–350/$450–500 DAD

Silver teapot, by Daniel Pontifex, the part-lobed body initialled 'CN' for Charlotte Nelthorpe, with everted collar and wooden handle, London 1802, 5in (12.5cm) high, 17oz. This piece came with a provenance explaining the engraved initials, which adds interest and can improve the value of a piece.
£400–480/$580–700 S(O)

The look without the price

With its wooden scrolled handle, spreading base and turned finial, this coffee pot is very similar in style to those produced in the reign of George II. An original George II coffee pot, however could be worth up to £1,500/$2,150.

Silver coffee pot, the spout with a hinged cover, wooden handle, maker's mark 'EJH' over 'CB', Chester 1921, 8½in (21.5cm) high, 17oz.
£260–300/$380–440 Bea(E)

Silver-plated four-piece tea and coffee service and tray, engraved with classical motifs, the covers with helmet finials, tray inscribed, c1880, tray 30in (76cm) wide.
£420–500/$600–720 S(O)

Miller's compares...

A. Silver three-piece tea service, with bent twig finials, handles and spouts, the bodies decorated with exotic birds among prunus, maker's mark 'O.G. & H.M.', teapot 4¾in (12cm) wide, 26.5oz.
£480–580/$700–850 DD

Item A is of similar quality to Item B, but Item A is less desirable due to the current poor demand for Oriental designs.

B. Silver three-piece tea service and sugar tongs, by Tiffany & Co, with embossed bands of putti surrounded by vines and flowers, New York c1880, 22oz.
£650–780/$950–1,150 S(O)

Silver teapot, by Samuel Meriton, with a crest and foliate engraving, wooden handle and button, on later ball supports, London 1783, 4¾in (12cm) high. Teapots are easily damaged and must be in perfect condition to fetch this price. The silver is very thin and wear is most likely on the corners, the cover joints and the spout end. The ball feet are easily bent inwards causing them to split.
£600–720/$870–1,000 S(O)

Coffee pots

A good Georgian coffee pot can cost well over £1000/$1,500. However it should be remembered that these pieces have been unfashionable since the late 1960s. Considering their attractiveness and usefulness, coffee pots should be worthy of greater appreciation and value, so now is a good time to collect. Look for examples of the later 18th century, which are often decorated with embossing. This treatment, usually of flowers, cartouches and scrolls can be dismissed as being later Victorian additions. However, a discerning eye can tell the difference.

The difference between a coffee pot and a hot water jug is often confused. The spout of a coffee pot emerges from the base whereas that of a hot water jug emerges from near the rim.

► **Silver three-piece tea service,** by Mitchell & Russell of Glasgow, comprising teapot and stand, sugar basin and cream jug, of part gadrooned circular shape, engraved, on a stand, Edinburgh 1817, 54oz. Many tea sets in the past were engraved and presented as prizes. The longer the inscription, the less desirable the set.
£800–950/$1,150–1,400 B(Ed)

Miscellaneous

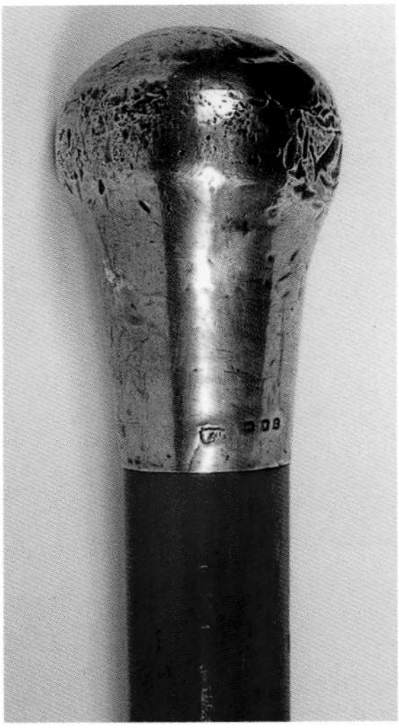

Silver-topped lacquered dress cane, Sheffield 1895, 36in (91.5cm) long. In the past 20 years canes have become highly collectable.
£45–50/$65–75 PSA

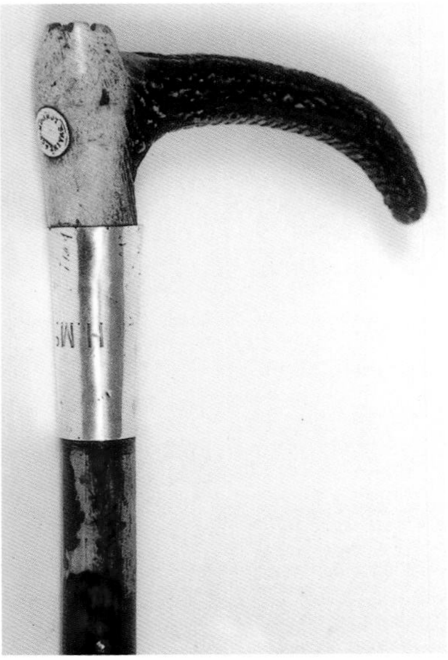

Silver-banded riding crop, with mottled bamboo shaft, and horn handle, c1880, 29in (73.5cm) long.
£65–75/$95–110 PSA

Pair of Victorian silver-plated tea canisters.
Tea canisters came in pairs, for the two types of tea available at the time – black and green. Pairs are more desirable and valuable than singles.
£80–95/$115–140 G(L)

◄ **Edwardian silver electric bell push,** of hexagonal shape, with engraved crest to button.
£80–95/$115–140 G(L)

► **Silver rose vase,** by Walker & Hall, with flared circular lip, blue glass liner, pierced tapered sides and scroll ornament decoration a circular base, Sheffield 1909. Check that the blue glass liner fits well inside the vase and is not damaged.
£85–95/$125–140 TRM

◄ **Set of George V silver and tortoiseshell piqué hair brushes,** hair brush 9in (23cm) long. These are in much demand even if the sets are incomplete.
£90–110/$130–160 G(L)

◄ **Pineapple-cut glass scent bottle,** with silver lid, 1886. If this scent bottle had a maker's mark and the lid was decorated rather than plain, it could have made up to three times this price at auction.
£90–110/$130–160 G(L)

Victorian silver sugar caster, 7¾in (19.5cm) high.
£100–120/£145–175 G(L)

George V silver *épergne*, of organic form, with seven vases, 11in (28cm) high.
£150–180/$220–260 G(L)

Pair of Sheffield-plated wine coasters, with scroll and shell cast rims, on circular turned wood bases, 1830–37, 7½in (19cm) diam. These coasters have obviously been used a great deal. The wood patina has been removed by absorbing wine spills and the silver plate has worn thin in some places. The greater the number in a set and the better the condition, the higher the price.
£100–125/$145–180 TMA

Sets/pairs

Unless otherwise stated, any description which refers to 'a set' or 'a pair' includes a guide price for the entire set or the pair, even though the illustration may show only a single item.

Late Victorian silver-plated inkstand, with a pair of hinged inkpots and a pen rest on a fan marquetry-inlaid Macassar ebony-veneered galleried base, with plated bun feet, 9in (23cm) wide. Inkstands tend to be expensive because they are so collectable.
£160–200/$230–290 WW

Pair of silver-rimmed vesta pots, in the form of glass custard glasses, the bodies ribbed for striking, Birmingham 1904, 2in (5cm) high.
£150–175/$220–255 TMA

Silver sugar caster, by F. Sibray & J. F. Hall, of baluster shape with embossed foliate decoration, London 1892, 4.8oz. This caster is good value.
£160–200
$230–290 Bea(E)

Silver nutmeg grater, with a crest, c1790, 2½in (6.5cm) high, 1oz. Nutmeg graters are a popular collecting area and because they are relatively uncommon they can be expensive.
£200–250/$290–360 S(O)

Silver wine funnel, part lobed, crested, with a detachable strainer, repaired, London 1809, 6in (15cm) high. Had this funnel not been damaged and restored, it could have been worth £600–700/$870–1,000.
£200–250/$290–360 S(O)

Miller's compares...

A. Late Victorian silver chatelaine, fitted with notecase, scissors, tape measure, pencil and incomplete needlecase.
£200–240/$290–350 G(L)

B. Late Victorian silver chatelaine, fitted with notecase, scissors, pincushion, pencil and needlecase.
£460–520/$660–740 G(L)

Item A is less ornate than Item B, and the needlecase is incomplete, which would explain the lower price. The individual items on each piece are probably worth more if sold separately, but the suspension piece would be rendered valueless on its own.

Silver nutmeg grater, by Peter and Ann Bateman, crested, damaged, 1¾in (4.5cm) wide, 1oz. Although this nutmeg grater is damaged, it is still of value because it is by Peter and Ann Bateman.
£250–300/$360–440 S(O)

◄ **Silver-plated Egyptian revival tea kettle,** 19thC, 12½in (32cm) high. Tea urns came in all shapes and sizes. Although they can be unusual and decorative, they have not been very popular with collectors and as a consequence they are not expensive to buy.
£220–260/$320–380 DD

Silver wine funnel, by George Burrows, with a pierced bowl and beaded edge, maker's mark, London 1876, 4¾in (12cm) long. Late 18thC funnels were made in two parts – a bowl and a funnel. Where the two pieces join there would have been a piece of muslin to help strain any sediment. It is very rare to find a funnel with an intact piece of muslin.
£300–350/$450–500 TMA

Child's silver whistle rattle, with eight bells and a coral teether, Birmingham 1883, 5¾in (14.5cm) long. When buying rattles, the silver must be crisp and unworn (difficult with a child's use!). There must be no bells missing or any damage. The marks must be good. Often they are marked on the edge of the ferrule next to the coral – this becomes broken with use and the marks disappear. 18thC rattles are of the greatest value.
£300–350/$450–500 TMA

George II three-bottle inkstand, with ink, pounce pot, sander and two pen rests, on a rectangular base with gadroon border, raised on four feet, 1791, 6in (15cm) wide. 18thC inkstands had glass bottles with silver collars and detachable silver tops. Check that all the parts match and fit together properly. Any damage or replacements will reduce the value.
£380–440/$575–650 TMA

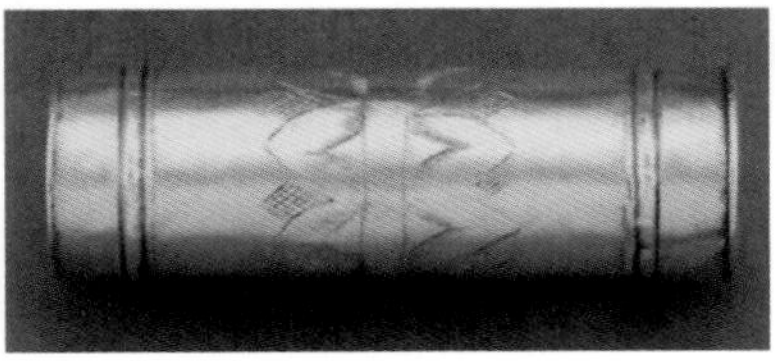

Silver nutmeg grater, with lozenge-engraved central band, the detachable cover with a flower motif, initialled to base, monogram, c1700, 3in (7.5cm) high. The fact that this is apparently unmarked has reduced the value. Similar marked graters can sell for £3,000–4,000/$4,400–5,800.
£475–575/$700–850 S(O)

Silver lemon strainer, by S. Herbert & Co, the concentrically pierced circular bowl with two scroll chiselled side handles, London 1763, 7½in (19cm) wide overall. Interesting small silver items such as this example, by a well-known maker, are very popular.
£300–360/$440–520 S(O)

The look without the price

The larger the set of matching coasters, the greater the value. A good, single coaster can fetch £400–500/ $580–720, a pair can fetch £1,200–1,500/ $1,750–2,200 and four can reach £3,000–4,000/ $4,400–5,800.

Silver wine coaster, by Robert Hennell, crested, with a pierced gallery decorated with floral medallions, tied foliate garlands and gadroon edging, London 1793, 4¾in (12cm) diam.
£450–500
$650–720 Bea(E)

Sheffield-plated wine cooler, with twin crest and motto, liner missing, double sun maker's mark, possibly Matthew Boulton or Mappin Bros, 10¼in (26cm) high. This single wine cooler is missing its liner but is, however, Sheffield plate and would make an imposing flower vase. Had it been one of a matching pair with original linings the value would be much higher.
£475–575/$700–850 S(O)

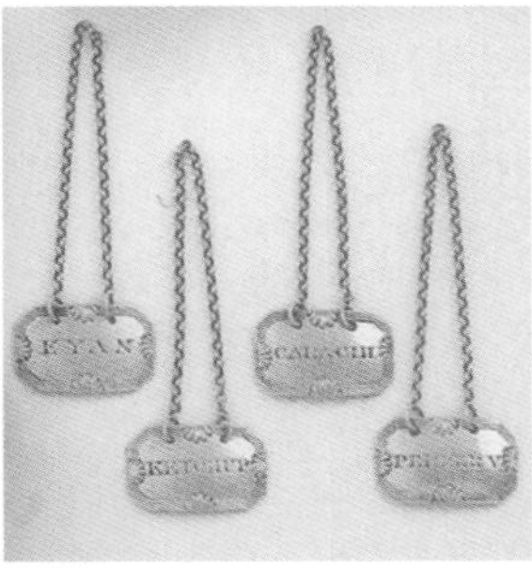

Four silver sauce labels, with canted corners and reeded and shell borders, incised Ketchup, Pepper V, Carachi and Kyan, maker's mark, c1800. Early 18thC ketchups were composed of anchovies, walnuts and mushrooms as opposed to the Ketchup we know today. On a set of four cut-glass bottles these labels would possibly add 10 to 20 per cent to the price of the bottles.
£600–650/$870–950 P(L)

Glass

It is not difficult to find glass that costs less than £1,000/$1,450. Many items which can be bought for only £100–500/$145–725 will make happy additions to any collection.

Glass is still relatively cheap in comparison with other collecting fields. One reason for this is that glass is still considered by some as a new subject for collecting, another is that the majority of people do not value it. Glass is utilitarian – to them a glass given away with petrol is much the same as an early wine glass or a Venini vase.

For those who are attracted to glass there is so much to choose from. The art of collecting, however, is deciding what really fascinates you and concentrating on buying the best you can afford. It is not quantity that matters but quality and there is plenty of quality available.

If damage does not offend you, buying glass that is not perfect is a way of building a collection that has little monetary value but huge value aesthetically. Let me illustrate this from my own collection. One item is a jug engraved by one of the great 19th-century Bohemian engravers, the lip of which is broken and stapled together. It is damaged but the engraving is wonderful. Another piece is an early 18th-century German goblet engraved and gilded to the highest standard but with a silver-gilt foot to replace the one broken perhaps 150 years ago.

The illustrations presented here show items that are excellent value for money. They also demonstrate that for those on a limited budget, glass is one field that can be explored quite freely. Those new to collecting glass should be able to take from these pages enough ideas to develop their own collections quite satisfactorily. **Brian Watson**

Baskets, Bowls & Dishes

Glass tea caddy bowl, with swags and lenses, c1830, 4½in (11.5cm) high. Tea caddy bowls were used to mix different blends of imported teas. They are becoming increasingly sought-after and can be attractively displayed with the tea caddy boxes with which they originally belonged.
£55–60/$80–90 JHa

Five Edwardian glass finger bowls, 3¼in (8.5cm) diam. Finger bowls have a greater value if found in complete sets of six or more, and can be attractive additions to the dining table. A set of six in perfect condition could cost £100–120/$145–175.
£60–70/$90–100 SWO

► **Cranberry glass salt,** c1900, 2½in (6.5cm) diam. This is probably one of a pair which may have had a plated metal holder. The condition of cranberry glass is important to collectors and any damage will reduce the price.
£70–80/$100–115 GRI

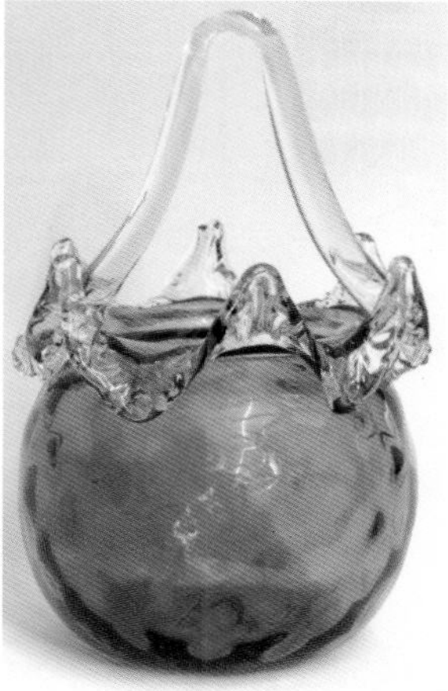

Dimpled cranberry glass basket, c1900, 6in (15cm) high. This piece is of very good quality. Always check for damage where the handle connects to the basket.
£115–125/$165–180 GRI ⊞

Cranberry glass comport, c1900, 6in (15cm) diam. The crimped top and clear knop add interest to this comport and make it more desirable than the common plainer examples.
£120–135/$175–195 GRI ⊞

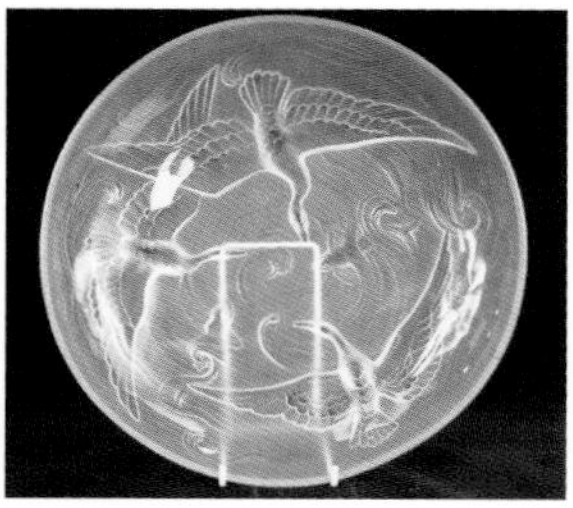

Verlys glass bowl, moulded with swans and carp in swirling water, signed to the centre, 1930s, 13¾in (35cm) diam.
£140–170/$200–250 SWO

► **Cranberry glass bonbon dish,** c1910, 6in (15cm) diam. These elegant bonbon or sweetmeat dishes can still be found by the resourceful collector. Always check the colour of cranberry glass as modern or reproduction pieces are often lighter in colour and lack the warmth and richness of the genuine article.
£115–130/$165–190 GRI ⊞

◄ **Glass bowl,** cut with diamonds and stars, c1830, 10in (25.5cm) wide. Diamond- and star-cut patterns were popular on this type of glass throughout the Georgian and Victorian periods. Chips are most likely to occur on the rim and may halve the value.
£125–140
$180–200 JHa ⊞

Verlys glass

Originally set up in 1920 to produce headlights for vehicles, the Société Holophane Français based in Rouen, northern France, expanded into making art glass vases and bowls, and established a department for these products which they named Verlys. Initially they made blown vessels with several layers of glass, smooth on the outside with internal decoration. From 1933 onwards they focussed on high quality press-moulded glass.

They produced clear, frosted, opalescent and coloured items with designs typical of Lalique-style glass of the 1930s – plants, flowers, birds, fish and abstract geometrical patterns. Each year they produced a catalogue with new designs. Their production normally has a moulded signature 'Verlys France' or 'Verlys Made in France'.

In 1935 they established 'Verlys of America' with a glassworks in Newark, Ohio. Moulds were supplied from France for the Ohio works, and the same items were made in France and in the USA, although not all the French designs were shared with the American works. Production in both France and the USA declined during the war, as the company focussed increasingly in industrial products.

The Verlys range was progressively abandoned in both countries from 1940 until it ceased altogether in 1951–52.

Lalique frosted and clear glass Jamaique *cendrier*, etched 'R. Lalique France', pre-1945, 5in (12.5cm) diam.
£190–230/$275–330 G(L)

Pair of cranberry glass preserve dishes, with petal edges and clear glass frills, probably by Thomas Webb, c1910, 5½in (14cm) diam. This is a good quality piece of cranberry glass in good condition and by a major glass maker so will always fetch a good price.
£270–300/$390–440 GRI

Clichy blue and white striped glass basket, French, 1845–50, 8in (20.5cm) high.
£270–300/$390–440 Del

Irish glass

Early 19th-century Irish cut glass has always held a fascination for English and American collectors. There is something about the style of cutting, deep and varied, which attracts. Irish glass also appeals because of its weight which is greater than that of most contemporary Continental pieces of similar design. Irish cut glass equates with quality as it was made originally for the best tables. It still commands good prices for the best pieces.

Piggin

A piggin is an Irish dish with an upright handle on one side of its rim. Sometimes bowls with two handles might be called piggins. The original piggin was a wooden milking pail with one stave extended above the rim to use as a handle. Glass piggins, which are usually quite small, were probably used for whipped creams, sauces, etc.

► **Cut-glass pedestal bowl,** with a hobnail-cut band and circular base, Irish, early 19thC, 8½in (21.5cm) diam. The quality of Irish glass makes it popular with collectors everywhere. This piece, with its double-stepped bowl and fine cutting, is an excellent example.
£450–550
$650–800 G(L)

► **Pair of diamond-cut glass bowls,** with fan-cut handles, Irish, c1815, 6in (15cm) diam. The fine cutting on these piggin bowls would make them an attractive addition to any early cut-glass collection.
£550–600/$800–870 Del

Candlesticks & Lustres

Glass candlestick, with facet-cut stem, c1770, 10in (25.5cm) high. 18thC glass candlesticks in good condition are becoming increasingly difficult to find. Examples with facet-cut stems tend to be less popular than those with balustroid, opaque or air-twist stems which can be worth three or four times more.
£450–500/$650–720 Del ⊞

Further reading

Miller's Collecting Glass: The Facts at Your Fingertips, Miller's Publications, 2000

The look without the price

These are beautiful, but having different sconces means they are not a pair, only the jasperware bases are the same. The damage to one is quite extensive and clearly some of the drops are not original. If they were in perfect condition and a pair they would be worth perhaps three to four times this amount.

Two Regency glass lustre candlesticks, the cut-glass sconces with serrated flat and shaped borders suspending festoons of four cut-glass drops, above a star-cut burst platform suspending further beaded drops on hobnail-cut capitals, the brass socles with friezes of blue jasperware, 13in (33cm) high.
£760–900/$1,100–1,300 RBB ⚒

◄ **Pair of green glass table lustres,** each decorated with a band of enamel panels, painted with flowers within gilt overlaid borders, hung with clear-cut glass drops, Bohemian, late 19th/early 20thC, 12in (30.5cm) high.
£850–1,000
$1,250–1,500 RTo ⚒

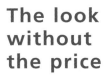

◄ **Pair of glass lustre candlesticks,** c1820, 7in (18cm) high. Always check that the drops match the main part of the lustre in both style and colour as later additions will reduce the value, however, new wires are acceptable to improve the appearance of the drops. The larger the lustre, the greater the value and these are a particularly fine example.
£850–900
$1,250–1,300 Del ⊞

Candlesticks

Eighteenth-century candlesticks are very desirable in pairs but less so as singles. This means that a single example should be proportionately much cheaper than a pair. Their shape, whether of the more common faceted form or of the other classic designs – baluster, air-twist etc – is attractive to many people. This is a good field for anyone who wants to put together a representative collection of 18th-century and early 19th-century glass without spending too lavishly.

Carafes & Decanters

Pair of Georgian glass carafes, of bulbous form, with split-cut bands, facet-cut shoulders and three-ring necks, one with slight rim chip, 5¼in (13.5cm) high. These are the most desirable of carafes and at this price they would be snapped up by the trade. A small rim chip can be polished out and a pair like this could easily command £120/$175.
£30–35/$45–50 TMA

Glass carafe, engraved with ferns, c1860, 6in (15cm) high. Carafes are generally robust, making them usable as well as affordable and attractive. Fern engraving was popular throughout the Victorian period.
£50–55/$75–80 JHa

Pillar and slice-cut glass carafe, c1840, 6in (15cm) high. Collectors look for different styles of cutting and the application of neck rings, while non-collectors will be attracted by the practicality and value of glass carafes.
£55–60/$80–90 JHa

◄ **Glass 'leather bottle' carafe,** late 19thC, 8in (20.5cm) high. This is a Powell design which is also known as 'rat tail'. This one has lost a bit of tail up to the frill. It could be called 'leather bottle' because of the shape, which is like a leather bottle of the 15th/16thC.
£100–110/$45–160 JHa

► **Pair of glass carafes,** c1820, 6in (15cm) high. Always try to find a matching pair, although they are becoming increasingly difficult to find. This does not add significantly to the value, but may well do so in the future.
£110–120/$160–175 Del

Olive green glass mallet-shaped bottle, probably 18thC, 10¼in (26cm) high. This has good colour which is always important with early bottles.
£110–140/$160–200 WW

Neck rings

Neck rings on 18th- and early 19th-century decanters were applied separately then moulded with a tool. The join in the neck ring was often carelessly made and could look like a crack. The neck rings on many middle to late 19th-century decanters are integral parts of the decanters. If a damaged neck has been replaced, it may be possible to feel a join on the inner surface.

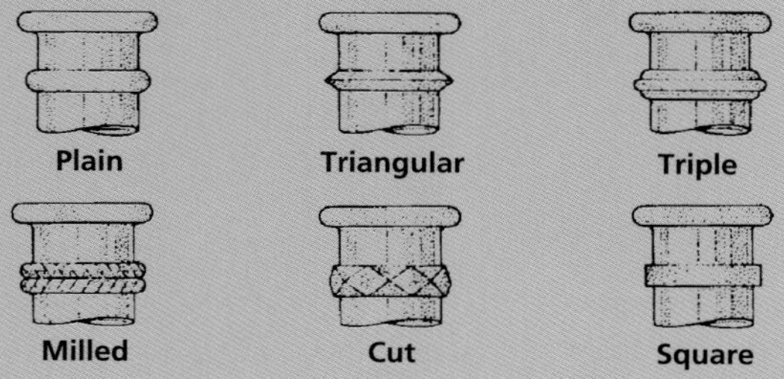

Cranberry glass liqueur decanter, Bohemian, c1900, 10in (25.5cm) high. One would expect to see a cranberry glass stopper in this decanter, so this clear glass one may well be matched.
£170–190/$250–275 GRI ⊞

Diamond flute-cut glass decanter, c1810, 10in (25.5cm) high. These came originally in sets of four in frames. They would be for Brandy, Rum, Hollands (Dutch gin) and Shrub (a sort of cordial made in the house which could be of different fruit bases).
£145–160/$210–230 JHa ⊞

Pair of facet-cut glass decanters, with facet-cut and compressed knop necks and star-cut bases, one with plated whisky label, 1820–30, 10½in (26.5cm) high. The plated whisky label is unlikely to belong to these. Whisky was not a drink for gentlemen until about 1840 – these are earlier in date.
£170–180/$250–260 TMA

► **Strawberry and diamond-cut glass decanter,** c1825, 9in (23cm) high. This is a particularly attractive piece with three symmetrical applied rings to the neck and stylized cutting. The stopper is well-proportioned to the decanter.
£200–220/$290–320 JHa ⊞

Glass hock decanter, probably Bohemian, c1895, 12in (30.5cm) high. This style of decanter can also be found in blue, green and amber glass, all of which have equal value.
£200–220/$290–320 GRI

Gilt-decorated overlaid glass decanter, decorated with gilt scrolling foliage on a white ground, raised on three feet, stopper missing, slight rubbing to neck, c1900, 7¼in (18.5cm) high. A small amount of rubbing to the gilt is acceptable and will not affect the value significantly. Severe rubbing and fading can reduce the price by 30 per cent. This piece would have fetched up to 50 per cent more with the original stopper and in better condition.
£200–250/$290–360 WW

► **Blue glass quart size decanter,** with gilt label for Brandy, c1790, 11in (28cm) high. Similar decanters for Gin, Shrub and Hollands can be found. They were also produced in green glass, but these are less desirable than the blue. The correct stopper can often be identified by noting that the gilt letter matched with the label on the decanter, for example B and Brandy. The value is significantly reduced by non-matching stopper and badly-rubbed gilt decoration.
£320–350/$465–500 Del

Further reading

Miller's Glass of the '20s & '30s: A Collector's Guide, Miller's Publications, 1999

Pair of cut-glass club decanters and stoppers, cut with panels of diamonds below a faceted triple-ring neck and mushroom stopper, on a star-cut base, minor chips, c1840, 11in (28cm) high. One would expect these items to have chips all over so be suspicious if the piece is not chipped at all. These are typical common-use cut decanters and cannot possibly be without some damage. A top price would be £400/$580.
£270–300/$390–440 S(O)

Stoppers

It is difficult to guarantee that a stopper is original except on Victorian clear glass decanters, which often have matching numbers etched on the stopper and decanter neck. Coloured glass decanters may have the number painted on the stopper and underside of the decanter. Generally a stopper is acceptable when it is the same cut and colour as the decanter, and of the right style and period. Broken stopper pegs can be replaced by glueing on a replacement, then grinding and polishing the whole peg. A very thin radial line will indicate where this has been done.

The look without the price

Engraved and cut-glass armorial decanter and stopper, cut with a circular panel and engraved with the arms of Sir George Griffin (1784–1878) of Pencraig, Anglesey, cut overall with raised diamonds below a step-cut neck, with a star-cut base and ball stopper, some typical chips, c1820, 10¼in (26cm) high.
£700–850/$1,000–1,250 S(O)

This is a very good example of a luxury cut-glass decanter of this period. A pair would be worth maybe three times as much. This is the ideal piece for anyone wanting an attractive decanter to use.

◀ **Glass decanter,** with applied turquoise studs and rim and finely engraved floral festoons, after a design by Joseph Keller, Stevens & Williams, Stourbridge, c1870, 11in (28cm) high.
£350–380/$500–565 LHo

Locate the source

The source of each illustration in Miller's can be found by checking the code letters below each caption with the Key to Illustrations, pages 286–290.

Joseph Keller

During the second half of the 19th century, a number of Bohemian engravers came to this country. Among the most important were Frederick E. Kny and William Fritsche, who worked for Thomas Webb & Sons at Stourbridge and, slightly later, Joseph Keller who worked in Birmingham. In about 1885 he produced *A Collection of Patterns for the Use of Glass Decorators* and thereby influenced the designs on glass vessels until WWI.

Semi-ship's glass decanter, c1820, 9in (23cm) high. Ship's decanters have wide, flat bases. They are desirable as they do not fall over. A semi-ship's decanter is similar in shape but not as wide. These decanters are always more expensive than contemporary ones of a more conventional design.
£450–500/$650–720 Del

Glass liqueur set, comprising a club-shaped decanter and stopper and six glasses, late 19thC, decanter 3½in (9cm) diam. This is an interesting design and is superb quality.
£780–930/$1,125–1,350 S

Drinking Glasses

Lens-cut dessert wine glass, c1890, 4½in (11.5cm) high. This type of glass is likely to have been part of a suite of various sized glasses. Sets of late Victorian glass can still be found and are both affordable and practical.
£7–8/$10–12 JHa ⊞

Miller's compares...

A. Slice-cut wine glass, c1820, 5in (12.5cm) high.
£10–15/$15–20 JHa ⊞

B. Slice-cut wine glass, engraved with swags including fouled anchors, c1820, 5in (12.5cm) high.
£70–80/$100–115 JHa ⊞

Item A is attractive but plain, whereas the naval interest on Item B makes it more popular, demanding the higher price.

Green wine glass, on a clear stem, Continental, c1900, 5in (12.5cm) high. This style of wine glass was also produced in cranberry, Bristol Blue and amethyst. The blue glasses cost £35–45/$50–65, and the rarer amethyst ones £40–45/$60–65.
£23–25/$33–35 JHa ⊞

White wine glass, acid-etched with passion flowers, c1890, 5in (12.5cm) high. The quality of the acid etching will enhance the value of this glass.
£27–30/$35–45 JHa ⊞

Engraved hock glass, Austrian, c1900, 8in (20.5cm) high. These are fine quality, elegant glasses. A set of six would be worth £300–350/$450–500.
£27–30/$35–45 JHa ⊞

Cut-glass port glass, with knop stem, c1820, 4in (10cm) high. The value of this type of glass is enhanced by good quality cutting and intricate patterns. The workmanship exemplified in the radial cutting to the underside of the foot is admirable, but not reflected in the price.
£27–30/$35–45 JHa ⊞

Lens-cut champagne saucer, late 19thC, 4in (10cm) high. Champagne saucers are particularly sought-after in sets of six or more, and are especially desirable if found with hollow stems. At present, champagne saucers are less popular than flutes.
£27–30/$35–45 JHa ⊞

Straight-sided pub rummer, c1890, 5½in (14cm) high. The different bowl shapes, styles of stems, facet cutting and knop formations of these rummers all appeal to collectors.
£30–35/$45–50 CAL ⊞

◄ **Frosted and cut-glass goblet,** c1850, 6in (15cm) high. The value of frosted and cut glass can be increased by more than half when decorated with patterns such as Water Lily found on some types of Richardson's glass.
£30–35
$45–50 JHa ⊞

Glass rummer, with a facet-cut stem, c1890, 6½in (16.5cm) high. Pub rummers were used extensively in Victorian pubs and taverns. They were produced in large quantities and many have survived, making them affordable. This, and their usefulness, makes them good value for money.
£35–40/$50–60 CAL ⊞

Cut glass

Lead glass is the most suitable type for cutting. Invented in England and Ireland, it was most fashionable during the late 18th and early 19th centuries. The object is held above an iron or stone wheel which cuts deep facets or grooves, which are then polished to create a brilliant sparkling surface.

Jelly glass, with bell bowl, c1820, 4¼in (11cm) high. The enormous range of jelly glasses makes them infinitely collectable. They would have been used to serve sweet dishes containing cream, wine and sugar to refresh the palate between courses.
£35–40/$50–60 JHa ⊞

Green wine glass, early 19thC, 5in (12.5cm) high. Although this example is a little plain, green wine glasses come in a variety of bowl shapes, sizes, cutting styles and knop formations. They were produced from the late Georgian period through to the Victorian era, the earlier pieces commanding higher prices.
£40–45/$60–65 JHa ⊞

OXO-engraved wine glass, with facet-cut stem, c1840, 5in (12.5cm) high. OXO engraving is very basic – normally a single band around the rim of the glass. Those with facet-cut stems are not particularly sought-after, hence the low price.
£50–60
$75–90 CAL ⊞

◄ **Pair of wine glasses,** each with geometrical cutting to the bowl and a glory star cut under the foot, c1880, 5¼in (13.5cm) high. A pair of good quality cut wine glasses will always be attractive to collectors and non-collectors alike. The fine cutting on the stem is particularly beautiful.
£50–55/$75–80 BrW ⊞

Types of drinking glass

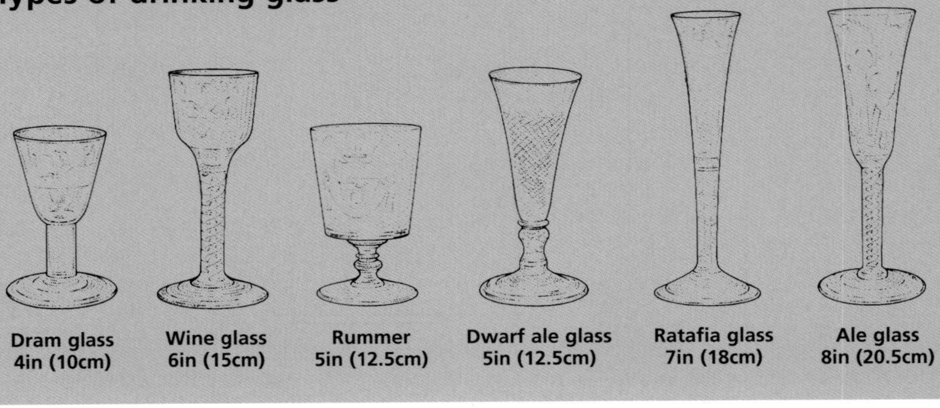

Dram glass 4in (10cm) | **Wine glass 6in (15cm)** | **Rummer 5in (12.5cm)** | **Dwarf ale glass 5in (12.5cm)** | **Ratafia glass 7in (18cm)** | **Ale glass 8in (20.5cm)**

Pair of cut wine glasses, c1900, 5in (12.5cm) high.
£55–60/$80–90 JHa ⊞

Shaded cranberry beer glass, c1930, 7in (18cm) high. Cranberry glass is collectable but plain shapes like this perhaps less so. Also, late pieces are less desirable than the decorative 19thC ones.
£60–70/$90–100 GRI ⊞

Dwarf ale glass, engraved with hops and barley, c1810, 5in (12.5cm) high. Collectors look for the subtle differences in the style of dwarf ale glasses made between the mid-18th and early 19thC. The height of the bowl, the subject and quality of the engraving, the knop formations and foot shape are all points to look out for.
£55–60/$80–90 JHa ⊞

Pair of intaglio-engraved tumblers, c1910, 4in (10cm) high.
£60–70/$90–100 JHa ⊞

Cranberry glass

Cranberry glass was probably originally produced in the early 18th century in Bohemia, although its heyday was in the late 19th/early 20th centuries, when it reached Britain, France, Belgium, Bavaria and the USA. Known originally as a type of ruby glass, cranberry glass derives its name from New England, USA, where cranberries are grown. The colour is produced with a thin layer of ruby over an inner layer of clear glass. Early pieces were comparatively simple in style, but later wares were often decorated with trailing, enamelling or overlay, in which the outer layer of glass is cut through to reveal the colour beneath. Some of the most collectable pieces today are British (notably Stourbridge).

◄ **Wrythen-moulded dwarf ale glass,** c1800, 4in (10cm) high. Collectors of wrythen-moulded dwarf ale glasses look for differences in the moulding and whether the bowl is full or part moulded. A folded foot would be found on earlier examples, and would fetch a higher price.
£65–70/$95–100 CAL ⊞

Amber wine glass, c1840, 5in (12.5cm) high. Amber and yellow glass are desirable colours.
£65–75/$95–110 JHa

► **Indented vaseline glass tumbler,** Stourbridge, c1890, 5in (12.5cm) high.
£70–80/$100–115 JHa

Coloured glass

The range of colours produced increased considerably during the 19th century. The best amber glass, was derived from gold, though not, as popular tradition has it, from the gold sovereigns that factory managers would fling into the pots of molten glass. Other colours were achieved by the addition, to the molten glass, or metal, of various amounts of metallic oxides, blue being the easiest to achieve, and yellow and orange the most complex.

Vaseline glass

Vaseline glass, so called because its colour resembles that of the ointment, was one of the types of coloured glass developed in Europe and the United States during the late 19th century. Glass workers had by then realized that they could experiment with their material and produced designs and colour which would have appeared completely revolutionary at the start of the century.

Glass rummer, with moulded flutes and engraved with hops and barley, c1800, 5¼in (13.5cm) high. This good example of a Georgian rummer is characterized by the moulded flutes. The fine quality engraving can increase the price by up to 40 per cent. Victorian rummers often retain the same style of engraving, but the moulded flutes would be replaced with scallop cutting to the base of the bowl.
£85–95/$125–140 BrW

Set of four green wine flutes and a set of eight clear wine glasses, with engraved borders, 19thC, 5in (12.5cm) high. These wine flutes do not have the rich, dark green glass which appeals to collectors, and the band of engraving on the wine glasses is very basic.
£75–90/$110–130 G(L)

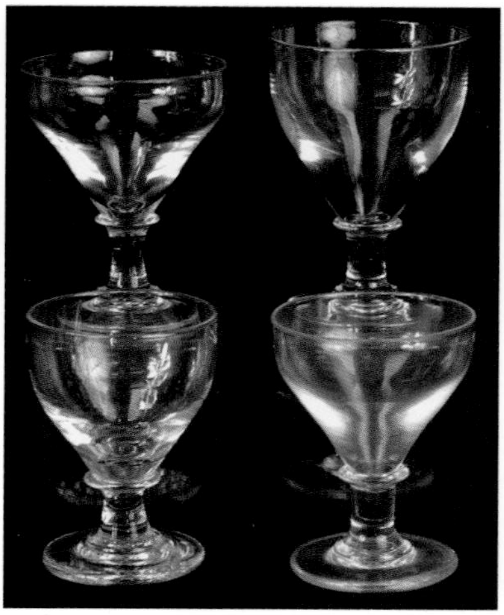

Four glass rummers, mid-19thC, largest 6in (15cm) high. Each glass rummer is unique due to the hand-blown features of the glass. This, with their practicality and value, makes them appealing to collectors.
£75–90/$110–130 each SWO

Pair of goblets, with flat-cut panels, c1900, 6in (15cm) high. This style of goblet is more likely to be purchased as a usable item than as part of a collection. Good quality engraving can increase the price by 40–50 per cent.
£90–100/$130–145 RUSK ⊞

Glass, with ogee bowl on a plain stem and folded foot, c1730, 5in (12.5cm) high. These glasses are often one of the first purchased when starting a collection of 18thC drinking glasses. Plain and elegant, with a folded foot, and approaching 300 years of age, it represents excellent value for money.
£110–120/$160–175 JHa ⊞

Double-walled trick tumbler, c1820, 3½in (9cm) high. This type of glass is also known as deceptive glass or toastmaster's glass – deceptive because it does not hold as much alcohol as it appears to, and popular with toastmasters who were anxious to remain sober until all the toasts had been made.
£90–100/$130–145 Del ⊞

► **Jelly glass,** with ribbed pan top and a ribbed, domed and folded foot, c1750, 3½in (9cm) high. A fine example of an early jelly glass. The moulded ribbing, pan top bowl and domed and folded foot date it to the mid-18thC, making it more sought-after than the widely-available Victorian examples.
£120–130/$175–190 JHa ⊞

Short ale glass, the bowl engraved with hops and one barley head, c1780, 6in (15cm) high. The value of this glass lies in the quality of the engraving and the folded foot. A plain glass on a conical foot would only be worth half as much.
£100–110/$145–160 BrW ⊞

◄ **Pair of goblets,** engraved with ferns, c1880, 6in (15cm) high. Engraved goblets are always popular, and quality fern engraving is sought-after on many other items such as jugs or vases.
£115–125/$165–180 LHo ⊞

The look without the price

Georgian wine glass, with a conical bowl and an air-twist stem, 6½in (16.5cm) high.
£180–220
$260–320 RBB

The bowl on this glass was discoloured and needed cleaning. A Georgian glass in perfect condition would normally be double the price.

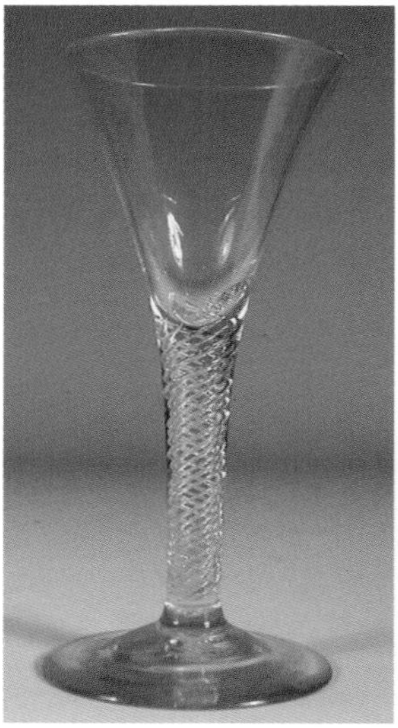

◄ **Wine glass,** with tapering conical bowl on an air-twist column, c1760, 6½in (16.5cm) high. This item carries a low price, possibly because the foot has been trimmed and polished, which reduces the value a little. **£140–170/$200–250** WW

Soda glass, with bell bowl and double-series opaque-twist stem, Dutch, c1765, 6in (15cm) high. 18thC Dutch glass has many similar features to English glass including opaque-twist stems and bell-shaped bowls. However, it is considerably lighter and not as highly-prized by the discerning collector. **£135–150/$195–220** JHa

Four glass rummers, c1850, largest 5½in (14cm) high. These glass rummers appear similar, but have unique hand-blown features which appeal to collectors. **£160–190/$230–275** SWO

◄ **Dram glass,** possibly Scandinavian, c1770, 3¾in (9.5cm) high. The design of the hollow stem looks more Scandinavian than English. Such glasses appear as schnapps glasses in catalogues of Norwegian and Danish glass. **£160–175/$230–255** BrW

Pair of engraved and gilded rummers, Bohemian, 1880–1900, 4¾in (12cm) high. **£180–200/$250–300** BrW

Pair of bucket rummers, engraved with fruiting vine, wheat ears and corn stooks, on plain stems with domed circular bases, c1840, 5½in (14cm) high. Rummers with bucket-shaped bowls are particularly popular with collectors. Engraving adds to their appeal and value.
£190–230/$275–330 TMA

Pair of rummers, with engraved zig-zag bands, on square lemon squeezer feet, c1810, 5¼in (13cm) high. These rummers are easily distinguished by the style of their feet and their similarity to lemon squeezers of the same period. Square lemon squeezer feet are also found on other styles of glass such as wine or ale flutes and are always a desirable feature. Look out for chips to the corners of the feet, or small feet which may have been trimmed or polished to hide chips.
£200–250/$300–360 WW

Georgian wine glass, with bell bowl and white enamel-twist stem, 6½in (16.5cm) high. This type of twist stem is also known as an opaque twist. The style of the twist and the shape of the bowl make it one of the more common designs to survive. A cloudy bowl reduces the value and makes this affordable piece an excellent starting point for new collectors.
£190–230/$275–330 RBB

Miller's compares...

A. Wine glass, with funnel-shaped bowl, on an opaque-twist stem, 1760–70, 5¼in (13cm) high.
£220–260/$320–380 WW

Both of these glasses have double-series opaque-twist stems and are of a similar date. Item B, however, is a cordial glass which is much rarer. Collectors look for the unusual and examples of cordial glasses are in limited supply and are always expensive.

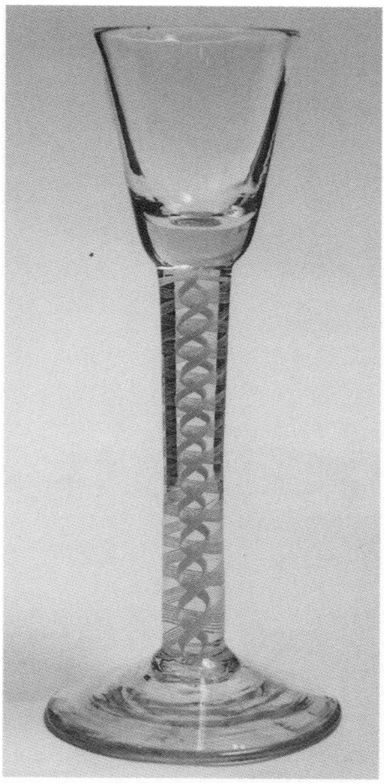

B. Cordial glass, the round funnel bowl with a solid base, on a double-series opaque-twist stem and conical foot, c1765, 6¼in (16cm) high.
£750–850/$1,100–1,250 GS

Four tall glasses, with fluted trumpet bowls, c1840, 6¾in (17cm) high. Fluted glasses were popular throughout the Victorian period for both wine and champagne, the latter being distinguished by their taller bowls.
£190–230/$275–330 SWO

Air-twist stemmed glasses

Air-twists were formed by denting a gather of molten glass and placing another gather on top, thereby creating air bubbles. The pattern made by the air was elongated and twisted by drawing and rotating the molten glass until it assumed the length and breadth needed for a stem.

Air-twist stemmed glasses proliferated between 1750 and 1760 as craftsmen sought to find a way to produce drinking glasses that were both light in weight and sufficiently decorative to have consumer appeal. Early air-twists were made in two pieces, the twist extending into the bowl.

Miller's compares...

A. Ruby glass beaker, Bohemian, c1840, 5in (12.5cm) high.
£250–300/$360–440 DORO

B. Ruby flashed tumbler, Bohemian, c1840, 4½in (11.5cm) high.
£320–350/$460–500 Del

These two beakers are similar in date, shape and the fact that they are both plain glass flashed with a thin layer of pink glass. This differs from cranberry glass which is usually just pink glass and often from the period 1880–1920. The more complex cutting of Item B makes it more interesting to collectors and therefore it commanded a higher price than Item A.

◄ **Set of five jelly glasses,** engraved with egg-and-tulip decoration, one foot trimmed, c1800, 6in (15cm) high. If one piece in a set has a smaller foot resulting from foot trim, this will reduce the overall value.
£280–320
$410–460 Som

Wine glass, with bell bowl and double-series opaque-twist stem, c1765, 6in (15cm) high.
£250–280/$360–410 JHa

Goblet, probably Lauenstein, engraved with a princely crown and the monogram FL, possibly for Friedrich Ludwig, the eldest son of George II, c1750, 6¼in (16cm) high. This goblet is not marked. The only sure sign is an engraved lion on the pontil.
£270–300/$400–440 BrW

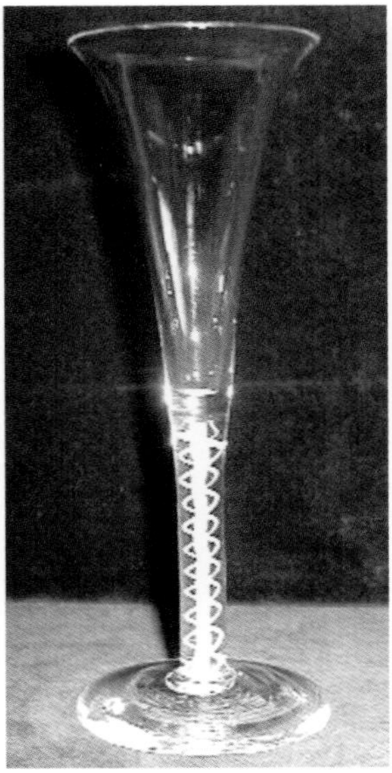

Glass wine flute, with double-series opaque-twist stem, c1760, 7¾in (19.5cm) high. Wine flutes are always popular and make an elegant contribution to any collection. They are less common than wine glasses but are of similar value.
£280–320/$410–460 BrW

Green rummer, c1800, 6in (15cm) high. 18thC coloured glass is rarer than colourless glass. However, fewer collectors look for it because most pieces are fairly indistinguished in shape. Those who have concentrated on this area have built collections of great interest for less money than traditional ones.
£400–450/$580–650 Del

Encased ruby goblet, decorated in gilding with formal scrollwork borders, slight rubbing to gilding, probably Bohemian, late 19thC, 15in (38cm) high.
£350–400/$500–580 S(O)

Sweetmeat glass, with lipped ogee bowl, moulded pedestal stem with diamonds on the shoulders, on a domed and folded foot, c1750, 6½in (16.5cm) high.
£380–420/$560–620 JHa

Sweetmeat glasses

Sweetmeat glasses were used to serve dry sweetmeats (chocolates, dried fruits etc), as opposed to desserts such as trifle and jelly, which were eaten from jelly glasses.

◄ **Engraved goblet and cover,** the round funnel bowl with an oval panel engraved and polished with a naked man and a hound flanked by birds and foliage, with German inscription to the reverse, on a baluster stem and broad conical foot, the cover engraved with scrolling foliage beneath a faceted finial, tip of finial chipped, Bohemian, mid-18thC, 9½in (24cm) high. Such goblets are excellent value in the UK. In Germany they would command a higher price even with a chipped finial. As much as £600/$870 might be achieved, assuming the cover actually belongs, and this is a good example of Bohemian engraving of the 1725–50 period. Most English collectors avoid such pieces, which means they ignore the possibility of owning some very fine pieces of 18thC glass.
£400–500/$580–720 DN

Potsdam goblet, the bowl engraved with dancers, the bowl, knop and foot cut with bands of stylized leaves, crizzling, c1720, 7¼in (18.5cm) high. The crizzling on this piece makes it less desirable and cheaper. Even if it was completely clear it would not be as expensive as a comparable period English glass.
£400–480/$580–700 S(O)

The look without the price

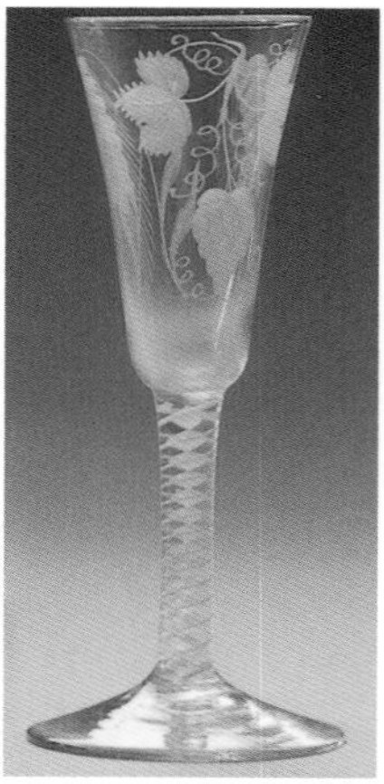

Pair of Georgian ale flutes, the bowls engraved with hops and barley, on double-series enamel-twist stems, 7½in (19cm) high.
£600–700/$870–1,000 RBB

Collecting ale glasses is a good area for those who do not have huge amounts of money to spend. There are three main groups: tall ales, short ales and dwarf ales. They all have bowls large enough to carry interesting engraving or moulding and ale glasses appear throughout the 18th and 19th centuries. A fine collection entirely of ale glasses could be built up over a number of years.

Wine glass, the ogee bowl with basal moulding, with multi-spiral air-twist stem, on a domed foot, c1750, 6½in (16.5cm) high. The moulding to the base of the ogee-shaped bowl and the domed foot make this glass worth 30–40 per cent more than a plain glass with a conical foot.
£500–550/$720–800 WMa

Wine glass, with engraved waisted bell bowl on a double-series mercury-twist stem and conical foot, c1755, 6¼in (16cm) high. The elegant shape of the bowl, the fine engraving and unusual stem make this a good example of a desirable wine glass which would enhance any collection.
£650–700
$950–1,000 BONN

Light baluster wine glass, the drawn trumpet bowl supported on a plain stem with two ball knops, on a conical foot, c1750, 7¼in (18.5cm) high. Light baluster and balustroid wine glasses of 1720–50 were made with many different and complex knop formations to the stem, and followed on from the heavy baluster goblets of the late 17th and early 18thC.
£800–1,000/$1,150–1,500 GS

Jugs

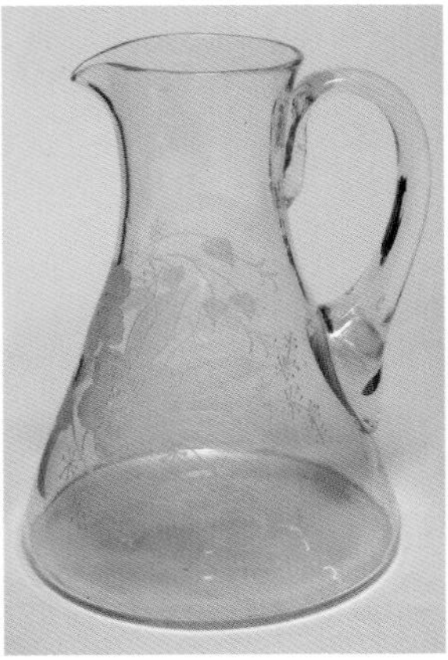

Glass cream jug, with acid-etched floral decoration, late 19thC, 6½in (16.5cm) high.
£70–80/$100–115 JHa ⊞

Glass jug, engraved with a fruiting vine, c1886, 8in (20.5cm) high. One of the signs of good quality engraving is when it extends behind the handle of the jug, and is possibly the signature of one of the better engravers of the period.
£130–145/$190–210 LHo ⊞

Handles on jugs

The method of fixing handles to jugs changed around 1860. Before that date handles were applied at the top first and secured at the bottom with an upward curl. Usually after 1860 the handle was applied at the bottom first, creating a large swelling, then drawn up to the top.

Diamond-cut glass cream jug, c1800, 4in (10cm) high. This Georgian cream jug illustrates the elegance of tableware from the period. It is an attractive piece, in good condition and free from any chips or defects.
£180–200/$250–300 Del ⊞

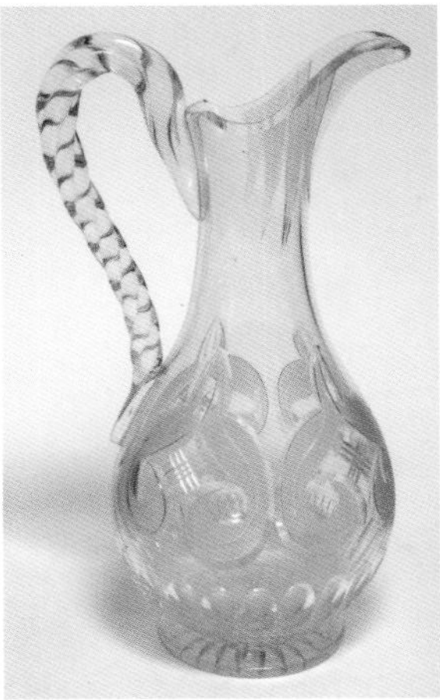

► **Cut- and frosted-glass jug,** with a rope-twist handle, c1860, 11in (28cm) high. The elegant shape of this jug and the style of the rope-twist handle almost certainly indicate that it was produced from one of the Stourbridge glassworks in the mid-19thC.
£200–220
$300–320 JHa ⊞

► **Glass water jug,** with simple moulded bands, c1830, 7in (18cm) high. Glass jugs of the late Georgian and early Victorian period were often more plain and simple in their form but still possess a unique attractiveness. One of the striking features of this type of jug is the applied loop handle with the upward curl. The handles should always be checked to ensure their detail is still intact. A useful tip for collectors is to gently tap the handle with a pen or pencil and listen for a ring – failure to achieve this may indicate a small defect or star crack at the point of application of the handle to the jug.
£225–250/$320–360 Del ⊞

Paperweights

Green glass dump, with flower spray inclusion and rising bubbles, c1860, 5½in (14cm) high. Although not possible to date exactly, these dumps were made from the mid-19thC through to the early 20thC. Glassmakers say that dark green ones were from Sunderland while the paler green ones such as this one were made at Nailsea, although huge numbers were made in the Castleford, Yorkshire area. Generally speaking dumps were not marked, although a few have an impressed mark. Traditionally they were thought to have been made by workers in their own time but the quality of these weights and the time they would have taken to produce question that theory.
£160–200/$230–300 JBL

The look without the price

This paperweight was probably made by Richardsons of Stourbridge c1912. However, the stopper is unlikely to be original as the majority of bottles were made with matching stoppers, although a few were made with one very simple cane. It is always advisable to question a bottle that does not have a clearly matching stopper. Stourbridge millefiori bottles with the correct stopper can range in price from £350–650/$500–950 depending on condition, number of rings, size and fineness of canes used.

Millefiori glass paperweight inkwell, with concentric rings of white, pink, red and blue canes, late 19thC, 5in (12.5cm) high.
£240–280/$350–400 G(L)

Clichy

The Clichy glassworks was originally founded at Sèvres, near Paris in 1838 but moved to Clichy, a suburb of Paris, in 1844. Between that date and 1885 the factory produced coloured glass of the highest quality. Clichy paperweights and vases with spirals of colour marvered into them are particularly sought after.

St Louis faceted flat bouquet glass paperweight, cut with a diced top and eight side printies, mid-19thC, 2½in (6.5cm) high. These are normally amber-flashed and ones that are not can be an inexpensive alternative. This one has four cane flowers and five green leaves. It is an interesting example of the St Louis use of a very restricted colour palette. In a wide variety of paperweights they constantly use four colours – chartreuse, salmon, red and royal blue with touches of white, the red being least used. These nosegays are used by both St Louis and Clichy and are hard to differentiate. The main differences to look for are the Clichy pastry mould canes and the St Louis colours and serrated-edge leaves.
£280–340/$400–500 B

Clichy concentric millefiori glass paperweight, with red, white, pink and blue canes on a translucent-green ground, c1850, 3¼in (8.5cm) high. The low price for this item is mainly due to three reasons. It is a late Clichy paperweight and these weights have rather flattened-out canes, the canes are not as carefully spaced, and they often do not have the popular 'rose' in the design. However, this is an interesting weight for a bargain hunter.
£500–600
$720–870 S(O)

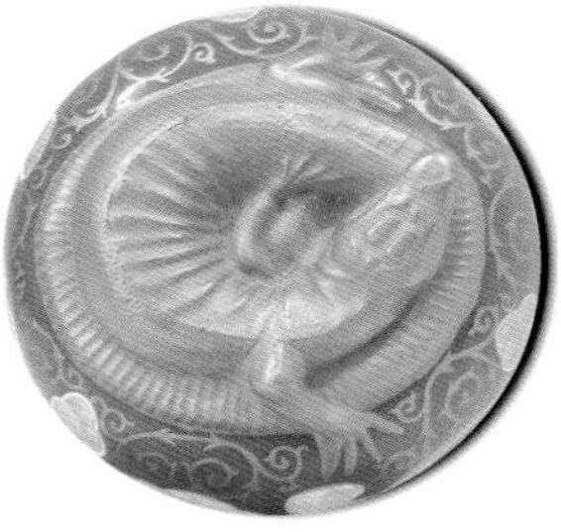

St Louis gilded lizard glass paperweight, No. 300, 1980, 3in (7.5cm) high. This is a modern version of the original antique and, while the word reproduction is not used in the paperweight world, both St Louis and Baccarat make good examples based on 19thC work. This is a beautiful weight and will be a good investment. There is a wide range of weights to be found on the lists of modern French makers.
£580–650/$850–950 SWB

Baccarat glass paperweight, enclosing a white double clematis with two rows of six striped petals around a stardust cane, on a stem with 11 serrated leaves, mid-19thC, 2¾in (7cm) high. Baccarat flowers without a garland are an excellent buy. This one fills the glass nicely – avoid examples with too much glass, conversely, avoid examples that have been over repolished resulting in the leaves 'falling' over the edge. Baccarat flowers with millefiori garlands are very beautiful, rather rare and can cost over £1,000/$1,500. However, there are some very good examples without a garland to be found, and it is possible to find a pretty dog rose in a rose or blue colour.
£580–700/$850–1,000 B

Miller's compares...

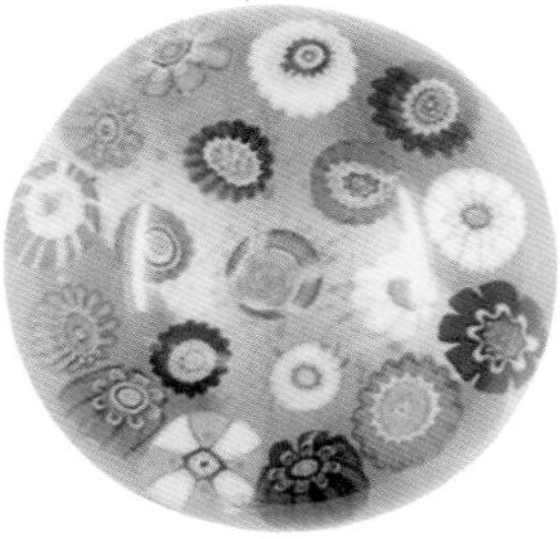

A. Clichy spaced millefiori glass paper-weight, the clear glass set with two concentric circles around a central rose, 19thC, 2¼in (6cm) diam.
£550–650/$800–950 B&L

B. Clichy spaced millefiori glass paperweight, with a pink and green rose above latticinio tubes, c1850, 1¾in (4.5cm) high.
£900–1,000
$1,300–1,500 S(O)

Item A is an excellent type of weight for a beginner. The clear glass is not as desirable as a muslin ground, however, with the pink rose cane in the centre and pink and white around the outer edge, this is very much worth buying. Item B, however, is considerabely more expensive due to the millefiori ground. It does also have a perfect Clichy 'rose' as its centre cane. Clichy roses are extremely popular among the international paperweight collecting community, and the existence of a Clichy rose in a paperweight makes it of immediate interest.

Baccarat glass paperweight, with interlaced trefoils, 1845–60, 3in (7.5cm) high. These types of weights are often priced at under £1,000/$1,500 as trefoils and Baccarat are not currently fashionable, with the result that some fine weights can be purchased by the alert collector. Without the coloured ground, prices are reduced. A good quality millefiori should be well-centred, fill the glass and have a pleasing colour balance.
£630–700/$900–1,000 SWB

St Louis glass paperweight, enclosing a fuchsia stem on spiralling latticinio threads, some surface wear, c1850, 2in (5cm) high. This is a very good price for a fuschia paperweight. The simplistic buds and thick stem may account for the low price, but this is still a real bargain for a paperweight of this quality by a well-known manufacturer.
£700–850
$1,000–1,250 S(O)

Vases

James Powell, Whitefriars amethyst ribbonware glass vase, 1930, 6in (15cm) high.
£40–50/$60–75 TCG

Art Nouveau iridescent green glass organic vase, Continental, 12½in (32cm) high.
£70–85/$100–125 G(L)

Faceted opalescent glass vase, with a domed and folded foot, late 18thC, 6¾in (17cm) high.
£100–120
$145–175 Bon(C)

◀ **Ruby glass pedestal vase,** with a central panel painted with a portrait of a young lady, within a gilt and black rope border, Bohemian, late 19thC, 12¼in (31cm) high. Portraits on this style of late 19thC Bohemian glass vase often depicted a family member. An artist may have been commissioned to paint a portrait which he would then transpose on to the blank panel of the vase.
£190–220/$275–320 Bea(E)

The look without the price

Richardson's pink-cased opaque white glass vase, chip and crack to rim, late 19thC, 11½in (29cm) high.
£200–250
$300–360 Bon(C)

Historically this is an important piece in that it was decorated by William Northwood, who experimented with glass at the end of the 19thC. If it had been perfect condition it would probably have sold for more than £1,000/$1,500.

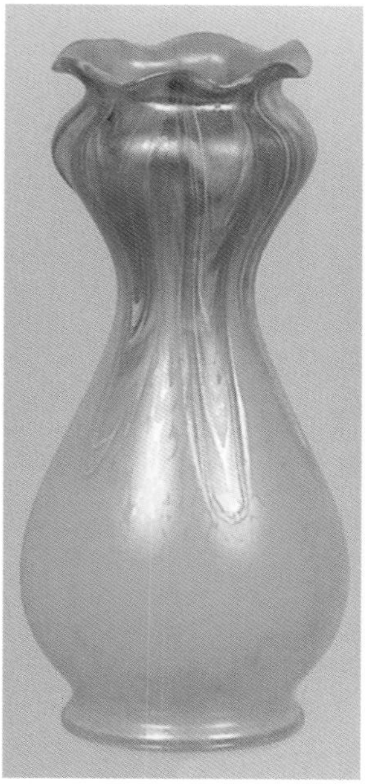

Iridescent glass vase, Bohemian, c1900, 11½in (29cm) high.
£200–250/$300–360 DORO

Cross Reference
See Baskets, Bowls & Dishes (page 168)

Glass vase, the trumpet body cut with a band of strawberry diamonds above flutes, with a knopped stem, on a star-cut foot, c1830, 8¼in (21cm) high.
£200–250/$300–360 Som

Clichy pink and white striped glass vase, French, 1845–50, 8in (20.5cm) high.
£270–300/$400–450 Del

Pair of Richardson's vitrified white opaline glass vases, sepia-painted with classical scenes, c1850, 10¼in (26cm) high. Unless covered with painting, white glass tends to be less appealing and this may explain the rather low price.
£400–475/$580–680 Bon(C)

Further reading

Miller's Glass Buyer's Guide, Miller's Publications, 2001

The look without the price

Double-overlay glass beaker, the opaque white glass cut with panels painted in enamels and gilding with bouquets of flowers and rocaille scrollwork, the gilded rim with a border of trailing flowers and scrolls, crack to base, Bohemian, 1840–45, 5¼in (13.5cm) high.
£350–420/$500–600 S(O)

This is another example of a piece that is damaged but still desirable. Cracks are only seen by those who are offended by them, but they do reduce the value when it comes to selling. If perfect, this piece would probably reach £450–550/$650–800.

Miscellaneous

Clear glass syphon, by the British Syphon Manufacturing Co, London, covered with wire mesh, early 20thC, 20in (51cm) high.
£60–75/$90–110 PFK

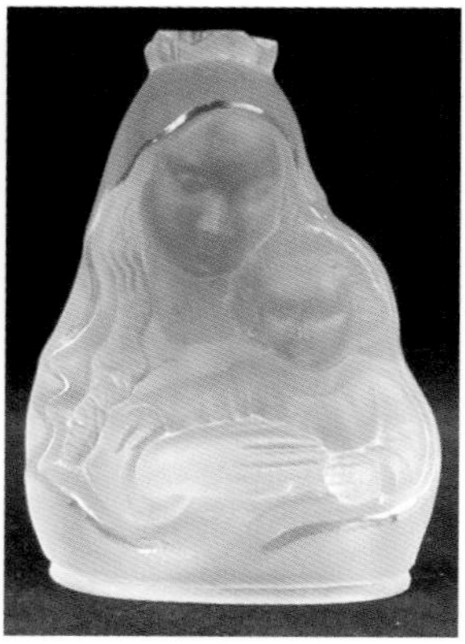

Lalique opalescent glass figure of the Madonna and Child, signed, pre-1945, 5¼in (13.5cm) high.
£85–100/$125–145 SWO

Pair of moulded green glass dogs, by John Derbyshire, c1860, 7in (18cm) wide.
£100–120/$145–175 Del

► Lalique frosted glass model of a bird preening, 'Moineau Coquet', engraved 'R. Lalique, France' in script, minor chips to wings, pre-1945, 4in (10cm) high.
£160–200/$230–300 G(L)

René Lalique

Starting his career as an innovative jewellery designer in the 1890s, René Lalique was to gain international recognition in the 1920s as a designer of beautiful mould-blown glass. Perhaps most recognized for his opalescent glassware, it is his coloured pieces, particularly in black or electric blue, that collectors seek out.

Care must be taken with Lalique pieces. 'R. Lalique, France' engraved on an item should mean that it was produced before his death in 1945. 'Lalique, France' is post-1945 and consequently worth less even though possibly made from the same mould. It is not unknown for 'R.' to be etched in front of 'Lalique' on a later piece to enhance the value in the eyes of the unwary.

Prices for Lalique glass stagnated in the early 1990s when the Japanese economy took a downwards turn. Today prices are stable, but collectors be particularly critical of polished areas where damage has been removed.

Three matching Bristol blue glass wine coolers, 19thC, 4in (10cm) high.
£140–175/$200–250 PFK

► Green glass table centrepiece, with gilt decoration, Bohemian, c1840, 6¼in (16cm) high.
£165–200
$250–300 DORO

The look without the price

Marbled glass ceiling dish, possibly by Dino Martens, in orange, brown, red and turquoise, the ogee strawberry shape with turnover rim above three handles on the shoulders, the domed base with strawberry print, Italian, Venice, 20thC, 11¾in (30cm) high.
£200–240/$300–350 CGC

It is always worthwhile if a modern piece can be attributed to a designer. Had this been by Dino Martens it would have been worth £2,500–3,500/$3,600–5,000.

Nailsea dark olive glass witch ball, with an opaque white marvered splashes, c1810, 4½in (11.5cm) diam.
£225–250/$325–360 Som

Glass ointment pot, commemorating George IV, crack to base, 1820–30, 2½in (6.5cm) diam, with associated shagreen case. This is an interesting and relatively low-priced item. Although slightly damaged, it is still attractive because of its case and its historical and social interest.
£320–385/$450–575 SWO

◄ **Nailsea glass model of a royal frigate,** 19thC, 7in (18cm) wide.
£350–400
$500–580 DQ

Glass ships

Sailing ships made of glass with rigging and sailors were popular decorative items in Victorian times. They were demonstrations of the manipulative skills of glassmakers. Because of their vulnerability they can be bought quite cheaply today.

Silver-mounted cut-glass brandy barrel, by Heath & Middleton, London, with three silver-plated bottle labels, 1897, 11in (28cm) wide.
£600–700/$870–1,000 S(O)

Clocks, Watches & Barometers

Sundials were first used to indicate the time of day over 4000 years ago. The Greeks and Romans measured time with sand-filled hour glasses and water-drip clepsydras. The search for new ideas to measure time in a standardized fashion, and to report its passage on a bell or 'glock', led at first to large public or tower clocks and later to portable clocks and watches.

Meteorologists in the late 17th century determined that a change in atmospheric pressure always accompanied a change in the weather. These scientists turned to the technical skill of clockmakers and the mercury tube or stick barometer was the result. In 1845 inventors found that by amplifying the small movements of a sealed metal canister they could accurately measure pressure changes, and by the late 19th century, cheap and portable aneroid barometers were available in all kinds of decorative wood casing. These were sold alongside clocks and watches in the clock maker's shop.

Early clocks, watches and barometers can fetch thousands of pounds and are sought-after by museums and advanced collectors. However, the prolific production of all of these objects after 1850 has left hundreds of thousands (if not millions) of examples, many of which are very affordable today.

Swiss and American watch companies produced millions of pocket watches in the last quarter of 19th century, so much so that many of the more common models are available now for less than £100/$150. A good Ingersoll 'Dollar' watch can still be bought for less than £35/$50, good railroad watches between £200–400/$300–600 and Swiss calendar watches less than £300/$450. Complicated watches that strike, repeat the quarters or with perpetual calendar indicators and chronographs can be more expensive, yet most watches are very affordable.

The 19th century clock factories also produced millions of clocks, including one-day cottage models, kitchen gingerbread clocks, imitation marble, mantel and shelf clocks, wall pendulum clocks, weight regulators and tall clocks. Two German factories alone, Gustav Becker and Lenzkirch, both passed the one million production mark around 1894. In France, Marti and Japy produced well over a million movements between 1850 and 1900. In America, a multitude of companies including Ansonia, Waterbury, New Haven, Gilbert, Ingraham, Seth Thomas and Welch, produced a myriad of models in quantities too large to count.

In 1983, the Swiss watch companies came up with the line of 'Swatch' watches to combat the competition of Japanese quartz wrist watches. The decorative vinyl bands of these watches have created a whole new 'art' market for watches. Special Swatch watches have been designed by celebrities, to celebrate films and events, as well as the current season's fashion. As a result these are fast becoming very collectable.

The net result of all this mass production is a plethora of affordable clocks, watches and barometers to tempt even the novice collector, the majority of which can still be acquired for less than £1,000/$1,500. These items can turn up at boot sales, garage sales, flea markets, auctions and dealers as well as the internet. But for those starting out, large online auction houses often have a good selection.

Robert Schmitt

Carriage Clocks

Brass-cased carriage clock, for Bailey, Banks & Biddle, Philadelphia, with lever platform, chip to dial, French, c1920, 5¼in (13.5cm) high, with travel case. To repair the dial, the entire enamel has to be replaced and this would be costly. Had this dial had the more popular Roman numerals it would have been worth more.
£140–165/$200–240 ROSc

Ormolu and brass carriage clock, with porcelain dial, the platform/cylinder escapement mounted on the backplate for easy access, the round case with bevelled lenticle, French, c1900, 5¼in (13.5cm) high. This clock is of poor quality. Roman numerals would have increased the value.
£150–185/$220–270 ROSc

Brass-cased carriage clock, with platform and strike, recently overhauled, French, c1900, 6¼in (16cm) high. This clock represents very good value. The recent restoration alone would have cost in the region of £120/$175.
£155–185/$225–270 ROSc

Miniature carriage timepiece, with white enamel dial, eight-day movement with cylinder escapement, polished brass corniche case, carrying handle missing, leather travelling case distressed, French, late 19thC, 3¼in (8.5cm) high. The missing handle would cost around £50/$75 to replace, making this clock good value.
£175–200/$250–300 S(O)

The look without the price

Gilt-brass carriage timepiece, by L'Epée, in a serpentine case, French, c1950.
£110–135/$160–200 G(L)

L'Epée are still making carriage clocks in Paris today and, therefore, it would not be cost effective to restore this example. Re-gilding would cost approximately £100/$150 and to restore the movement would cost as much again. However, if you are just after the look then this is good value.

Miniature carriage clocks

Miniature carriage clocks, also known as *mignonettes*, or 'little darlings', were produced mainly during the late 19th century. They were made by French makers, but not in large numbers. Miniatures are more sought after today than examples of standard size.

Gorge-cased carriage clock, by J. Soldano, with a seconds hand in lieu of the numeral 12, striking movement, platform signed JS in a stretched octagon frame and numbered 729, matching number on movement, case polished to brass, small crack to dial, French, c1875, 7¼in (18.5cm) high. The second dial makes this clock attractive. It is very good value.
£240–290/$350–425 ROSc

Checklist

There are several things to bear in mind when identifying porcelain and cloisonné panelled carriage clocks. The following are all good signs of quality:

- Are the frame and handle made of brass?
- If there are porcelain panels, do these show pastoral scenes?
- Do the cloisonné panels depict patterns of abstract or stylized foliage?
- Is there a bevelled glass panel over the dial panel itself and the top of the case?
- Are the side panels decorated instead of glazed?
- Does the piece have a serial number?

Brass carriage clock, the porcelain dial with Arabic numerals, with lever platform escapement and push repeat on a gong, the moulded glazed case with a swing handle, 19thC, 6¼in (16cm) high. The cleaning and servicing of this clock would cost approximately £150/$220, making it still very good value for money. Restoring clocks after purchase is always advisable.
£250–300/$360–440 B(Ed)

Alarm carriage clock, the white dial and the movement signed 'Futvoye, Paris', striking on a bell, in a brass case moulded with foliate scrolls, c1850, 8¼in (21cm) high. The case engraving on this example is of poor quality and would not restore well.
£280–320/$410–460 GH

Eight-day brass-cased carriage clock, the two-train movement with lever escapement, striking on a gong, French, late 19th/early 20thC, 7in (18cm) high. This is a very popular type of clock and a very good buy. It has an attractive case with an original platform and a silvered dial.
£250–325/$360–470 DN

Brass and *champlevé* carriage clock, the white porcelain dial with Roman numerals surrounded by enamel arabesques, with a lever platform escapement, the glazed bevelled case with fluted pillars and swing handle, French, late 19thC, 6in (15cm) high. The quality of the *champlevé* is very good, and it is always popular. Had this clock sold in London rather than Edinburgh, it could have achieved a higher price as *champlevé* is more sought after in the south.
£260–300/$380–400 B(Ed)

Miller's compares...

A. Silver-cased carriage timepiece, the later enamel dial signed 'Dubois Geneve', the French movement with a lever escapement, in a polished case with handle, on bun feet, London hallmark 1905, 4¼in (11cm) high.
£320–380/$470–570 Bon

B. Silver-cased carriage timepiece, with enamel dial, the frosted gilt movement with a lever escapement, in a machine-striped case, with carrying case, Swiss, 1920, 2¾in (7cm) high.
£425–525/$620–750 Bon

Item B is in perfect condition and has a protective carrying case, whereas Item A shows some denting to the case. Silver dents easily and is expensive to repair. Item B also has machining to the case which makes it more attractive.

Silver-cased repeating carriage clock with alarm, by Wurtel, Paris, the enamel dial set with a foliate gilt surround, the bell-striking movement signed, with ratchet tooth level escapement and plain steel balance, the one-piece case with elaborate scroll handle and engraved overall with flowers and leaves, restoration required, French, c1845, 5½in (14cm) high. This clock is great value and once restored, it could fetch £2,000/$3,000.
£400–450/$580–650 S(O)

Strike/repeat carriage clock, the cream dial with concentric calendar dial and subsidiary day and month dials with gilt filigree centres, the brass case surmounted by spires, late 19thC, 6in (15cm) high. Due to the extra dials, this is a quality carriage clock and a very good buy.
£550–650/$800–950 GH

Gilt-brass barometer and thermometer combination timepiece, with an enamel chapter ring, the movement with a cylinder escapement, top-mounted compass, French, early 20thC, 6¼in (16cm) high. In this restored condition this is a good buy. If unrestored it would be very expensive to overhaul.
£600–750/$870–1,100 Bon

Brass repeating carriage clock, the enamel dial signed 'Hamilton & Co', the gong-striking movement No. 12968 with the gong-maker's stamp 'PM', with ratchet-tooth lever escapement, French, c1885, 6¼in (16cm) high. This clock is a good shape and, even after restoration costs of around £180/$250, would still be a good buy.
£750–850
$1,100–1,250 S(O)

Longcase Clocks

Oak grandmother clock, with eight-day striking movement and arched top, German, 20thC, 73in (185.5cm) high.
£120–145/$175–210 TAY

Oak longcase clock, with square brass dial, 30-hour movement, signed 'Henry Baker', in an arch-topped case with a long trunk door, late 17thC, 80¼in (204cm) high.
£400–480/$580–700 B(W)

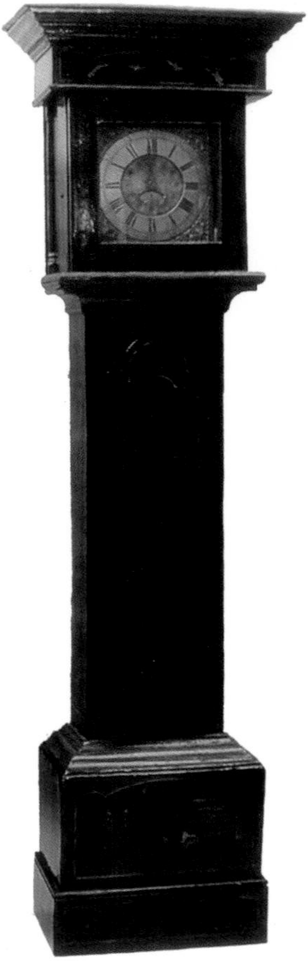

► **Pine longcase clock,** the square brass dial with black Roman and Arabic numerals within cast spandrels, the milled centre with draught-turned detail and calendar aperture inscribed 'Stonehouse Whitby', 30-hour movement striking on a bell, the case chinoiserie-decorated and painted with scrolled foliage and Oriental figures in landscapes, outlined with painted stringing, early 19thC, 81¾in (207.5cm) high. Chinoiserie decoration should never be cleaned as it will rub off and destroy the value of the piece.
£600–700/$870–1,000 DD

George III oak and mahogany longcase clock, the painted arched dial marked 'C. Prosser, Broneth', with seconds dial and calendar aperture, the eight-day movement striking on a bell, Walker & Finnemore false-plate, the hood with swan-neck pediment, dial retouched, case associated, 91¼in (232cm) high. This is a good-looking clock with correct proportions. It is an inexpensive price because the movement has been put into an associated case, however, it is still a good buy.
£850–1,000/$1,250–1,500 CGC

Mantel Clocks

Black mantel clock, with gilt dial, movement by Marti & Co, 1894, 17½in (44.5cm) high. The restoration costs for this clock would be expensive and must be taken into account when buying.
£75–90/$110–130 GH

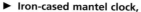

Art Nouveau inlaid oak mantel clock, with convex enamelled dial and gong-striking movement, side moulding missing, 10in (25.5cm) high. The side moulding is easy to repair, making this a good buy.
£160–190/$230–275 G(L)

Further reading

Miller's Clocks & Barometers Buyer's Guide, Miller's Publications, 2001

► **Iron-cased mantel clock,** by Bradley & Hubbard, Meriden, Connecticut, with 30-hour movement, the case retaining some of the original gold decoration, minor paint loss, dial numerals repainted, brass bezel replaced, original maker's label inside the case, American, c1865, 10¾in (27.5cm) high. This clock requires too much expensive restoration to be of great value, even at this price.
£85–100/$145–150 ROSc

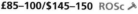

White marble mantel clock, the two-part porcelain dial with visible escapement and bevelled glass, with eight-day bell-striking movement, repair to right side of base, minor chips, French, c1880, 12¼in (31cm) high. Prices for marble mantel clocks have not risen for the last fifteen years.
£170–200/$250–300 ROSc

Mahogany mantel timepiece, the painted dial with fleur-de-lys hands, the fusee movement with anchor escapement and off-set pendulum, the case with brass cupboard handles to the sides, applied leaf carving at the front, the hinged top inset with a coin shute, opening to reveal a circular tin tray with 12 compartments, driving mechanism to the tray incomplete, c1850, 19¾in (50cm) high. This clock is a very good buy as it will cost very little to restore.
£250–300/$360–440 S(O)

◄ **Mahogany mantel clock,** by Seth Thomas Clock Co, with porcelain dial, the eight-day movement striking on a coiled flat wire cathedral gong, the inlaid case with pierced brass side frets, on brass ball feet, silk needs replacing, minor corner abrasion, American, c1909, 13½in (34.5cm) high.
£260–300/$380–440 ROSc

Mahogany arched-top mantel clock, the white convex dial signed 'Rowell, Oxford', the movement stamped 'G.B. & E.' and striking on a gong, the case inlaid with satinwood and ebony, c1920, 16in (40.5cm) high.
£280–320/$410–460 GH

Art Nouveau bronze Fan on Easel mantel clock, the bronze dial with porcelain cartouche numerals, with eight-day pendulette movement, the fan case with chinoiserie decoration, small chip to numeral, French, c1900, 18in (45.5cm) high. This type of novelty clock is very popular with collectors.
£300–350/$450–500 ROSc

Gilt-metal mantel clock, the movement with Brocot trademark, the dial within a baroque case flanked by caryatids and inset with foliate damascene panels, French, c1890, 17½in (44.5cm) high. Cases made of gilt ormolu are much better quality than spelter. This clock is a quality piece and it is a good investment which will rise in price.
£300–380/$440–560 GH

White marble and bronzed-spelter garniture, by Japy, the clock with porcelain dial, with a bronzed-spelter figure, a mask lying at the foot, and a pair of five-branch bronzed-spelter candelabra on marble bases, French, c1870, 6¼in (16cm) high. Beware when buying brass or bronze that it is not spelter. It can look very similar to the untrained eye and is not as valuable.
£300–350/$440–500 ROSc

► **Oak mantel clock,** by Dent, London, with painted white dial, the twin-train fusee movement striking and repeating on a bell, the case with brass side frets, dial chipped, mid-19thC, 14½in (37cm) high. Dent was a very good maker and it is well worth repairing the dial.
£400–450/$580–650 PFK

Red boulle mantel clock, with 12-piece enamel cartouche dial, the gong-striking movement by A. D. Mougin, the straight-sided case with concave-sided cresting veneered with red-stained tortoiseshell inlaid with brass, a glazed pendulum aperture, ebonized sides and applied gilt mounts, French, c1890, 16¼in (41.5cm) high. This clock is good value as it is ready to place on the mantelpiece and needs no restoration.
£400–450/$500–580 S(O)

► **Black marble and bronze Egyptian-style mantel clock,** by Vincenti, with marble dial, the bell-striking movement No. 820 with Brocot escapement, the breakfront case surmounted by a bronze sphinx flanked by seated figures and embellished with incised decoration, French, c1885, 15½in (39.5cm) high.
£480–520/$700–775 S(O)

◄ **Walnut drumhead mantel timepiece,** the painted dial signed 'Samuel Dixon, Cornhill, London', the associated single fusee movement with turned pillars and formerly with a passing strike, c1880, 16in (40.5cm) high. This clock is a good buy at this price. Quality English clocks will always prove a good investment.
£480–580
$700–850 Bon

Mahogany drumhead timepiece, signed 'R. Passmore, Sidmouth', with subsidiary seconds dial, the single fusee movement with anchor escapement, late 19thC, 21in (53.5cm) high). This is a good-quality English clock and an excellent buy.
£500–600/$720–870 Bea(E)

Maintenance

Clocks can suffer wear due to lack of maintenance. It is advisable to overhaul movements every seven to ten years.

► **Louis XV-style boulle-work mantel clock,** with ormolu mounts, the Japy Frères movement countwheel striking on a bell, on a serpentine plinth, dial chipped, French, 19thC, 14in (35.5cm) high. This clock would be expensive to repair. Be sure to get a quote before you buy as restorations can sometimes push the price of a clock beyond its value.
£550–650/$800–950 G(L)

The look without the price

Gilt-metal mantel clock, the dial painted with a water landscape, the twin-train movement stamped 'R & C', striking on a bell, the case mounted with Sèvres-style porcelain panels, with a lion mask and ribbon-tied ornament, surmounted by a classical two-handled urn, on a giltwood plinth under a glass dome, French, 19thC, 15in (38cm) high.
£650–750/$950–1,100 P(S)

This is a good-quality clock and a very good buy for the price. The case is mounted with Sèvres-style porcelain panels and if they had been orginal Sèvres panels the clock could be worth at least £3,000/$4,350.

Porcelain-panelled mantel clock, the porcelain face with landscape decoration, striking on a bell, French, late 19thC, 11¾in (30cm) high.
£700–850/$1,000–1,250 BLH

Set of six oak National Line shelf clocks, by the E. Ingraham Clock Co, with eight-day striking movements, entitled 'Peerless', 'Capitol', 'Mt Vernon', 'Banner', 'Freedom' and 'Union', all cases refinished, one clock with re-papered dial, one with new pendulum and two with replaced tablets, American, c1910, 22in (56cm) high. These clocks were marketed by Ingraham with six to a box, no two are alike. They were also marketed in 1904 by the St Louis Clock & Silverware Co, as the World's Fair Assortment. Individually, these clocks should fetch around £60/$90, but as a set they are worth much more.
£750–900/$1,100–1,300 ROSc

Mahogany bracket clock, the dial signed 'Frodsham, London', the twin fusee movement striking on a bell, with ring handles to the sides, 19thC, 16¼in (41.5cm) high. This clock is good quality and by a very good maker which helps retain the value.
£800–950
$1,150–1,400 Bea(E)

Gilt-brass mantel clock, the two-piece enamel dial with visible Brocot escapement, the bell-striking movement with a polished disc pendulum, on a moulded base, French, 1880s, 15¾in (40cm) high. This is a good-quality two-week duration clock at a very good price.
£850–1,000
$1,250–1,500 Bon

Power

Clocks are powered in two ways:
- Weight-driven – by the pull of hanging weights, found in lantern, longcase and some wall clocks.
- Spring-driven – by the release of energy in a coiled spring, found in bracket, carriage, skeleton, novelty and some wall clocks.

Wall Clocks

Two slave wall timepieces, by Standard Electric Time Co, Springfield, Mass, in brushed aluminium cases, stains and loss to one dial, American, c1920, 15in (38cm) diam.
£50–60/$75–90 ROSc

◄ **Rosewood-veneered wall clock,** with printed dial and inlaid brass roundel to the trunk, German, late 19thC, 11½in (29cm) high. This clock is a good buy.
£110–130/$160–190 G(L)

Arts and Crafts inlaid oak wall clock, with silver-coloured dial and pendulum, the eight-day mechanism striking on a single long rod, some staining to dial, German, c1915, 24in (61cm) high.
£70–85/$100–115 ROSc

◄ **Vienna wall clock,** with gilt-metal dial and enamelled chapter ring, surmount missing, early 20thC, 18in (45.5cm) high. This clock is still a good buy even though the inlaid eagle surmount is missing.
£130–160/$200–230 PFK

The look without the price

Eight-inch lever time calendar wall clock, by New Haven Clock Co, with double-spring movement, water-stained label on the reverse, some veneer loss, calendar hand replaced, numerals repainted, c1890, 11in (28cm) high.
£145–175/$210–255 ROSc

This clock would have been worth £200/$300 if it had been in perfect order.

Wall clock, with glass dial, the 30-hour time/strike and alarm on a wooden plate, spring-driven movement, German, c1870, 10in (25.5cm) high.
£140–165/$200–240 ROSc

Miller's compares...

A. Mahogany octagonal wall timepiece, the painted convex dial signed 'Hanson & Son, Windsor', the single fusee movement with shaped plates, inlaid with brass foliage, 15in (38cm) diam.
£280–340/$410–500 Bon

B. Rosewood wall timepiece, by Charles Maggs, Axbridge, with later single fusee movement, inlaid with mother-of-pearl, back restored, 19thC, 12¾in (32.5cm) diam.
£450–550/$650–800 Bon

Item A is an unpopular shape, and the face requires cleaning and repair, while the face of Item B is in good condition. Satinwood, rosewood, maple and brass are popular inlays, but mother-of-pearl is less so. Despite the mother-of-pearl in Item B, the round form and the use of rosewood make this the more desirable piece.

Pressed-brass wall clock, for Roehm & Wright, Detroit, the open brass dial with French inset numerals, with eight-day movement, rococo hands and a sunburst pendulum bob, French, c1900, 22in (56cm) high. This clock would not suit all tastes, but if you like it, it is a good buy.
£300–350/$450–500 ROSc

North American wall clocks

Wall clocks were produced in the United States from c1780. From c1850 exports of inexpensive North American wall clocks contributed to the decline in popularity of English wall clocks.

All North American wall clocks are weight-driven, with an anchor escapement and a long pendulum with a brass bob. Typical features include a white-painted metal dial, as well as a panel of *verre eglomisé*. The banjo case is the most sought-after American wall clock.

Advertising drop dial wall timepiece, by Baird Clock Co, Plattsburg, the white dial signed 'D. Collins, Sadler', the case impressed 'Vanner and Prest's Embrocation', early 20thC, 31in (78.5cm) high. This clock could also be of interest to collectors of advertising memorabilia.
£340–400/$500–580 GH

◄ **Gallery wall clock,** by A. D. Smith, Cincinnati, Ohio, with a Hubbel eight-day marine movement in an S. B. Jerome patented case, simulated leather over pine with a brass trim, the front decorated with pressed stars, cavalry bugles and crossed swords, label to reverse, second hand missing, possibly made to commemorate the Civil War, American, c1868, 13in (33cm) diam.
£450–550/$650–800 ROSc

Mahogany drop-dial wall timepiece, with painted dial, the single fusee movement in a case with a turned surround and pegged back, the lower dropped trunk with a glazed pendulum aperture, 19thC, 21in (53.5cm) high. This clock is in very good condition and is a good buy.
£500–550/$720–800 Bon

◄ **Rosewood office calendar wall clock,** by Ithaca Clock Co, 'No. 4 Hanging Office', with a nickel-plated 30-day movement, case stripped, age crack on upper bezel, upper dial re-papered, date rollers darkened with age, in need of overhaul, American, c1880, 29in (73.5cm) high. This clock would be expensive to repair due to work that is necessary to restore the calendar.
£550–650/$800–950 ROSc

Miller's compares...

A. Rosewood trunk-dial wall timepiece, with a painted dial, fusee movement with anchor escapement, the case inlaid with mother-of-pearl leaves, the similarly-decorated trunk inset with a brass-framed lenticle, flanked by carved leaf sprays and with undercurved trunk incorporating a door, c1850, 28¾in (73cm) high.
£700–850
$1,000–1,250 S(O)

B. Rosewood drop-dial wall clock, by George Esplin, Wigan, with a single fusee movement, c1840, 12in (30.5cm) diam.
£900–1,000
$1,300–1,500 Mit

Item A is unsigned and the colour of the rosewood is not as rich as that of Item B, which is of excellent quality. Item A is also a much larger clock which might not suit the smaller, modern home, thus resulting in a lower price compared to Item B.

Mahogany wall clock, the eight-day striking movement with two brass weights, the case with an octagonal hood, 19thC, 48in (122cm) high. This English clock is a good buy as one would expect to pay much more for a clock in this condition.
£600–700/$870–1,000 SWO

Further reading

Miller's Clocks Antiques Checklist, Miller's Publications, 2001

Miscellaneous

Ironclad cast-iron alarm clock, by Westclox, with 24-hour movement, alarm-set hand missing, c1935, 5¼in (13.5cm) high.
£55–65/$80–90 ROSc

Cast-iron door stop clock, the 30-hour movement with back winder and centre-set stem, the case depicting a young woman flanked by floral decoration, the clock set within sun rays, paper dial renewed, small chip to crystal, the whole case sprayed with gold paint, American, c1900, 13½in (34.5cm) high.
£85–100/$125–145 ROSc

Bulkhead timepiece, with silvered dial inscribed 'Chelsea Clock Co, Boston', American, probably early 20thC, 7in (18cm) diam. This item would appeal to a specialist marine collector.
£120–140/$175–200 G(L)

Rosewood cottage clock, by Atkins Clock Co, Bristol, Connecticut, with 30-hour time/alarm movement, original rose tablet beneath the dial, some veneer missing, paint loss to dial, American, c1865, 10in (25.5cm) high. The veneer on this clock would be easy and relatively inexpensive to replace so this is a good price.
£155–185/$225–270 ROSc

► **Shelf clock,** by C. & N. Jerome, Bristol, Connecticut, with 30-hour movement, the white dial with Roman numerals, the case with rounded sides, backboard painted red, with label, dial has some paint loss, some veneer chips, American, c1838, 22in (56cm) high.
£190–220/$275–325 ROSc

► **Gilded-spelter figural clock,** with bell-strike movement, the case depicting a young girl holding a skein of yarn, left index finger missing, French, c1890, 12½in (32cm) high. This clock represents good value.
£190–220/$275–325 ROSc

Spelter

Spelter is impure zinc, usually containing about three per cent of lead and other impurities. It was used as a much cheaper version of brass and bronze from c1860s.

Shelf clock, by Riley Whiting, Winchester, Connecticut, with 30-hour movement, case carved, with label, stripping work incomplete, some veneer missing, door lock and escutcheon missing, American, c1835, 35in (89cm) high. This clock is a good price and would make an interesting restoration project.
£225–275/$325–400 ROSc

► **White metal mantel clock,** by Seth Thomas, with paper dial, the eight-day movement striking on a gong on the hour and a bell on the half-hour, entire clock painted gold, in need of restoration, American, c1905, 12in (30.5cm) high. This clock is by a named maker which makes it a good buy. It would especially be of interest to those who collect Art Nouveau pieces.
£240–290/$350–425 ROSc

Seth Thomas Company

The Seth Thomas Company was incorporated in 1853. They started making longcase clocks with wooden movements before branching out into shelf clocks, phasing in brass movements in 1842, and ceasing wooden movements two years later.

Seth Thomas was very conservative, and after his death in 1859 his sons introduced many new types of clock, including regulators, perpetual calendar clocks and tambour clocks. Most Seth Thomas clocks date between 1881 and 1918 and have the date stamped in ink – often the year is in reverse and followed by a letter representing the month of manufacture.

◄ **Burr-walnut-veneered George III-style bracket clock,** the engraved dial signed 'John Smith, London', the movement with count wheel striking on a bell, German, c1900, 15in (38cm) high.
£260–300
$380–440 G(L)

Oak picture frame clock, by Werner Clock Manufacturing Co, with intricate lithograph dial on paper by Werner Litho, Akron, Ohio, the 30-hour alarm clock movement in a red leather case, American, c1900, 9in (23cm) high. This clock is good value.
£275–3250/$400–470 ROSc

Victorian brass desk timepiece, in the shape of a kettle drum, by G. B. & Sons, the silvered Roman numeral dial with a chased floral rim, registration mark, 7in (18cm) high. This clock is unusual and good value. Items such as this are popular with collectors.
£300–350/$440–500 G(L)

The look without the price

Admiral Blinking Eye clock, by Bradley & Hubbard, Meriden, Connecticut, with new paper dial and hands, original movement, repainted, American, c1875, 16in (40.5cm) high.
£380–450
$550–650 ROSc

These novelty clocks usually sell well and if this example had been in perfect condition it could be worth in the region of £1,000–1,400/$1,500–2,000

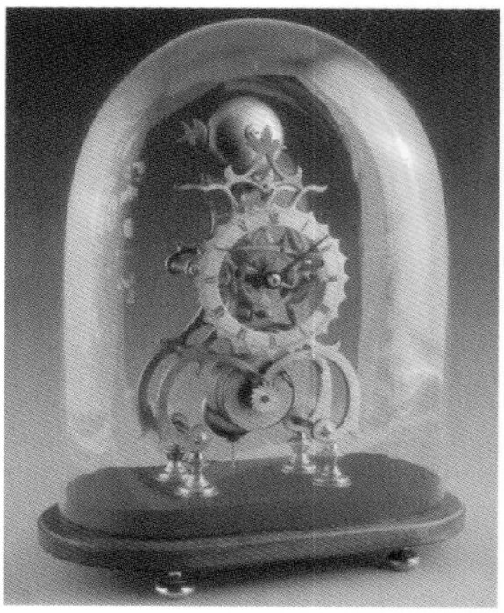

► **Brass skeleton clock,** with later bell strike, restored, c1850, 12¼in (31cm) high.
£500–600/$720–870 HAM

Miller's compares...

A. Shelf cuckoo clock, with a wooden plate, two-day movement, dial numerals replaced, minute hand repaired, bellows in need of attention, replacement pendulum bob, German, c1880, 21in (53.5cm) high.
£400–500/$600–720 ROSc

B. Shelf cuckoo clock, the heavy 56-hour movement with cast lyre-shaped plates, with original dial, bone hands and bone grommets to the winding holes, German, c1920, 15in (38cm) high.
£600–700/$870–1,000 ROSc

The repair costs to restore the bellows, numerals and hands on Item A would be expensive and must be added to the overall cost of the item. Item B is in good original condition and thus commanded the higher price.

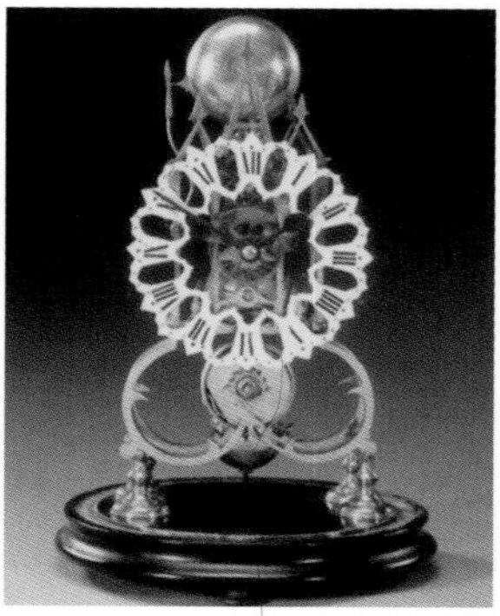

Skeleton timepiece, with painted and pierced chapter ring, the fusee movement with anchor escapement and passing strike, 13in (33cm) high. This clock is a good buy and would have been £200–300/$290–430 more if it had the original dome.
£600–700/$870–1,000 S(O)

Pocket Watches

Lady's silver pocket watch, with polychrome and gilt-on-enamel dial, and key-wound bar movement, c1880, 1½in (4cm) diam. Pocket watches are not particularly fashionable or sought after at present, and it is possible to buy them at a very reasonable price such as this one.
£60–70/$90–100 AOH

► **Calendar watch,** with porcelain dial indicating day, date, month and seconds on subsidiary dials, with stem-wound, pin-set, lever movement in a gun-metal case, dial chipped, Swiss, c1880, 1½in (4cm) diam.
£100–125
$150–180 ROSc

Watches

Watches rank alongside scientific instruments as functional, mechanical items. Remember, if the watch is not working, parts may be unavailable, repairs expensive, and 'a good clean' is unlikely to improve matters. Perhaps because of this, watches under £1,000/$1,500 remain undervalued but, if well maintained, will give many years of pleasure and excellent service.

Because of the complexity of the subject, collectors should only buy from reputable sources; quality dealers will warrant their watches, whilst many auctioneers will give condition reports prior to the auction.

George V silver-mounted travelling watch case, with a nickel pocket watch, 4in (10cm) wide. This watch and case are very good value.
£180–220/$260–320 G(L)

► **Pair-cased watch with eccentric dial,** by John Reilly, Dublin, the white enamel dial with outer minute track and subsidiary hour dial at twelve and seconds dial at six, the signed gilt movement with pierced and engraved cock now with lever escapement (formerly verge) over circular turned pillars, in plain inner and outer cases, mid-18thC, 2¼in (5.5cm) diam. Eccentric dial watches are sought-after and can make high prices at auction. This example, however, is not very expensive because it has been altered by changing the verge to a lever escapement, and this has devalued the object considerably.
£260–300/$380–440 B(Kn)

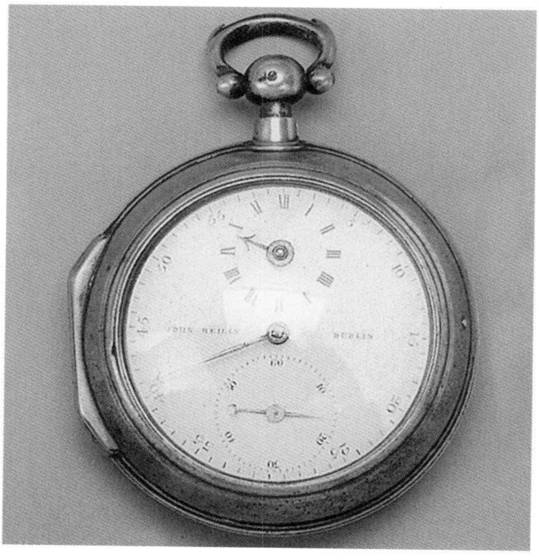

Collecting pocket watches

Pocket watches are seldom worn today, as men tend not to wear waistcoats, and so currently represent good value. Although the earliest examples are over £1,000/$1,500, it is possible to buy excellent 18th-century silver pair-cased verge watches, late 18th- and 19th-century English, American and Continental lever and cylinder watches, all under £1,000/$1,500.

Themed collections may include, among others, movement types, mechanical complexity, case styles, makers or hallmarks. Look for condition of casework and dial, originality of hands and working condition. Damage, other than fair wear and tear, seriously detracts from the price.

◄ **Gun-metal calendar pocket watch,** by John Hall & Co, the white enamel dial with Roman numerals, subsidiary seconds and moonphase dials, the reverse with calendar dials for days and date, with central indicating hand and month indicating aperture, c1900. John Hall was a retailer who dealt in timepieces with Swiss imported movements. Other notable watchmakers of this type of timepiece were the Universal Watch Co, and Benson & Co.
£340–400/$500–580 Bea(E)

Gentleman's 18ct gold hunter pocket watch, by Arnold Frodsham, the white enamel dial numbered 7275, with Roman numerals and subsidiary seconds dial, the movement with backplate inscribed 'J. R. Arnold. Chas Frodsham, London 7275', in a *guilloche* case with a crest and an attached curb-link chain with a vesta case, c1850. The price for this watch reflects the fact that the chain, key, vesta case and watch are all original and in very good condition.
£360–420/$520–620 Bea(E)

18k gold pair-cased verge watch, Leslie, No. 124, with enamel dial, Roman numerals, gold hands, beetle hour hand, full plate verge movement, baluster pillars, pierced and engraved balance cock, replaced minute hand, signed and numbered, hallmarked London 1782, IR, gilt outer case, 2¼in (5.5cm) diam. It can be expensive to restore pocket watches, so it is important to bear this in mind when considering buying an unrestored watch at what appears to be a cheap price.
£260–320/$380–470 S(O)

18ct gold half-hunter case keyless lever watch, with white enamel dial, Roman numerals, and subsidiary seconds, the gilt three-quarter plate lever movement signed 'Chas Frodsham, 84 Strand, London, No. 06875', with bi-metallic compensation balance, the polished case with initials to the reverse and blue enamel numerals surrounding the glazed aperture, case maker HMF, hallmarked London 1883. This is a well-priced example from a famous maker. The double 'swell' on the hour hand means that a half hunter can be read without opening the case, unlike a full hunter, which must be opened.
£375–425/$560–620 S(O)

Gun-metal open-faced annual calendar watch with moonphases, the white enamel dial with subsidiary dials, day, date, month and constant seconds combined with an aperture for moon phases, with a nickel lever movement and mono-metallic compensation balance, in a polished case, c1900, 3¼in (8cm) diam. Gun-metal-cased watches are a good way to buy complicated functions inexpensively.
£420–500/$620–720 S(Am)

Gilt and tortoiseshell pair-cased verge pocket watch, by John Rogers, Leominster, No. 2578, the white enamel dial with Roman numerals and Arabic five minutes, the signed and numbered movement with pierced and engraved cock over square baluster pillars, in a plain inner case, the outer case with mottled tortoiseshell, dial cracked, 1750–1800, 2in (5cm) diam. Tortoiseshell pair cases in undamaged condition attract a premium and the cracked dial can be expertly repaired.
£500–600/$720–870 B(Kn)

Enamel easel timepiece, the dial painted with a scene of a house by a river, the central panel painted with a Bacchic scene, surmounted by a gilt brass and enamelled crown, the flanking panels painted with classical maidens and cherubs, on four gilt-brass scrolling feet cast with bird maskheads, the back of the panels chased with scrolling foliage, the enamel back painted with a scene of a classical maiden and a cherub, Austrian, late 19thC, 8¼in (21cm) wide. This is a good and inexpensive example of a boudoir timepiece.
£550–650/$800–950 B

Miller's compares...

A. 14ct pink gold hunting-cased keyless lever watch, by Audemars Frères, No. 151766, the enamel dial with Arabic numerals and subsidiary seconds, the gilt lever movement with screwed-down chatons, bi-metallic compensation balance, precision regulator, signed and numbered cuvette, in an engine-turned case, the front cover with a central cartouche with an engraved monogram, French, c1900, 2¼in (5.5cm) diam.
£580–650/$850–950 S(O)

B. 14ct gold hunting-cased quarter-repeating chronograph watch, by Audemars Frères, the white enamel dial with Roman numerals and subsidiary seconds, the gilt lever movement with bi-metallic compensation balance, push repeat and gold cuvette, the engine-turned case with applied disc with monogram L. K., French, c1900, 2¼in (5.5cm) diam.
£750–900/$1,100–1,300 S(AM)

These two watches are by the same maker, however, there is a premium for Item B because of the quarter repeating chronograph. However, both Item A and B are still excellent value.

Insurance values

Always insure your valuable antiques for the cost of replacing them with similar items, regardless of the original price paid. Both dealers and auctioneers can provide a valuation service for a fee.

Japanese-style lacquerwork purse watch, by Movado, the silvered dial with applied Arabic numerals, lever movement, the gilt-silver case with lacquerwork of the three monkeys See No Evil, Hear No Evil, Speak No Evil, with presentation case, c1950, 1¾in (4.5cm) wide. This example is by a good-quality maker, with a Swiss movement. The lacquerwork adds to the value.
£600–700/$870–1,000 S(O)

Miller's compares...

A. Gold and enamel open-faced cylinder watch, the silver engine-turned dial with Roman numerals, subsidiary seconds, gilt cylinder movement and gold cuvette, the case with blue *champlevé* enamel with flora and fauna motif, c1940, 1½in (4cm) diam.
£250–300/$360–440 S(O)

Item B has a verge movement and is older than Item A, making it more desirable and expensive, even though they have similarly ornate cases.

B. Gold and enamel verge watch, the silver regulator dial with steel indicator, the engine-turned silver dial with Roman numerals and gold Breguet hands, the full plate gilt fusee movement with finely pierced and engraved bridge cock with a polished steel coqueret, the gold consular case decorated with foliate black *champlevé* enamel, the back with white *champlevé* enamel flowers, Swiss, early 19thC, 1¾in (4.5cm) diam.
£650–750/$950–1,100 PT

18ct gold open-faced duplex watch, by James McCabe, No. 01119, the white enamel dial with Roman numerals, subsidiary seconds, signed on the three-quarter plate movement 'Jas. McCabe Royal Exchange London', with fixed cuvette, the cuvette and back of the case with the number repeated and stamped 'IMC', hallmarked 1856, 2in (5cm) diam, in original velvet-lined leather case. This duplex watch by McCabe represents particularly good value at this price and is a good example of an open-faced pocket watch by a good English maker.
£600–720/$870–1,000 S

18ct pink gold open-faced keywind jump hour watch, with engine-turned silver dial, eccentric minute ring, subsidiary seconds, aperture for hours, gilt cylinder movement, plain three-arm balance, gilt cuvette, in an engine-turned case, c1830, 2in (5cm) diam. Jump hour watches are highly collectable.
£700–850
$1,000–1,250 S(AM)

Wristwatches

Longines Flagship Automatic 9ct gold wristwatch, the signed dial with centre seconds and baton markers, on a leather strap. This is an affordable classic with elegant proportions.
£230–270/$330–400 Bea(E)

Collecting wristwatches

Wristwatches date from the early 20th century and continue to be worn today. In general, women do not like to wind watches and so automatic movements will bring a premium. Early manual watches, even those by the best makers, remain highly affordable and those such as Omega, who have made their parts widely available, deserve their reputation for quality and service. Look out for government issue watches as a collection theme, but remember wristwatches are generally newer than pocket watches and condition is even more critical.

Favre Leuba reversible metal wristwatch, the silvered dial with Arabic numerals and subsidiary seconds, 1950. This offers Jaeger Le Coultre Reverso functionality at a fraction of the price.
£250–300/$360–440 S(Am)

Omega Seamaster Chronostop stainless steel chronograph wristwatch, the black dial with applied baton hour markers, outer tachymetre scale, the gilt 17 jewel Cal.865 movement in a polished case with stop/start push button and screw down back, the case, dial and movement signed, 1970s, 1½in (4cm) diam. Always bear in mind that if the strap is original this will add to the value.
£250–300/$360–440 Bon

► **Nickel Mickey Mouse wristwatch,** the paper dial inscribed 'Ingersoll Mickey Mouse', with Arabic numerals, centred with Mickey Mouse, his arms providing the hands, subsidiary seconds with one figure only, in a tonneau-shaped case, c1935. Early Mickey Mouse watches are highly collectable and this example exceeded the estimate almost tenfold.
£280–320/$410–460 S(O)

International Watch Company steel wristwatch, the silvered dial with applied Arabic numerals and subsidiary seconds, the nickel lever movement with mono-metallic compensation balance, in a water-resistant-style case, with signed dial and movement, c1950, 1¼in (3cm) diam. International Watch Company watches are always of exceptionally high quality.
£280–320/$410–460 S(Am)

Omega 14ct gold sweep seconds wristwatch, the silvered dial with applied triangular and Arabic numerals, the 15 jewel movement with mono-metallic compensation balance and gilt metal cover, in a water-resistant-style case, dial, movement and case signed, c1940, 1¼in (3cm) diam. These watches, if in need of repair, are easily restored.
£280–320/$410–460 S(Am)

Miller's compares...

A. Rolex Oyster Solar Aqua stainless steel waterproof wristwatch, No. 2784, the two-tone dial with Arabic numerals and red inner 13–24 hour ring, subsidiary seconds and luminous hands, 17 jewel nickel movement, the polished case with raised bezel, screw down Oyster patent crown and screw back, dial and case signed, 1930s, 1¼in (3cm) diam.
£280–320/$410–460 B

B. Rolex Oyster Perpetual Chronometer Bubble-back stainless steel wristwatch, the silver matt dial with applied Arabic numerals and outer minute track divided for fifths of a second, the chronometer movement with patent trigger screw, the polished case with a chamfered bezel, Super Oyster winding button and screw-down rear cover, dial, movement and case signed, c1950, 1¼in (3cm) diam.
£675–750/$950–1,100 B(Kn)

Rolex Bubble-back watches, such as Item B, are affordable and very collectable. Item B easily outsold Item A even though Item A was in better condition.

◄ **A lady's Art Deco diamond-set platinum cocktail watch,** 1920s.
£340–380/$500–575 G(L)

► **Tudor Oyster Prince stainless steel Date-Day wristwatch,** the silvered dial with applied baton numerals and apertures for day and date, the nickel lever movement with 25 jewel mono-metallic compensation balance, in a water-resistant-style case with screw-down crown, date quick-set, dial, movement and case signed, with stainless steel Tudor bracelet and clasp, c1990, 1¼in (3cm) diam. This wristwatch is fine quality and with Rolex association, as Tudor is owned by Rolex.
£350–400/$500–580 S(AM)

► **Silver wristwatch,** with Swiss movement, retailed by Harrods, 1930s. This watch shape is rare.
£400–450/$580–650 TEM ⊞

Jaeger Le Coultre stainless steel wristwatch, with two-tone silvered dial, luminous Arabic numerals and hands, aperture for day, outer ring calibrated for date, central date indicator hand, subsidiary seconds, with Geneva striped tonneau-form nickel lever movement with compensation balance, in a polished steel case, dial movement and case signed, c1940, 1¼in (3cm) diam). Early calendar wristwatches from Jaeger Le Coultre, Movado and Gubelin are highly collectable, particularly with moonphase function.
£500–600/$720–870 S(O) ⚒

◄ **Diamond-set 14ct gold wristwatch,** the silvered dial painted with Arabic numerals and retouched signature, with pocket watch movement by Longines, No. 2148925, in a lozenge-shaped case set with eight diamonds, 1930s, 1in (2.5cm) diam. Longines is a good maker, but in this instance the value of the item is in the gems.
£400–480/$580–700 B ⚒

Heuer single button yachting recorder wristwatch yacht timer, Ref. No. 503.512, with large colour-coded central five minute register, reverse second division facilitates countdown, single button in the band with three functions, with seven jewel shock-protected movement, dial, movement and case signed, with blue and red fabric strap, 1960s. Heuer has a long association with sports timers and recorders, particularly for motor sport.
£500–600
$720–870 B(Mon) ⚒

Longines stainless steel military wristwatch, ref. No. 4870, the dial with military arrow mark and Arabic numerals, the matt gilded movement with 15 jewels and shock-resistant balance, with screw back to the case, dial and movement signed, c1955, 1½in (4.cm) diam. In 1953, Longines refined this jewel movement and fitted a shock-resist balance for a series of British and military scientific expeditions to the Arctic regions.
£470–550/$700–800 S(O) ⚒

Pierce anti-magnetic stainless steel chronograph wristwatch, anti-magnetic, No.1630, the copper dial with Arabic numerals, outer telemetric scale, sweep centre seconds, subsidiaries for running seconds and 60-minute recording, with jewelled nickel movement, the polished case with two push buttons in the band, the case held by 8 screws, with original fitted velvet case, 1940s, 1½in (4cm) diam. A watch in fine condition and with its original case always attracts a significant premium.
£880–1,000/$1,300–1,500 B(Mon) ⚒

Barometers

Oak barometer and thermometer with mirror, by H. O. Quinn, for public display, c1935, 22in (56cm) high. Public display barometers are becoming very collectable, especially when there is a maker's name on the dial. This example would have been hung in the lobby of a hotel, guest house or club. Although this one is missing the glass bezel and set hand on the barometer, there are specialists who can replace these at a modest cost.
£80–100/$115–145 RTW

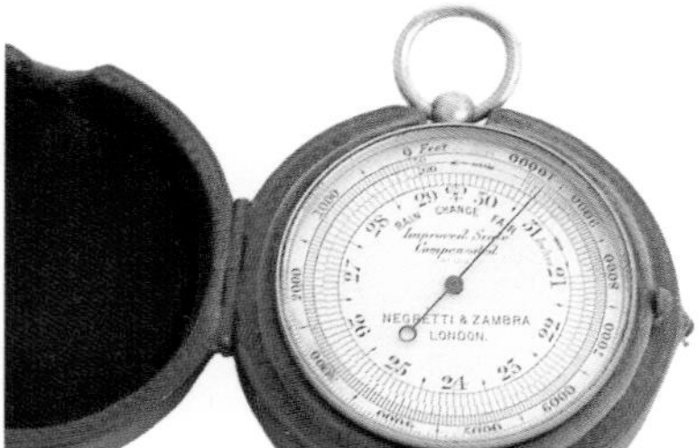

Pocket barometer, by Negretti & Zambra, with silvered dial, in a folding leather case, c1890, 2in (5cm) diam. This barometer has a scale up to 10,000 feet in increments of 50 feet. Those which still retain their original case, especially when signed by the maker, are usually in much better condition and will always fetch 40 to 50 per cent more than those sold without. Pocket barometers are quite sturdy instruments but can be almost impossible to repair if the internal diaphragm 'blows'.
£200–240/$290–350 G(L)

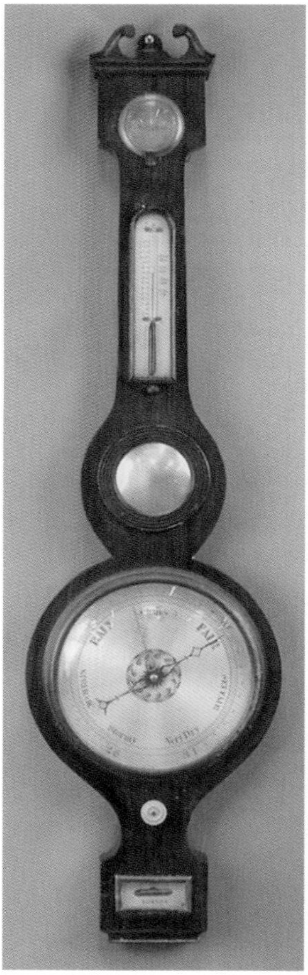

◄ **Rosewood wheel barometer,** inscribed D. Fagioli, London, with silvered dial, hygrometer, alchohol thermometer, convex mirror and bubble level, the case with a swan-neck pediment, late 19thC, 37¾in (96cm) high. D. Fagioli of London was a prolific manufacturer of barometers and this one can be dated at around the second quarter of the 19th century. Rosewood is a particularly high-quality wood and is especially collectable as fewer barometers were produced in this species after the Victorian era. Barometers decorated with swan necks or scroll pediments at the top are attractive, but look out for replacements as this delicate part often becomes damaged during transportation.
£160–190/$230–275 RTo

► **Rosewood wheel barometer,** with a silvered dial, subsidiary hygrometer, alchohol thermometer, mirror and spirit level, c1880, 40in (101.5cm) high. This five-glass barometer has an onion or tulip-style top which was common for that period. Although this one is clearly unsigned on the barometer face, some manufacturers do put their name below the levelling plate at the base of the instrument.
£200–250/$290–360 PFK

Mahogany wheel barometer, by M. Riva, Glasgow, the boxwood-strung case with hydrometer, thermometer, mirror, brass face and level, c1840, 40¼in (102cm) high. This five-glass barometer has all the original component parts. While it retains its urn-style finial at the top, the swan necks either side have broken off and this will detract from its true value by around £150/$220. However, this is a good purchase as it is signed and can be dated to the second quarter of the 19thC.
£240–280/$350–400 TRM

Miller's compares...

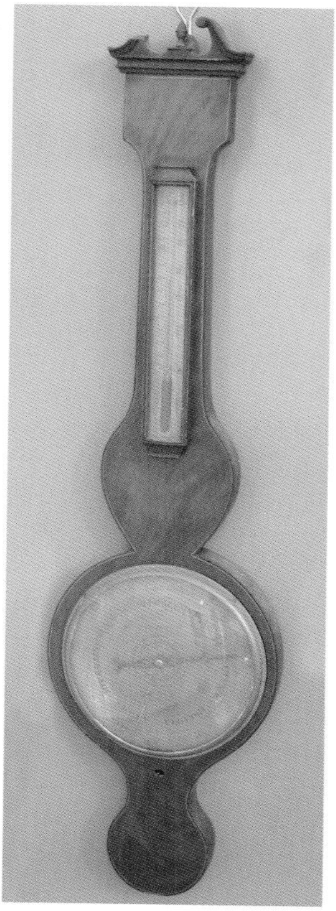

A. Victorian mahogany wheel barometer, by F. Primavesi, Reading, with silvered dials and swan-neck cresting, cresting damaged, 37in (94cm) high.
£280–320/$410–460 G(L)

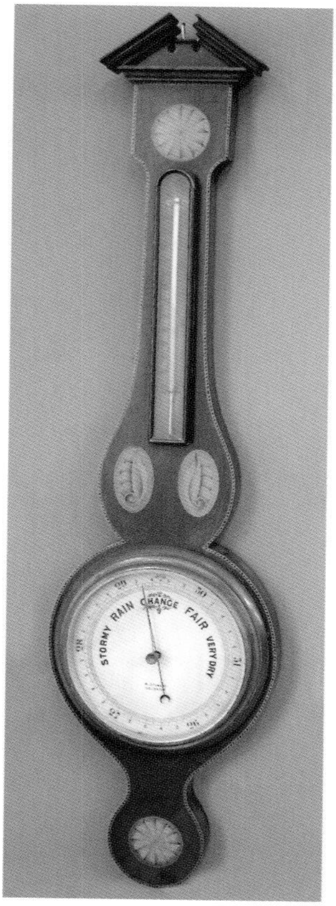

B. Edwardian inlaid mahogany wheel barometer, by A. Steward, Leicester, the case inlaid with bats' wings and conch shells, broken arch pediment, 38in (96.5cm) high.
£460–520/$675–725 G(L)

Item A, by Primavesi of Reading, is in need of some repairs which could prove expensive. Re-silvering the dial and thermometer plate could cost £80–100/$115–145; add to that the cost of repairing the swan-neck pediment and replacing the mercury tube and one could pay double the original purchase price. Item B is much more recent and is in excellent condition. There is no apparent damage to the perimeter inlaid stringing. It has a broken arch pediment, copied from a style of over a century earlier, an elegant mercury thermometer and the shape of the instrument has very pleasing proportions. Inlays of bats' wings and conch shells show that the Edwardians seemed to prefer these decorative features rather than the hygrometer, convex mirror and levelling plate favoured by their Victorian predecessors.

Oak hall barometer, by Chadburns of Liverpool, c1920, 36in (91.5cm) high. This would have retailed at about £2–3/$4–6 when originally sold. The round moulded pediment and scroll effect is drawn from the style of mercury wheel barometers from around the 1860s. It has a white porcelain dial and thermometer plate which are undamaged. Always be aware that if cracked they cannot successfully be repaired.
£250–300/$360–440 RTW

Useful tips

To check whether a barometer is working, gently incline it to 45 degrees and the mercury should rise smoothly up the tube with a light 'smack' as it touches the top. Great care must be taken as new glass tube replacements for these instruments can be expensive.

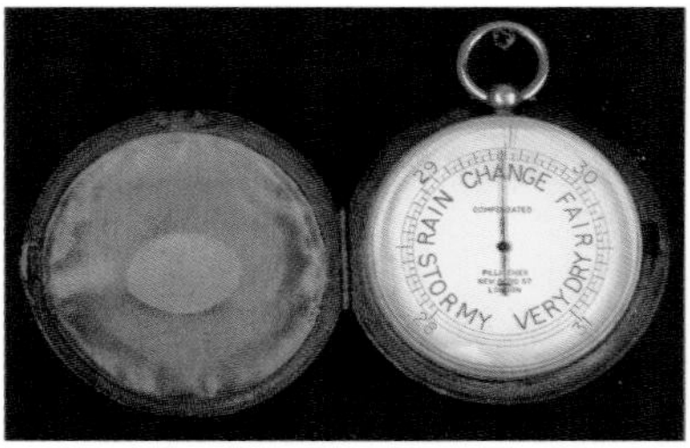

Pocket aneroid barometer, by Moritz Pillischer, London, c1880, 3¼in (8cm) diam. This unusual pocket barometer has a very open scale, similar to that of a normal size instrument. It is particularly desirable as it is signed and is complete with its original case.
£300–350/$440–500 AW

Walnut five-glass wheel barometer, with porcelain dial, c1900, 36in (91.5cm) high.
£400–450/$580–650 RTW

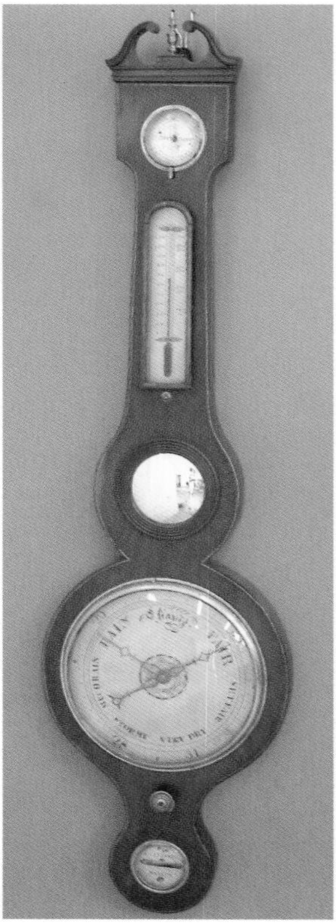

Early Victorian mahogany wheel barometer, by A. Cattanio, Malton, with silvered level, hygrometer, thermometer and barometer dials and a convex mirror, 38in (96.5cm) high.
£300–360/$440–550 G(L)

Silver-mounted combined desk timepiece and barometer, by William Comyns, 1900, 8½in (21.5cm) wide. The clock and barometer were probably made by Negretti & Zambra, who were prolific manufacturers at that time. This is worth collecting providing the clock and barometer are both functioning, as repairs are expensive.
£400–500/$580–720 G(L)

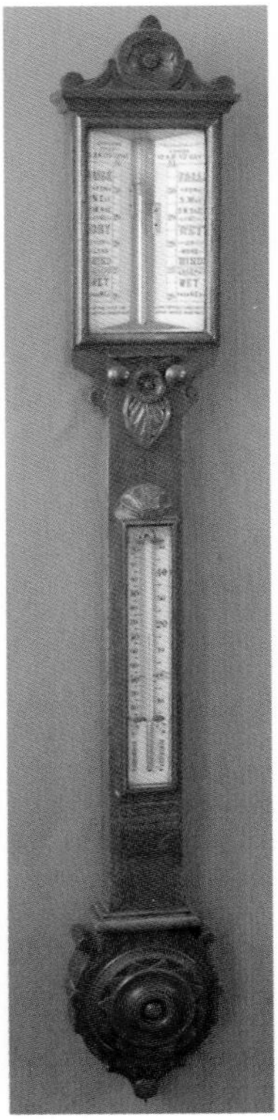

Purchasing barometers

Below are things to look for when purchasing a good quality barometer:

- ◆ It should be in working condition
- ◆ Signed and of good provenance
- ◆ Minimal damage – try to avoid cracks or scratches to dials or register plate
- ◆ Matching barometer and set hands
- ◆ Be aware of the popularity of woods – rosewood being the most popular, then mahogany and lastly oak
- ◆ Ornate or 'plump' thermometer reservoir
- ◆ Stringing to the perimeter
- ◆ A knowledgeable dealer will have plugged the mercury tube ready for transportation.

◄ **Victorian oak stick barometer,** by J. H. Steward, with glazed porcelain scales and thermometer, 41in (104cm) high. This barometer represents excellent value and would retail for between $800–1,000/$1,150–1,500. It looks to be in excellent condition and has been well maintained. The porcelain backplates are undamaged and the red lettering shows only minor fading. This style of instrument is increasing in popularity but check for damage and that the set knobs are not missing.
£500–600/$720–870 G(L)

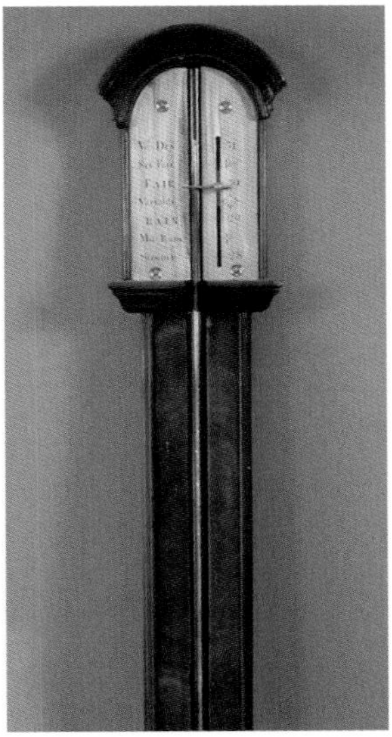

Mahogany stick barometer, with a silvered register, restored, early 19thC, 37in (94cm) high. If this instrument were signed it would be worth 15 to 20 per cent more.
£610–730
$885–1,000 SWO

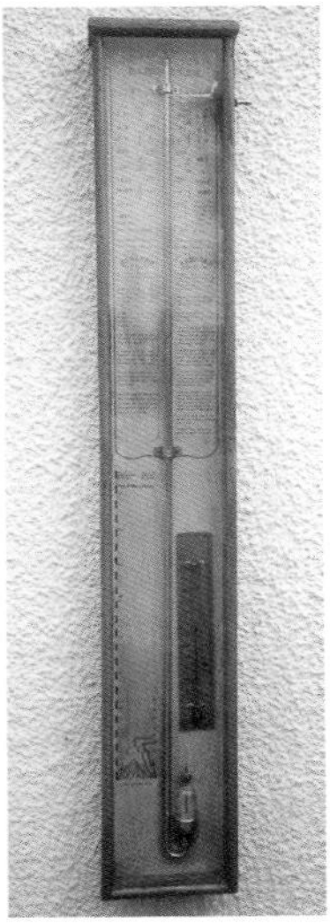

Mahogany Admiral Fitzroy barometer, with glazed charts, c1890, 36in (91.5cm) high.
£700–850
$1,000–1,250
RAY

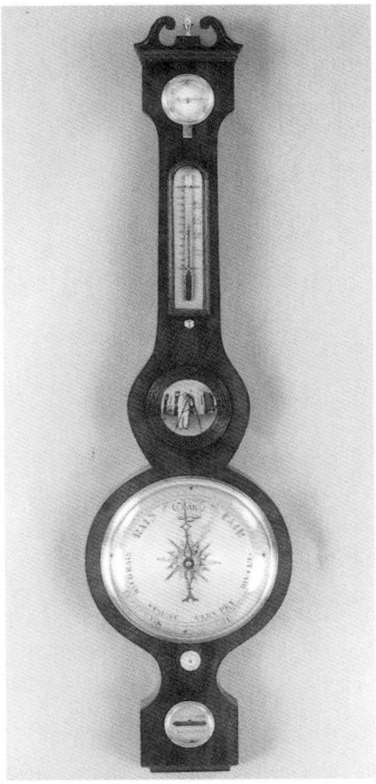

Mahogany wheel barometer, by Thatcher, Lambourn, with silvered brass scale, thermometer, hygrometer, spirit level and mirror, c1840, 38in (96.5cm) high.
£850–950/$1,250–1,400 PAO

Other Antiques

Since no two items are exactly the same, the reasons for price variations will be due to one or more of the following criteria: age, authenticity, condition, and the vendor's knowledge of its value and availability. Comparing like with like, whether it be two Persian carpets or a pair of brass candlesticks, requires the collector to balance all of these five basic criteria to determine the article's true value.

Collecting inexpensively-priced antiques within the price range covered by this book can, with a certain degree of self-discipline, produce not only a collection giving personal satisfaction, but one that will, eventually, give the collector a financial reward to compensate (if necessary) for the time taken to acquire the items.

The catalysts that trigger a collection can be as diverse as a long-forgotten item from childhood that has suddenly come to light, or a misjudged wedding gift that is never given. Whatever your chosen field, the first premise for a successful long-term collection must be a degree of personal empathy with the items being acquired. If, for instance, one is collecting antiquities, a knowledge of the times in which the articles were used gives the acquired item a fresh meaning and value.

Architectural recycling can bring the discarded fabric of our forefathers' buildings and homes back to life and, when presented in a modern setting, may allow the object to acquire new intrinsic and financial values.

Deciding what to collect, whether you are a teenage novice collector or an octogenarian veteran, is an Aladdin's cave of choice, with infinite fields and innumerable sub-sections of specialization on which you may wish to concentrate.

The home is an ideal vehicle for the collector, requiring carpets on the floor, lights, tapestries and paintings on the walls, chandeliers on the ceilings and textiles in the bedroom, all displayed in their natural surroundings. The fact that you don't have the money to fully decorate can be cleverly hidden, and may generate some unusual collections.

Some collectors may wish to narrow their acquisitions to very specific fields in order to increase the difficulty of obtaining items within that collecting sphere while, at the same time, increasing the satisfaction of acquiring that special item. This creates the buzz that makes collecting the great hobby that it has become.

Finally, a few simple home truths: only buy what you can afford (plus a little); only buy the best you can afford; buy a damaged item if it is rare, fills a gap in a collection and will one day be replaced with a better example, or if you simply like it and want a purely decorative object; collect items that are relatively common, giving you the chance of acquiring without too much difficulty; enjoy the hunt whether it be through antique fairs, auction rooms, dealers' shops or the internet; enjoy what you buy.

Do not buy for financial gain, but for the pleasure of putting together your collection, and the joy of acquiring that sought-after item. Remember, one item is an object and two is a collection. Finally, try to theme your collecting, however broad or narrow the parameters you may wish to put your collecting criteria.

John Proops

Antiquities

◄ **Five flint instruments,** western Asian, Neolithic, largest 4¼in (11cm) long.
£25–30
$35–45 HEL ⊞

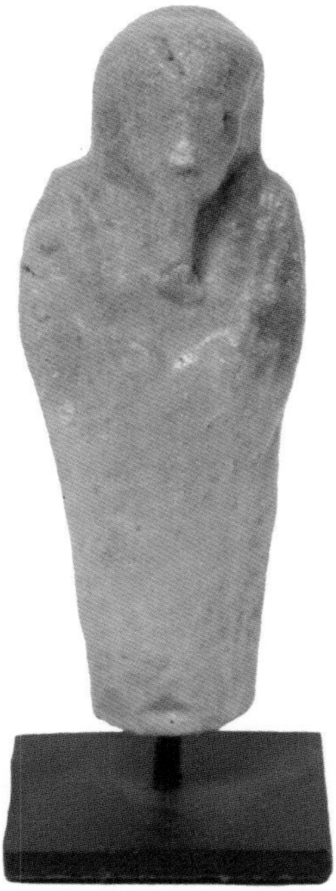

Faïence upper part of an ushabti figure, glaze intact, feet missing, 750–332BC, 3in (7.5cm) high. This particular figure is late period, has little or no inscription, was mass produced and is damaged and would therefore not attract the attention of the serious collector. It would have been customary to fill the tomb with 50 to 100 of this type of piece.
£35–40/$50–60 HEL ⊞

The Shabti

The Shabti (Answerer) was cast in the image of the deceased and placed in the tomb as Osiris, to answer for, and do the work of, the deceased in the afterlife, it being the belief that work carried on after death. The earlier and better pieces often have attribution to an owner – a court official, a priest or even a member of the ruling family – and can command high prices from the serious specialist, according to the period, owner's details, condition and size. Later period items are mainly of curiosity value and would be suitable for the collector who wants a low budget collection.

Anthropomorphic orangeware pottery bowl, with vestigial limbs and male anatomical details, decorated with incised geometric ornament, cracks and old repair, pre-Columbian, probably Mayan, Late Classic. If undamaged, the price would be over £100/$145.
£45–50/$65–75 F&C

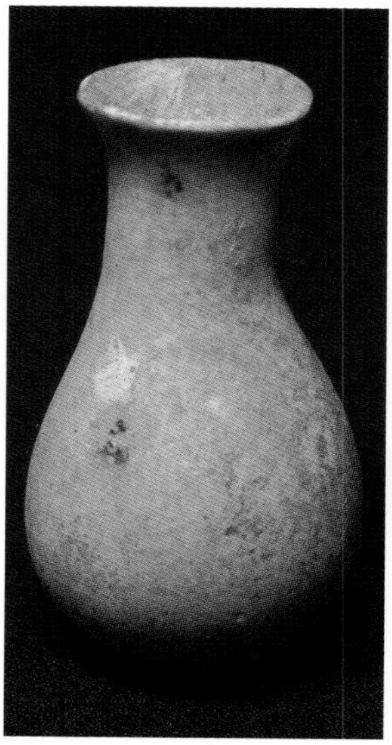

Pale green glass tear flask, Roman, 3rdC BC, 2¾in (7cm) high.
£55–60/$80–90 HEL ⊞

Collection of carved steatite scarab amulets, Egyptian, 1st millennium BC, largest ½in (1.5cm) long. Scarabs are usually seals in the shape of the sacred scarab beetle and can be made of steatite, faïence or any hardstone.
£55–60/$80–90 HEL ⊞

Collection of 13 moulded faïence amulets, Egyptian, 1st millennium BC, largest 1¼in (3cm) high. Small groupings such as these are a good way to start collecting. It also gives the buyer a selection of items to research without spending an enormous amount of money.
£55–60/$80–90 HEL ⊞

Bronze skyphate disc brooch, dark patina, with stylized animal design to the centre, five recesses originally set with glass, found in Spain, Visigothic Kingdom, 5th–7thC AD. The Goths who contributed to the collapse of the Roman Empire were, in fact, a civilized Christian race.
£60–65/$90–95 ANG ⊞

◄ **Certosa brooch,** with a highly arched bow and long gutter-type catch plate, Etruscan, 6th–5thC BC, 2¼in (5.5cm) long.
£60–65/$90–95 ANG ⊞

Bronze bow brooch, with highly arched bow and simple coil spring, pin and shaped catch plate, Greek, 3rdC BC, 2in (5cm) wide.
£60–65/$90–95 ANG ⊞

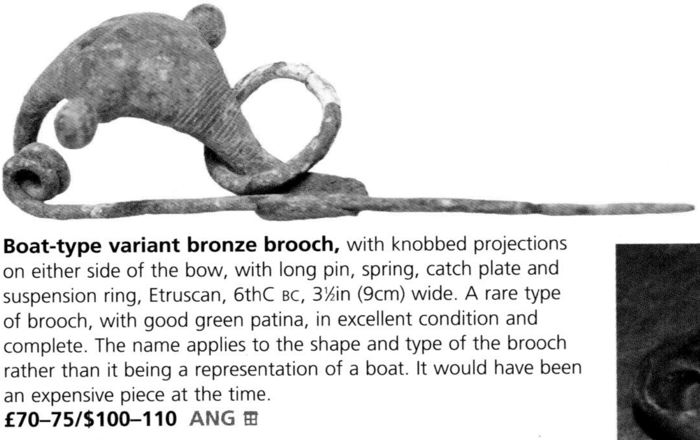

Boat-type variant bronze brooch, with knobbed projections on either side of the bow, with long pin, spring, catch plate and suspension ring, Etruscan, 6thC BC, 3½in (9cm) wide. A rare type of brooch, with good green patina, in excellent condition and complete. The name applies to the shape and type of the brooch rather than it being a representation of a boat. It would have been an expensive piece at the time.
£70–75/$100–110 ANG ⊞

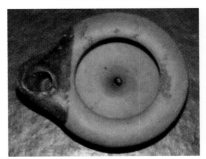

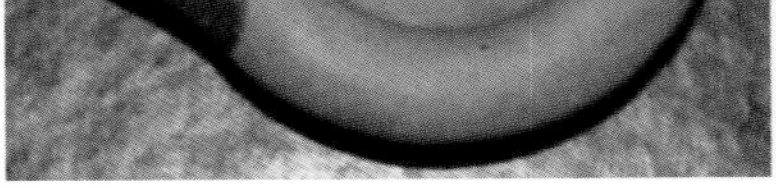

Oil lamp, with round flattened bowl, central conical projection and decorated protruding nozzle, Greek, c5th–4thC BC, 3¼in (8.5cm) diam. These lamps would have been used with olive oil. It would be easy to build a collection as several pieces can be obtained in one lot from auction or individually from dealers.
£85–95/$125–140 CrF ⊞

◄ **Pottery bowl,** Egyptian, c3000 BC, 4in (10cm) diam.
£70–80
$100–115 HEL ⊞

◄ **Pottery bowl,** with a flared rim, Jordanian, 2nd millennium BC, 7in (18cm) diam.
£90–100
$130–145 HEL ⊞

Decorated pot, Persian, small chip to rim, 10th–12thC, 2¼in (5.5cm) high.
£115–125/$165–180 CrF ⊞

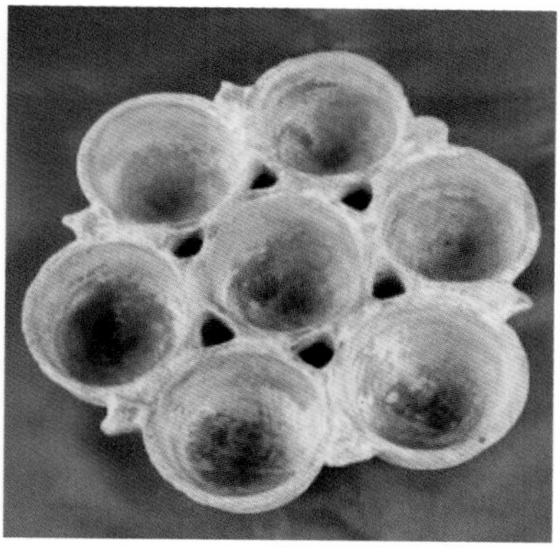

◄ **Pottery sweetmeat dish,** comprising a central bowl and six outer bowls, worn, Islamic, 11thC CE, bowls 2¾in (7cm) diam.
£115–125/$165–180 CrF ⊞

► **Pottery storage jar,** the cylindrical body with twin looped handles and everted rim decorated with encircling bands in orange slip, rim chipped, encrustation, Mycenaean, c12thC BC, 3¼in (8.5cm) high. This item is priced very competitively.
£120–135/$175–195 CrF ⊞

Bronze stamp seal, with the *Agnus Dei* (Lamb of God) as the central motif surrounded by a legend, with handle and suspension loop, 15thC, ½in (1.5cm) high. This would have been owned by someone of standing. It is in fact a matrix and would have been used for making the seal impression. It is quite a rare piece.
£180–200/$260–290 ANG ⊞

► **Bronze figure of a woman,** wearing a headdress and a long skirt, one foot and both hands missing, Etruscan, 6th–5thC BC, 4¼in (11cm) high. Damage to this extent would have an impact on the price.
£270–300/$390–440 ANG ⊞

Pale blue glass bottle, the body with five irregular vertical indentations, a wavy amber collar applied around the base of the short cylindrical neck, with a thickened infolded rim, Roman, 3rdC AD, 3in (7.5cm) high.
£300–360 $440–525 Bon

Anthropomorphic bronze key, the upper part modelled as a bust of Mercury in winged cap and cloak, with suspension loop on head, the ward in the form of a rectangular loop, Roman, 1st–3rdC AD, 4¾in (12cm) long. This could have originated in Italy. It would probably have been the key for a strongroom rather than an ordinary shop door.
£400–450/$580–650 ANG

Pale green glass juglet, with silvery iridescence, the cylindrical body mould-blown with vertical fluting, slightly indented at the base, with a cylindrical neck, everted mouth with infolded rim and applied handle, c4thC AD, 3½in (9cm) high.
£300–360/$440–525 Bon

Green glass bowl, with curved walls and everted rim with thickened lip and applied pie-crust handles, on a thick base-ring, Roman, 2nd–3rdC AD, 4¾in (12cm) diam.
£400–480/$580–700 Bon

Bronze cruciform mount, cast in high relief with a male face, his hair centrally parted with a distinctive downward curving moustache and prominent elliptical eyes, three arms of the cross incised with scroll decoration and a beaded border, Celtic, 5thC BC, 1in (2.5cm) square. Facing moustached male heads appear to have been widely used in the adornment of Celtic metalwork and frequently appear in varying guises.
£420–500/$620–720 Bon

Carnelian intaglio, engraved with Apollo holding a laurel branch in his left hand and leaning on one elbow against a column, set in a Georgian gold ring, the band chased with a scrolling foliate design, Roman, 1st–2ndC AD, 1in (2.5cm) diam. Roman antiquities were popular in the Georgian period and were often reset, such as this piece.
£450–550/$650–800 Bon

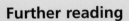

Further reading

Miller's Antiques Price Guide 2003, Miller's Publications, 2002

► **Stone head,** European, 13th–14thC BC, 9in (23cm) high.
£450–500/$650–720 OCH

Black-on-red ware *oinochoe*, with conjoined handle, trefoil lip, spherical body and ring base decorated with numerous concentric circles and three intersecting strokes at the front, handle repaired, chipped rim and some pitting to the body, Cypriot, c750–650 BC, 13¼in (33.5cm) high.
£500–600/$720–870 Bon

Pottery stirrup vessel, Mycenaean, c12thC BC, 5in (12.5cm) high. These false-necked jars known as stirrup jars were used to hold liquids such as scented oil. This modern name is derived from the shape of the handle, which resembles upside-down stirrups and the type is believed to have originated in Crete.
£550–625/$800–925 CrF

Bronze figure of the god Osiris, Egyptian, 730–332 BC, 6¾in (17cm) high. Osiris was the God of the dead, and was represented by a mummy holding a crook and flail, wearing the Atef crown and Uraeus serpent. They were usually tomb figures. Condition will obviously vary, but they are usually inexpensive.
£550–600/$800–870 HEL

◀ **Naqada burnished pottery vessel,** with black top, Egyptian, 3500–3200 BC, 9¾in (25cm) high.
£550–600/$800–870 HEL

Hollow terracotta figure of Aphrodite, shown naked with a *naos*, holding her drapery behind her, her hair beneath a diadem, some pink and white slip remaining, mainly to columns, the reverse unmodelled, Roman, c2nd–3rdC AD, 8in (20.5cm) high. These figures were used in household shrines and were on display to visitors, people having their favourite gods and gods of the House. These items are now scarce.
£700–850
$1,000–1,250 Bon

Fakes

There are very few outright fakes of antiquities – and these would mostly be higher-priced rarities which are usually known about. More problematical are the altered pieces, that is, broken and damaged pieces which have been restored, possibly using modern materials, but more usually similar ancient material which has been taken from a different piece.

Some restored pieces are honest attempts at improvement, others are dishonest attempts to present something as a better piece than it really is.

▶ **Glass cup,** with rounded sides, flattened base and cut-off rim, the body decorated with two groups of three dark blue blobs applied to form a triangle, alternating with two applied dark blue blobs, Rhineland, c4th–5thC AD, 2½in (6.5cm) high.
£850–1,000/$1,250–1,500 Bon

Architectural

Wall tile, c1900, 3¼in (8cm) square. The small size of the tile is often an indicator that it was part of a larger multi-design scheme.
£4–5/$5–7 C&R ⊞

Two tiles, c1900, 6in (115cm) square and 6 x 2½in (15 x 6.5cm).
£18–20
$25–30 C&R ⊞

Tiles

With plain tiles the value often depends on the quantity that is available – a larger quantity can have more uses and is therefore at a premium.

Cast-iron soap dish, French, c1900, 5 x 4in (12.5 x 10cm). Re-enamelling of this piece would be prohibitively expensive. Modern waterproof paints can provide an excellent alternative if you do not like the antique appearance.
£27–30/$35–45 C&R ⊞

Washstand tile, c1900, 6in (15cm) square. Tiles such as this add an interesting and affordable period touch.
£18–20/$25–30 C&R ⊞

Brass light switch, with a ceramic base, c1910, 3in (7.5cm) diam.
£27–30/$35–45 WRe ⊞

Safety first

If you are intending to use electrical equipment, make sure it is in a safe condition – if in doubt ask a sympathetic electrician.

► **Victorian brass letter plate,** 3 x 6in (7.5 x 15cm). Brass letter plates, if bought new, can be the same price as antique ones, but far less decorative. This kind of door furniture would complement a Victorian house perfectly.
£35–40/$50–60 WRe ⊞

Kitten-in-a-basket cast-iron door stop, 7in (18cm) high. The low price suggests that this is possibly not old. Many simply-made pieces like this are being reproduced – the more desirable and 'kitsch', the more likely it is to be a reproduction.
£38–42/$50–60 MLL

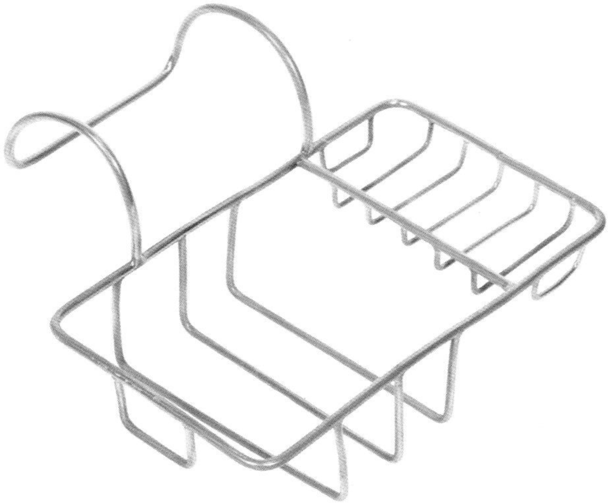

Polished brass soap bath rack, original, c1900, 12½ x 8in (32 x 20cm). This item has classic styling which will hold value, unlike the modern equivalent.
£45–50/$65–75 C&R

Brass jelly-mould light switch, with ceramic base, 1910–30, 4in (10cm) diam. This decorative light switch is more desirable due to the ribbing, which is less common.
£45–50/$65–75 WRe

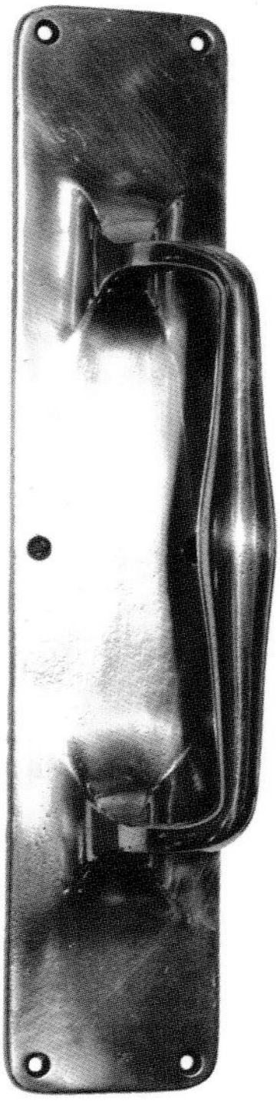

◄ **Pair of brass door-pulls,** 1930s, 15in (38cm) high.
£55–60/$80–90 WRe

Door furniture

Antique door furniture is an effective and economical way to complement a period house or to disguise a modern door. A protective coating of lacquer will serve to protect the finish of door furniture.

Brass wirework fender, with brass rail and bun feet, mid-19thC, 24½in (62cm) wide. This was a good buy as there is often a premium on small pieces. The large amount of 'antique' fire furniture made in the 1920s and 1930s has ensured that prices are often surprisingly affordable, especially when compared to modern reproductions.
£50–60/$75–90 WW

► **Arts and Crafts cylindrical copper coal bin,** c1900, 19in (48cm) high. With a little application this item could be easily cleaned at home for minimal cost. Alternatively it is excellent 'shabby chic'.
£70–85/$100–125 SWO

Pair of inlaid mahogany bellows, 1875–1910, 16in (40.5cm) high. Bellows are rarely used as functional items these days, therefore, the more decorative the piece the more desirable. Some have wonderful tooled leather and if this is in good condition it will add to the value, as do engraved brass fittings.
£90–100/$130–145 F&F ⊞

Victorian servants' brass and black ceramic bell-pull, 5in (12.5cm) wide.
£110–120/$160–175 OLA ⊞

► **Cast-iron door knocker,** in the form of a hand, French, 19thC, 5in (12.5cm) wide.
£110–120
$160–175 OLA ⊞

◄ **Coach door handle,** engraved, 1860–70, 4in (10cm) wide.
£110–125
$160–180 RGe ⊞

◄ **Cast-iron stove,** late 19thC, 49½in (126cm) high. As pieces of sculpture in their own right, testament to the skill of iron founders and as a functional heater, pound for pound old stoves are great value.
£130–160
$190–230 SWO

► **Cast-iron lamp heater,** French, c1900, 14 x 21in (35.5cm x 53.5cm).
£100–150
$145–220 C&R ⊞

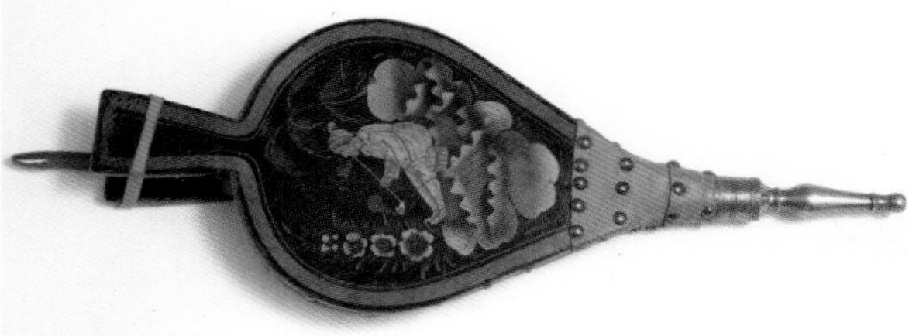

Pair of lacquer bellows, decorated in English chinoiserie, probably early 19thC, 14in (35.5cm) high.
£120–130/$175–190 F&F

Pair of rosewood door handles with matching fingerplates, 11in (28cm) long. Rosewood has always been an expensive and rare wood, so its use for door furniture is a good indicator of quality.
£135–150/$195–220 OLA

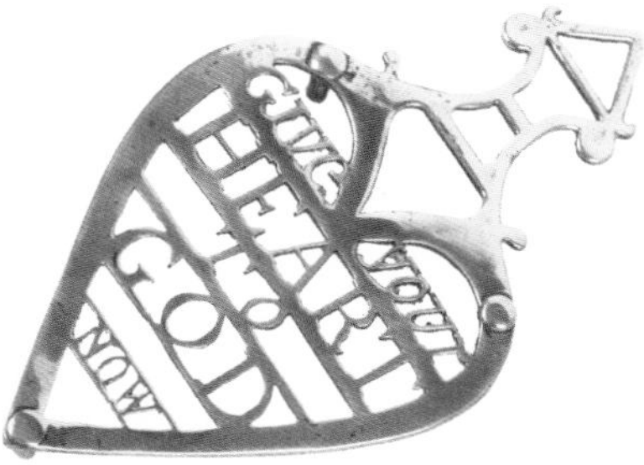

◄ **Brass trivet,** reading 'Give your heart to God now', c1850, 9in (23cm) long. The value of this item rests on the inscription. Plainer examples can be much cheaper.
£135–150
$195–220 RGe

Victorian cast-iron door knocker, 7in (18cm) high.
£145–160/$210–230 OLA

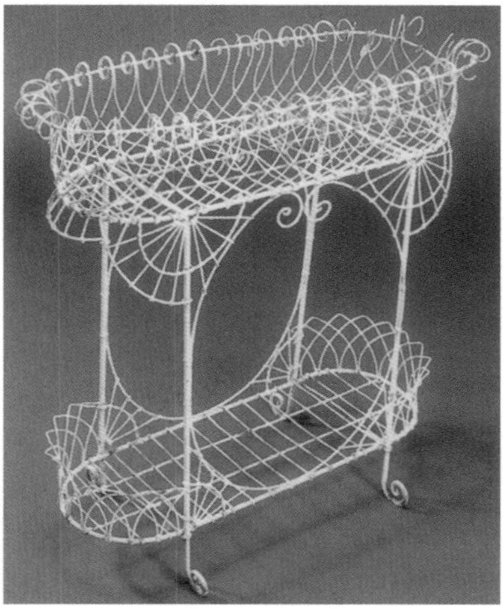

Wirework, two-tier jardinière stand, with overscroll arcading, scrolling brackets and feet, early 20thC, 32¼ in (82cm) high. The price of genuine examples is low because of the number of reproductions. Look out for touches such as tapering on the feet which only tend to appear on genuine examples.
£140–170/$200–250 DN

Locate the source

The source of each illustration in Miller's can be found by checking the code letters below each caption with the Key to Illustrations, pages 286–290.

◄ **Cast-iron round two-tier table,** with three sabre legs surmounted by male masks, the later top pierced all over with foliate scrolls, late 19thC, 27½ (70cm) high. These items are commonly referred to as pub tables and the basic design came with wooden, cast-iron or marble tops and were normally found in public houses. The most common have 'Brittannia' stamped on the legs. Some are collectable, such as the W.G. Grace commemorative table and command a higher price.
£160–200/$230–290 DN

◄ **Regency iron trivet,** 13in (33cm) high. People often buy these to display their copper kettles and pan warmers etc.
£160–175
$230–255 SEA ⊞

Pair of Victorian servants' brass and ceramic bell pulls, 5in (12.5cm) wide. The comparatively low price is because these bell pulls are not quite a perfect pair.
£160–180/$230–260 OLA ⊞

► **Brass fire irons rest,** 19thC, 7½in (19cm) wide.
£160–175
$230–255 SEA ⊞

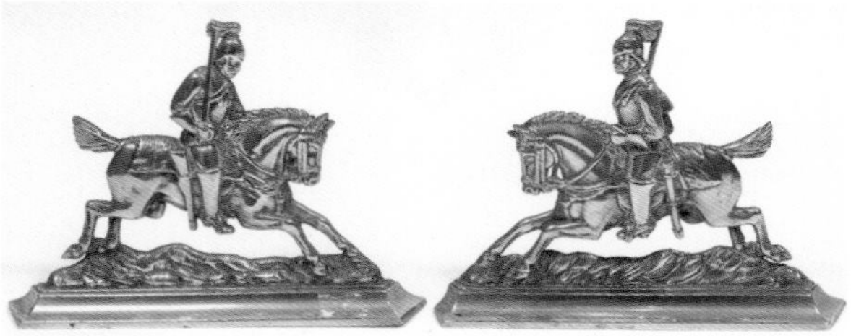

Pair of Victorian brass chimney pieces, No. 218993, 12 x 10in (30.5 x 25.5cm).
£160–180/$230–260 PICA ⊞

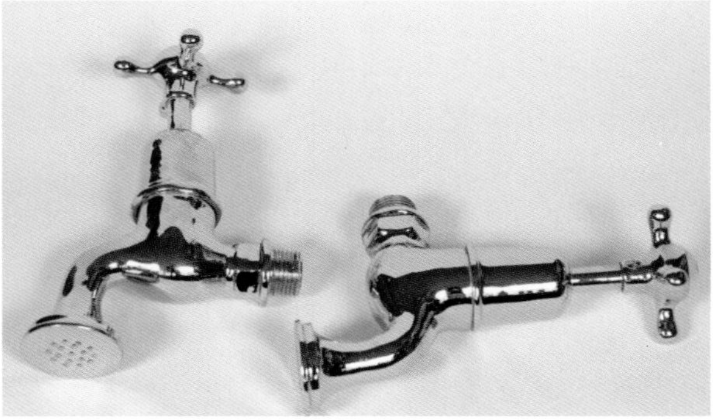

Pair of nickel-plated kitchen spray taps, reconditioned, 1930s, 7in (18cm) high. Antique taps may have non-standard threads. Ask the supplier if they can recommend a plumber who can fit them.
£180–200/$260–290 WRe ⊞

Victorian pine front door, with five panels, 84in (213.5cm) high.
£160–180/$230–260 WRe ⊞

Victorian pine quarter-glazed door, 29in (74cm) wide. With their etched glass and classic styling, these doors are often a cheaper alternative to a modern reproduction and are normally built much more solidly. Always check that the wood is sound, especially around the bottom edge. Doors which have had only one set of furniture are the better choice as less wood would have been cut away.
£215–240/$310–350 WRe

► **Victorian copper scuttle and shovel,** 18in (45.5cm) high. The en suite shovel adds to the desirability and price.
£225–250
$325–360 DOA

Extendable cast-iron and brass fender, 1870, 38in (96.5cm) wide.
£225–250/$325–360 PICA

Fenders

Machine dye-stamping enabled even quite elaborate pieces to be made quickly and cheaply. The mellow colour of old brass ensures it will fit in with most surroundings, unlike harsher modern brass, making fenders good value for money.

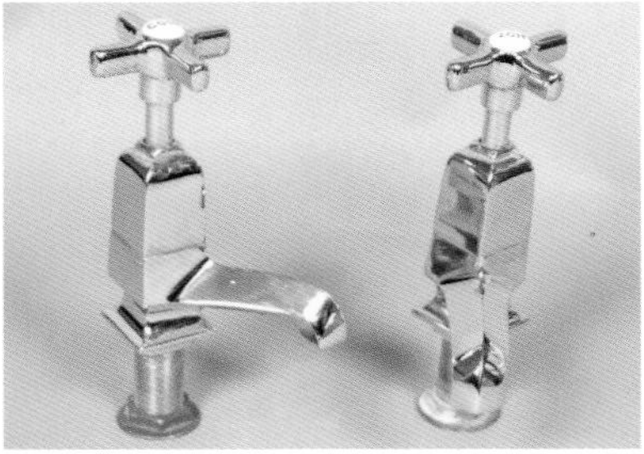

Pair of Art Deco nickel-plated taps, fully reconditioned, 1930s, 7in (18cm) high. The much sought-after shape of these Art Deco taps means there will always be a willing buyer.
£225–250/$325–360 WRe

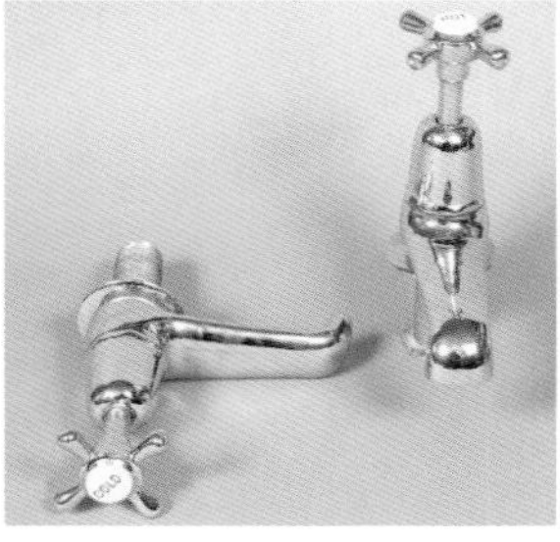

Pair of nickel-plated bath taps, fully reconditioned, c1915, 1in (2.5cm) thread.
£230–270/$330–390 WRe

Art Nouveau floral greenhouse heater, by Fletcher Russell & Co Ltd, Warrington, 36in (91.5cm) high.
£225–250/$325–360 OLA

Georgian steel and brass rim lock, with key, 16in (40.5cm) wide.
£250–280/$360–410 OLA

► **Pair of large polished brass taps,** fully reconditioned, c1901, large 1in (2.5cm) thread. These large taps with their classic styling would fit in with most surroundings.
£270–300
$390–440 WRe

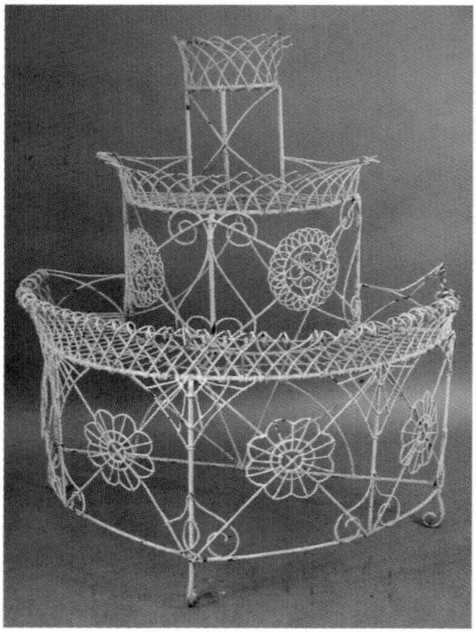

Wirework three-tier demi-lune conservatory stand, 19thC, 46¾in (119cm) high.
£300–360/$440–525 SWO

Brass door knocker, c1840, 8in (20.5cm) long.
£315–350/$450–500 RGe

► **Brass door stop,** stamped Coalbrookdale, c1840, 16in (40.5cm) high.
£360–400/$525–580 RGe

Pair of brass fire dogs, French, c1910, 14in (35.5cm) wide.
£325–360/$470–550 PICA

Oak chicken coup or carrying case, with hinged lid, the open front with 14 turned spindles, side handles, the end stiles extending as feet, 19thC, 62½in (159cm) wide.
£350–420/$500–620 PFK

Serpentine-shaped decorative cast-iron fender, c1850, 48in (122cm) wide. Adjustable fenders are much more desirable as they fit a variety of chimneypieces and can be taken with you when you move house.
£380–420/$560–610 ASH

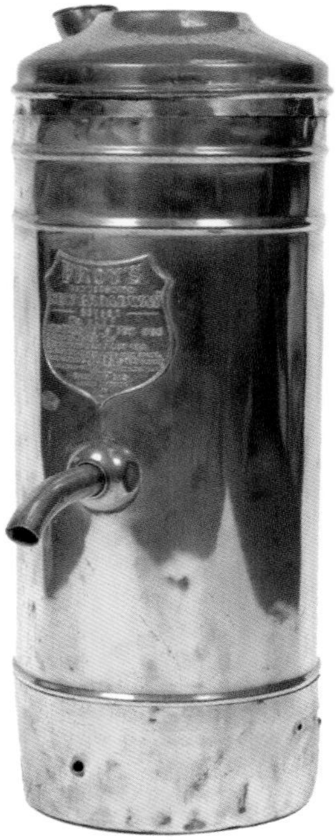

Froy's copper geyser, c1900, 26¾in (68cm) high.
£360–400/$500–580 C&R

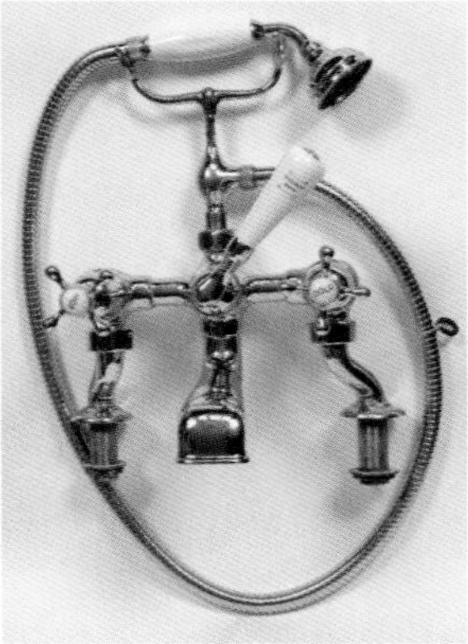

Nickel-plated bath mixer set, with shower attachment, fully reconditioned, c1930, 11in (28 cm) wide.
£380–420/$560–610 WRe

White wash-down lavatory, by Oeneas, with concealed S-trap, c1892, 16in (40.5cm) high.
£400–450/$580–650 OLA

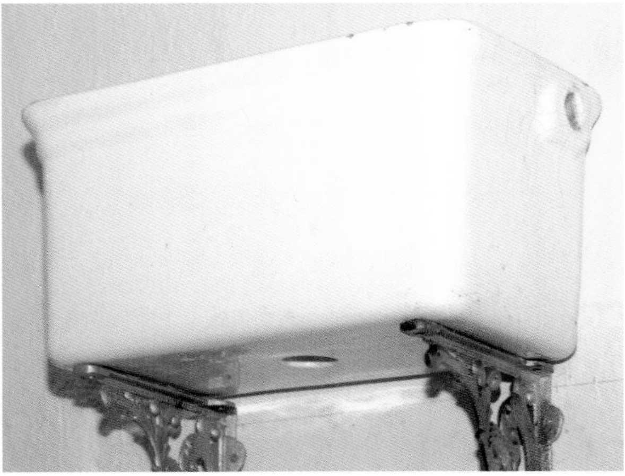

Ceramic high-level cistern, c1900, 17in (43 cm) wide.
£400–600/$580–870 C&R

Victorian cast-iron door stop, in the shape of an owl, 13in (33cm) high.
£420–470/$600–680 S(O)

◄ **Pair of elm bellows,** c1780, 18in (45.5cm) long. It is, in this case, the age of the bellows and the simple design that makes these more expensive than Edwardian ones which would not suit a cottage so well.
£430–475/$625–700 SEA

Pair of brass fire jambs, 1780–1800, 5in (12.5cm) high.
£430–475/$620–690 SEA ⊞

Sets/pairs

Unless otherwise stated, any description which refers to 'a set' or 'a pair' includes a guide price for the entire set or the pair, even though the illustration may show only a single item.

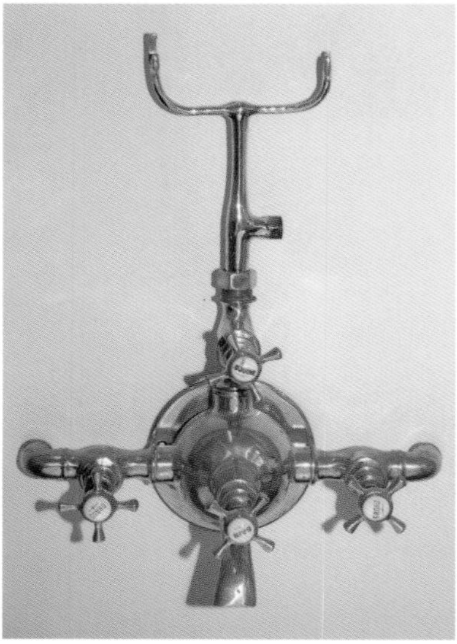

Polished brass wall tap mixer set, French, c1900, 18in (45.5cm) high.
£500–750/$720–1,100 C&R ⊞

Cast-iron fireplace, with grate and original tiles, c1880, 37in (94cm) wide.
£450–500/$650–720 WRe ⊞

Bronze garden sundial, on an inscribed limestone base, c1860, 15in (38cm) square.
£450–500/$650–720 HUM ⊞

Brown and white floral lavatory, by Trent, with concealed s-trap, c1885, 16in (40.5cm) high.
£450–500/$650–720 OLA ⊞

Pair of wrought iron fire dogs, French, c1780, 30in (76cm) high.
£500–550/$720–800 SEA ⊞

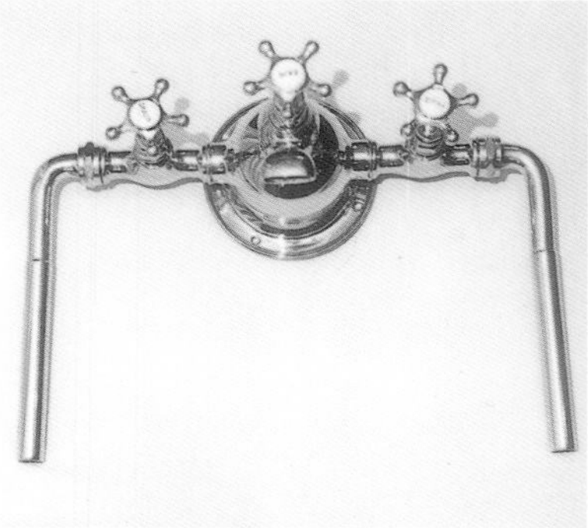

Nickel-plated bath filler, fully restored, French, 19th–early 20thC, 9in (23cm) wide.
£450–570/$650–825 ACT ⊞

Mahogany and lead-lined high-level cistern, c1900, 21in (53.5cm) wide.
£450–500/$650–720 C&R

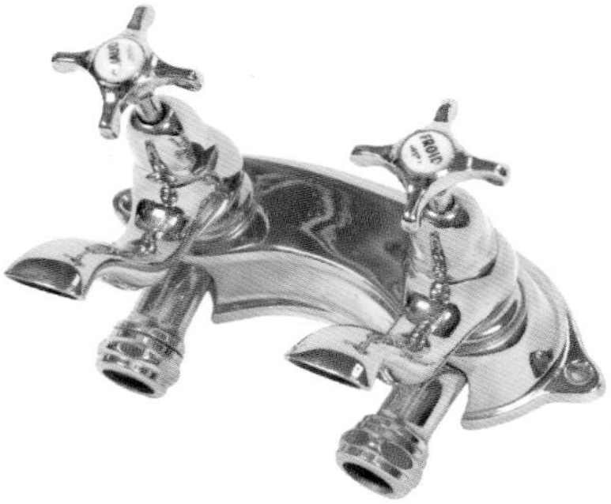

Set of nickel bath filler taps, c1900, 10in (25.5cm) wide. The stylish design combined with nickel, which is more expensive than brass, accounts for the higher price.
£500–750/$720–1,100 C&R

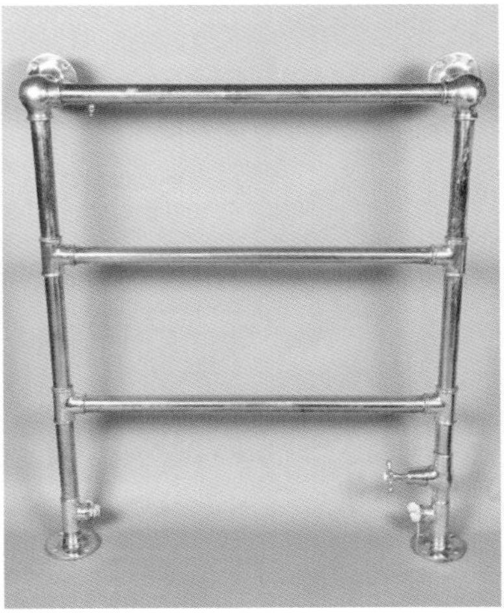

Copper and brass heated towel rail, reconditioned, c1915, 42in (106.5cm) high.
£675–750/$975–1,100 WRe

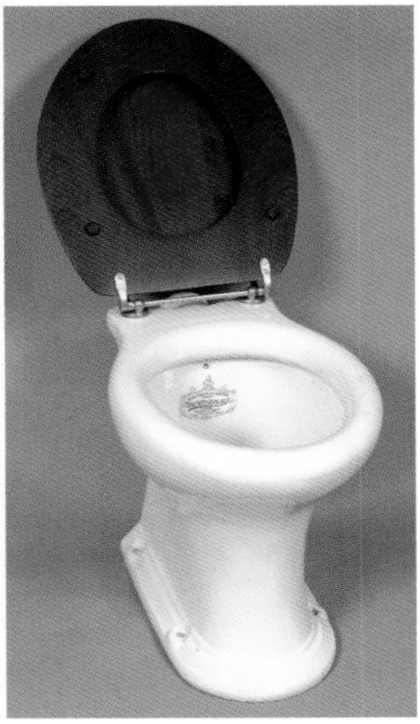

Lavatory pan, by Doulton, 'Waverley', c1900, 16in (40.5cm) high.
£675–750/$975–1,100 C&R

Blue and white floral-decorated wash-down lavatory pan, 'The Torrent', c1885, 16in (40.5cm) high. When buying lavatory pans, check the condition carefully, especially the glaze, as repairs are difficult to make.
£720–800
$1,050–1,150 OLA

Pair of gilt double rim locks, for double doors, original, French, c1880, 10in (25.5cm) wide.
£720–800/$1,050–1,150 OLA

Further reading

Miller's Antiques Price Guide,
Miller's Publications

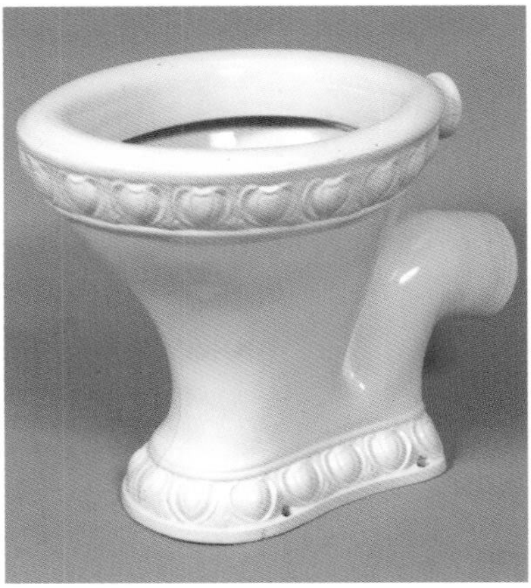

► **Lavatory pan,** by Stroud, London, c1900, 16in (40.5cm) high.
£750–1,000
$1,100–1,500
C&R

Arms & Armour

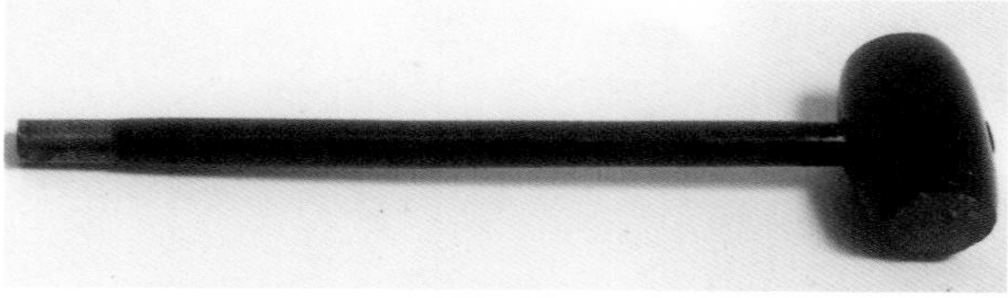

Ebony pistol mallet and rod, with leather and brass, from a set of flintlock duelling pistols, c1810, 9in (23cm) long. This item is part of the accessories contained within gun and pistol cases, which also includes bullet moulds, and makes an interesting subject for collection on their own. The hammer is used for starting the bullet into the barrel and the bullet is then pushed down and into the barrel using the rod.
£40–50/$60–75 ARB

Hunting knife, with horn handle, folding steel blade and steel shoulder, with carrying ring, 19thC, 14in (35.5cm) long.
£100–120/$145–175 TMA

Enfield breech loading rifle, no ramrod, missing collar, faults, 1872, 37½in (95.5cm) long. This is in poor condition, but suitable for mounting on a wall. Remember that some calibres of breech loaders require a firearms certificate.
£100–120/$145–175 SWO

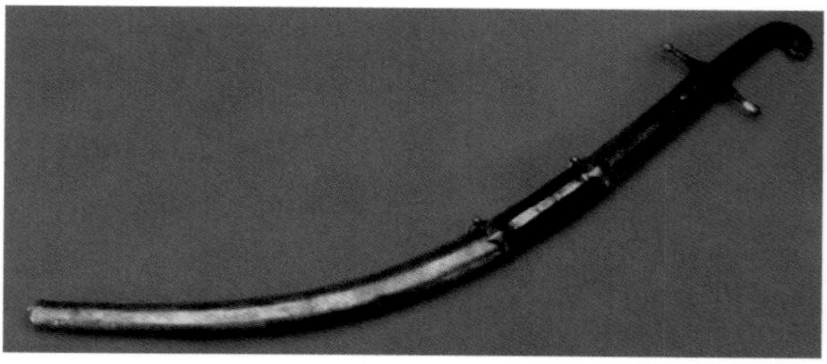

► **Tulwar sword,** with curved nickel-plated blade, silver and velvet sheath, horn hilt, c1900, blade 30in (76cm) long. Mameluke hilted swords are originally of Islamic derivation and became generally popular as dress swords during the late 18th and 19th centuries.
£120–150/$175–220 LCM

Collecting antique arms & armour

While a fascinating subject for collecting, the novice collector should observe the following rules:

- Quality and condition are paramount. Make allowances for condition respective to age. Some restoration can be tolerated if properly done but avoid over-restoration and excessive cleaning.
- A collection of one or two good pieces is better than a larger quantity of dubious quality.
- Keep your collection clean and stored or displayed in secure conditions.
- No licence is required to own, buy, sell, exchange or display any genuine antique muzzle-loading firearm. Most obsolete cartridge weapons do not require a licence either but professional advice should be sought before purchase. This applies to the UK only, other countries will have their own laws.
- Should a collector wish to fire any of his pieces, the relevant licences will be required. Deactivation totally destroys the value of antique firearms and should never be considered.

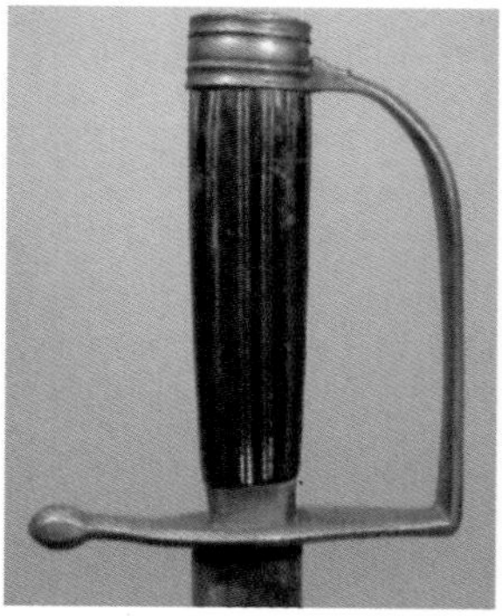

Brass-hilted hanger, with ribbed wood grip, blade stamped 'Woolley', c1780, blade 23¾in (60.5cm) long. Hanger is the name given to a short sidearm. It is similar to a hunting sword but is a service weapon.
£120–150/$175–220 WW

Flintlock & percussion pistols

In England, ignition for firearms by means of flint and steel dates from the beginning of the 17th century to the dawn of the 19th century. The Reverend Alexander Forsyth discovered that the properties of the fulminates of certain elements exploded when struck with a sharp blow.

Alexander Forsyth was a keen wildfowler and amateur chemist, and he knew from experience the shortcomings of loose powder priming in flintlocks in wet and windy conditions. His discovery and development led to the perfection of the copper percussion cap, which subsequently made a self-contained cartridge feasible.

12 bore manstopper percussion pistol, with Birmingham proofs, rounded walnut butt, trigger mechanism box frame with foliate engraving, turn off tightly closed, butt restored, c1850, 9¼in (23.5cm) long. Box lock percussion pistols of this type, both pocket and travelling size, were mass-produced mainly in Birmingham by numerous small workshops during the 19thC. The quality is frequently poor and, although they make interesting decorations, they have no place in a serious collection.
£175–200/$255–300 CrF

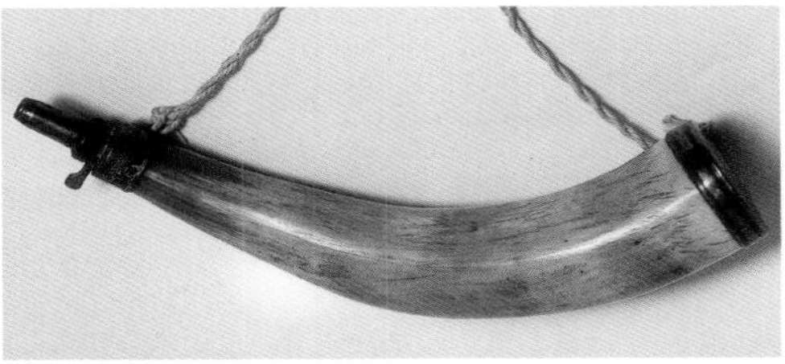

► **Powder horn,** for a rifle, with brass nozzle, c1800, 13in (33cm) long. Powder flasks and horns provide plenty of scope for collection on their own and are still very affordable.
£220–260/$320–380 ARB

Hunting knife and sheath, the ivory handle with three acorns to each side, the blade etched with deer and hunting dogs, by G. Eckenhoff, German, 19thC, 17¾in (45cm) long.
£220–260/$320–380 SWO

Victorian infantry officer's 1845 pattern sword, by Hawkes & Co, London, the brass four-bar basket hilt with crowned VR monogram, the curved single-edged blade etched with panels of foliage and royal cypher at the forte, in a black lacquered scabbard, blade 32in (81.5cm) long. Victorian military swords are still very common and offer an interesting field for the novice collector. Buy a good book on the subject and always remember that condition matters.
£240–280/$350–400 ASB

Fireman's brass helmet, by Merryweather & Sons, London, embossed with dragons and with applied badge of crossed axes within a scrolling cartouche, leather inset and adjustable-link chin strap, c1900. This is not as valuable as military helmets of the period, but still of interest.
£300–350/$440–500 B(Ed)

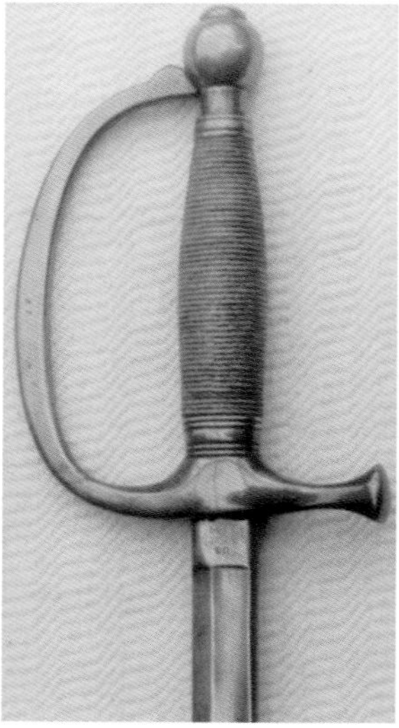

American Civil War officer's sword, the hilt with brass grip, pommel and knucklebow, blade marked 'US 1864, Ames Mfg co', in black leather scabbard with brass mounts, minor cracking to scabbard, blade 28in (71cm) long. American Civil War items are popular on both sides of the Atlantic, but are much rarer in Britain.
£300–350/$440–500 ASB

Miller's compares...

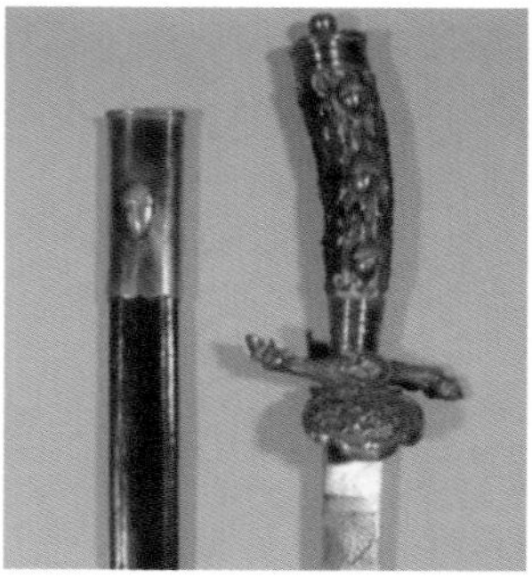

A. Hunting sword, with copper-mounted hilt, etched blade by ACS and copper-mounted scabbard, early 20thC, blade 15¾in (40cm) long. Hunting swords and associated accoutrements provide an interesting field for collecting as a group, and quality is usually good.
£280–340/$400–500 WW

B. Hunting sword, the silver-mounted hilt with green-stained ivory grip, c1760, blade 24¼in (61.5cm) long.
£380–420/$570–620 WW

Item A has a stag-horn grip and brass mounts, and although complete with scabbard and in very good condition, it is very late. Item B has an ivory grip and pewter mounts and dates from 150 years earlier. It is therefore not only more valuable but of greater interest to collectors.

◄ **Silver-mounted Skean Dhu,** the stag-horn hilt with silver ferrule engraved with strapwork and owner's name 'Evan Fraser-Campbell', the pommel with silver cap engraved with a crest and motto, the blade with faceted back edge, in a leather scabbard with silver mounts engraved with strapwork, hallmarked Edinburgh 1898, blade 3¼in (8.5cm) long. Highland regalia experienced a renaissance following the visit to Scotland in 1822 by King George IV. Scottish items are always popular.
£320–360/$450–500 P(Ed)

Travelling flintlock pistol, by Brander & Potts, hammer replaced, c1800, barrel 6in (15cm) long. This is an attractive pistol by a good London maker who was a contractor to the Board of Ordnance. It is in rather poor condition but represents good value at this price.
£360–440/$550–650 SWO

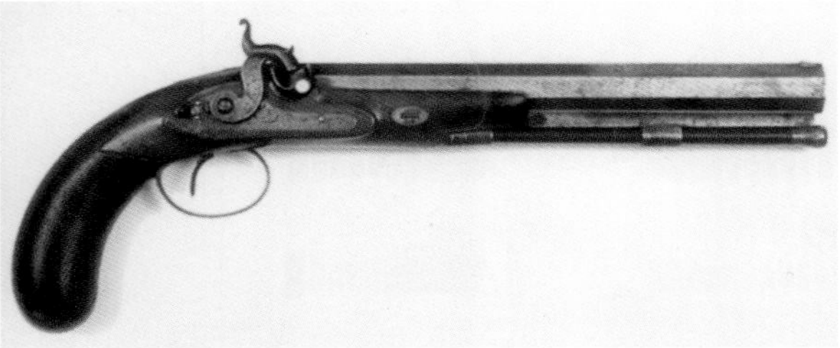

40 bore percussion duelling pistol, by Robert Wheeler & Son, Birmingham, with Birmingham proofs, the twist octagonal sighted barrel signed on the top flat, the scroll-engraved breech with pierced platinum plug, the scroll-engraved tang incorporating the back-sight, with signed scroll-engraved bolted detented lock, figured walnut half-stock, rounded chequered escutcheon, horn fore-end cap and original steel-tipped ramrod, some wear and light pitting to barrel, mid-19thC, 15in (38cm) long. This pistol is one of a pair originally contained in a wooden case with the necessary accessories. It is of good quality and in fairly good condition. These pistols are still quite easy to find and the collector can afford to be choosy.
£500–600/$720–870 Bon

Snaphaunce pistol, with associated octagonal barrel, the lock engraved with monster-head scrolls, chiselled with a grotesque mask on the tail, and fitted with sliding pan-cover, moulded figured walnut stock, chiselled iron mounts including side-plate incorporating a grotesque mask and associated iron ramrod, top-jaw replaced, battery refaced, cracks and repairs to stock, trigger-guard replaced, belt hook missing, Italian, c1750, 13in (33cm) long. This is an interesting early type of mechanism on a good quality pistol, but it would need a considerable sum spent to really make it worthwhile.
£750–900/$1,100–1,300 S(O)

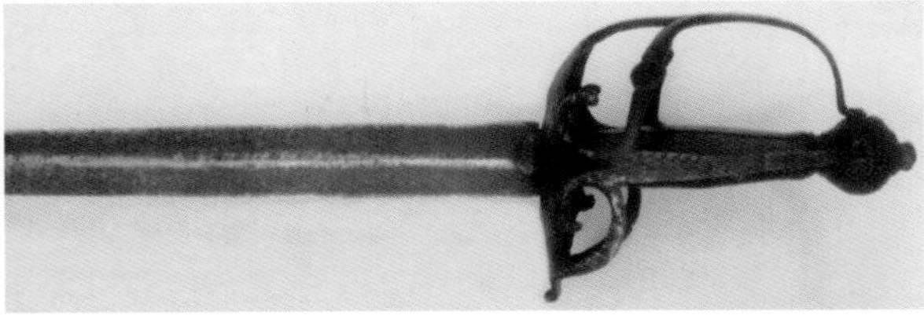

Iron mortuary sword, with tapering double-edged flattened diamond blade, semi-basket hilt, guard chiselled with six stylized human masks, chiselled ovoid pommel, wood grip, grip cover missing, one bar of guard loose at pommel, age pitting overall, 17thC, blade 32in (81.5cm) long. The mortuary sword was so-called because the guard bowls of the hilts are often crudely engraved with busts supposedly of King Charles I and his Consort. Condition is usually not good, which is understandable given the age of these pieces.
£850–1,000/$1,250–1,500 WAL

Duelling pistols

The practice of duelling with pistols, as opposed to swords, came about with a change in gentlemen's fashion in the 1760s. Initially, a pair of riding holster pistols or travelling pistols was the new weapon of choice, but soon one or two entrepreneurial gunsmiths saw a gap in the market and started to produce a specialized weapon.

Duelling was never lawful in this country; theoretically a duel ending in death could lead to the gallows. The practice gradually fell out of favour with the accession of Queen Victoria who strongly disapproved of it and by 1850 duelling had, to all intents and purposes, ceased in England.

Basket-hilted military broadsword, with double-fullered blade, the steel hilt composed of flattened bars and junction plates pierced with hearts and circles connected to a ring beneath the pommel, leather-covered wood grip, some old repairs, Scottish, c1770, 30in (76cm) long. 18thC Scottish swords are always desirable and would be hard to find under £1,000/$1,500. Many of these swords were hidden in the thatched roofs of bothies after the defeat at Culloden in 1746.
£750–850/$1,100–1,250 P(Ed)

Boxes

Sorrento ware book-shaped box, c1910, 5in (12.5cm) wide.
£52–58/$75–90 MLL

Walnut sarcophagus-shaped tea-caddy, with chevron parquetry banding and interior mahogany covers, 19thC, 8in (20.5cm) wide. A good, late box with original finish/age on turned bun feet. Slight wear to extreme corners.
£65–100/$95–145 G(L)

Victorian hanging oak candle box, carved with oak leaves, 16in (40.5cm) high. An attractive piece but the lid may be a replacement as all the other facets are carved.
£70–85/$100–125 G(L)

Collecting advice

The interest in collecting boxes, especially tea caddies, over the last ten years has inevitably also seen a sizable rise in the price of many examples.

Tortoiseshell, ivory and fruitwood tea caddies have increased the most over this period. However, there are still many good boxes to be found for under £1,000/$1,500 and before purchasing a box, one should follow these guidelines:

- Originality – Ensure that the object is an antique, not 'cobbled' together from old timber, or an out-and-out fake. These are, unfortunately, quite common at auction and unfortunately also seen in some dealer's stock, marked and priced as period.
- Quality is difficult to define but includes proportion, style, workmanship and the materials that the object is made from. These factors, and also the object's rarity, will determine the price.
- Colour and patination are what makes an antique! Patination is not dirt, but the accumulation of dust, wax and age over the object's life. Glassy, repolished and over-restored boxes should be avoided. The only exception to this rule is that tortoiseshell may be cleaned to bring out its natural lustre, markings and colours.
- Price – Bearing in mind the above points, two boxes, that initially appear to be similar may be valued differently. A good rule is to buy one quality item rather than three or four lesser ones, but always buy because you like the item.

◀ **Regency brass-bound coromandel decanter box,** with four rectangular spirit decanters, one initialled 'B', another 'S' and two other odd decanters, three of the plated stoppers marked Gin, Rum and Whiskey, with brass swing-handle, and a rectangular japanned coal bucket. This box has been forced open at some time, damaging the lock and keep and the area around it. The escutcheon plate also appears out of proportion and may be of a later date.
£70–100/$100–145 BR

Victorian Tunbridge ware stamp box, with facsimile 'Receipts' stamp, c1860, 1¾in (4.5cm) wide.
£75–100/$110–145 VB

Tunbridge ware stamp box, with Victorian facsimile postage stamps, c1860, 1¾in (4.5cm) square. Slight damage to the transfer print, otherwise a very good box.
£75–100/$110–145 VB

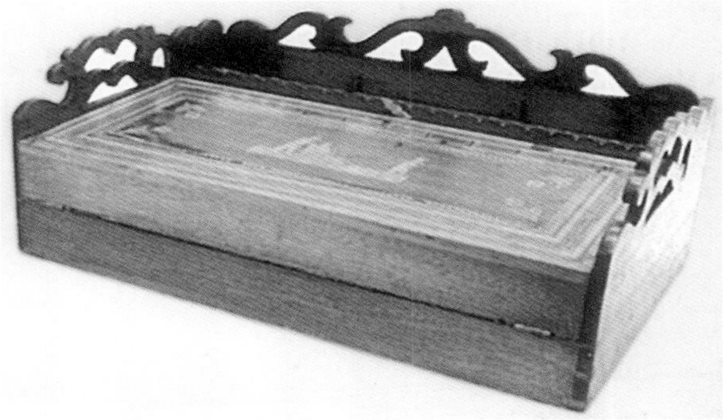

Mahogany writing slope, the pierced, scrolled gallery over a marquetry–inlaid rising top with figures pulling a sleigh, the interior silk-lined and fitted with twelve small lidded compartments, early 20thC, 18in (45.5cm) wide.
£85–100/$125–145 DA

Miller's compares...

A. Tunbridge ware pen box, with floral border, damaged, c1860, 10½in (26.5cm) wide.
£90–110/$130–160 G(L)

B. Tunbridge ware rosewood glove box, with floral-decorated top and sides, c1850, 11¼in (28.5cm) wide.
£220–265/$320–385 G(L)

Item B is in good condition and is a much better buy than the distressed box, Item A. Although Item A could be restored, it would be a costly job and would make the final price of the box higher than the example in good condition.

Victorian papier mâché snuff box, decorated with two seaside donkeys and motto 'When shall we three meet again', 3in (7.5cm) wide.
£90–110/$130–160 G(L)

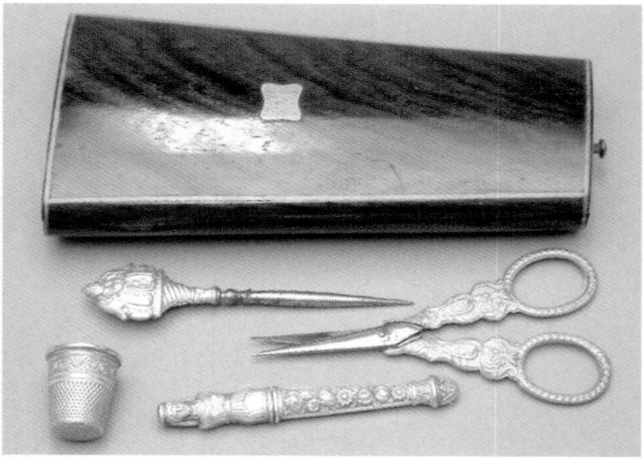

Rosewood étui, fitted with white metal needlecase, stiletto, pair of scissors and thimble, French, 19thC, 4in (10cm) long.
£95–115/$140–165 G(L)

Papier mâché circular box, the cover painted with a portrait of an Italian woman wearing national costume, Continental, 19thC, 3¾in (9.5cm) diam.
£100–110/$145–160 WW

► Mahogany tea chest, with a brass swing handle, a lift-up secret compartment with an oak drawer for a caddy spoon, mid-18thC, 9½in (24cm) wide. A rather heavy-set tea caddy.
£110–120
$160–175 WW

Victorian rosewood-veneered tea chest, the recessed panel cover and front with reel mouldings, the interior with a later shallow glass bowl flanked by a pair of caddies, side handles missing, 14in (35.5cm) wide. Although missing the turned ring side-handles and possibly feet – this is still a good quality box, having good markings on the rosewood.
£110–120/$160–175 WW

Porcupine quilled and ebony-work box, with bone inlay, the interior with a fitted tray and nine cupboard compartments, 19thC, 12in (30.5cm) wide. Although not to everyone's taste, it is a good box at the price. Avoid those boxes with warped/twisted lids as they give an unsightly 'smile' to the front and are expensive to correct.
£110–130/$160–190 G(L)

Burr-yew wood work box, damaged, tray missing, 19thC, 10¼in (26cm) wide. This box has suffered from sun and/or water damage. However, it is restorable and is an attractive piece.
£140–170/$200–250 SWO

Victorian figured-walnut two-compartment tea caddy, 9in (23cm) wide. These are quite common, so pick and choose a good example. Beware of shrinkage in the carcase pulling apart the veneers.
£160–180/$230–260 TMA

Miller's compares...

A. Mahogany paint box, with chequer stringing, the fitted interior with a paper trade label for Reeves & Inwood, To the Royal Family and Acadamies At The Kings Arms, the frieze drawer with a later Dutch drop handle, early 19thC, 9in (23cm) wide.
£140–200/$200–290 WW

B. Victorian mahogany paint box, the interior of the lid with a trade label for Winsor & Newton, with fitted interior, a frieze drawer with a sunken brass handle, and a ceramic artist's palette, 8½in (21.5cm) wide.
£200–250/$290–350 WW

Item A appears to have the original finish/patination and the trade label is a nice feature. However the interior is just a little worn, whereas Item B is a much better box for not much more money. It has a nicer interior and, although it is of a later date, it is a better buy.

◀ **Mahogany box,** with lower drawer and ivory escutcheons, c1770, 17in (43cm) wide. The ring marks and splits to the top detract from what is quite a good box.
£170–200
$250–290 OTT

Carved mahogany shoe-shaped snuff box, with piqué decoration, 19thC, 4in (10cm) wide. This item appears to have the original finish/patination. Avoid snuff-shoes that have been ruined and devalued by over restoration and refinishing.
£170–210/$250–300 G(L)

Miller's compares...

A. Regency rosewood tea caddy, with two lidded compartments and cast brass ring handles, 13in (33cm) wide. A good, honest box which, although of simple form, has good markings in the veneers.
£170–220/$250–320 SWO

B. Rosewood tea caddy, with cut brass escutcheon, brass rail line and angular handle to the hinged cover, enclosing two lift-out tea boxes, both with hinged covers, early 19thC, 10in (25.5cm) wide.
£300–330/$440–475 TMA

Both are good boxes. Item B has the more decorative escutcheon and handle, but lacks the nice fluted bun feet of Item A. Not visible in the picture of Item A are the cast brass ring handles to either side.

Mahogany tea caddy, with brass handle, escutcheon and lion paw feet, interior altered, 18thC, 9½in (24cm) wide. This is a good original piece even though the lid is slightly displaced and the bottom plinth is possibly of a later date. Other tips to check for are any damage or poor restoration around the hinges.
£180–220/$260–320 SWO

► **Victorian walnut stationery box,** the burr-veneered sloping flaps reveal a fitted interior above a drawer, 16in (40.5cm) wide. This box has good markings to the veneer, faded to a good mellow colour to make this an attractive piece.
£200–220
$290–320 WW

◄ **George III mahogany box,** 10in (25.5cm) wide. This caddy, once a good Georgian box, has been totally over-restored and has lost its patination due to being stripped and re-polished. The keyhole escutcheon is also missing.
£200–250
$290–360 OTT

◄ **Treen snuffbox,** with inlaid silver wirework scrolled decoration and similar decoration to the heel and sole, 19thC, 3½in (9cm) long.
£200–230/$290–330 Bea(E)

Black lacquer gaming box, decorated with pagoda landscape scenes, with fitted interior of lidded boxes with mother-of-pearl gaming counters, 19thC, 11¾in (30cm) wide. The lid has become detached from its base. Check around the hinges for damage, old poor restoration, etc, as this will affect the price.
£220–300/$320–440 Bea(E)

Burr yew tea caddy, with sycamore and mahogany banding and a domed top, with lidded compartments, 19thC, 11¾in (30cm) wide. The brass ring handle needs re-shaping, but otherwise this is a very good caddy.
£250–300/$360–440 SWO

Oak Bible box, with carved front frieze, 17thC, 27¼in (69cm) wide. This appears to be a good, original box, but be careful of boxes made up from old fragments of carvings and timber etc.
£350–400/$500–580 S(O)

► **Regency-style penwork work-box,** with chinoiserie figures and motifs against a black ground, on cast brass feet, 9in (23cm) wide.
£260–300
$380–440 G(L)

◄ **Pressed horn box,** by John Obriset, with the arms of Sir Francis Drake, early 18thC, 4in (10cm) wide. John Obriset (d1731) made many boxes in pressed horn and tortoiseshell. Always check carefully for splits, chips and poor repairs when contemplating buying items made from tortoiseshell and horn.
£450–500/$650–720 HUM

Tortoiseshell tea caddy, with pewter stringing, the interior with two lidded compartments, on bun feet, some damage, mid-19thC, 6in (15cm) wide. The price of tortoiseshell items, including tea caddies, are dependant upon condition, shape, style and rarity and quality of the tortoiseshell veneer used. This example scores relatively low on all these accounts. However, it is an honest box that has not suffered from incompetent restoration, which makes it a better buy than many others on the market.
£380–450/$565–650 WW

Mahogany travelling work box, with side carrying handles, the crossbanded moulded hinged top enclosing a compartmented interior above two graduated drawers, on a plinth base, c1780, 22¾in (58cm) wide. Some water damage to the top, good veneers to the front. The handles with traces of original gilding. An attractive and useful piece.
£650–800/$950–1,150 S(S)

Dolls, Teddy Bears & Toys

Bassett-Lowke G1 wooden truck, c1914, 7in (18cm) long. This Bassett-Lowke truck represents fine value as although it is quite play-worn its early date, popular maker and solid structure hold it in good stead. A 1950s metal gauge 0 first-class Bassett-Lowke carriage can make around £120–150/$175–220, while a 1930s metal locomotive would make around £700/$1,000. Look out for individual carriages, track sections and locomotives of the same gauge and maker to build up an affordable collection.
£30–32/$45–47 VJ

Clockwork pecking bird, in plush and metal, c1900, 5in (12.5cm) long. While items like this are visually appealing, if not working it is worth consulting an expert before buying as restoration can cost more than the item is worth. However, there is a market for visually appealing toys that do not work for use as display items.
£70–75/$100–110 Beb

What is a shelf piece?

A shelf piece is a toy that can be used for decorative purposes even though it has some damage or missing parts. The decorative attributes of the toy will not have been diminished even though its value may have.

► **Lithographed tinplate toy snake,** with flywheel mechanism, German, c1920, 16in (40.5cm) long. If tinplate toys do not work, make sure the toy is otherwise in excellent condition to have as a shelf piece.
£75–90
$110–130 G(L)

Three pairs of leather shoes, to fit large dolls. The boots appear to be Victorian and the shoes 1900–30.
£90–100/$130–145 a pair Beb

Doll's towel and a soap doll, the towel boxed with labels, the doll in a French box, 1900s, boxes 6in (15cm) long. Anything made of soap is rare because of its vulnerable composition.
Towel £75–100/$110–145
Soap £100–150/$145–220 Beb

► **Child's laundry set,** c1900, mangle 8in (20.5cm) high. Sets can easily be separated, so it can be worth keeping an eye out at fairs and junk shops for individual pieces that can be put together to achieve a similar look.
£150–175/$220–255 SMI ⊞

Dolls' furniture

When buying dolls' furniture it is worth considering if the piece is handmade or mass-produced. If it is handmade, is it well made? What is the condition? If it is a dolls' vanity or bureau, is the mirror cracked or missing? Do the knobs match? Are any missing? Are the proportions of the piece correct? If it is part of a set, are all the parts there? Are the proportions of the complete set correct? Do they match? Is the piece signed and dated by the maker? Was the piece made for a famous child or a well-known person? Overall, consider if you like the piece and feel it will fit in with the rest of your collection. Purchasing an item you love is usually the best way to buy.

Doll's *faux* bamboo chair, probably beech, with cane seat, c1900, 14in (35.5cm) high. It appears that little, if any, restoration is required on this chair, making the price very attractive.
£220–245/$320–355 MLL ⊞

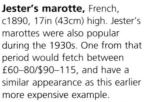

Jester's marotte, French, c1890, 17in (43cm) high. Jester's marottes were also popular during the 1930s. One from that period would fetch between £60–80/$90–115, and have a similar appearance as this earlier more expensive example.
£225–250/$325–360 AUTO ⊞

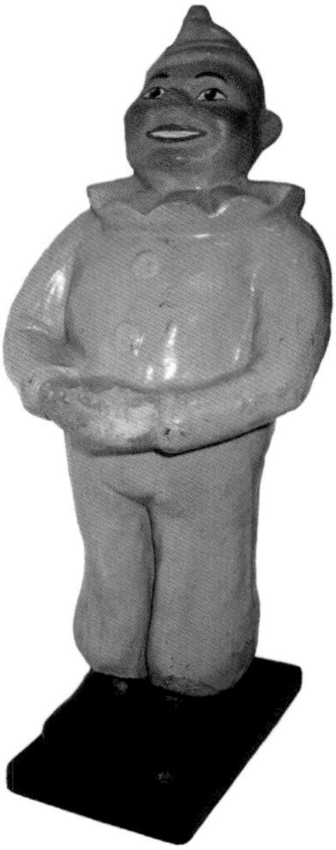

Papier mâché fairground clown, on a tilting wooden base, c1900, 12in (30.5cm) high. Papier mâché toys are often found in poor condition, unlike this item. Good condition adds to the value.
£225–250/$325–360 Beb ⊞

What makes a toy collectable?

- ◆ Clarity of design
- ◆ Clever mechanisms
- ◆ Comic or appealing facial features
- ◆ Condition
- ◆ Rarity
- ◆ Signature of the maker

The look without the price

Teddy bear, with boot button eyes and original outfit, c1930, 6in (15cm) high. The bear and his clothes show some wear, which is usual for a toy of this age.
£270–300/$390–440 Beb ⊞

An unmarked teddy bear from the 1930s with a pleasing expression will cost less than a Steiff bear of the same size but often the same appeal. A Shuco stuffed toy from Germany is usually less expensive than a Steiff, as is a Shackman, distributed through the United States. The attention to detail in the colouring of the fur etc is not the same, but it will still be a good, decorative item. Remember, just because a toy is old does not mean that it is valuable. A broken or worn toy with missing or altered parts is not valuable just because it is old.

► **Lehmann Tut-Tut clockwork automobile,** EDL 490, unboxed, one front wheel missing, 1905–35. The missing front wheel has been taken into account in the price.
£350–450/$500–650 N

Considerations when buying toys

- ◆ There should be no missing parts.
- ◆ If the toy is made of plastic, it should not be cracked or misshapen.
- ◆ Cast-iron toys should not be heavily rusted or have worn paint.
- ◆ Do not buy a rubber toy that is dry or brittle.
- ◆ A toy is usually worth more if it still has its original box.
- ◆ Not all reproductions are marked.
- ◆ Rare means just that. Only a limited number were made and a few survived years of being played with by children.
- ◆ If a toy is owned or made by someone famous, it is usually more valuable because of its provenance.

► **Beige mohair teddy bear,** with brown velvet pads, amber eyes, together with a golden mohair bear, repaired, 1920s, 28in (71cm) and 18in (45.5cm) high. Mohair bears are more desirable than plush ones as long as they are in reasonable condition.
£425–500/$620–720 G(L)

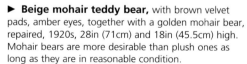

Miller's compares...

A. Clockwork rabbit, covered with rabbit fur, playing a bell, c1930, 12in (30.5cm) high.
£400–450/$580–650 AUTO

B. Clockwork drumming polar bear, by Roullet et Decamps, covered in goat fur, c1910, 10in (25.5cm) high.
£520–580/$750–850 AUTO

Item A is less expensive than Item B as it cannot be attributed to a maker, but it is French. At 12in (30.5cm) high it is small for a rabbit automaton and larger, named ones can fetch between £11,000–12,000/$16,000–17,500. This model has a simple jumping mechanism that produces a comic jerking action. It is however, covered in real rabbit fur, strengthening the price and authenticity.

Both Item B and Item C are by Roullet et Decamp. Item C still has the original label around its neck bearing the stock number and the Decamp stamp, and Item B is listed in a design catalogue. Item B is rare and has a more complex jumping mechanism than Item A as both the arms move, beating the drum and cymbal. The goat fur was chosen to represent polar bear fur, and the overall impression is one of a comic parody.

Item C has an extremely complex motor that moves the head left to right and back, lifts the glasses up to the nose and fans gently all at once. Unlike the jumping mechanism of the other two items, this automaton has a smooth, deliberate, realistic movement which accounts for its higher price. The rabbit fur covering and the glass eyes are both in good condition but a musical accompaniment would make this model worth even more.

◄ **C. Automaton cat,** covered in rabbit fur, by Roullet et Decamps, with stock label round the neck, c1930, 12in (30.5cm) high.
£750–1,000/$1,100–1,500 AUTO

Kitchenware

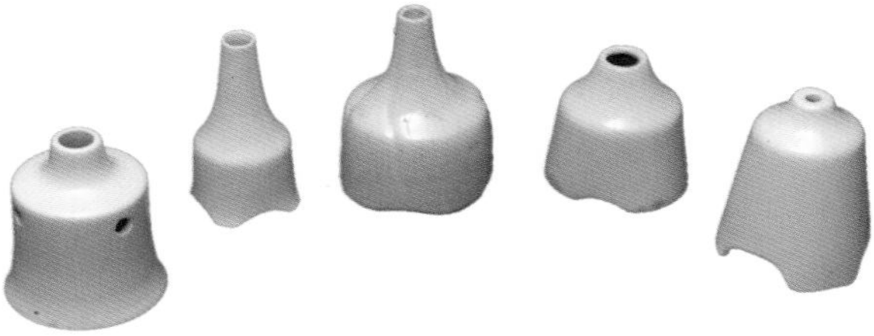

Five ceramic pie funnels, 1930s, 3in (7.5cm) high. Pie funnels are easy to find and relatively inexpensive.
£4–5/$5–7 AL

Derbyshire brown salt-glazed mould, c1840, 4in (10cm) diam.
£10–12/$15–18 IW

Salter cast-iron quadrant scale, with brass trim, hook missing, c1880, 10in (25.5cm) high. This is an unusual scale and very sought-after.
£20–30/$30–45 ET

Oak and copper-bound jug, c1900, 12in (30.5cm) high. Originally used for carrying cider or wine, this would look good filled with dried flowers.
£32–35/$47–50 MLL

Bretby butter dish, slight damage, 1930s, 7½in (19cm) diam. Bretby manufactured storage jars, rolling pins, mixing bowls etc in the same design, making them a good subject for collecting.
£34–38/$48–58 B&R

Miller's compares...

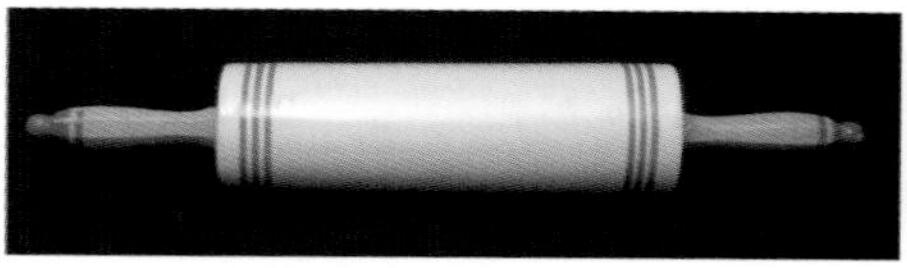

A. Streamline rolling pin, by T. G. Green, with wooden handle and ceramic body, c1930, 18in (45.5cm) long.
£30–35/$45–50 AL

B. Cornishware rolling pin, stamped T. G. Green, 1950s, 17in (43cm) long.
£85–95/$125–140 HSt

Rolling pins are very collectable; as well as being functional they are also decorative. Both these rolling pins served the same purpose when new but now, years later, they have to be compared on their collectable merits. Item B can be incorporated into a larger collection of virtually every china kitchen item, and the quality has resulted in them being in the same condition now as when first purchased. Item A can be prone to crazing and discolouration, making it less decorative, less desirable and consequently cheaper.

Mixing bowl, by T. G. Green, 1940s, 10in (25.5cm) diam.
£40–45/$60–65 HSt ⊞

Mahogany cutlery tray, with two sections, c1820, 14in (35.5cm) wide. This is a good, deep tray.
£70–80/$100–115 F&F ⊞

Enamel jug, French, c1930, 11in (28cm) high.
£50–55/$75–80 AL ⊞

◄ **Enamel bread bin,** 1930, 11in (28cm) high. Coloured bread bins are more desirable – the more unusual the colour the higher the price.
£55–60/$80–90 AL ⊞

Wooden grain measure, c1860, 12in (30.5cm) high. This item is in good condition and could be used to hold plants or dried flowers.
£50–75/$75–110 WaH ⊞

► **Lightning pottery egg-beater,** size 1, steel and brass beater missing, c1900, 9in (23cm) high. Black and white pottery is collectable and this original beater would make an attractive addition to a kitchen.
£60–80/$90–115 B&R ⊞

◄ **Steel and brass milk strainer,** by John Tyler & Sons, Highbridge, c1900, 16½in (42cm) wide.
£70–80/$100–115 B&R ⊞

Salter brass spring balance, c1880, 11in (28cm) high. This scale is for weighing bread and is more unusual than most.
£55–60/$80–90 SMI ⊞

◄ **Grocer's butter crock,** c1890, 8in (20.5cm) diam.
£80–90
$115–130 WeA

► **Teak and steel grain measure,** 1880, 9in (23cm) high. This is possibly European, hence the low price.
£90–100
$130–145 MLL

Copper cream skimmer, 19thC, 20in (51cm) long.
£135–150/$195–220 SEA

Set of four enamel storage jars, French, c1930, 7in (18cm) high. French enamel items are very desirable because of their colours and shapes.
£120–135/$175–195 AL

► **Copper lobed and turreted shallow ring mould,** stamped 522, 19thC, 6in (15cm) diam. This is a nice, decorative mould at a good price.
£140–170/$200–250 TMA

The look without the price

A similar set of measures made in the late 18th or early 19th century would command a price of £350–450/$500–650 at auction and would retail in excess of £500/$720. These later good-quality measures realized £100/$145 at auction – newer sets can be bought for considerably less.

Three Victorian copper measures, two-gallon, two-quart and one-quart capacities, 20thC.
£100–120/$145–175 G(L)

Copper pan, with copper handles, 19thC, 16in (40.5cm) wide. Copper pans are generally preferred over a modern pan for jam making etc and are very attractive when hung in the kitchen.
£150–165/$220–240 PICA

Tin cutlery tray, with painted lid and brass carrying handle, c1890, 12in (30.5cm) wide. One side of the tray is for teaspoons and the other for dessertspoons. It is unusual and in very good condition.
£155–175/$225–255 SMI

Oak coopered jug, c1800, 17in (43cm) high. This jug was used for beer, wine or cider.
£160–175/$230–255 F&F

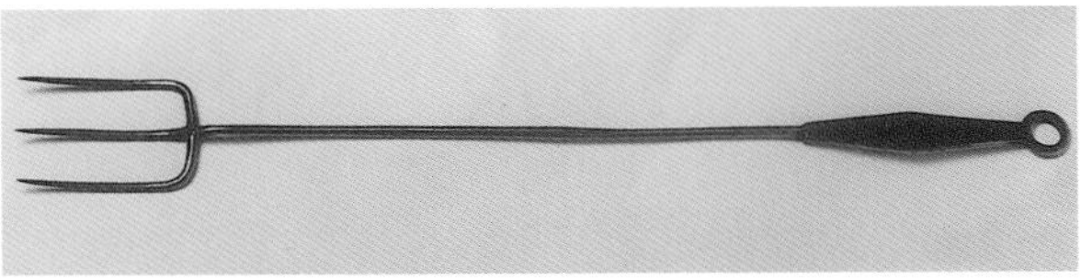

Iron toasting fork, c1800, 24in (61cm) long.
£165–175/$240–255 SEA

► **Doulton salt-glazed water filter,** c1880, 18in (45.5cm) high. This is a very unusually shaped filter with a good coloured glaze. Rarely found complete with the lid, this is a very good buy.
£180–200/$260–290 AL

Ceramic milk barrel, c1920, 10in (25.5cm) high. This is rare and in good condition.
£180–200/$260–290 SMI

Two copper saucepans and lids, with iron handles, late 19thC, larger 10¾in (27.5cm) diam.
£190–225/$275–325 SWO

***Tôle peinte* oval bread basket,** with pierced gallery, early 19thC, 10½in (27cm) wide.
£200–250/$290–360 S(O)

► **Iron peel,** c1780, 19in (48.5cm) long. This was probably used on a domestic range.
£250–275/$360–400 RGe ⊞

Locate the source

The source of each illustration in Miller's can be found by checking the code letters below each caption with the Key to Illustrations, pages 286–290.

Mahogany tapering candle box, c1800, 18in (45.5cm) high. This is a very nice example with a heart motif, popular with the American market.
£250–280/$360–410 F&F ⊞

Mahogany wall-mounted salt box, with a drawer, c1820, 14in (35.5cm) high. This salt box has a lovely patina and a drawer which is unusual.
£255–285/$365–415 F&F ⊞

Coopered wine jug, French, Burgundy, late 19thC, 15in (38cm) high.
£265–275/$385–400 AMS ⊞

Steel dairy can, by C. Hull of Shaftesbury, early 20thC, 20in (51cm) high.
£265–295/$385–420 B&R ⊞

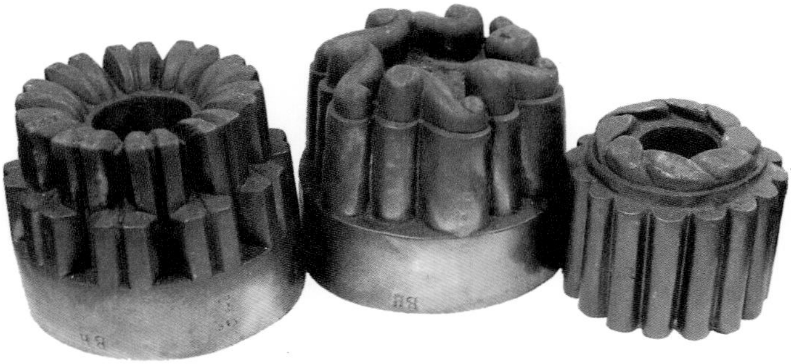

Two copper jelly moulds, with orb and cross stamps, numbered 343 and 363, 19thC, 6in (15cm) diam, and a smaller jelly mould, 4in (10cm) diam. Cleaned and restored, these moulds would fetch £200/$300 each.
£260–310/$380–450 G(L) ⚒

Dairy cans

Milk delivery cans were used to take milk to the householders where it could be ladled out as required.

Cornishware

Cornishware has grown more and more popular over the last two years. Jars with unusual wording such as Granulated Sugar, Brown Sugar or with titles out of the ordinary are fetching anything from £80–200/$115–290, and even more for rarer examples. Everyday jars with labels such as Flour, Sugar and Tea realize £40–50/$60–75. Cornishware is still a very good investment as it is usable as well as decorative.

Cornishware Flour storage jar, 8in (20.5cm) high, and four similar storage jars.
£325–375/$470–560 G(L)

Wrought-iron game crown, French, c1780, 11in (28cm) diam. This crown can be used for a variety of other purposes, such as displaying dried flowers or herbs.
£340–375/$490–560 SEA

George III mahogany candle box, with an arched back plate, sliding panelled lid with parquetry banding and marquetry paterae with oak leaves and acorns, 18in (45.5cm) high. This is a good example with good quality inlay.
£470–570/$680–850 AH

Wooden spice tower, with four sections, Mace and Nutmeg, two labels missing, c1810, 8in (20.5cm) high.
£355–400/$500–580 F&F

Sycamore apple press, 19thC, 24in (61cm) wide. It is rare to find this type of press in such good condition.
£430–475/$625–690 SEA

► **Pottery oil jar,** with incised floral decoration under honey-amber glaze, fitted with a spigot and bunghole, French provincial, c1900, 54in (137cm) high. This is a rare item. Condition and colour are important.
£600–700/$870–1,000 NOA

Lighting

◄ **Victorian painted spelter vase-shaped oil lamp,** with original glass shade and two applied painted metal swan side handles, 26in (66cm) high. The value is reduced by up to 50 per cent if, when electrifying this type of oil lamp, the oil reservoir is drilled.
£100–120/$145–175 SWO

► **Pair of base metal table lustres,** with original drops, late 19thC, 10¼in (26cm) high.
£150–180/$220–260 SWO

◄ **Double masthead lamp,** the polished copper and brass lamp with ribbed glass reflectors and brass carrying handle, 19thC, 27in (68.5cm) high.
£180–215/$260–310 S(O)

Base metal hall lantern, now with crude electric bulb socket, missing glass, late 19thC, 27½in (70cm) high. The material and the size of this lantern has great bearing on the value. Larger brass hall lanterns would command a 100 per cent premium.
£170–200/$250–290 SWO

► **Table oil lamp,** with an opaque lilac-coloured glass vase-shaped column, enamelled with flowers a bird and a butterfly, on an ebonized plinth base, with an embossed frosted glass shade with a frill trim, the double burner marked with a ship, funnel missing, 21¼in (54cm) high. Electrification of this style of table lustre can reduce the value by up to 50 per cent.
£190–230/$275–330 FHF

Brass and horn oil lamp, the blue glass oil reservoir and original matching shade above the horn with cast decoration, late 19thC, 31in (78.5cm) high. Oil lamps that display the tasteful use of horn and ivory command a premium, the use of excessively large items of horn and/or ivory commands a proportionally larger premium.
£200–240/$290–340 TAY

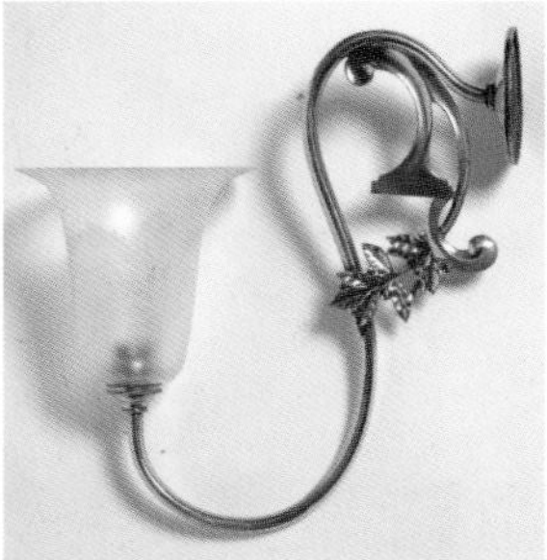

Pair of Edwardian brass wall lamps, with original etched glass shades.
£225–250/$320–360 EAL

Period lighting

The tendency for High Street shops and departmental stores to sell reproduction Victorian and even later lighting has resulted in an appreciable increase in the value of original and period lighting. By purchasing from a specialist lighting shop, the buyer will not only be able to obtain authentication, but also make an informed choice about investing in the type of lighting that best suits the style of their home.

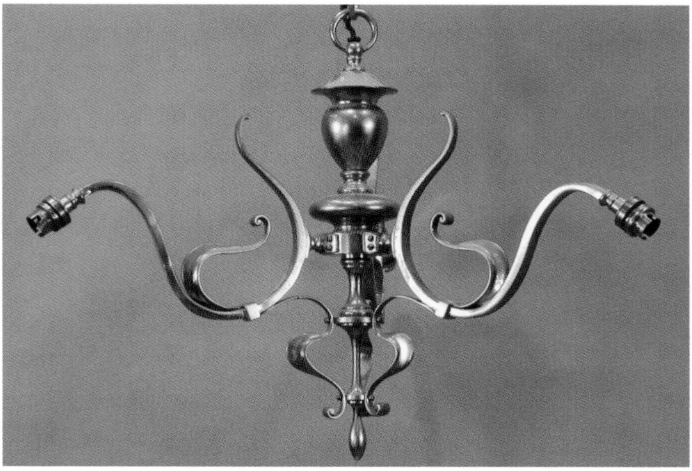

Art Nouveau three-branch brass chandelier, with original etched shades, rewired, 18in (45.5cm) high. Lack of original shades would reduce the value by up to 50 per cent.
£200–250/$290–360 SWO

The look without the price

Brass student oil lamp, with lower secondary candle holder, new green glass shade, late 19thC, 31in (78.5cm) high.
£225–275/$325–400 TAY

Original shades add about £80–100/115–145 to the value, therefore one could achieve the look with an original base and a new shade. However, having the original funnel is not nearly so important to the value of the piece.

◀ **Table oil lamp,** the cranberry oil reservoir body with applied crystal petals, c1895, 5in (12.5cm) diam. It is important that the piece retains its original oil wick holder and burner. If not, the value could be reduced by at least 50 per cent.
£250–300/$360–440 GRI ⊞

Holophane glass pendant lamp, with original bronze fittings, early 20thC, 12in (30.5cm) diam.
£270–300/$390–440 EAL ⊞

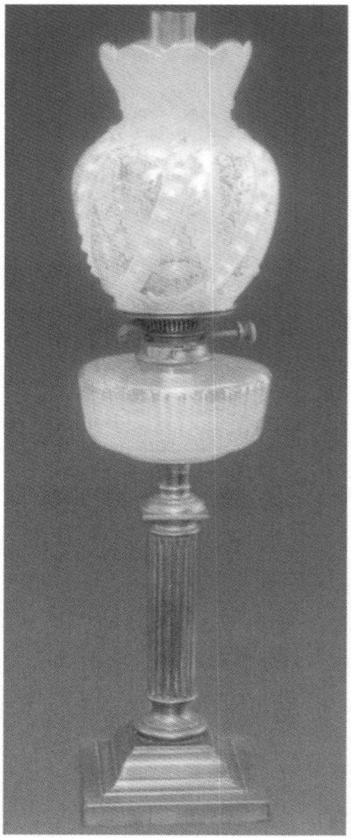

Brass Doric column table oil lamp, on a stepped square base, with a cut and clear glass reservoir and clear and frosted glass shade decorated with floral and foliate motifs and with a deep yellow tinted rim, the burner marked Hinks Duplex No. 2, 29in (73.5cm) high including funnel.
£280–320/$410–460 FHF

Pair of Victorian metal-framed red glass-bodied lamps, with original etched glass shades, 27½in (70cm) high. The lack of electrification adds up to 25 per cent to the value, and a matching pair adds up to 50 per cent to the value.
£280–350/$410–500 SWO

Purchasing advice

Certain points should be considered when buying period lighting.

- Original glass drops and shades enhance the value by up to 50 per cent.
- Drip trays on wall and ceiling lights can add up to 25 per cent in value.
- Rewiring, if done competently, should not affect the value.
- Fashion is the overall dictator of value. However, a good quality and original light fitting, whether an oil lamp or a chandelier, will invariably retain value.
- Wall lights, and to a certain extent oil lamps, benefit from being purchased in pairs, and in the case of wall lights, sets of four. Compared with the price of sets, single lights can be purchased for disproportionately lower amounts.
- The use of gilded bronze (ormolu) as opposed to polished brass increases the value dramatically, even though the outward appearance may be similar.

Gilded metal and porcelain basket six-branch chandelier, with hooped suspension and gilded metal sconces, the porcelain flowers hand-painted, French, 1930s, 22in (56cm) high. Minimal damage to porcelain flowers is acceptable, and subtle colouring can add up to 25 per cent to the value of the piece.
£350–400/$500–580 JPr

► **Silver plated three-branch ceiling lamp,** with etched glass tear drop shades, c1910, 20in (51cm) high. Lack of colour in shades reduces the value by up to 25 per cent.
£350–400
$500–580 EAL ⊞

Art Nouveau polished brass three-arm light fitting, with Vaseline glass shades, c1900, 23in (58.5cm) high. The retention of original coloured shades adds up to 25 per cent.
£400–450/$580–650 EAL ⊞

◄ **Metal-framed four-branch chandelier,** with a central glass column, cut-glass drops and crystal swags, French, early 20thC, 22in (56cm) high. The replacement of damaged drops with good-quality new ones does not, unless done excessively, effect the value. The affect of the glass central column as opposed to a metal one adds 25 per cent to the value.
£400–450
$580–650 JPr ⊞

► **Pair of mounted brass carriage lamps,** surmounted with a winged eagle, adapted for electricity, on later wrought-iron wall frames, c1920, 40in (101.5cm) high. Lamps retaining their original candle sconces and un-electrified would be worth 50 per cent more.
£650–750/$9570–1,100 ASH ⊞

◄ **Six-branch chandelier,** with cut-glass drops, and a cast-brass frame, rewired, French, early 20thC, 25½in (65cm) high. It is essential that the rewiring of this type of chandelier is carried out by a competent qualified electrician. Rewiring should be done sensitively as wires showing outside the metal frame can reduce the value.
£500–550/$720–800 JPr ⊞

Metalware

Copper brandy warmer, with rolled rim and turned wood handle, 19thC, 9in (23cm) wide. It is important to look at the handle on brandy warmers to see if it is original (usually turned fruitwood) as a replacement handle will affect the value.
£65–80/$95–110 TMA

◄ **Pewter sports trophy tankard,** with glass bottom and pewter lid, engraved with a coat-of-arms, 1865, 10in (25.5cm) high. The value of this item is helped by the coat-of-arms engraved on it.
£75–85/$110–125 HO

Circular brass jewellery box, with inset porcelain portrait medallion on lid, interior lined in velvet, 19thC, 6in (15cm) high. The porcelain plaque enhances the appeal of this piece to collectors.
£70–85/$100–130 G(L)

Starting a collection

Antique metalware is still very underrated in terms of value, which is good news for the collector. To the new collector metalware can seem daunting. Good places to start with are specialist dealers who are often happy to share valuable advice with novice collectors. Visiting good-quality vetted fairs where metalware is authenticated is another way to start to get a feel for the subject without worrying about making a mistake with initial purchases.

Miller's compares...

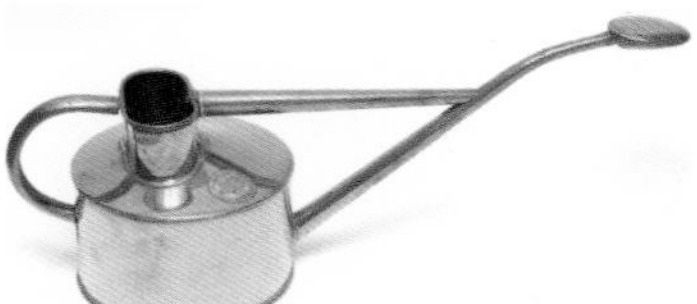

A. Copper Haws watering can, c1950, 16in (40.5cm) long.
£25–30/$35–45 AL

B. Copper watering can, c1910, 24in (61cm) long.
£110–120/$160–175 AL

Both watering cans are attractive shapes and in good condition. Item B is Edwardian. Like Victoriana, Edwardian items have become extremely collectable and are now being allowed into dateline fairs. Item A does not have significant age to be of great value at the moment but no doubt it soon will and it still is a decorative piece.

Copper bowl, stamped with Imperial duty marks for 1889 and 1896, Russian, 17in (43cm) diam, with later wall fixing.
£100–130/$120–180 WW

Copper one-gallon harvest measure, 19thC, 12½in (32cm) high. Verdigris, although unattractive, can be cleaned off. Prices are affected more by dents and damage to the base on these measures.
£120–145/$175–230 SWO

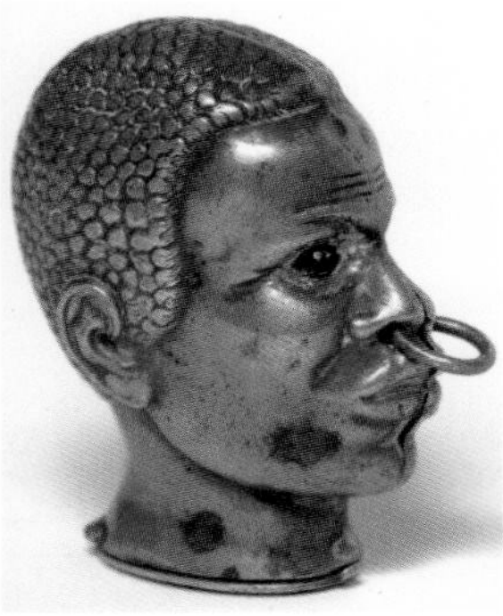

Brass vesta case, in the form of head, 19thC, 2in (5cm) high. Vesta cases have become very collectable and can today command high prices. The most popular are early and novelty; for example anything that depicts animals, popular scenes and golfing,
£200–220/$300–320 HUM

The look without the price

These candlesticks look very Art Nouveau in style and would certainly fetch at least £110/$160 and as much as £200–300/$300–330 on a good day at auction. If, however, they were by Liberty this pair could be worth as much as £500–800/$720–1,200.

Pair of brass candlesticks, on turned knopped stems set with rings and onyx cabochons applied to the bases, late 19thC, 7in (18cm) high.
£110–140/$170–220 WW

Pair of brass Brighton buns candlesticks, c1880, 2in (5cm) high. This style of candlestick was popular throughout the 19thC with people who travelled a lot and was used by soldiers during the Crimean war. These were known as Brighton buns because when the two sconces are unscrewed the bases thread together to look like a Brighton bun.
£160–175/$240–270 SEA

Brass vase, 19thC, 8in (20.5cm) high. This shape is unusual for a vase – it could have been used in a church or chapel.
£165–185/$250–270 SEA

◄ **Four-gallon copper measure,** with riveted handle, 19thC, 15in (38cm) high. This has a clear '4 gallon' stamp but is also dented. Dents such as these do affect the price but can sometimes be removed.
£220–265/$320–400 SWO

The look without the price

This Georgian-style wine cooler dates from c1920 and could be by Pearson-Page who made all kinds of household items from 1920 onwards in various different styles. If this wine cooler dated from c1800 it could be worth £500–800/$725–1,150. Stylistically very similar, the price of a Georgian cooler allows for wear and tear due to age, which would be unacceptable in the later item.

Georgian-style copper and brass wine cooler, possibly by Pearson-Page, c1920, 14in (35.5cm) diam.
£200–220/$300–320 PICA

Pair of Regency-style brass candelabra, with four sconces on scroll supports, bronze winged griffin stems on mask terminals, 19thC, 20½in (52cm) high.
£225–270/$325–400 G(L)

Copper baluster-form coffee pot, with circular raised base, swan neck spout, domed lift-off lid with hinged vent cover and turned wood handle, 1780–1800, 7in (18cm) high. Hinged vent covers are quite unusual and thus more desirable.
£230–280/$330–425 TMA

Pair of brass candlesticks, with central *faux* marble stems, 19thC, 7in (18cm) high.
£280–320/$400–460 SWO

◄ **Patinated-bronze and coconut shell inkwell/table bell,** in the form of an Native American sitting crosslegged and holding a club, with hinged head and coconut shell body, with mechanical bell, 19thC, 8in (20.5cm) high. It would be worthwhile having this piece restored sympathetically. This subject matter is particularly popular in the USA.
£340–375/$450–550 TMA

Set of four brass candlesticks, each with inscription to base, 'Friendly Brothers of The St Mary of Eygpt's Tontine Benefit Society', 19thC, 12in (30.5cm) high. Being a set of four and having the inscription will add to the value, although how much is difficult to say. Friendly societies were set up in the UK from 1875 to provide relief for members in times of need. Cash was provided by voluntary subscriptions or donations. Societies also helped members looking for work and provided a form of fire insurance.
£340–400/$500–630 SWO

Glasgow School brass jardinière, embossed with roses, c1910, 16¾in (42.5cm) wide. Beware of later pieces in this style. Pearson-Page of Birmingham and London produced many household items such as candlesticks, fenders and jardinières in the 1920s, these pieces are now 60 to 70 years old and they can be mistaken for early examples.
£300–350/$460–540 DAD ⊞

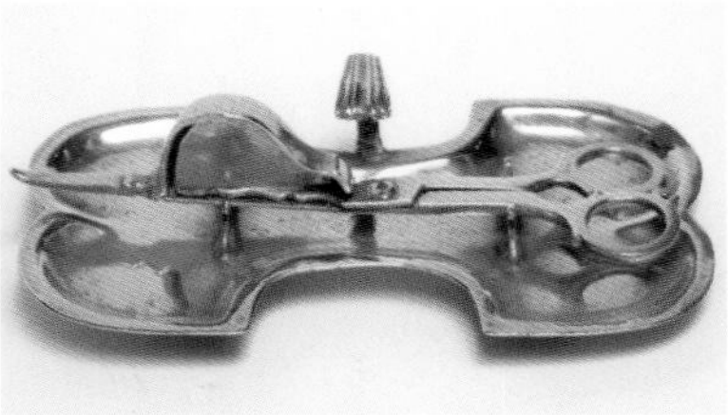

Pair of brass candle snuffers and tray, early 18thC, 8in (20.5cm) wide. The fact that the snuffers have their original tray is reflected in the price. Very often the two have been separated and the value is decreased. When purchasing an item such as this, make sure the tray is original – look for a piece of decoration that ties the two together such as embossing, or the design.
£440–485/$640–700 SEA ⊞

Spiral iron candlestick with turned pine base, c1780, 9in (23cm) high. Dating from early 18thC through to 19thC, spiral or coil candlesticks can be found all over England and Europe. French ones are more common and they were used in the home, barn or cellar, using the hook to hang them from a nail on the wall or as a handle for carrying. This one is made more collectable because the well turned wooden base has the original paint on it.
£315–350/$480–500 SEA ⊞

Miller's compares...

A. Brass warming pan, with wrought-iron handle, c1660, 35in (90cm) long.
£380–420/$575–625 F&F ⊞

B. Brass warming pan, with turned red walnut handle and embossed lid, c1690, 45in (114.5cm) long.
£625–700/$950–1,000 F&F ⊞

Warming pans with wrought–iron handles are not as desirable as those with wooden handles as collectors prefer unusual and better-quality items. Plainer warming pans are quite common whereas heavily decorated ones with wooden handles are less so. Even so, when looking at plainer ones watch the condition as pans were often dropped and many are badly dented or cracked, lowering their value further. The red walnut handle on Item B is well turned and the lid decoration is well embossed, all making this item highly desirable and more valuable than Item A which is plainer.

Rugs & Carpets

Beshir rug, with a large octagonal medallion in indigo, reds, gold and ivory on a blue and red all-over stellar field, enclosed by triple narrow borders, wear and slight losses, southwest Turkestani, c1880, 171 x 86in (434 x 218.5cm). The obvious wear, damage to sides and format account for the price, but Beshir carpets are uncommon and this is a good design and colour. Hand-cleaning and sewing in the edges with linen thread and tapestry wool would transform it.
£120–145/$175–210 WW

Rug, based on a Saryk Turkoman *ensi*, with a triple prayer panel with geometric columns on either side, in crimson, ivory and grey, with multiple prayer panel above and tulip *elem* panel below, wear, slight damage and losses, Indian, possibly Yeravda Jail, Poona, late 19th/early 20thC, 80 x 54in (203 x 137cm). Indian Jail carpets are well made with good materials and dyes. This rug has good colours and design. Hand-cleaning and sewing in the ends and edges would lighten it up.
£150–200/$220–300 WW

Lilihan rug, with a central lobed medallion in ivory, blues and browns with matching spandrels on an abrashed pale red field, enclosed by floral and navy main border and two meander red subsidiary borders, west Persian, 1900–20, 75 x 59in (190.5 x 150cm). Lilihan rugs are well made with thick pile. This rug would have been very red, but has had a chemical wash to mellow it which accounts for the price (the trade does not like chemical washes). However, it is still an attractive rug.
£200–250/$300–360 WW

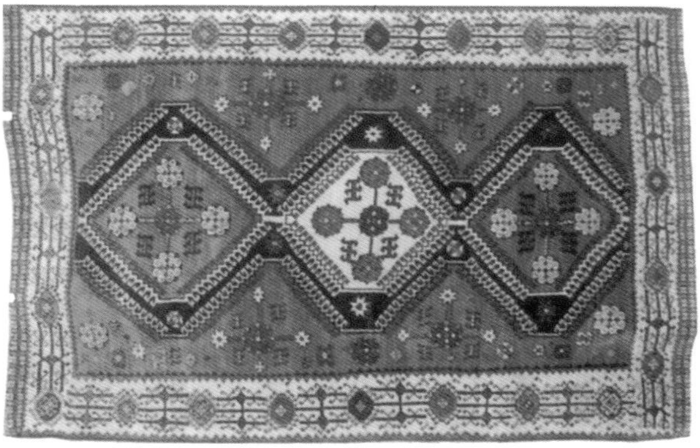

Kashgai rug, the blush red field of flowerheads and stellar motifs centred by three pole link ivory and red hooked lozenge medallions, enclosed by an ivory hooked gul and angular vine and X-motif border, with typical Kashgai endstripes, southwest Persian, dated AH 1329, 97¼ x 65in (247 x 165cm). This appears to be in good condition for a 90-year-old rug and with good drawing and design. The rather hard red may have affected the price, which is low for a good size rug.
£250–300/$360–440 B(Ba)

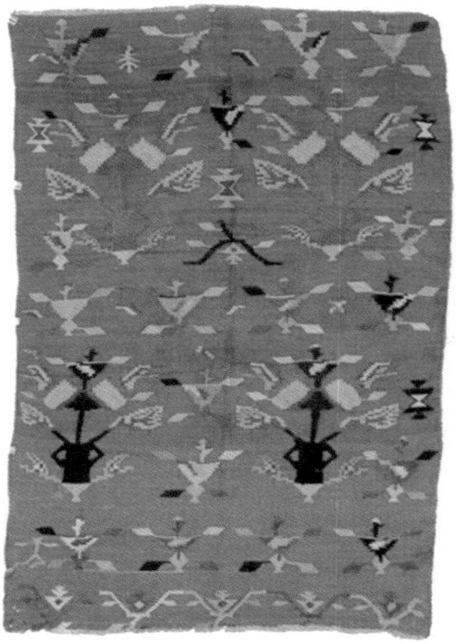

Bessarabian *kilim*, Balkan, c1920, 64 x 44in (162.5 x 112cm). Bessarabian *kilims* are popular because of their designs and colours. This one is no exception and is a useful size and an attractive price.
£240–300/$350–440 S(O)

Khotan silk rug, with a rosette medallion, pomegranates and rosettes in gold, ivory and brown on an apricot field, enclosed by a flowerhead and ivory border, eastern Turkestani, c1920, 59 x 37in (150 x 94cm). This silk rug looks in good condition with attractive colour and design, although silk does not wear well.
£300–375/$440–560 WW

► **Afshar rug,** southwest Persian, c1890, 67 x 47in (170 x 119.5cm). Afshar rugs are always popular, as is an all-over design such as here. It is a useful size and is in good condition. Hand-cleaning should brighten it up.
£350–400/$500–580 S(O)

Condition

Overall wear should not deter buyers providing colour, design, size and structural condition are acceptable. Avoid larger holes, bare patches, jagged splits, missing borders and bad and obvious repairs, all of which would cost disproportional sums to put right.

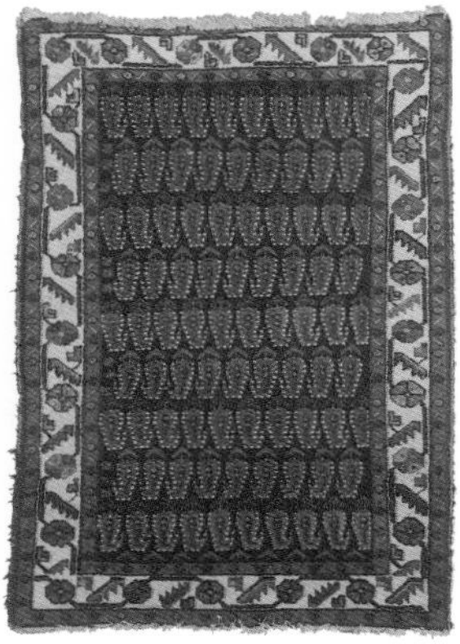

Hamadan rug, the dark blue field with horizontal rows of *boteh* in blues, reds and ivory, enclosed by a main flowerhead and leaf ivory border and two red floral subsidiary borders, part of border missing at one end, Persian, c1920, 58 x 42in (147.5 x 106.5cm). Hamadan rugs are hard-wearing and an all-over design with well-balanced border makes this an attractive rug at a reasonable price.
£350–380/$500–575 DNo

► **Afshar rug,** with a trellis design of stylized leaves, flowerheads and stems in blues, reds and gold on an ivory field, enclosed by an Afshar red border and twin blue floral subsidiary borders, some wear, Persian, c1900, 54 x 45in (137 x 114.5cm). A good all-over design Afshar rug of square format. The slight wear is reflected in the price which is what one would expect.
£350–400/$500–580 DNo

Colour & dyes

Avoid orange, hard red, pink, purple and vivid green. These are probably aniline or chrome chemical dyes. Orange and red are prone to seeping into ivory, black and brown are prone to dye corrosion, and blue and brown in preponderence can be dull, and are therefore not popular with the British market, which prefers light colours as they are more favourable in that climate.

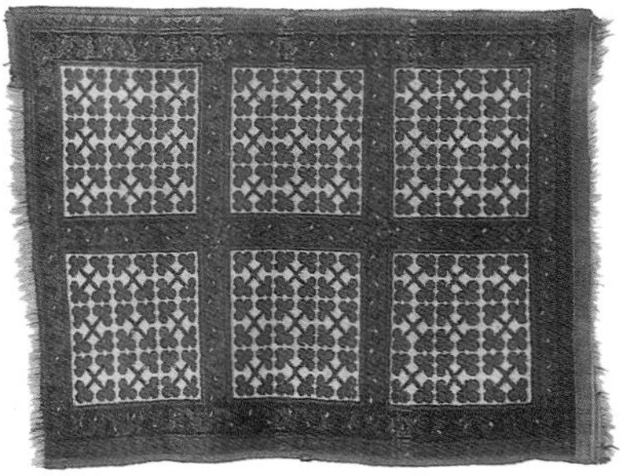

Ersari Turkoman rug, with six ivory panels with a trellis design of trefoil clovers in reds and browns, divided by floral and indigo bands and an outer saw-tooth border, part missing at one end, southwest Turkestani, c1880, 51 x 40in (129.5 x 101.5cm). An attractive rug with an unusual design. The price reflects the condition.
£350–400/$500–580 DNo

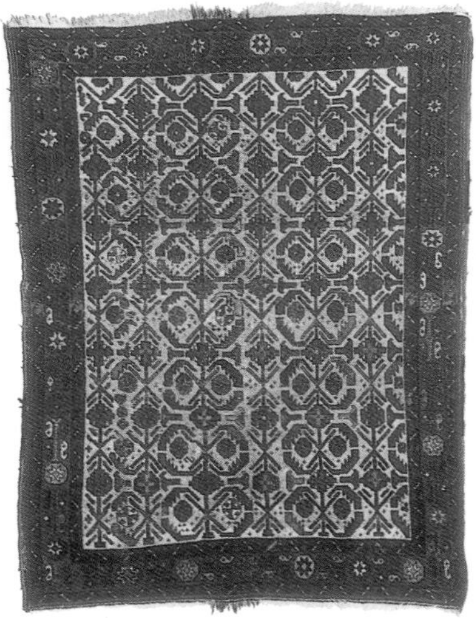

Malayer *khelleh*, west Persian, dated AH1317/1899, 156 x 77in (396 x 195.5cm). This attractive well-drawn Malayer gallery carpet looks in good condition. The pink-red colour and the unwieldy format (long and narrow) are reflected in the price, which is a good price for a hardwearing carpet.
£410–500/$600–720 S(O)

Design

Low-piled finely-knotted rugs have more distinct patterns and are generally to be preferred. All-over field designs are more desirable and popular than medallion designs in today's market. Prayer rugs are popular and look good on walls.

Shirvan wool rug, the central midnight blue field filled with cruciforms and rosettes and stylized animals, enclosed by geometric guard stripes and border, Caucasian, 62 x 45in (157.5 x 114.5cm). This is a good price for an attractive all-over design Shirvan rug with a *Kufic* border which is in reasonable condition.
£450–540/$650–800 CGC

Carpet, Chinese, c1930, 116 x 96in (294.5 x 244cm). This Chinese carpet has a good design with a pretty border and looks in good condition. The predominance of blue and brown, together with the medallion may not be to everyone's taste but this is nevertheless a good buy for the price.
£500–550/$720–800 S(O)

Size/shape

Square shapes are more popular than narrow rugs, except with runners where those under 36in (91.5cm) wide are sought after. A 'shaped' rug e.g one with undulating edges making one end narrower than the other, may be difficult to place. Avoid rugs that don't lie flat.

Malayer hand-woven rug, in ivory, black, blue, green and pink on a red ground, west Persian, c1920, 76 x 49in (193 x 114.5cm). Malayer rugs are hardwearing with good quality dyes. The all-over design with well-balanced border on this example, plus the size, makes it attractive and the price is acceptable. A good clean would improve it.
£500–600/$720–870 JAA

► **Tabriz rug,** with petal anchor medallion in light red, blues, ivory and gold on an abrashed blue-black field decorated with flowers and shrubs in light colours, enclosed by a light red and floral main border and two light blue floral minor borders, some wear, northwest Persian, c1920, 78 x 53in (198 x 134.5cm). A well-designed hardwearing rug of useful size with good colour. It is perhaps rather dark but the price is attractive.
£550–600/$800–870 DNo

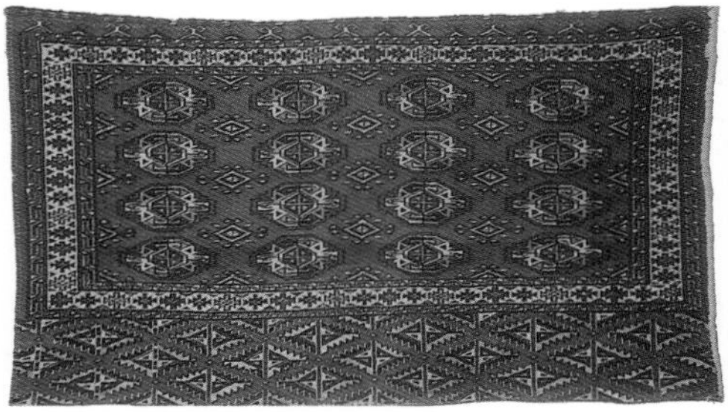

Yomud Turkoman bagface, with 16 *guls* in four rows in reds, ivory and indigo on a madder field enclosed by an Ashik and ivory border and twin running-dog guard stripes, the madder skirt with Dyrnak *guls*, northwest Turkestani, c1880, 51 x 27in (129.5 x 68.5cm). This bagface appeals equally to collectors and private buyers. It is very finely knotted with excellent wool, good colours and is in good condition.
£675–750/$975–1,100 DNo

► **Heriz runner,** northwest Persian, 1900–20, 154 x 32in (391 x 81.5cm). This runner has good colours and well-balanced design. It is a good length, lies straight and flat and is only 32in (81.5cm) wide – a much sought-after size, so the price is good.
£700–850/$1,000–1,250 S(O)

Belouch rug, northeast Persian, Khorassan Province, c1900, 58 x 34in (147.5 x 86.5cm).
£750–850
$1,100–1,250 LIN

Types to look for

- Village and tribal rugs from Persia, Afghanistan, the Caucasus, Turkestan.
- Persia (Iran since 1928): Hamadan, Kurdistan, Sarabend, Shiraz, Afshar, Kashgari, Baktiari, Belouch.
- Afghanistan: Daoulatabad, Dali, Taghan, Kazan, Solarman, Kizilayak, Belouch.
- The Caucasus: Shirvan, Kuba, Karabagh, Daghestan, Derbend, Lesghi
- Turkestan: Turkoman: Tekke, Salor, Yomud, Saryk, Chodor bokharas
- Avoid silk rugs – they corrode too easily and are usually too expensive. Avoid rugs made in Kashmir, India or Pakistan during the last 60 years. Kelims are generally impractical; they tend to wrinkle up, won't lie flat and are difficult to mend.

Marasali Shirvan rug, with reciprocal *boteh* in light colours on a dark blue field, enclosed by a red and ivory reciprocal trefoil main border and several guard stripes, northeast Caucasian, c1890, 106 x 56in (269 x 142cm). A very attractive rug of good size and, assuming good condition, it is a good price.
£750–900
$1,100–1,300 S(O)

◄ **Afshar rug,** with rows of flowers in pots above and below on an abrashed field, some wear, southeast Persian, c1890, 78 x 60in (198 x 152.5cm). A classic Afshar rug of square shape. The wear is reflected in the price.
£800–900
$1,150–1,300 DNo

Scientific Instruments

◄ **Kodak Autographic Junior camera,** No. 2C, 1916–27, 3 x 5in (7.5 x 12.5cm). Although these cameras were produced in their thousands, they are rarely found in good condition. They are always worth buying when in good condition and with their original case. Certain models of folding cameras have bellows in red leather rather than the more usual black, and this is always an added attraction. Although in today's market they are an inexpensive item, they are still interesting and attractive display and conversation pieces.
£23–25/$30–35 HEG

Philip's terrestrial globe, on a bronzed metal stand, c1930, 6in (15cm) high.
£45–55/$65–80 G(L)

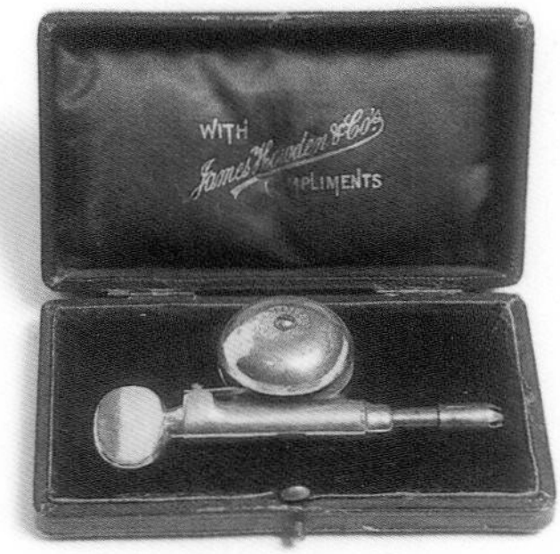

Rev. counter, by Greene Tweede & Co, New York, bell counter chimes every 100 revolutions, patent date 1894, 5in (12.5cm) wide. These rev. counters for calculating machine speeds were made at the end of the 19thC, usually to a very high quality and in many varied designs. They have been largely ignored by collectors, but are worth buying at today's low prices. There is interest among some dealers/collectors who are buying and putting them away with an eye to the future.
£50–55/$75–80 WAC

Le Merveilleux brass-mounted mahogany plate camera, by J. Lancaster & Son, Birmingham, with two plates, 19thC. These mahogany and brass cameras make superb collectors' items and can often fetch £140–200/$200–300 in auction. They must, however, be in really good condition; particular note should be taken of the condition of the bellows, as a replacement set of bellows will cost more than the camera itself.
£55–65/$80–95 BR

► **1in refracting leather-covered telescope,** with five drawers, eyepiece missing, 19thC, 4in (10cm) long, with another smaller example signed 'Gilbert & Wright, London' around the eyepiece, in an associated case. Telescopes have a long and interesting history of development and use and have been collected for almost as long as they have been made. Buyers should take particular care to check that the lenses are the correct ones and are not damaged, as they are extremely difficult to replace.
£60–70/$90–100 S(O)

Pair of collapsible binoculars, French, presented 28 April 1887, 6in (15cm) wide closed. Very little information has been published on the history and development of binoculars and yet many unusual and interesting designs and patents have been registered, which makes them interesting items to collect. Collectors should ensure any binoculars they buy are in sound optical condition as repairs can be difficult and expensive.
£125–140/$180–200 PHo

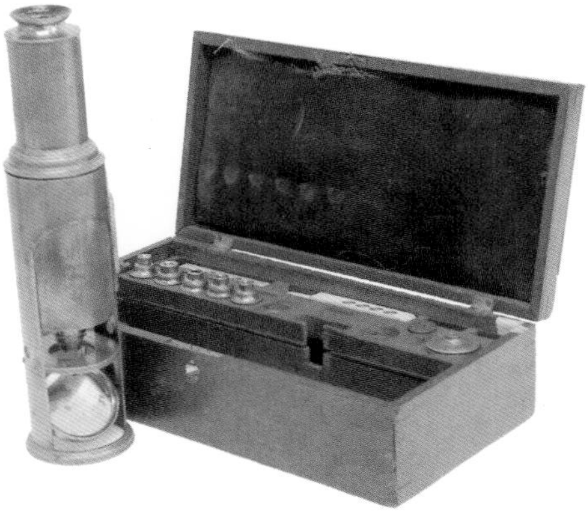

Brass microscope, with adjustable body tube, five additional objectives and various bone specimen slides, in a fitted mahogany case, early 19thC, 7in 18cm) wide. This Martin-type microscope would normally fetch £250–300/$360–440 in restored condition, but it is always worth checking with a specialist the cost of such work before buying.
£130–155/$200–225 G(L)

Nimrod Automan bellows camera, by Thornton Pickard, c1910, 6½in (16.5cm) long, with a Mackenzie-Wishart day slide, 7in (18cm) long. The quality of construction, together with the red bellows and polished mahogany interior, make this leather-covered plate camera particularly attractive as a collector's piece.
£170–200/$250–300 G(L)

Brass dip circle, by Phillp Harris, London, c1900, 8in (20.5cm) high. This is a demonstration instrument which measures the vertical component of the earth's magnetic field.
£180–200/$260–300 PHo

◄ **Pair of plated binoculars,** by Dollond, London, presented by the RNLI in 1888, 7in (18cm) long, in a leather case. Optical instruments and binoculars given as presentation pieces, engraved and dated, usually have an enhanced value.
£200–220/$300–320 HUM

Mahogany apothecary's box, the hinged lid enclosing a fitted interior with 18 stoppered glass bottles, above a single fitted drawer with further glass bottles, plated handles to side, c1906, 12½in (32cm) wide. Extremely sought-after as collectors' and decorative pieces. Buyers should check that glass containers and stoppers match and that the contents are as original as possible, as it will often be found that they are later replacements.
£220–260/$320–380 G(L)

Weather service barograph, by Bendix Aviation Corporation, Baltimore, in a metal case, American, 1950s, 11in (28cm) wide. Barographs make interesting functional and/or decorative pieces; they are also highly sensitive instruments. It is always advisable to check with a specialist before buying at auction as restoration can be expensive.
£250–300/$360–440 RTW

◄ **Diptych sundial compass,** in a boxwood case, with scale divided 0-12-0 and stamped on the interior lid with a further scale, glass covering compass cracked, late 18thC, 4in (10cm) square. The value of an instrument of this type is greatly affected by its condition, and also the fact that it has no maker's name.
£300–350
$440–500 S(O)

Locate the source

The source of each illustration in Miller's can be found by checking the code letters below each caption with the Key to Illustrations, pages 286–290.

Prismatic compass, by Negretti & Zambra, with hinged mirror and sight, late 19thC, 3in (7.5cm) diam, in a folding leather case. Instruments of quality in original condition should never be cleaned or polished without first seeking specialist advice, as this can greatly reduce their value.
£320–385/$460–575 G(L)

► **Lacquered brass compound microscope,** by Baker, London, on a black enamel stand, late 19thC, 13in (33cm) high, in a mahogany case. It is always worth carrying a pocket magnet as an easy way to check whether the metal is brass or steel. A similar microscope but with a blackened steel base instead of black and brass would have an auction price of £80–120/$115–175.
£430–480
$630–700 WAC

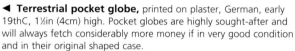

◀ **Terrestrial pocket globe,** printed on plaster, German, early 19thC, 1½in (4cm) high. Pocket globes are highly sought-after and will always fetch considerably more money if in very good condition and in their original shaped case.
£400–450/$580–650 HUM

Collapsible portable terrestrial globe, by Betts, with cartouche reading 'By the Queens Royal Letters Patent Betts's New Portable Terrestrial Globe compiled from latest and best authorities London, John Betts, 115 Strand', printed on waxed cloth with umbrella-style frame, within a fitted maker's box with trade label to lid interior, mid-19thC, 28½in (72.5cm) long. These unusual globes are frequently subject to wear and tear. The stitching, in particular, should be carefully checked and any rust staining from the frame.
£400–450/$580–650 S(O)

◀ **Silver equinoctial dial,** c1700, 2½in (6.5cm) diam. This comprises a compass and a sundial for telling the time.
£450–500/$650–720 DJH

Tunbridge ware thermometer and compass, by Thomas Barton, c1870, 5in (12.5cm) high. This item is of greater interest to collectors of Tunbridge ware than to collectors of scientific instruments, and this is reflected in the price.
£550–600/$800–870 AMH

Miller's compares...

A. Oak-cased barograph, by M. W. Dunscombe, Bristol, with chart drawer, c1935, 15in (38cm) wide.
£550–600/$800–870 RTW

B. Mahogany-cased barograph, by Army & Navy, London, with bevelled glass and chart drawer, dated 1924, 14in (35.5cm) wide.
£650–750/$950–1,100 RTW

While both these barographs are desirable, the difference in the quality of Item B is reflected in the higher price. The use of mahogany against oak for the base and case, the bevelled glass, the presentation plaque and general appearance all contribute to the higher price of Item B.

Sculpture

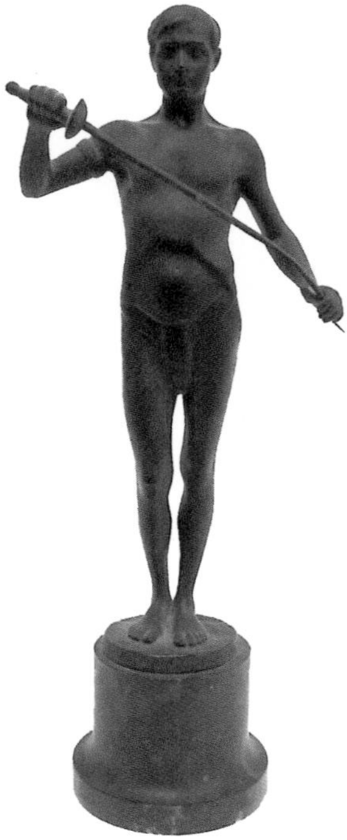

Bronze figure of a fencer, on a marble socle, signed H. Muller, c1900, 11in (28cm) high. A good clean and wax would make this shine. The marble socle looks original but the German 'health and beauty' look is not currently in fashion, therefore works by good artists can be found at very affordable prices.
£110–135/$160–195 G(L)

Ormolu paperweight group of a dog guarding a sleeping child, on a marble base, French, 1870, 6in (15cm) high.
£320–385/$470–570 G(L)

◄ **Alabaster bust of a young woman,** semi-clad and wearing a headband, raised on a waisted green plinth, possibly Continental, late 19th/early 20thC, 11½in (29cm) high.
£200–250/$300–360 AH

Bronze group of a cockerel, hen and chicks, by Alphonse-Alexandre Arson, c1900, 9½in (24cm) high. Arson is one of the greatest bird sculptors. However, this cast is probably posthumous and therefore much less valuable.
£260–315/$380–450 G(L)

◄ **Bronze group of an Austrian huntsman with rifle and hound,** on a marble base, 19thC, 12in (30.5cm) high. Austrian patinated bronzes (unlike their very popular cold-painted cousins) can look old-fashioned today.
£300–375/$440–560 G(L)

► **Bronze figure of a partridge,** by Alphonse-Alexandre Arson, on a naturalistic oval base, c1880, 9½in (24cm) high. This model is dirty, but close inspection might show that the detail on the bird is a little crisper and closer to the standard expected of his work.
£380–460/$560–675 G(L)

Italian marble/alabaster c1900

Italian families like Pugi and Cipriani produced signed and unsigned highly decorative pieces in the 30-year period around 1900. Busts and full-length figures of girls in a classical or contemporary pose now cost very little and are genuine period art that creates a real look. However, don't rely on the signatures since names can be incised at any time.

You can expect restoration, especially on vulnerable extended hands and long necks. Minor abrasions are normal signs of age, but if you see an area of white sheen and/or you feel areas of different textures/temperatures it may be air-brushed white paint hiding serious rework. Remember these pieces are solid, and therefore heavier than bronze.

Bronze group of an old man being dragged/carried out of his home, clutching the two things he holds most dear, his grand-daughter and the image of his household god, French, 1870, 16in (40.5cm) high. This piece is very dirty and would be much more impressive when cleaned.
£400–480/$580–700 G(L)

Insurance values

Always insure your valuable antiques for the cost of replacing them with similar items, regardless of the original price paid. Both dealers and auctioneers can provide a valuation service for a fee.

Oak statuette of St Christina, holding a serpent, Continental, early 19thC, 19¾in (50cm) high. Religious works, even early ones, are a more Continental taste than English, so can be good value if damage is limited and restoration sympathetic.
£425–500/$620–720 S(O)

► **Bronze bust of Napoleon III,** by E. Debannes-Gardonne, depicted as a young man with his head turned to the right, raised on a waisted socle base, signed, inscribed with foundry 'S. Martin fondeur' and 'Salon 1874 No. 2657', 19thC, 12½in (32cm) high. Had this been a bust of Napoleon I it would have made a higher price.
£450–550/$650–800 B

Bronze model of an Arab horseman, the turbanned figure sitting astride the horse, on a naturalistically cast base, set on an ebonized wood base, sword missing to right hand, late 19thC, 15¾in (40cm) high. This looks like a high-quality cast, but the posture is rather stiff and the subject-matter is currently out of fashion, so it would be a bargain for those who like it.
£450–550/$650–800 B

Marble torso of Psyche, attributed to Giuseppe Vacca, after the Antique, signed, Italian, dated 1861, 19in (48.5cm) high. A quality Italian work of which a 23½in (60.5cm) version was estimated elsewhere at £2,000/$2,900.
£470–560/$680–800 S(O)

Painted terracotta bust, by Ernst Wahlis, the face with bulging eyes, wearing a shell on his head, inscribed 'Cyklon', numbered 200, Austrian, early 20thC, 28¾in (73cm) high. Undamaged antique terracotta is relatively rare and perhaps only the idiosyncratic subject kept the price under £800/$1,150.
£500–600/$720–870 B

Spelter group of a woman and child, after Kinsburger, the female figure seated on a tree trunk holding a bough, the child at her feet sailing a boat, set on a circular plinth, signed, entitled 'Jeune Mère', converted to an electrical lamp, French, late 19thC, 29¼in (74.5cm) high. Figural lamps are often speltre and this attractive model is from a good artist. Damage is important since speltre is not easily restored, and the lamp conversion should be sympathetic. Spelter, selling for around one-fifth the price of bronze, makes this affordable.
£480–575/$700–850 S(S)

Alabaster figure of a girl, by G. Cipriani, the naked figure seated on a bench, holding a cloth over one breast, signed to back, Italian, late 19thC, 23¾in (60.5cm) high. A charming model if in undamaged condition. Lift before you buy, as marble, being solid should be heavy.
£500–600/$720–870 B

Bronze model of a retriever, the dog holding a bird in its mouth, raised on a naturalistically cast base, signed in Cyrillic and stamped with foundry mark 'FABR. G.F. Woerffel, St. Petersburg', late 19thC, 9½in (24cm) high. Russian sculpture is not always as popular as their remarkable craftsmanship deserves. However, the dead bird reduces desirability and therefore the price.
£600–720/$870–1,050 B

◄ **Bronze figure of a youth,** with a seated dog to one side and a boar's head trophy on a tree trunk to the other, after the Antique, late 19thC, 17¾in (45cm) high. Classical, after the Antique, figures were made in large numbers towards the end of the 19thC. Although rather out of fashion at present, the well-cast ones of an interesting subject can be good value.
£600–720/$870–1,050 P(S)

◀ **Bronze model of the Dying Gladiator,** after the Antique, with rich dark green patination, 19thC, 24½in (62cm) wide.
£600–720/$870–1,050 PFK

Dying Gladiator/Gaul

First discovered in the Ludovici Collection in 1623, the original is now in the Capitoline Museum. It has two different titles but it is age, casting quality and size that are needed to push this common model over £1,000/$1,450, although a greenish patina will also add to its appeal. If it has a Collas stamp this means that it was part of a long production run by Barbedienne in several sizes

◀ **Bronze model of the Dying Gaul,** by Barbedienne Fondeur, after the Antique, inscribed, French, late 19thC, 7¼in (18.5cm) high.
£650–750/$950–1,100 P

Bronze figure of a girl, by Victor Rousseau, holding a mask in one hand, a fan, violin, pair of opera glasses and sheet music at her feet, signed, Belgian, c1900, 21¾in (55cm) high. This bronze sold for a relatively low price. It is beautifully modelled and finished in a warm rich colour.
£700–850/$1,000–1,250 P

Pair of ivory grotesque figures, carved as medieval musicians, on turned wooden stands, German, late 19thC, 9½in (24cm) high. Ivory is highly collectable as it is no longer widely poached, but is most popular in Art Deco works. This earlier, somewhat Gothic, German pair would be very interesting to those of a slightly Gormenghast turn of mind.
£750–900/$1,100–1,300 S(O)

Bronze figure of a young sailor dancing, entitled 'La Gigue', on a seashore base, French, late 19thC, 16½in (42cm) high. Although Garnier is a known decorative sculptor, non-English military, especially naval, subjects are not commercial. The dance however gives this piece something extra.
£800–1,000
$1,150–1,500 RBB

Textiles

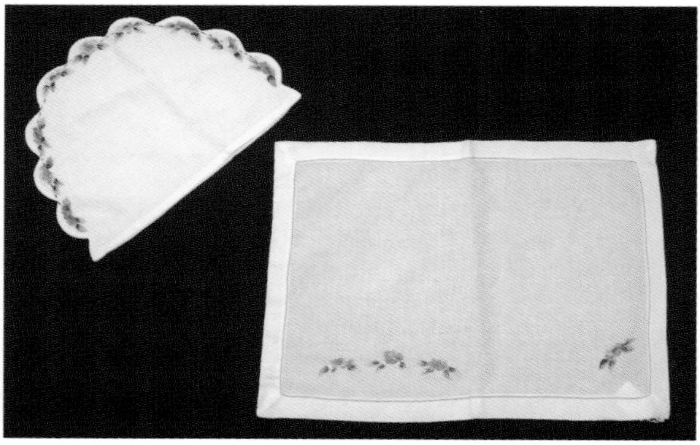

Matching tea cosy and tray cloth set, hand-embroidered in silks with roses and foliage, c1910, tray cloth 18½in (47cm) wide.
£8–12/$10–16 AL

Crochet and embroidered tray cloth, c1900, 23½in (59.5cm) square.
£15–20/$20–30 AL

Crochet and embroidered tray cloth, with machine-made lace border, 11½in (29cm) wide. Cloths with highly embroidered centres, especially with cutwork and cherubs, command premium prices. However, a plain cloth with a deep crochet edge can be valued lower, as would those with machine embroidery, while retaining the look of the more valuable hand-made versions.
£18–20/$25–30 AL

Ribbon-worked purse, with colourful ribbons on a black velvet body, with drawstring and tassel, c1880, 8in (20.5cm) long. Ribbon-work is collected, but near-perfect condition is essential to maintain value.
£70–100/$100–145 JPr

Crewelwork fragment, worked on a linen ground in brightly-coloured wools with long and short stitch, speckling stitch, and button-hole outlining stitch, depicting scrolling flowers and foliage, c1700, 17 x 6½in (43 x 16.5cm).
£80–100/$115–145 WW

Crewelwork

When looking to buy crewelwork it is important to consider the condition. Look for pieces that have not been washed and have strong bright colours. The quality of the stitching should also be considered, as should the condition of the fabric – look out for holes. When displaying your purchase, keep it out of direct sunlight to minimize the risk of colours fading.

Crazy hand-stitched quilt, in silks and velvets with a frill of faded green cotton, slight damage, c1880, 34in (86.5cm) square.
£85–95/$125–140 JPr

The look without the price

A dated sampler always commands a premium as opposed to an authentic although undated one. The inclusion of more unusual and well-represented animals and houses adds a large premium – as much as £500/$720. The religious aspect of a sampler is less important than the quality of stitch-work.

Silk-worked sampler, with alphabet, numerals, strawberry band and baskets of fruit, by Harriet Roper, Walsham, faded, framed, 1847, 10 x 8in (25.5 x 20.5cm).
£85–100/$125–145 G(L)

Wool paisley shawl, colourfully printed, slight damage, mid-19thC, 47¼ x 26¾in (120 x68cm). Damage, if slight, in the body colour affects the value less than when apparent in the central coloured panel.
£85–120/$125–175 DE

Wool narrow-loom blanket, black and cream plaid, Welsh, 84 x 70in (203.5 x 178cm).
£90–100/$130–145 JJ

► **Embroidered silk-work picture,** depicting an English thatched cottage and garden, using a variety of stitches, early 20thC, 6 x 8in (15 x 20.5cm). The value of a silk-work picture can be diminished by up to 50 per cent when the scene is only of a garden.
£100–120/$145–175 JPr

Samplers

When buying samplers look at the condition of the piece, check whether it has been washed or kept in the sun, and whether it has any holes in it. A few small holes may bring down a price without affecting the look of the piece. The material is also important as silk is preferable to wool. Subject matter is also a factor to consider as alphabets and pictures are more desirable than religious text.

Beaded bag, with flower and foliage decoration, with a brass frame and beaded knop, early 19thC, 4in (10cm) long. Larger bags tend to be more expensive, up to five times, so the smaller bags, which are usually earlier, can be a good starting point for the collector. Generally, the size of the beads is an indication of age – small being earlier.
£110–120/$160–175 JPr

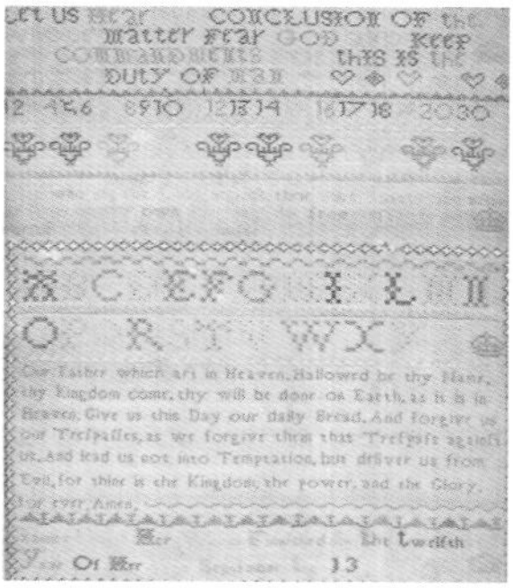

Sampler, worked in polychrome silk with the alphabet, numerals, pattern bands, The Lord's Prayer and two religious verses by Hannah Wood, framed, part faded, 1740, 12 x 9½in (30.5 x 24cm). Over-cleaning and the religious context has reduced the value of this sampler by 50 per cent; the fact that it is 18thC has added 25 per cent.
£150–200/$220–290 G(L)

Needlepoint embroidered picture, depicting a young girl, a dog and two puppies, in a maple frame, mid-19thC, 11 x 8½in (28 x 21.5cm). Sentimental embroideries without any religious connections command a 50 per cent premium – even more with animals and children.
£120–150/$175–225 SWO

► **Crewelwork panel,** with birds, rabbits and deer worked in brightly-coloured wools, probably removed from a fire screen, c1920, 20 x 48in (51 x 122cm).
£160–200/$230–290 JPr

Needlework and beadwork tea cosy, c1880, 14in (35.5cm) wide.
£135–150/$195–220 HUM

Blue and white hand-stitched double size quilt, with tartan centres in the flower garden design, slight damage, late 19thC. The continuing popularity of the use of tartan in antique textiles with both the American and Japanese public sometimes results in over-large premiums.
£180–200/$260–290 JPr

Silk patchwork quilt, with overstitch design and bobble fringing, hand-stitched, slightly damaged, mid–19thC.
£225–250/$320–360 JPr ⊞

General factors

- Many quilts are backed but those that are not can cost around half the price.
- Beadwork with roses is always a popular buy, but other flowers can achieve a similar effect for less money.
- On linen and handmade lace, hand-embroidered decoration adds to the value, especially if in perfect condition.
- Shawls are an inexpensive way to buy decorative textile pieces. Look for wool ones from the 19th century when Paisley print was very popular.

The look without the price

Wool and silk often look similar. However, silk can command a premium when used in samplers and embroideries.

Woolwork sampler, 1850, 19in (48.5cm) square.
£250–280/$360–410 JPr ⊞

Part casket of five drawers, the front embroidered in silk with colourful geometric designs, the sides and back densely embroidered in satin stitch on linen with biblical scenes, trimmed with silver braid and pink paper-lined, distressed, lid and feet missing, 11¼in (28.5cm) wide. The condition of all types of stumpwork is paramount to its value. Had this item been in mint condition the value would have been up to ten times that shown. The rarity of stumpwork and the increasing collectability of this form of early textile will ensure that this disparity will increase.
£350–420/$500–600 TMA

◄ **Sampler,** worked in wool with verse within a foliate border with butterflies, in a burr-maple frame, 19thC, 19 x 21in (48.5 x 53.5cm). The excessive discolouration of this sampler reduces the value by up to 50 per cent.
£550–600
$800–870 P(NW)

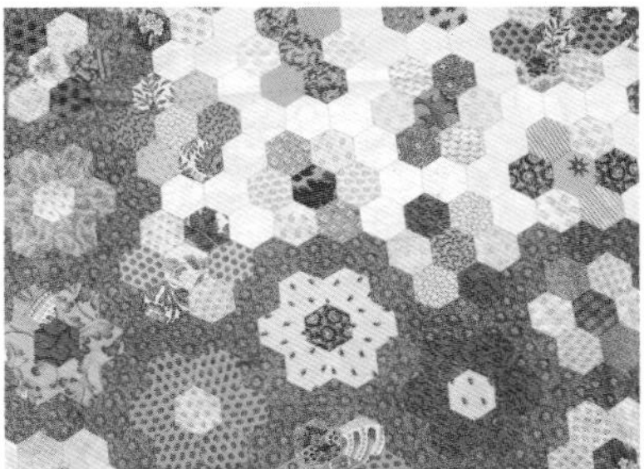

► **Patchwork quilt,** in green, red and brown, unfinished, mid-19thC, 120 x 110in (305 x 279.5cm). The importance of finishing this type of quilt in relation to its value is far outweighed by the intricacy and condition of the patchwork. Modern-day quilters would pay a premium to be able to finish such a quality quilt, using old cottons, in the same way as those of the mid-19thC. Finished, this quilt should realize £800–1,000/$1,150–1,500.
£750–850/$1,100–1,250 JPr ⊞

Wooden Antiques

Mahogany wig or bonnet stand, c1825, 10in (25.5cm) high. Used for displaying antique bonnets. These are also popular with barristers for court wigs and treen collectors as a larger piece.
£52–58/$75–85 F&F

Ashwood brass-banded gill measure, c1840, 4in (10cm) high.
£70–75/$100–110 F&F

Mahogany wig or bonnet stand, c1830, 9in (23cm) high.
£70–75/$100–110 F&F

Miller's compares...

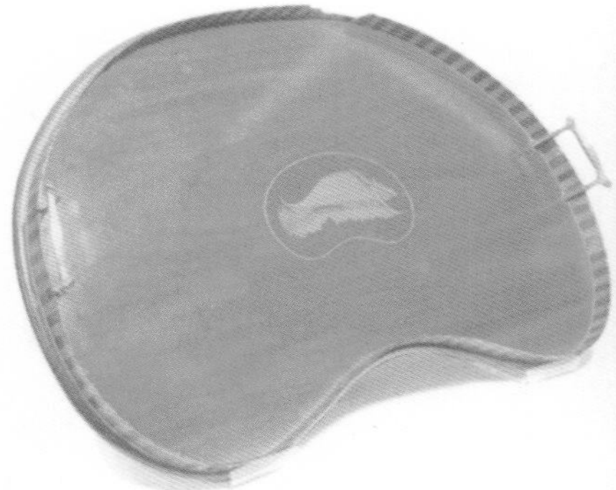

A. Mahogany tea tray, the centre inlaid with a conch shell, with a raised chequer border, two brass handles, border chipped, c1905, 24in (61cm) wide.
£80–90/$115–130 WW

B. Satinwood tea tray, with Sheraton revival-style painted decoration of putti holding garlands in the clouds, a ribbon and entwined foliage border, the shaped gallery with two brass handles, c1880, 27½in (70cm) wide.
£200–250/$290–360 WW

These two tea trays are typical examples produced in the Sheraton revival style spanning the period 1880–1920. Item A is made of the more usual mahogany with a conch shell inlaid to the centre and has sustained slight damage to the gallery. Item B commanded a higher price as it is far more decorative, with the use of more exotic satinwood and painted ornamentation.

Sycamore ladle, with initials 'OE', dated 1853, 5in (12.5cm) long.
£85–95/$125–140 SEA ⊞

Turned walnut towel rail, c1900, 22in (56cm) wide.
£90–100/$130–145 MLL ⊞

► **Carved oak baguette tray,** French, late 19thC, 17in (43cm) long.
£90–110/$130–160 AMR ⊞

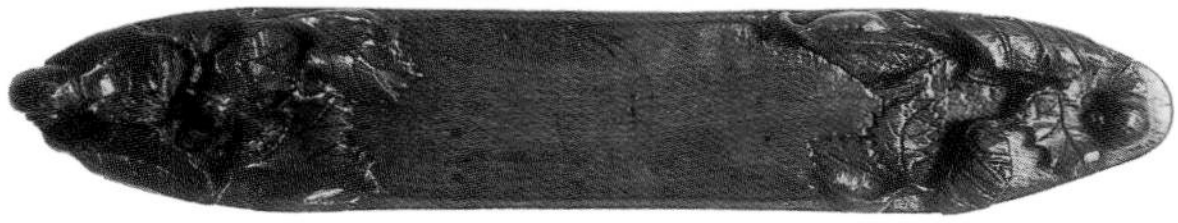

◄ **Victorian Tunbridge ware rosewood ring stand,** with three branches on a ring-turned tapering column, on a circular base with a geometric pattern, 3in (7.5cm) high.
£100–120/$145–175 TMA ⚒

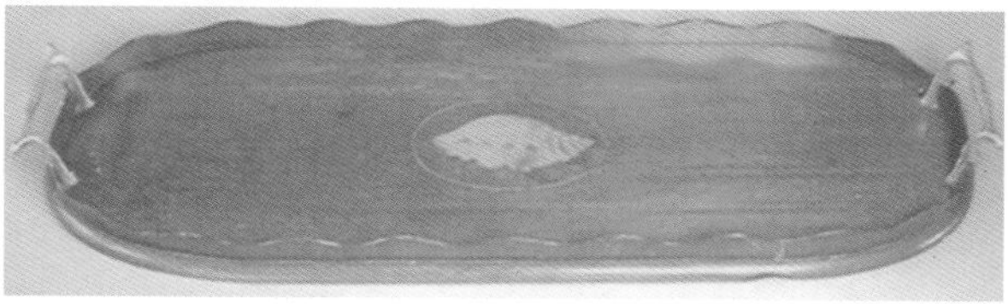

Edwardian inlaid mahogany tray, with two brass handles and wavy-edged gallery, the field centred by an oval conch shell paterae, 23in (58.5cm) wide.
£120–145/$175–210 PFK ⚒

Sycamore bowl, with sloping sides and flat bottom, 19thC, 16in (40.5cm) diam. This bowl is simple enough to appeal to collectors with modern aesthetic tastes as well as those interested in period pieces.
£120–145/$175–210 PFK ⚒

Edwardian mahogany tray, with marquetry conch shell inlay and stringing, 30in (76cm) wide.
£150–180/$220–260 SWO ⚒

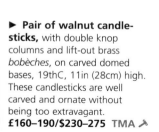

► **Pair of walnut candlesticks,** with double knop columns and lift-out brass *bobèches*, on carved domed bases, 19thC, 11in (28cm) high. These candlesticks are well carved and ornate without being too extravagant.
£160–190/$230–275 TMA ⚒

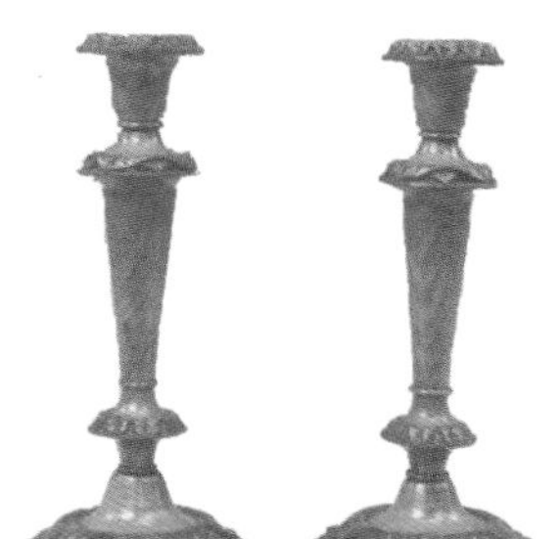

Fruitwood sweetmeat bowl, c1820, 5in (12.5cm) diam.
£180–200/$260–290 SEA ⊞

Rosewood connoisseur's magnifying glass, for viewing pictures, c1820, 17in (43cm) long.
£250–275/$360–400 F&F

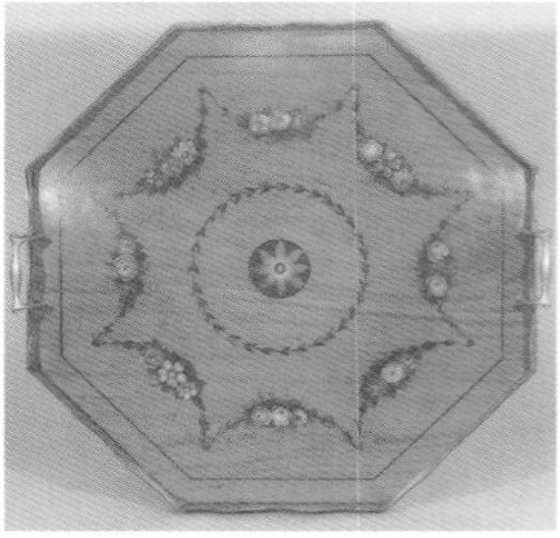

Satinwood tea tray, painted with garlands centred by a stylized flowerhead, with stringing, waved gallery and brass loop handles, c1905, 20in (51cm) wide.
£300–350/$440–500 AH

Miller's compares...

A. Lignum vitae pestle and mortar, c1730, 7in (18cm) long.
£330–365/$475–550 F&F

B. Lignum vitae pestle and mortar, c1720, 7in (18cm) long.
£535–600/$750–870 F&F

Lignum vitae (wood of life) is one of the hardest woods known. It was first imported to Europe from South America in the 16th century and was much favoured by wood turners for producing high-status vessels. Although Item A is well-figured, the crisp turning to Item B required greater skill from the turner and would therefore command a higher price.

◄ **Rosewood magnifying glass,** with turned stickware handle, c1880, 5½in (14cm) long.
£300–350/$440–500 VB

Carved wood mastiff head inkwell, with glass inset eyes and leather collar, Black Forest, late 19thC, 3in (7.5cm) high.
£420–500/$600–720 G(L)

Sycamore spice pot, c1790, 5in (12.5cm) high.
£430–475/$630–690 SEA

Oak tobacco jar, with lead liner and tamper, c1820, 8in (20.5cm) high. Unusual tobacco-related items such as this jar command a higher price.
£675–750
$975–1,100 SEA

Locate the source

The source of each illustration in Miller's can be found by checking the code letters below each caption with the Key to Illustrations, pages 286–290.

◄ **Coromandel vanity case,** with vacant mother-of-pearl cartouche fitted with two sprung drawers, the interior with silver-topped glass jars, c1860, 12in (35.5cm) wide.
£800–880
$1,150–1,275 RAN

Tunbridge ware walnut tea caddy, with a panel depicting Penshurst Place, Kent, and foliate banding, c1850, 12½in (32cm) wide.
£880–1,000/$1,275–1,500 G(L)

Tunbridge ware box, with floral mosaic, c1870, 12in (30.5cm) wide.
£900–1,000/$1,300–1,500 AMH

◄ **Oyster olivewood lace box,** c1690, 16in (40.5cm) wide.
£900–1,000/$1,300–1,500 F&F

Glossary

We have defined here some of the terms that you will come across in this book. If there are any terms or technicalities you would like explained or you feel should be included in future, please let us know.

abrashed: A slight shift in colour tone caused by the weaver running out of one batch of yarn and continuing with another: each batch of a natural dye will differ slightly from others.

armorial: A full coat-of-arms. Also a term used for any object decorated with the owner's coat-of-arms, especially silver or silver plate.

astragal: Moulding into which are set the glass panes of a cabinet or bookcase.

bergère chair: Originally any armchair with upholstered sides, now more often used to describe a chair with a square or round caned back and sides.

bevelled glass: Where a slope is cut at the edge of a flat surface. Usually associated with the plate glass used in mirrors.

boteh: The Paisley motif which may also be found in stylized form. It probably represents a leaf.

bright-cut engraving: Whereby the metal surface is cut creating facets that reflect the light.

bust: A sculpture of the head, shoulders and upper chest of a person.

cabriole leg: Tall curving leg subject to many designs and produced with club, pad, paw, claw-and-ball, and scroll feet.

canapé: A large settee with upholstered back and arms.

cartouche: A decorative frame, surrounded by scrollwork and foliage, often bearing an inscription, monogram or coat-of-arms.

chasing: Method of decorating using hammers and punches to push metal into a relief pattern – the metal is displaced, not removed.

corbel: Projecting moulding at the top of tall cabinet furniture.

cornishware: Blue- and white-striped kitchen china produced from c1926.

coromandel: Yellow- and black-striped wood from South America which is used mainly for crossbanding.

credenza: Elaborately decorated Victorian side cabinet, sometimes with rounded ends, and often with glazed or solid doors.

dip circle: A dip needle with a vertical circular scale of angles used for measuring dip. Also called an inclinometer.

enamel: Coloured glass, applied to metal, ceramic or glass in paste form and then fired for decorative effect.

field: The large area of a rug or carpet usually enclosed by borders.

finial: An ornament, often carved in many forms from animal figures to obelisks, and used to finish off any vertical projection.

gesso: Composition of plaster of Paris and size which was used as a base for applying gilding and usually moulded in bas relief.

intaglio: Incised gemstone, often set in a ring, used in antiquity and during the Renaissance as a seal. Any incised decoration; the opposite of carving in relief.

kilim: A simple, pileless rug or carpet.

lithography: Method of polychrome printing in which a design is drawn in ink on a stone surface and transferred to paper. Lithographic prints were also used to decorate ceramics.

marotte: Doll on a stick which plays a tune when spun round.

marquetry: Design formed from different coloured woods veneered onto a carcase to give a decorative effect. Many early examples are Dutch.

meiping: Chinese for cherry blossom. A term referring to a tall vase, with high shoulders, small neck and narrow mouth, used to display flowering branches.

nacreous: Made from mother-of-pearl, or having the lustre of, mother-of-pearl.

naos or cella: The inner room of a temple housing the statue of a deity.

ogee: Double curved shape which is convex at the top and becomes concave at the bottom. It is often found on the feet of Georgian furniture. Also known as cyma reversa.

papier mâché: Paper pulp usually combined with a glue and moulded into boxes, trays and ornaments, painted or japanned. Also used to make furniture building up layers of paper with pitch and oil over an iron frame.

parquetry: Decorative veneers laid in a geometric pattern.

patera: Small flat circular ornament, often in the form of an open flower or rosette, used as a ceiling or furniture ornament.

patina: Surface colour of genuinely old wood resulting from the layers of grease, dirt and polish built up over the years, and through handling. Differs from wood to wood and difficult to fake.

piecrust: Carved and scalloped edge found on tripod tables. It resembles the rim of a crusty pie.

pilaster: Decorative flat-faced column projecting from a wall.

plush: Warp pile fabric with a long loosely-woven cut pile used to imitate fur.

prie-dieu: Chair with a low seat and a tall back. They were made during the 19th century and were designed for prayer.

putti: Cupids or cherubs used as decoration.

retipping: Replacing the tips of chair legs.

salt glaze: Hard transluscent glaze used on stoneware and achieved by throwing common salt into the kiln at high temperatures. Produces a silky, pitted appearance like orange peel.

secrétaire: Writing cabinet with a flat front and a deep drawer hinged to open and form a writing surface.

socle: Another name for a plinth.

spelter: Zinc treated to look like bronze. An inexpensive substitute used in Art Nouveau appliqué ornament and Art Deco figures.

spigot: A stopper or tap, usually wood, and fitted to a cask.

splat: Central upright in a chair back.

strapwork: Repeated carved decoration suggesting plaited straps. Originally used in the 16th and 17th centuries and revived in the 19th century.

tamper: An instrument for packing down tobacco in a pipe.

tine: The prong of a fork; early ones have two, later ones three.

tôle peinte: French 18th-century method of varnishing sheet iron vessels so that the surface could be painted upon. And by derivation, painted metal panels applied to furniture.

Tunbridge ware: Objects decorated with wooden inlay made of bundles of coloured wood cut into sections; usually simple geometric designs, but sometimes whole scenes; mid-17th to late 19th century.

verdigris: Greenish or blueish patina formed on copper, bronze or brass.

wrought-iron: A pure form of iron often used for decorative purposes.

wucai: Type of five-colour Chinese porcelain decoration.

Directory of Specialists

If you wish to be included in next year's directory, or if you have a change of address or telephone number, please contact Miller's Advertising Department. We advise readers to make contact by telephone before visiting a dealer, therefore avoiding a wasted journey.

ANTIQUITIES
Dorset
Ancient & Gothic Tel: 01202 431721
Antiquities from before 300,000 BC to about 1500 AD

London
Helios Gallery, 292 Westbourne Grove, W11 2PS Tel: 077 11 955 997
heliosgallery@btinternet.com
www.heliosgallery.com
Roman, Greek, Egyptian, Chinese, ancient art

ARCHITECTURAL
Cheshire
Nostalgia, Hollands Mill, 61 Shaw Heath, Stockport, SK3 8BH
Tel: 0161 477 7706
www.nostalgia-uk.com
Antique fireplaces

Devon
Adrian Ager Ltd, Great Hall, North Street, Ashburton, TQ13 7QD
Tel/Fax: 01364 653189
afager@tinyworld.co.uk
www.adrianager.co.uk

Gloucestershire
Olliff's Architectural Antiques, 19–21 Lower Redland Road, Redland, Bristol, BS6 6TB
Tel: 0117 923 9232
marcus@olliffs.com
www.olliffs.com

Kent
Catchpole & Rye, Saracens Dairy, Jobbs Lane, Pluckley, Ashford, TN27 0SA
Tel: 01233 840457
info@crye.co.uk www.crye.co.uk
Antique bathroom ware

Somerset
Walcot Reclamations, 108 Walcot Street, Bath, BA1 5BG
Tel: 01225 444404

ARMS & MILITARIA
Gloucestershire
Q & C Militaria, 22 Suffolk Road, Cheltenham, GL50 2AQ
Tel/Fax: 01242 519815
Mobile: 07778 613977
john@qc-militaria.freeserve.co.uk
www.qcmilitaria.com

Surrey
West Street Antiques, 63 West Street, Dorking, RH4 1BS
Tel: 01306 883487
weststant@aol.com
www.antiquearmsandarmour.com

BAROMETERS
Berkshire
Alan Walker, Halfway Manor, Halfway, Nr Newbury, RG20 8NR
Tel/Fax: 01488 657670
Mobile: 07770 728397
www.alanwalker-barometers.com

Cheshire
Derek & Tina Rayment Antiques, Orchard House, Barton Road, Barton, Nr Farndon, SY14 7HT
Tel: 01829 270429 Mobile: 07860 666629 and 07702 922410
raymentantiques@aol.com

BEDS
Wales
Seventh Heaven, Chirk Mill, Chirk, Wrexham, County Borough, LL14 5BU Tel: 01691 777622/773563
requests@seventh-heaven.co.uk
www.seventh-heaven.co.uk

Worcestershire
S.W. Antiques, Abbey Showrooms, Newlands, Pershore, WR10 1BP
Tel: 01386 555580
sw-antiques@talk21.com
www.sw-antiques.co.uk

BOXES & TREEN
Berkshire
Mostly Boxes, 93 High Street, Eton, Windsor, SL4 6AF Tel: 01753 858470

Somerset
Alan & Kathy Stacey Appointment only Tel: 01963 441333
sales@antiqueboxes.uk.com
ww.antiqueboxes.uk.com
Tortoiseshell, ivory, shagreen and mother of pearl tea caddies and boxes

CAMERAS
Kent
Stuart Heggie, 14 The Borough, Northgate, Canterbury, CT1 2DR
Tel: 01227 470422

CLOCKS
Surrey
Antique Clocks by Patrick Thomas, 62a West Street, Dorking, RH4 1BS
Tel: 01306 743661
clockman@fsmail.net
www.antiqueclockshop.co.uk
Clocks, scientific instruments, sporting antique

Wiltshire
P A Oxley Antique Clocks, The Old Rectory, Cherhill, Nr Calne, SN11 8UX Tel: 01249 816227
info@paoxley.com
www.british-antiqueclocks.com

USA
R. O. Schmitt Fine Art, Box 1941, Salem, New Hampshire 03079
Tel: 603 893 5915
bob@roschmittfinearts.com
www.antiqueclockauction.com
Specialist antique clock auctions

DECORATIVE ARTS
Gloucestershire
Ruskin Decorative Arts, 5 Talbot Court, Stow-on-the-Wold, Cheltenham, GL54 1DP
Tel: 01451 832254
william.anne@ruskindecarts.co.uk
Decorative Arts 1860–1930

Kent
Delf Stream Gallery, 14 New Street, Sandwich, CT13 9AB Tel: 01304 617684 www.delfstreamgallery.com
19th–20thC European and American art pottery

Scotland
decorative arts @ doune, Stand 26, Scottish Antique and Arts Centre, By Doune, Stirling, FK16 6HD
Tel: 01786 461 439
Mobile: 07778 475 974
decorativearts.doune@btinternet.com

DOLLS
Kent
Barbara Ann Newman, London House Antiques, 4 Market Square, Westerham, TN16 1AW
Tel: 01959 564479
Mobile: 07850 016729

Scotland
Bébés et Jouets, c/o Post Office, Edinburgh, EH7 6HW
Tel: 0131 332 5650
Mobile: 0771 4374995
bebesetjouets@u.genie.co.uk
www.you.genie.co.uk/bebesetjouets
Antique French bébés and German dolls, teddy bears, juvenilia and related items

EPHEMERA
Oxfordshire
Michael Jackson Antiques, The Quiet Woman Antiques Centre, Southcombe, Chipping Norton, OX7 5QH Tel: 01608 646262
mjcig@cards.fsnet.co.uk
www.our-web-site.com/cigarette-cards
Cigarette cards

FURNITURE
Hampshire
Millers Antiques Ltd, Netherbrook House, 86 Christchurch Road, Ringwood, BH24 1DR
Tel: 01425 472062
mail@millers-antiques.co.uk
www.millers-antiques.co.uk
English and continental country furniture, 19thC Majolica, Quimper, treen

Kent
Pantiles Spa Antiques, 4, 5, 6 Union House, The Pantiles, Tunbridge Wells, TN4 8HE Tel: 01892 541377
Mobile: 07711 283655
psa.wells@btinternet.com
www.antiques-tun-wells-kent.co.uk

Lincolnshire
David J Hansord & Son, 6 & 7 Castle Hill, Lincoln, LN1 3AA
Tel: 01522 530044
Mobile: 07831 183511
18thC English furniture, works of art and objects

Middlesex
Phelps Antiques, 133–135 St Margaret's Road, Twickenham, TW1 1RG Tel: 020 8892 1778/7129
antiques@phelps.co.uk
www.phelps.co.uk

Nottinghamshire
No.1 Castlegate Antiques, 1–3 Castlegate, Newark, NG24 1AZ
Tel: 01636 701877
Mobile: 07850 463173
18th–19thC furniture, clocks, barometers

Ranby Hall-Antiques, Barnby Moor, Retford, DN22 8JQ
Tel: 01777 860696
Mobile: 07860 463477
paul.wyatt@virgin.net
www.ranbyhall.antiques-gb.com

Oxfordshire
The Country Seat, Huntercombe Manor Barn, Henley-on-Thames, RG9 5RY Tel: 01491 641349

Dorchester Antiques, 3 High Street, Dorchester-on-Thames, OX10 7HH
Tel: 01865 341 373
Georgian furniture, country pieces

West Sussex
Dycheling Antiques, 34 High Street, Ditchling, Hassocks, BN6 8TA Tel: 01273 842929
Mobile: 07785 456341
www.antiquechairmatching.com
Sets of Georgian to Victorian dining furniture, upholstered furniture, chiffoniers, dining tables

Wales
Collinge Antiques, Old Fyffes Warehouse, Conwy Road, Llandudno Junction, LL31 9LU
Tel: 01492 580022
General antiques, Georgian–Edwardian furniture

West Midlands
Martin Taylor Antiques, 323 Tettenhall Road, Wolverhampton, WV6 0JZ Tel: 01902 751166
Mobile: 07836 636524
enquiries@mtaylor-antiques.co.uk
www.mtaylor-antiques.co.uk

Worcestershire
Fenwick & Fenwick, 88–90 High Street, Broadway, WR12 7AJ
Tel: 01386 853227/841724
17th–early 19thC oak, mahogany, walnut furniture and works of art. Treen, boxes, pewter, lace bobbins, Chinese porcelain, corkscrews, early metalware

GLASS
Gloucestershire
Grimes House Antiques, High Street, Moreton-in-Marsh, GL56 0AT
Tel/Fax: 01608 651029
grimes_house@cix.co.uk
www.grimeshouse.co.uk
www.cranberryglass.co.uk
Cranberry glass

London
Andrew Lineham Fine Glass, The Mall, Camden Passage, N1 8ED Tel: 020 7704 0195
wed & sat 01243 576241
Mobile: 07767 702722
andrew@andrewlineham.co.uk
www.andrewlineham.co.uk
19th–20thC glass

Norfolk
Brian Watson Antique Glass, Foxwarren Cottage, High Street, Marsham, Norwich, NR10 5QA
Tel: 01263 732519

Somerset
Somervale Antiques, 6 Radstock Road, Midsomer Norton, Bath, BA3 2AJ Tel/Fax: 01761 412686
Mobile: 07885 088022
ronthomas@somervaleantiquesglass.co.uk
www.somervaleantiquesglass.co.uk

JEWELLERY
London
Shapiro & Co, Stand 380, Gray's Antique Market, 58 Davies Street, W1Y 5LP Tel: 020 7491 2710
Jewellery, silver, objets d'art

KITCHENWARE
Gloucestershire
Bread & Roses, Durham House Antique Centre, Sheep Street, Stow on the Wold, GL54 1AA
Tel: 01451 870404 or 01926 817342
Kitchen antiques 1800–1950s

Lincolnshire
Skip & Janie Smithson Antiques
Tel/Fax: 01754 810265
Mobile: 07831 399180

East Sussex
Ann Lingard, Ropewalk Antiques, Rye, TN31 7NA Tel: 01797 223486
ann-lingard@ropewalkantiques.freeserve.co.uk
Large selection of hand finished English antique pine furniture, kitchen shop and complementary antiques

LIGHTING
Devon
The Exeter Antique Lighting Co., Cellar 15, The Quay, Exeter, EX2 4AP Tel: 01392 490848
Mobile: 07702 969438
www.antiquelightingcompany.com

MARKETS & CENTRES
Derbyshire
Chappells Antiques Centre, King Street, Bakewell, DE45 1DZ
Tel: 01629 812496
ask@chappellsantiquescentre.com
www.chappellsantiquescentre.com
Open Monday to Saturday 10am to 5pm, Sunday 12 to 5pm. Antique furniture and furnishings, decorative and collectors items from 17th to the 20th century

Gloucestershire
Durham House Antiques Centre, Sheep Street, Stow-on-the-Wold, GL54 1AA Tel: 01451 870404
30+ dealers with an extensive range of town and country furniture, metalware, books, pottery, porcelain, kitchenalia, silver, jewellery and art. Mon–Sat 10am–5pm, Sunday 11am–5pm. Stow-on-the-Wold, Cotswold home to over 40 antique shops, galleries and bookshops

Hampshire
Dolphin Quay Antique Centre, Queen Street, Emsworth, PO10 7BU
Tel: 01243 379994/379994
www.dolphin-quay-antiques.co.uk
30 plus dealers, antique furniture, porcelain, clocks, watches, jewellery, silver

Northamptonshire
Brackley Antique Cellar, Drayman's Walk, Brackley, NN13 6BE
Tel: 01280 701393
30,000 sq ft of floor space with over 100 antique dealers specialising in ceramics, porcelain, clocks, glass, books, dolls, jewellery, militaria, linen, lace, victoriana, kitchenalia and furniture

Nottinghamshire
Dukeries Antiques Centre, Thoresby Park, Budby, Newark, NG22 9EX
Tel: 01623 822252
Antique furniture, paintings, porcelain, glass, silver

Newark Antiques Warehouse, Old Kelham Road, Newark, NG24 1BX
Tel: 01636 674869
enquiries@newarkantiques.co.uk

Wales
Offa's Dyke Antique Centre, 4 High Street, Knighton, Powys, LD7 1AT Tel: 01547 528635/528940
General antiques and ceramics

Worcestershire
Worcester Antiques Centre, Reindeer Court, Mealcheapen Street, Worcester, WR1 4DF
Tel: 01905 610680
Porcelain, early Worcester, furniture, silver, jewellery, Art Nouveau, Arts and Crafts

OAK & COUNTRY
Cambridgeshire
Mark Seabrook Antiques, PO Box 396, Huntingdon, PE28 0ZA
Tel: 01480 861935 Mobile: 07770 721931 enquiries@markseabrook.com
www.markseabrook.com

Surrey
The Refectory, 38 West Street, Dorking, RH4 1BU
Tel: 01306 742111
www.therefectory.co.uk

ORIENTAL
Buckinghamshire
Glade Antiques, PO Box 873, High Wycombe, HP14 3ZQ
Tel: 01494 882818
sonia@gladeantiques.com
www.gladeantiques.com
Oriental porcelain, bronzes, jades, antiquities

Devon
Mere Antiques, 13 Fore Street, Topsham, Exeter, EX3 0HF
Tel: 01392 874224
Oriental porcelain

Norfolk
Roger Bradbury Antiques, Church Street, Coltishall, NR12 7DJ
Tel: 01603 737444
Chinese porcelain cargoes, 18th–19thC furniture, pictures and objets d'art

Somerset
Orient Expressions, Assembly Antiques Centre, 5–8 Saville Row, Bath, BA1 2QP Tel: 01225 313399
Mobile: 0788 1588 314
Early 19thC provincial Chinese furniture

PAPERWEIGHTS
Cheshire
Sweetbriar Gallery Ltd, Robin Hood Lane, Helsby, WA6 9NH
Tel: 01928 723851
Mobile: 07860 907532
sweetbr@globalnet.co.uk
www.sweetbriar.co.uk

USA
The Dunlop Collection, PO Box 6269, Statesville, NC 28687 Tel: (704) 871 2626 or Toll Free Tel: (800) 227 1996

PERFUME BOTTLES
Somerset
Lynda Brine, Assembly Antiques, 6 Saville Row, Bath, BA1 2QP
Tel: 01225 448488
lyndabrine@yahoo.co.uk
www.scentbottlesandsmalls.co.uk
Perfume bottles, vinaigrettes, pomanders, objects of vertu

PINE
Hampshire
Pine Cellars, 39 Jewry Street, Winchester, SO23 8RY
Tel: 01962 777546/867014

Republic of Ireland
Bygones of Ireland Ltd, Lodge Road, Westport, County Mayo
Tel: 00 353 98 26132/25701

Delvin Farm Antiques, Gormonston, Co Meath Tel: 00 353 1 841 2285
info@delvinfarmpine.com
john@delvinfarmpine.com
www.delvinfarmpine.com

Somerset
Westville House Antiques, Westville House, Littleton, Nr Somerton, TA11 6NP Tel/Fax: 01458 273376
Mobile: 07941 510823
antique@westville.co.uk
www.westville.co.uk

East Sussex
Ann Lingard, Ropewalk Antiques, Rye, TN31 7NA Tel: 01797 223486
ann-lingard@ropewalkantiques.freeserve.co.uk
Large selection of hand finished English antique pine furniture, kitchen shop and complementary antiques

Warwickshire
Pine & Things, Portobello Farm, Campden Road, Nr Shipston-on-Stour, CV36 4PY
Tel: 01608 663849

PORCELAIN
London
Diana Huntley Antiques, 8 Camden Passage, Islington, N1 8ED
Tel: 020 7226 4605
diana@dianahuntleyantiques.co.uk
www.dianahuntleyantiques.co.uk
19thC porcelain

POTTERY
Buckinghamshire
Gillian Neale Antiques, PO Box 247, Aylesbury, HP20 1JZ
Tel: 01296 423754
Mobile: 07860 638700
gillianneale@aol.com
www.gilliannealeantiques.co.uk
English blue printed pottery 1780–1900

Kent
Serendipity, 125 High Street, Deal, CT14 6BB Tel: 01304 369165/01304 366536 dipityantiques@aol.com

London
Jonathan Horne, 66 Kensington Church Street, W8 4BY
Tel: 020 7221 5658
JH@jonathanhorne.co.uk
www.jonathanhorne.co.uk
Early English pottery

Somerset
Peter Scott, Stand 39, Bartlett Street Antiques Centre, Bath, BA1 2QZ
Tel: 01225 310457 or 0117 986 8468
Mobile: 07850 639770
Blue & white transferware pottery

Suffolk
John Read, 29 Lark Rise, Martlesham Heath, Ipswich, IP5 7SA Tel: 01473 624897

Surrey
Judi Bland Tel: 01276 857576
Toby jugs

East Sussex
Tony Horsley, PO Box 3127, Brighton, BN1 5SS Tel: 01273 550770

Tyne & Wear
Ian Sharp Antiques, 23 Front Street, Tynemouth, NE30 4DX
Tel: 0191 296 0656
iansharp@sharpantiques.demon.co.uk
www.sharpantiques.demon.co.uk

Wales
Islwyn Watkins, Offa's Dyke Antique Centre, 4 High Street, Knighton, Powys, LD7 1AT Tel: 01547 520145
18th and 19thC pottery, 20thC country and Studio pottery, small country furniture, treen and bygones

Wiltshire
Andrew Dando, 34 Market Street, Bradford on Avon, BA15 1LL
Tel: 01225 865444
www.andrewdando.co.uk
Pottery and porcelain 1750–1870

PUBLICATIONS
West Midlands
Antiques Magazine, H.P. Publishing, 2 Hampton Court Road, Harborne, Birmingham, B17 3AE
Tel: 0121 681 8000
Weekly guide to buying and selling antiques

RUGS & CARPETS
Kent
Desmond & Amanda North, The Orchard, 186 Hale Street, East Peckham, TN12 5JB
Tel: 01622 871353
Oriental rugs and carpets

Republic of Ireland
Peter Linden, Georges Avenue, Blackrock, Dublin
Tel: 00 3531 288 5875
lind@indigo.ie
www.peterlinden.com
Oriental rugs, carpets, kilims, tapestries

SCIENTIFIC INSTRUMENTS
Scotland
Early Technology, Monkton House, Old Craighall, Musselburgh, Midlothian, EH21 8SF
Tel: 0131 665 5753
michael.bennett-levy@virgin.net
www.earlytech.com

Somerset
Richard Twort
Tel/Fax: 01934 641900
Mobile: 07711 939789
Science and technology

SERVICES
USA
Go Antiques, 2330 Aubin Lane, Baton Rouge, LA 70816
Tel: UK 01423 771122
US 1 877 481 5750
sales@goantiques.com
www.goantiques.com
AOL Keyword: GoAntiques
Antiques, art, collectables & more

SILVER
London
Daniel Bexfield, 26 Burlington Arcade, W1J 0PU
Tel: 020 7491 1720
antiques@bexfield.co.uk
www.bexfield.co.uk
Specialising in fine quality silver, jewellery and objects of vertu dating from the 17th to the 20thC

Republic of Ireland
J. W. Weldon, 55 Clarendon Street, Dublin 2 Tel: 00 353 1 677 1638
Jewellery, antique and provincial Irish silver

West Sussex
Nicholas Shaw Antiques, Virginia Cottage, Lombard Street, Petworth, GU28 0AG
Tel: 01798 345146/01798 345147
Mobile: 07885 643000/07817 572746 silver@nicholas-shaw.com
www.nicholas-shaw.com
Scottish and Irish silver

TEXTILES
Lancashire
Decades, 20 Lord St West, Blackburn, BB2 1JX Tel: 01254 693320
Costumes, textiles, accessories, pottery, small furniture, pictures, glass, curios and collectables

Somerset
Joanna Proops Antique Textiles & Lighting, 34 Belvedere, Lansdown Hill, Bath, BA1 5HR
Tel: 01225 310795
antiquetextiles@uk.online.co.uk
www.antiquetextiles.co.uk

Wales
Jen Jones, Pontbrendu, LLanybydder, Ceredigion, SA40 9UJ Tel: 01570 480610
Welsh quilts and blankets, small Welsh country antiques

USA
Antique European Linens, PO Box 789, Gulf Breeze, Florida 32562-0789
Tel: 001 850 432 4777
Cell: 850 450 463
name@antiqueeuropeanlinens.com
www.antiqueeuropeanlinens.com

M. Finkel & Daughter, 936 Pine Street, Philadelphia, Pennsylvania 19107-6128
Tel: 001 215 627 7797
mailbox@finkelantiques.com
www.finkelantiques.com
Americas leading antique sampler and needlework dealer

TRIBAL ART
Yorkshire
Gordon Reece Galleries, Finkle Street, Knaresborough, HG5 8AA Tel: 01423 866219
www.gordonreecegalleries.com

TUNBRIDGE WARE
London
Amherst Antiques, Monomark House, 27 Old Gloucester Street, WC1N 3XX Mobile: 07850 350212
amherstantiques@monomark.co.uk
Tunbridge ware, 19thC English ceramics, glass, silver

WATCHES
Kent
Tempus, Union Square, The Pantiles, Tunbridge Wells, Tel/Fax: 01932 828936
www.tempus-watches.co.uk

London
Pieces of Time, (1–7 Davies Mews), 26 South Molton Lane, W1Y 2LP
Tel: 020 7629 2422 info@antique-watch.com www.antique-watch.com

Directory of Auctioneers

Auctioneers who hold frequent sales should contact us on 01580 766411 for inclusion in the next edition.

Bedfordshire
W&H Peacock, 26 Newnham Street, Bedford, MK40 3JR Tel: 01234 266366

Berkshire
Dreweatt Neate, Donnington Priory, Donnington, Newbury, RG14 2JE Tel: 01635 553553 fineart@dreweatt-neate.co.uk

Law Fine Art, Firs Cottage, Church Lane, Brimpton, RG7 4TJ Tel: 0118 971 0353 info@lawfineart.co.uk www.lawfineart.co.uk

Special Auction Services, The Coach House, Midgham Park, Reading, RG7 5UG Tel: 0118 971 2949 www.invaluable.com/sas/

Buckinghamshire
Amersham Auction Rooms, 125 Station Road, Amersham, HP7 0AH Tel: 01494 729292

Cambridgeshire
Rowley Fine Art, The Old Bishop's Palace, Little Downham, Ely, CB6 2TD Tel: 01353 699177 mail@rowleyfineart.com www.rowleyfineart.com

Channel Islands
Bonhams and Langlois, Westaway Chambers, 39 Don Street, St Helier, Jersey, JE2 4TR Tel: 01534 722441

Cheshire
Bonhams, New House, 150 Christleton Road, Chester, CH3 5TD Tel: 01244 313936

Cumbria
Penrith Farmers' & Kidd's plc, Skirsgill Salerooms, Penrith, CA11 0DN Tel: 01768 890781 penrith.farmers@virgin.net

Devon
Bonhams, Dowell Street, Honiton, EX14 1LX Tel: 01404 41872

Taylors, Honiton Galleries, 205 High Street, Honiton, EX14 8LF Tel: 01404 42404

Dorset
Hy Duke & Son, Dorchester Fine Art Salerooms, Dorchester, DT1 1QS Tel: 01305 265080

Essex
Ambrose, Ambrose House, Old Station Road, Loughton, IG10 4PE Tel: 020 8502 3951

Cheffins, 8 Hill Street, Saffron Walden, CB2 4BW Tel: 01799 513131 www.cheffins.co.uk

Sworders, 14 Cambridge Road, Stansted Mountfitchet, CM24 8BZ Tel: 01279 817778 www.sworder.co.uk

Gloucestershire
Mallams, 26 Grosvenor Street, Cheltenham, GL52 2SG Tel: 01242 235712

Tayler & Fletcher, London House, High Street, Bourton-on-the-Water, Cheltenham, GL54 2AP Tel: 01451 821666 bourton@taylerfletcher.com www.taylerfletcher.com

Herefordshire
Brightwells Fine Art, The Fine Art Saleroom, Ryelands Road, Leominster, HR6 8NZ Tel: 01568 611122 fineart@brightwells.com www.brightwells.com

Hertfordshire
Tring Market Auctions, Brook Street, Tring, HP23 5EF Tel: 01442 826446 sales@tringmarketauctions.co.uk www.tringmarketauctions.co.uk

Kent
Bonhams, 49 London Road, Sevenoaks, TN13 1AR Tel: 01732 740310

Bracketts, Auction Hall, Pantiles, Tunbridge Wells, TN2 5QL Tel: 01892 544500 www.bfaa.co.uk

The Canterbury Auction Galleries, 40 Station Road West, Canterbury, CT2 8AN Tel: 01227 763337 canterbury_auction_galleries@compuserve.com www.thecanterburyauctiongalleries.com

Mervyn Carey, Twysden Cottage, Benenden, Cranbrook, TN17 4LD Tel: 01580 240283

London
Bonhams, Montpelier Street, Knightsbridge, SW7 1HH Tel: 020 7393 3900 www.bonhams.com

Bonhams, 101 New Bond Street, W1S 1SR Tel: 020 7629 6602 www.bonhams.com

Bonhams, 10 Salem Road, Bayswater, W2 4DL Tel: 020 7229 9090 www.bonhams.com

Bonhams, 65–69 Lots Road, Chelsea, SW10 0RN Tel: 020 7393 3900 www.bonhams.com

Dix-Noonan-Webb, 1 Old Bond Street, W1X 3TD Tel: 020 7499 5022

Sotheby's, 34–35 New Bond Street, W1A 2AA Tel: 020 7293 5000 www.sothebys.com

Sotheby's Olympia, Hammersmith Road, W14 8UX Tel: 020 7293 5000

Nottinghamshire
Neales, 192 Mansfield Road, Nottingham, NG1 3HU Tel: 0115 962 4141 fineart@neales.co.uk www.neales-auctions.com

Oxfordshire
Bonhams, 39 Park End Street, Oxford, OX1 1JD Tel: 01865 723524

Holloway's, 49 Parsons Street, Banbury, OX16 5PF Tel: 01295 817777 enquiries@hollowaysauctioneers.co.uk www.hollowaysauctioneers.co.uk

Scotland
Bonhams, 65 George Street, Edinburgh, EH2 2JL Tel: 0131 225 2266

Thomson, Roddick & Medcalf, 60 Whitesands, Dumfries, DG1 2RS Tel: 01387 255366

Shropshire
Walker, Barnett & Hill, Cosford Auction Rooms, Long Lane, Cosford, TF11 8PJ Tel: 01902 375555 wbhauctions@lineone.net www.walker-barnett-hill.co.uk

Somerset
Bonhams, 1 Old King Street, Bath, BA1 2JT Tel: 01225 788 988

Gardiner Houlgate, The Bath Auction Rooms, 9 Leafield Way, Corsham, Nr Bath, SN13 9SW Tel: 01225 812912 gardiner-houlgate.co.uk www.invaluable.com/gardiner-houlgate

Lawrences Fine Art Auctioneers, South Street, Crewkerne, TA18 8AB Tel: 01460 73041

Staffordshire
Wintertons Ltd, Lichfield Auction Centre, Fradley Park, Lichfield, WS13 6NU Tel: 01543 263256 Photos: Courtesy of Crown Photos 01283 762813

Suffolk
Olivers, Olivers Rooms, Burkitts Lane, Sudbury, CO10 1HB Tel: 01787 880305 oliversauctions@btconnect.com

Surrey
Ewbank, Burnt Common Auction Rooms, London Road, Send, Woking, GU23 7LN Tel: 01483 223101 www.ewbankauctions.co.uk

Hamptons International, 93 High Street, Godalming, GU7 1AL Tel: 01483 423567 fineartauctions@hamptons-int.com www.hamptons.co.uk

East Sussex
Gorringes Auction Galleries, Terminus Road, Bexhill-on-Sea, TN39 3LR Tel: 01424 212994 bexhill@gorringes.co.uk www.gorringes.co.uk

Gorringes inc Julian Dawson, 15 North Street, Lewes, BN7 2PD Tel: 01273 472503 auctions@gorringes.co.uk www.gorringes.co.uk

Wallis & Wallis, West Street Auction Galleries, Lewes, BN7 2NJ Tel: 01273 480208 auctions@wallisandwallis.co.uk www.wallisandwallis.co.uk

West Sussex
Rupert Toovey & Co Ltd, Star Road, Partridge Green, RH13 8RJ Tel: 01403 711744

Sotheby's Sussex, Summers Place, Billingshurst, RH14 9AD Tel: 01403 833500

Warwickshire
Locke & England, 18 Guy Street, Leamington Spa, CV32 4RT Tel: 01926 889100 www.auctions-online.com/locke

West Midlands
Bonhams, The Old House, Station Road, Knowle, Solihull, B93 0HT Tel: 01564 776151

Wiltshire
Woolley & Wallis, Salisbury Salerooms, 51–61 Castle Street, Salisbury, SP1 3SU Tel: 01722 424500

Yorkshire
Bonhams, 17a East Parade, Leeds, LS1 2BH Tel: 0113 244 8011

Dee, Atkinson & Harrison, The Exchange Saleroom, Driffield, YO25 6LD Tel: 01377 253151 exchange@dee-atkinson-harrison.co.uk www.dee-atkinson-harrison.co.uk

David Duggleby, The Vine St Salerooms, Scarborough, YO11 1XN Tel: 01723 507111 auctions@davidduggleby.freeserve.co.uk www.davidduggleby.com

Andrew Hartley, Victoria Hall Salerooms, Little Lane, Ilkley, LS29 8EA Tel: 01943 816363 info@andrewhartleyfinearts.co.uk www.andrewhartleyfinearts.co.uk

Tennants, The Auction Centre, Harmby Road, Leyburn, DL8 5SG Tel: 01969 623780 enquiry@tennants-ltd.co.uk www.tennants.co.uk

Austria
Dorotheum, Palais Dorotheum, A-1010 Wien, Dorotheergasse. 17 Tel: 0043 1 515 60 354

Australia
Leonard Joel Auctioneers, 333 Malvern Road, South Yarra, Victoria 3141 Tel: 03 9826 4333 decarts@ljoel.com.au jewellery@ljoel.com.au www.ljoel.com.au

Shapiro Auctioneers, 162 Queen Street, Woollahra, Sydney, NSW 2025 Tel: 00 612 9326 1588

China
Sotheby's, Li Po Chun Chambers, 18th Floor, 189 Des Vouex Road, Hong Kong Tel: 852 524 8121

Mexico
Galeria Louis C. Morton, GLC A7073L IYS, Monte Athos 179, Col. Lomas de Chapultepec, CP11000 Tel: 52 5520 5005 glmorton@prodigy.net.mx www.lmorton.com

Monaco
Bonhams, Le Beau Rivage, 9 Avenue d'Ostende, Monte Carlo, MC 98000 Tel: +41 (0)22 300 3160 www.bonhams.com

Netherlands
Sotheby's Amsterdam, De Boelelaan 30, 1083 HJ, Amsterdam Tel: 00 31 20 550 22 00

Republic of Ireland
Hamilton Osborne King, 4 Main Street, Blackrock, Co. Dublin Tel: 353 1 288 5011 blackrock@hok.ie www.hok.ie

Sweden
Bukowskis, Arsenalsgatan 4, Stockholm Tel: 00 46 (0)8 614 08 00 info@bukowskis.se www.bukowskis.se

USA
Jackson's Auctioneers & Appraisers, 2229 Lincoln Street, Cedar Falls, IA 50613 Tel: 00 1 319 277 2256

New Orleans Auction Galleries, Inc., 801 Magazine Street, AT 510 Julia, New Orleans, Louisiana 70130 Tel: 00 1 504 566 1849

Sotheby's, 1334 York Avenue, New York, NY 10021 Tel: 00 1 212 606 7000

Key to Illustrations

Each illustration and descriptive caption is accompanied by a letter code. By referring to the following list of auctioneers (denoted by ⚒) and dealers (⊞), the source of any item may be immediately deter-mined. Inclusion in this edition no way constitutes or implies a contract or binding offer on the part of any of our contributors to supply or sell the goods illustrated, or similar articles, at the prices stated. Advertisers in this year's directory are denoted by †.

If you require a valuation, it is advisable to check whether the dealer or specialist will carry out this service and if there is a charge. Please mention Miller's when making an enquiry. A valuation by telephone is not possible. Most dealers are willing to help you with your enquiry; however, they may be very busy and consideration of the above points would be welcomed.

AAR	⚒	Amersham Auction Rooms, 125 Station Road, Amersham, Buckinghamshire, HP7 0AH Tel: 01494 729292
ACT		No longer trading
AH	⚒†	Andrew Hartley, Victoria Hall Salerooms, Little Lane, Ilkley, Yorkshire, LS29 8EA Tel: 01943 816363 info@andrewhartleyfinearts.co.uk www.andrewhartleyfinearts.co.uk
AL	⊞†	Ann Lingard, Ropewalk Antiques, Rye, East Sussex, TN31 7NA Tel: 01797 223486 ann-lingard@ropewalkantiques.freeserve.co.uk
ALA	⊞	Alexander Antiques, Post House, Small Dole, Henfield, West Sussex, BN5 9XE Tel: 01273 493121
ALiN	⊞	Andrew Lineham Fine Glass, The Mall, Camden Passage, London, N1 8ED Tel: 020 7704 0195 or 01243 576241 andrew@andrewlineham.co.uk www.andrewlineham.co.uk
AMH	⊞	Amherst Antiques, Monomark House, 27 Old Gloucester Street, London, WC1N 3XX Tel: 07850 350212 amherstantiques@monomark.co.uk
AMR	⊞	Amron Antiques Tel: 01782 566895
AMS	⊞	Andy & Margaret Shannan, 28 Plymouth Road, Buckfastleigh, Devon, TQ11 0DB Tel: 01364 644624
ANG	⊞†	Ancient & Gothic Tel: 01202 431721
AnS	⊞	No longer trading
AOH	⊞	Antiques on High, 85 High Street, Oxford, OX1 4BG Tel: 01865 251075
ARB	⊞	Arbour Antiques Ltd, Poet's Arbour, Sheep Street, Stratford-upon-Avon, Warwickshire, CV37 6EF Tel: 01789 293453
ASB	⊞	Andrew Spencer Bottomley, The Coach House, Thongs Bridge, Holmfirth, Yorkshire, HD7 2TT Tel: 01484 685234 andrewbottomley@compuserve.com
ASH	⊞	Adrian Ager Ltd, Great Hall, North Street, Ashburton, Devon, TQ13 7QD Tel/Fax: 01364 653189 afager@tinyworld.co.uk www.adrianager.co.uk
AUTO	⊞	Automatomania, Stand 124, Grays Antique Market, 58 Davies Street, London, W1K 5LP Tel: 020 7495 5259 magic@automatomania.com www.automatomania.com
AW	⊞	Alan Walker, Halfway Manor, Halfway, Nr Newbury, Berkshire, RG20 8NR Tel/Fax: 01488 657670 www.alanwalker-barometers.com
B	⚒	Bonhams, 101 New Bond Street, London, W1S 1SR Tel: 020 7629 6602 www.bonhams.com
B(Ba)	⚒	Bonhams, 10 Salem Road, Bayswater, London, W2 4DL Tel: 020 7229 9090 www.bonhams.com
B(Ch)	⚒	Bonhams, 65–69 Lots Road, Chelsea, London, SW10 0RN Tel: 020 7393 3900 www.bonhams.com
B(Ed)	⚒	Bonhams, 65 George Street, Edinburgh, EH2 2JL, Scotland Tel: 0131 225 2266 www.bonhams.com
B(Kn)	⚒	Bonhams, Montpelier Street, Knightsbridge, London, SW7 1HH Tel: 020 7393 3900 www.bonhams.com
B(L)	⚒	Bonhams, 17a East Parade, Leeds, Yorkshire, LS1 2BH Tel: 0113 244 8011 www.bonhams.com
B(Mon)	⚒	Bonhams, Le Beau Rivage, 9 Avenue d'Ostende, Monte Carlo, MC 98000, Monaco Tel: +41 (0)22 300 3160 www.bonhams.com
B(NW)	⚒	Bonhams, New House, 150 Christleton Road, Chester, CH3 5TD Tel: 01244 313936 www.bonhams.com
B(O)	⚒	Bonhams, 39 Park End Street, Oxford, OX1 1JD Tel: 01865 723524 www.bonhams.com
B(S)	⚒	Bonhams, 49 London Road, Sevenoaks, Kent, TN13 1AR Tel: 01732 740310 www.bonhams.com
B(W)	⚒	Bonhams, Dowell Street, Honiton, Devon, EX14 1LX Tel: 01404 41872 www.bonhams.com
B(WM)	⚒	Bonhams, The Old House, Station Road, Knowle, Solihull, West Midlands, B93 0HT Tel: 01564 776151 www.bonhams.com
B&L	⚒	Bonhams and Langlois, Westaway Chambers, 39 Don Street, St Helier, Jersey, JE2 4TR, Channel Islands Tel: 01534 722441
B&R	⊞	Bread & Roses, Durham House Antique Centre, Sheep Street, Stow on the Wold, Gloucestershire, GL54 1AA Tel: 01451 870404 or 01926 817342
BaN	⊞	Barbara Ann Newman, London House Antiques, 4 Market Square, Westerham, Kent, TN16 1AW Tel: 01959 564479
Bea(E)	⚒	Bearnes, St Edmund's Court, Okehampton Street, Exeter, Devon, EX4 1DU Tel: 01392 422800
Beb	⊞	Bébés et Jouets, c/o Post Office, Edinburgh, EH7 6HW, Scotland Tel: 0131 332 5650 bebesetjouets@u.genie.co.uk www.you.genie.co.uk/bebesetjouets
BES	⊞	Bear Steps Antiques, Fish Street, Shrewsbury, Shropshire, SY1 1UR Tel: 01743 344298 Mobile: 07720 675813 englishporcelain@aol.com www.bear-steps-antiques.co.uk
BEX	⊞†	Daniel Bexfield, 26 Burlington Arcade, London, W1J 0PU Tel: 020 7491 1720 antiques@bexfield.co.uk www.bexfield.co.uk
BLH	⚒	Ambrose, Ambrose House, Old Station Road, Loughton, Essex, IG10 4PE Tel: 020 8502 3951
Bon		See **B(Kn)**
Bon(C)		See **B(Ch)**
Bon(O)		See **B(O)**
BONN	⊞	Bonnons Antique Glass Tel: 02380 273900 www.bonnonsantiqueglass.co.uk
BR	⚒	Bracketts, Auction Hall, The Pantiles, Tunbridge Wells, Kent, TN2 5QL Tel: 01892 544500 www.bfaa.co.uk
BRU	⊞	Brunel Antiques, Bartlett Street Antiques Centre, Bath, Somerset, BA1 2QZ Tel: 0117 968 1734

BrW Brian Watson Antique Glass, Foxwarren Cottage, High Street, Marsham, Norwich, Norfolk, NR10 5QA Tel: 01263 732519

BUK Bukowskis, Arsenalsgatan 4, Stockholm, Sweden-SE111 47 Tel: 00 46 (0)8 614 08 00 info@bukowskis.se www.bukowskis.se

BWL Brightwells Fine Art, The Fine Art Saleroom, Ryelands Road, Leominster, Herefordshire, HR6 8NZ Tel: 01568 611122 fineart@brightwells.com www.brightwells.com

Byl Bygones of Ireland Ltd, Lodge Road, Westport, County Mayo, Republic of Ireland Tel: 00 353 98 26132/25701

C&R Catchpole & Rye, Saracens Dairy, Jobbs Lane, Pluckley, Ashford, Kent, TN27 0SA Tel: 01233 840457 info@crye.co.uk www.crye.co.uk

CAG The Canterbury Auction Galleries, 40 Station Road West, Canterbury, Kent, CT2 8AN Tel: 01227 763337 canterbury_auction_galleries@compuserve.com www.thecanterburyauctiongalleries.com

CAL Cedar Antiques Ltd, High Street, Hartley Wintney, Hampshire, RG27 8NY Tel: 01252 843252

CF Country Furniture, 79 St Leonards Road, Windsor, Berkshire, SL4 3BZ Tel: 01488 683986

CGC Cheffins, 8 Hill Street, Saffron Walden, Essex, CB2 4BW Tel: 01799 513131 www.cheffins.co.uk

CoA Country Antiques (Wales), Castle Mill, Kidwelly, Carmarthenshire, SA17 4UU, Wales Tel: 01554 890534

CoHA Corner House Antiques and Ffoxe Antiques Tel: 01793 762752 jdhis007@btopenworld

COLL Collinge Antiques, Old Fyffes Warehouse, Conwy Road, Llandudno Junction, LL31 9LU, Wales Tel: 01492 580022

CrF Crowdfree Antiques, Fairview, The Street, Stanton, Suffolk, IP31 2DQ Tel: 0870 444 0791 info@crowdfree.com www.crowdfree.com

DA Dee, Atkinson & Harrison, The Exchange Saleroom, Driffield, Yorkshire, YO25 6LD Tel: 01377 253151 exchange@dee-atkinson-harrison.co.uk www.dee-atkinson-harrison.co.uk

DAC David Cardoza Antiques, Lewes Road, Laughton, Lewes, East Sussex, BN8 6BN Tel: 01323 811162 sales@davidcardozaantiques.co.uk www.davidcardozaantiques.co.uk

DAD decorative arts @ doune, Stand 26, Scottish Antique and Arts Centre, By Doune, Stirling, FK16 6HD, Scotland Tel: 01786 461 439 decorativearts.doune@btinternet.com

DAN Andrew Dando, 34 Market Street, Bradford on Avon, Wiltshire, BA15 1LL Tel: 01225 865444 www.andrewdando.co.uk

DD David Duggleby, The Vine St Salerooms, Scarborough, Yorkshire, YO11 1XN Tel: 01723 507111 auctions@davidduggleby.freeserve.co.uk www.davidduggleby.com

DE Decades, 20 Lord St West, Blackburn, Lancashire, BB2 1JX Tel: 01254 693320

DeA Delphi Antiques, Powerscourt Townhouse Centre, South William Street, Dublin 2, Republic of Ireland Tel: 00 353 1 679 0331

DEE Dee's Antique Pine, 89 Grove Road, Windsor, Berkshire, SL4 1HT Tel: 01753 865627/850926

Del Delomosne & Son Ltd, Court Close, North Wraxall, Chippenham, Wiltshire, SN14 7AD Tel: 01225 891505

DFA Delvin Farm Antiques, Gormonston, Co Meath, Republic of Ireland Tel: 00 353 1 841 2285 info@delvinfarmpine.com john@delvinfarmpine.com www.delvinfarmpine.com

DHA Durham House Antiques Centre, Sheep Street, Stow-on-the-Wold, Gloucestershire, GL54 1AA Tel: 01451 870404

DHu Diana Huntley Antiques, 8 Camden Passage, Islington, London, N1 8ED Tel: 020 7226 4605 diana@dianahuntleyantiques.co.uk www.dianahuntleyantiques.co.uk

DJH David J. Hansord & Son, 6 & 7 Castle Hill, Lincoln, LN1 3AA Tel: 01522 530044

DMa David March, Abbots Leigh, Bristol, Gloucestershire, BS8 Tel: 0117 937 2422

DMC Diamond Mills & Co, 117 Hamilton Road, Felixstowe, Suffolk, IP11 7BL Tel: 01394 282281

DN Dreweatt Neate, Donnington Priory, Donnington, Newbury, Berkshire, RG14 2JE Tel: 01635 553553 fineart@dreweatt-neate.co.uk

DNo Desmond & Amanda North, The Orchard, 186 Hale Street, East Peckham, Kent, TN12 5JB Tel: 01622 871353

DOA Dorchester Antiques, 3 High Street, Dorchester-on-Thames, Oxfordshire, OX10 7HH Tel: 01865 341 373

DORO Dorotheum, Palais Dorotheum, A-1010 Wien, Dorotheergasse. 17, 1010 Austria Tel: 0043 1 515 60 354

DQ Dolphin Quay Antique Centre, Queen Street, Emsworth, Hampshire, PO10 7BU Tel: 01243 379994/379994 www.dolphin-quay-antiques.co.uk

DSG Delf Stream Gallery, 14 New Street, Sandwich, Kent, CT13 9AB Tel: 01304 617684 www.delfstreamgallery.com

DUK Dukeries Antiques Centre, Thoresby Park, Budby, Newark, Nottinghamshire, NG22 9EX Tel: 01623 822252

DY Dycheling Antiques, 34 High Street, Ditchling, Hassocks, West Sussex, BN6 8TA Tel: 01273 842929 www.antiquechairmatching.com

E Ewbank, Burnt Common Auction Rooms, London Road, Send, Woking, Surrey, GU23 7LN Tel: 01483 223101 www.ewbankauctions.co.uk

EAL The Exeter Antique Lighting Co, Cellar 15, The Quay, Exeter, Devon, EX2 4AP Tel: 01392 490848 www.antiquelightingcompany.com

ET Early Technology, Monkton House, Old Craighall, Musselburgh, Midlothian, EH21 8SF, Scotland Tel: 0131 665 5753 michael.bennett-levy@virgin.net www.earlytech.com

F&C Finan & Co, The Square, Mere, Wiltshire, BA12 6DJ Tel: 01747 861411

F&F Fenwick & Fenwick, 88–90 High Street, Broadway, Worcestershire, WR12 7AJ Tel: 01386 853227/841724

FHF Frank H. Fellows & Sons, Augusta House, 19 Augusta Street, Hockley, Birmingham, West Midlands, B18 6JA Tel: 0121 212 2131

FRY Curiosities and Collectables, Gloucester Antiques Centre, The Historic Docks, 1 Severn Road, Gloucester, GL1 2LE Tel: 01452 529716

FST See **FRY**

G(B) Gorringes Auction Galleries, Terminus Road, Bexhill-on-Sea, East Sussex, TN39 3LR Tel: 01424 212994 bexhill@gorringes.co.uk www.gorringes.co.uk

G(L) Gorringes inc Julian Dawson, 15 North Street, Lewes, East Sussex, BN7 2PD Tel: 01273 472503 auctions@gorringes.co.uk www.gorringes.co.uk

GBr Geoffrey Breeze Antiques, 6 George Street, Bath, Somerset, BA1 2EH Tel: 01225 466499

GH Gardiner Houlgate, The Bath Auction Rooms, 9 Leafield Way, Corsham, Nr Bath, Somerset, SN13 9SW Tel: 01225 812912 gardiner-houlgate.co.uk www.invaluable.com/gardiner-houlgate

GKe Gerald Kenyon, 6 Great Strand Street, Dublin 1, Republic of Ireland Tel: 00 3531 873 0625/873 0488

GLa Glassdrumman Antiques, 7 Union Square, The Pantiles, Tunbridge Wells, Kent, TN4 8HE Tel: 01892 538615

GLD Glade Antiques, PO Box 873, High Wycombe, Buckinghamshire, HP14 3ZQ Tel: 01494 882818 sonia@gladeantiques.com www.gladeantiques.com

GN Gillian Neale Antiques, PO Box 247, Aylesbury, Buckinghamshire, HP20 1JZ Tel: 01296 423754 Mobile: 07860 638700 gillianneale@aol.com www.gilliannealeantiques.co.uk

GRG Gordon Reece Galleries, Finkle Street, Knaresborough, Yorkshire, HG5 8AA Tel: 01423 866219 www.gordonreecegalleries.com

GRI Grimes House Antiques, High Street, Moreton-in-Marsh, Gloucestershire, GL56 0AT Tel/Fax: 01608 651029 grimes_house@cix.co.uk www.grimeshouse.co.uk www.cranberryglass.co.uk

GS Ged Selby Antique Glass Tel: 01756 799673

HAM Hamptons International, 93 High Street, Godalming, Surrey, GU7 1AL Tel: 01483 423567 fineartauctions@hamptons-int.com www.hamptons.co.uk

HCA Hilltop Cottage Antiques, 101 Portobello Road, London, W11 Tel: 01451 844362 noswadp@AOL.com

HCFA Henry T. Callan, 162 Quaker Meeting House Road, East Sandwich, MA 02537-1312, USA Tel: 508-888-5372

HEB Hebeco, 47 West Street, Dorking, Surrey, RH4 1BU Tel: 01306 875396

HEG Stuart Heggie, 14 The Borough, Northgate, Canterbury, Kent, CT1 2DR Tel: 01227 470422

HEL Helios Gallery, 292 Westbourne Grove, London, W11 2PS Tel: 077 11 955 997 heliosgallery@btinternet.com www.heliosgallery.com

HO Houghton Antiques, Houghton, Cambridgeshire Tel: 01480 461887

HOK Hamilton Osborne King, 4 Main Street, Blackrock, Co. Dublin, Republic of Ireland Tel: 353 1 288 5011 blackrock@hok.ie www.hok.ie

HOLL Holloway's, 49 Parsons Street, Banbury, Oxfordshire, OX16 5PF Tel: 01295 817777 enquiries@hollowaysauctioneers.co.uk www.hollowaysauctioneers.co.uk

HSt High Street Antiques, 39 High Street, Hastings, East Sussex, TN34 3ER Tel: 01424 460068

HUM Humbleyard Fine Art, Unit 32 Admiral Vernon Arcade, Portobello Road, London, W11 2DY Tel: 01362 637793

HUN The Country Seat, Huntercombe Manor Barn, Henley-on-Thames, Oxfordshire, RG9 5RY Tel: 01491 641349

HYD Hy Duke & Son, Dorchester Fine Art Salerooms, Dorchester, Dorset, DT1 1QS Tel: 01305 265080

IS Ian Sharp Antiques, 23 Front Street, Tynemouth, Tyne & Wear, NE30 4DX Tel: 0191 296 0656 iansharp@sharpantiques.demon.co.uk www.sharpantiques.demon.co.uk

IW Islwyn Watkins, Offa's Dyke Antique Centre, 4 High Street, Knighton, Powys, LD7 1AT, Wales Tel: 01547 520145

JAA Jackson's Auctioneers & Appraisers, 2229 Lincoln Street, Cedar Falls, IA 50613, USA Tel: 00 1 319 277 2256

JACK Michael Jackson Antiques, The Quiet Woman Antiques Centre, Southcombe, Chipping Norton, Oxfordshire, OX7 5QH Tel: 01608 646262 mjcig@cards.fsnet.co.uk www.our-web-site.com/cigarette-cards

JAK Clive & Lynne Jackson Tel: 01242 254375

JBL Judi Bland Tel: 01276 857576

JHa Jeanette Hayhurst Fine Glass, 32a Kensington Church Street, London, W8 4HA Tel: 020 7938 1539

JHo Jonathan Horne, 66 Kensington Church Street, London, W8 4BY Tel: 020 7221 5658 JH@jonathanhorne.co.uk www.jonathanhorne.co.uk

JJ Jen Jones, Pontbrendu, LLanybydder, Ceredigion, SA40 9UJ, Wales Tel: 01570 480610

JO Jacqueline Oosthuizen, 23 Cale Street, Chelsea, London, SW3 3QR Tel: 020 7352 6071

JOA Joan Gale Antiques Dealer, Tombland Antiques Centre, 14 Tombland, Norwich, Norfolk, NR3 1HF Tel: 01603 619129 joan.gale@ukgateway.net

JP Paull's of Kenilworth, Beehive House, 125 Warwick Road, Old Kenilworth, Warwickshire, CV8 1HY Tel: 01926 855253 janicepaull@btinternet.com www.janicepaull-ironstone.com

JPr Joanna Proops Antique Textiles & Lighting, 34 Belvedere, Lansdown Hill, Bath, Somerset, BA1 5HR Tel: 01225 310795 antiquetextiles@uk.online.co.uk www.antiquetextiles.co.uk

JRe John Read, 29 Lark Rise, Martlesham Heath, Ipswich, Suffolk, IP5 7SA Tel: 01473 624897

JUP Jupiter Antiques, P.O. Box 609, Rottingdean, East Sussex, BN2 7FW Tel: 01273 302865

L Lawrences Fine Art Auctioneers, South Street, Crewkerne, Somerset, TA18 8AB Tel: 01460 73041

LBr Lynda Brine, Assembly Antiques, 6 Saville Row, Bath, Somerset, BA1 2QP Tel: 01225 448488 lyndabrine@yahoo.co.uk www.scentbottlesandsmalls.co.uk

LCM Galeria Louis C. Morton, GLC A7073L IYS, Monte Athos 179, Col. Lomas de Chapultepec, CP11000, Mexico Tel: 52 5520 5005 glmorton@prodigy.net.mx www.lmorton.com

LFA Law Fine Art, Firs Cottage, Church Lane, Brimpton, Berkshire, RG7 4TJ Tel: 0118 971 0353 info@lawfineart.co.uk www.lawfineart.co.uk

LHo Lin Holroyd Antique Glass Tel: 01924 848780

LIN Peter Linden, Georges Avenue, Blackrock, Dublin, Republic of Ireland Tel: 00 3531 288 5875 lind@indigo.ie www.peterlinden.com

MAA Mario's Antiques Tel: 0207 226 2426 marwan@barazi.screaming.net www.marios_antiques.com

MAL Mallams, 26 Grosvenor Street, Cheltenham, Gloucestershire, GL52 2SG Tel: 01242 235712

MAR Frank R. Marshall & Co, Marshall House, Church Hill, Knutsford, Cheshire, WA16 6DH Tel: 01565 653284

MB Mostly Boxes, 93 High Street, Eton, Windsor, Berkshire, SL4 6AF Tel: 01753 858470

MCC M.C. Chapman Antiques, Bell Hill, Finedon, Northamptonshire, NN9 5NB Tel: 01933 681260

MER Mere Antiques, 13 Fore Street, Topsham, Exeter, Devon, EX3 0HF Tel: 01392 874224

MIL No longer trading

MIN Ministry of Pine, The Ministry, St James Hall, Union Street, Trowbridge, Wiltshire, BA14 8RU Tel: 01225 719500 ministryofpine.uk@virgin.net

Mit Mitchells, Fairfield House, Station Road, Cockermouth, Cumbria, CA13 9PY Tel: 01900 827800

MLL Millers Antiques Ltd, Netherbrook House, 86 Christchurch Road, Ringwood, Hampshire, BH24 1DR Tel: 01425 472062 mail@millers-antiques.co.uk www.millers-antiques.co.uk

MLu	⊞	Michael Lucas Antiques, Admiral Vernon Antiques Arcade, Portobello Road, London, W11 Tel: 020 8650 1107
MTay	⊞	Martin Taylor Antiques, 323 Tettenhall Road, Wolverhampton, West Midlands, WV6 0JZ Tel: 01902 751166 Mobile: 07836 636524 enquiries@mtaylor-antiques.co.uk www.mtaylor-antiques.co.uk
MURR	⊞	Murrays' Antiques & Collectables Tel: 01202 309094
N	🔨	Neales, 192 Mansfield Road, Nottingham, NG1 3HU Tel: 0115 962 4141 fineart@neales.co.uk www.neales-auctions.com
NAW	⊞	Newark Antiques Warehouse, Old Kelham Road, Newark, Nottinghamshire, NG24 1BX Tel: 01636 674869 enquiries@newarkantiques.co.uk
NOA	🔨	New Orleans Auction Galleries, Inc., 801 Magazine Street, AT 510 Julia, New Orleans, Louisiana 70130, USA Tel: 00 1 504 566 1849
NoC	⊞	No.1 Castlegate Antiques, 1–3 Castlegate, Newark, Nottinghamshire, NG24 1AZ Tel: 01636 701877
NS	⊞	Nicholas Shaw Antiques, Virginia Cottage, Lombard Street, Petworth, West Sussex, GU28 0AG Tel: 01798 345146/01798 345147 silver@nicholas-shaw.com www.nicholas-shaw.com
OD	⊞	Offa's Dyke Antique Centre, 4 High Street, Knighton, Powys, Wales, LD7 1AT Tel: 01547 528635/52894
OE	⊞	Orient Expressions, Assembly Antiques Centre, 5–8 Saville Row, Bath, Somerset, BA1 2QP Tel: 01225 313399
OFM	⊞	The Old French Mirror Company, Nightingales, Greys Green, Rotherfield Greys, Henley on Thames, Oxon, RG9 4QQ Tel: 01491 628080 bridget@debreanski.freeserve.uk www.oldfrenchmirrors.com
OKK	⊞	Nadine Okker, 8 The Mall, 359 Upper Street, Islington, London, N1 0PD Tel: 020 7354 9496
OLA	⊞	Olliff's Architectural Antiques, 19–21 Lower Redland Road, Redland, Bristol, Gloucestershire, BS6 6TB Tel: 0117 923 9232 marcus@olliffs.com www.olliffs.com
Oli	🔨	Olivers, Olivers Rooms, Burkitts Lane, Sudbury, Suffolk, CO10 1HB Tel: 01787 880305 oliversauctions@btconnect.co
OTT	⊞	Otter Antiques, 20 High Street, Wallingford, Oxon, OX10 0BP Tel: 01491 825544
P		See **B**
P(L)		See **B(L)**
P(S)		See **B(S)**
P(NW)		See **B(NW)**
P(WM)		See **B(WM)**
P&T	⊞	Pine & Things, Portobello Farm, Campden Road, Nr Shipston-on-Stour, Warwickshire, CV36 4PY Tel: 01608 663849
PAO	⊞	P. A. Oxley Antique Clocks, The Old Rectory, Cherhill, Nr Calne, Wiltshire, SN11 8UX Tel: 01249 816227 info@paoxley.com www.british-antiqueclocks.com
PFK	🔨	Penrith Farmers' & Kidd's plc, Skirsgill Salerooms, Penrith, Cumbria, CA11 0DN Tel: 01768 890781 penrith.farmers@virgin.net
PHo	⊞	Paul Howard Tel: 07881 862 375 scientificantiques@hotmail.com
PICA	⊞	Piccadilly Antiques, 280 High Street, Batheaston, Bath, BA1 7RA Tel: 01225 851494 piccadillyantiques@ukonline.co.uk
POT	⊞	Pot Board Tel: 01834 842699 Gill@potboard.co.uk www.potboard.co.uk
PSA	⊞	Pantiles Spa Antiques, 4, 5, 6 Union House, The Pantiles, Tunbridge Wells, Kent, TN4 8HE Tel: 01892 541377 psa.wells@btinternet.com www.antiques-tun-wells-kent.co.uk
PT	⊞	Pieces of Time, (1–7 Davies Mews), 26 South Molton Lane, London, W1Y 2LP Tel: 020 7629 2422 info@antique-watch.com www.antique-watch.com
PVD	⊞	Puritan Values at the Dome, St Edmunds Business Park, St Edmunds Road, Southwold, Suffolk, IP18 6BZ Tel: 01502 722211 sales@puritanvalues.com www.puritanvalues.com
RAN	⊞	Ranby Hall-Antiques, Barnby Moor, Retford, Nottinghamshire, DN22 8JQ Tel: 01777 860696 paul.wyatt@virgin.net www.ranbyhall.antiques-gb.com
RAV	⊞	Ravenwood Antiques Tel: 01886 884 456 alan@arthur81.freeserve.co.uk
RAY	⊞	Derek & Tina Rayment Antiques, Orchard House, Barton Road, Barton, Nr Farndon, Cheshire, SY14 7HT Tel: 01829 270429 Mobile: 07860 666629 and 07702 922410 raymentantiques@aol.com
RBA	⊞	Roger Bradbury Antiques, Church Street, Coltishall, Norfolk, NR12 7DJ Tel: 01603 737444
RBB		See **BWL**
RdeR	⊞	Rogers de Rin, 76 Royal Hospital Road, London, SW3 4HN Tel: 020 7352 9007
REF	⊞	The Refectory, 38 West Street, Dorking, Surrey, RH4 1BU Tel: 01306 742111 www.therefectory.co.uk
RGe	⊞	Rupert Gentle Antiques, The Manor House, Milton Lilbourne, Nr Pewsey, Wiltshire, SN9 5LQ Tel: 01672 563344
ROSc	🔨	R. O. Schmitt Fine Art, Box 1941, Salem, New Hampshire 03079, USA Tel: 603 893 5915 bob@roschmittfinearts.com www.antiqueclockauction.com
RPh	⊞	Phelps Antiques, 133–135 St Margaret's Road, Twickenham, Middlesex, TW1 1RG Tel: 020 8892 1778/7129 antiques@phelps.co.uk www.phelps.co.uk
RTo	🔨	Rupert Toovey & Co Ltd, Star Road, Partridge Green, West Sussex, RH13 8RJ Tel: 01403 711744
RTW	⊞†	Richard Twort Tel/Fax: 01934 641900
RUSK	⊞	Ruskin Decorative Arts, 5 Talbot Court, Stow-on-the-Wold, Cheltenham, Gloucestershire, GL54 1DP Tel: 01451 832254 william.anne@ruskindecarts.co.uk
S	🔨	Sotheby's, 34–35 New Bond Street, London, W1A 2AA Tel: 020 7293 5000 www.sothebys.com
S(Am)	🔨	Sotheby's Amsterdam, De Boelelaan 30, 1083 HJ, Amsterdam, Netherlands Tel: 00 31 20 550 22 00
S(HK)	🔨	Sotheby's, Li Po Chun Chambers, 18th Floor, 189 Des Vouex Road, Hong Kong, China Tel: 852 524 8121
S(NY)	🔨	Sotheby's, 1334 York Avenue, New York, NY 10021, USA Tel: 00 1 212 606 7000
S(O)	🔨	Sotheby's Olympia, Hammersmith Road, London, W14 8UX Tel: 020 7293 5000
S(S)	🔨	Sotheby's Sussex, Summers Place, Billingshurst, West Sussex, RH14 9AD Tel: 01403 833500
SAS	🔨	Special Auction Services, The Coach House, Midgham Park, Reading, Berkshire, RG7 5UG Tel: 0118 971 2949 www.invaluable.com/sas/
SCO	⊞	Peter Scott, Tel: 0117 986 8468 Mobile: 07850 639770
SEA	⊞	Mark Seabrook Antiques, PO Box 396, Huntingdon, Cambridgeshire, PE28 0ZA Tel: 01480 861935 enquiries@markseabrook.com www.markseabrook.com

SeH ⊞ Seventh Heaven, Chirk Mill, Chirk, Wrexham, County Borough, Wales, LL14 5BU Tel: 01691 777622/773563 requests@seventh-heaven.co.uk www.seventh-heaven.co.uk

SER ⊞ Serendipity, 125 High Street, Deal, Kent, CT14 6BB Tel: 01304 369165/01304 366536 dipityantiques@aol.com

SHa ⊞ Shapiro & Co, Stand 380, Gray's Antique Market, 58 Davies Street, London, W1Y 5LP Tel: 020 7491 2710

SHSY ⚒ Shapiro Auctioneers, 162 Queen Street, Woollahra, Sydney, NSW 2025, Australia Tel: 00 612 9326 1588

SIL ⊞ The Silver Shop, Powerscourt Townhouse Centre, St Williams Street, Dublin 2, Republic of Ireland Tel: 00 3531 6794147

SMI ⊞ Skip & Janie Smithson Antiques Tel/Fax: 01754 810265

Som ⊞ Somervale Antiques, 6 Radstock Road, Midsomer Norton, Bath, Somerset, BA3 2AJ Tel/Fax: 01761 412686 ronthomas@somervaleantiquesglass.co.uk www.somervaleantiquesglass.co.uk

SQA ⊞ Squirrel Antiques, Scottish Antique and Arts Centre, Carse of Cambus, Doune, Perthshire, FK16 6HD, Scotland Tel: 01786 841203

SSW ⊞ Spencer Swaffer, 30 High Street, Arundel, West Sussex, BN18 9AB Tel: 01903 882132

SuA ⊞ Suffolk House Antiques, High Street, Yoxford, Suffolk, IP17 3EP Tel: 01728 668122

SWA ⊞ S.W. Antiques, Abbey Showrooms, Newlands, Pershore, Worcestershire, WR10 1BP Tel: 01386 555580 sw-antiques@talk21.com www.sw-antiques.co.uk

SWB ⊞ Sweetbriar Gallery Ltd, Robin Hood Lane, Helsby, Cheshire, WA6 9NH Tel: 01928 723851 sweetbr@globalnet.co.uk www.sweetbriar.co.uk

SWO ⚒ Sworders, 14 Cambridge Road, Stansted Mountfitchet, Essex, CM24 8BZ Tel: 01279 817778 www.sworder.co.uk

TAY ⚒ Taylors, Honiton Galleries, 205 High Street, Honiton, Devon, EX14 8LF Tel: 01404 42404

TCG ⊞ 20th Century Glass, Nigel Benson, Kensington Church Street Antique Centre, 58–60 Kensington Church Street, London, W8 4DB Tel: 020 7938 1137 Tel/Fax: 020 7729 9875

TDS ⊞ The Decorator Source, 39a Long Street, Tetbury, Gloucestershire, GL8 8AA Tel: 01666 505358

TEM ⊞ Tempus, Union Square, The Pantiles, Tunbridge Wells, Kent Tel/Fax: 01932 828936 www.tempus-watches.co.uk

TEN ⚒ Tennants, The Auction Centre, Harmby Road, Leyburn, Yorkshire, DL8 5SG Tel: 01969 623780 enquiry@tennants-ltd.co.uk www.tennants.co.uk

TF ⚒ Tayler & Fletcher, London House, High Street, Bourton-on-the-Water, Cheltenham, Gloucestershire, GL54 2AP Tel: 01451 821666 bourton@taylerfletcher.com www.taylerfletcher.com

TH ⊞ Tony Horsley, PO Box 3127, Brighton, East Sussex, BN1 5SS Tel: 01273 550770

TMA ⚒ Tring Market Auctions, Brook Street, Tring, Hertfordshire, HP23 5EF Tel: 01442 826446 sales@tringmarketauctions.co.uk www.tringmarketauctions.co.uk

TPC ⊞ Pine Cellars, 39 Jewry Street, Winchester, Hampshire, SO23 8RY Tel: 01962 777546/867014

TRI ⊞ Trident Antiques, 2 Foundry House, Hall Street, Long Melford, Suffolk, CO10 9JR Tel: 01787 883388 tridentoak@aol.com

TRM ⚒ Thomson, Roddick & Medcalf, 60 Whitesands, Dumfries, DG1 2RS, Scotland Tel: 01387 255366

US ⊞ Ulla Stafford Tel: 0118 934 3208

VB ⊞ Variety Box Tel: 01892 531868

VJ ⊞ Ventnor Junction, 48 High Street, Ventnor, Isle of Wight, PO38 1LT Tel: 01983 853996 shop@ventjunc.freeserve.co.uk

WAC ⊞ Worcester Antiques Centre, Reindeer Court, Mealcheapen Street, Worcester, WR1 4DF Tel: 01905 610680

WaH ⊞ The Warehouse, 29–30 Queens Gardens, Worthington Street, Dover, Kent, CT17 9AH Tel: 01304 242006

WAL ⚒ Wallis & Wallis, West Street Auction Galleries, Lewes, East Sussex, BN7 2NJ Tel: 01273 480208 auctions@wallisandwallis.co.uk www.wallisandwallis.co.uk

WBH ⚒ Walker, Barnett & Hill, Cosford Auction Rooms, Long Lane, Cosford, Shropshire, TF11 8PJ Tel: 01902 375555 wbhauctions@lineone.net www.walker-barnett-hill.co.uk

WELD ⊞ J. W. Weldon, 55 Clarendon Street, Dublin 2, Republic of Ireland Tel: 00 353 1 677 1638

WilP ⚒ W. & H. Peacock, 26 Newnham Street, Bedford, MK40 3JR Tel: 01234 266366

WL ⚒ Wintertons Ltd, Lichfield Auction Centre, Fradley Park, Lichfield, Staffordshire, WS13 6NU Tel: 01543 263256 Photos: Courtesy of Crown Photos 01283 76281

WMa ⊞ William Macadam, Edinburgh, Scotland Tel: 0131 466 0343

WRe ⊞ Walcot Reclamations, 108 Walcot Street, Bath, Somerset, BA1 5BG Tel: 01225 444404

WV ⊞ Westville House Antiques, Westville House, Littleton, Nr Somerton, Somerset, TA11 6NP Tel/Fax: 01458 273376 antique@westville.co.uk www.westville.co.uk

WW ⚒ Woolley & Wallis, Salisbury Salerooms, 51–61 Castle Street, Salisbury, Wiltshire, SP1 3SU Tel: 01722 424500

WWW ⊞ W W Warner, The Forge, The Green, Brasted, Kent, TN16 1JL Tel: 01959 563698

Index to Advertisers

Index

Bold numbers refer to information and pointer boxes.

D